GAO VILLAGE

Rural Life in Modern China

Mobo C. F. Gao

UNIVERSITY OF HAWAI'I PRESS
HONOLULU

Published in the U.S.A in 1999 by
University of Hawai'i Press
2840 Kolowalu Street
Honolulu, Hawai'i 96822

First published in Great Britain by
C. Hurst & Co. (Publishers) Ltd.

Printed in Malaysia

Library of Congress Cataloging-in-Publication Data

Gao, Mobo C. F. 1952-
    Gao Village / Mobo C.F. Gao

    Includes bibliographical references and index.
    ISBN 0-8248-2123-8 (alk. Paper)
    ISBN 978-0-8248-3192-9 (Pbk)
    1. Villages--China--Gao Village (Kiangsi Province, China)--Case
studies.   2. Gao Village   (Kiangsi Province, China)--Social
conditions--Case studies   3. Kiangsi Province, (China)-Rural
conditions--Case studies   I. Title.
HN740.G36G36   1999
307.72'0951'222--dc21   98-32124
                                                                CIP

CONTENTS

v

ILLUSTRATIONS

MAP IN TEXT

XINJIANG

HEILUNJIANG

JILIN

GANSU

LIAONING

INNER MONGOLIA

HEPEI

NINGXIA

SHANXI

SHANDONG

QINGHAI

SHAANXI

HENAN

JIANGSU

TIBET

SICHUAN

HUBEI

ANHUI

Shanghai

JIANGXI

ZHEJIANG

HUNAN

Nanchang

GUIZHOU

FUJIAN

YUNNAN

GUANGXI

GUANDONG

Location of
Gao Village

HAINAN

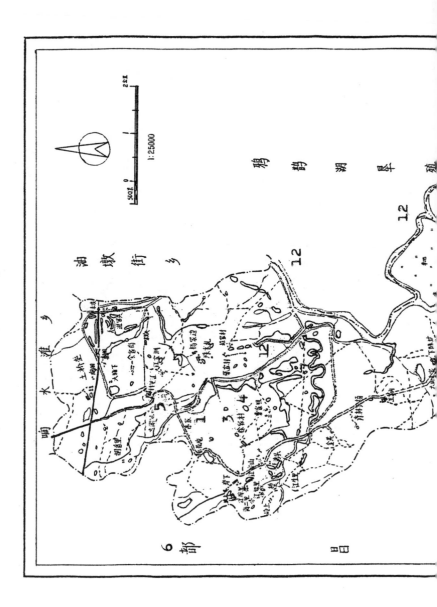

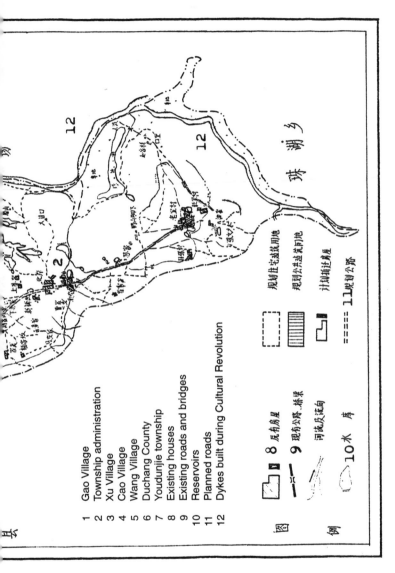

1 Gao Village
2 Township administration
3 Xu Village
4 Cao Village
5 Wang Village
6 Duchang County
7 Youdunjie township
8 Existing houses
9 Existing roads and bridges
10 Reservoirs
11 Planned roads
12 Dykes built during Cultural Revolution

Township map (1994), including Gao Village

PREFACE AND ACKNOWLEDGEMENTS

This is about Gao Village, the village in which I was born and brought up, and lived until I was twenty-one years old. I left the village in 1973 and went to Xiamen University to study English. Thereafter I went back to the village once a year until 1977, when I left China for Britain. In 1980, I returned to China and taught English at Xiamen University until 1985, during which time my contact with the village was frequent. In 1985 I left China again and stayed in Britain till 1990 when I emigrated to Australia. In 1992 a Griffith University Research Grant enabled me to make a research trip to the village, which I visited again in 1994, 1995, 1996 and 1997. One of my brothers still lives there. For all the time since I have been away from Gao Village I have kept in touch with developments there.

By making my background clear I hope to have adequately declared my personal interest and involvement in writing this book. I had not realised to what extent I was involved in the village until I started thinking very hard of an approach towards writing about it. Should I stand aside and avoid any personal involvement, the approach taken in a standard academic work, or allow myself to be personally involved in the text? Is the book to be semi-autobiographical or completely impersonal? What stories are to be told and in what way? To what extent is personal involvement detrimental to analytical presentation? Does the fact of its being personal add insights to critical analysis?

Since to avoid personal involvement would be a pretence, I have decided to take the personal approach. However, as the reader will detect, tensions and difficulties arising from this choice appear from time to time. As an academic I would like the book not only to be relevant to the field but also to address some important theoretical and political issues. Therefore, the chapters are written in such a way that each addresses a theme such as education, health, the Great Leap Forward or the Cultural Revolution. The statistical information is presented and analysed in a way that I think is relevant to the current state of the field. As a Gao villager who witnessed and participated in village life for a large portion of the book's study, I have also included personal stories and experiences relevant to the themes addressed.

Ever since I came to the "West"[1] and established myself as an overseas Chinese, I have devoured books and materials that described and interpreted China. Almost anything about China said by anyone in the "West" arouses my interest. It has been a process of self-awakening and self-identification. I learned and admired the analytical techniques and methodology practiced by English-speaking academics, but have also realised that personal experiences inevitably influence one's perception, interpretation and analysis of a person, an event or a state of affairs.

During my years in the village, ever since I had any knowledge of myself and any awareness of choice, I felt lonely, hopeless and alienated. I wanted to work in a factory; I wanted to be recruited into the army; I wanted to do anything just to leave the village. I hated the darkness at night, the severe cold in winter and extreme heat in summer, the back-breaking manual labour, the dirt, the mud, and the "superstitious" practices, all of which I considered backward and despicable. But now, after two decades away, I feel a strange kind of attachment. When a beggar approaches me in the streets of London or New York for some money, the first idea that comes to mind is that I had better save it for the people I know in the village. Whenever my daughter takes things such as food and school stationery for granted, I cannot help but think of my childhood and that of other children in Gao Village.

I have been in the West for so many years; and yet my dreams invariably either have the village as background or villagers as characters in "Western" settings. I have profound misgivings about the attitudes towards and presentations of what has happened and what is happening in China by the establishment intellectuals in China, by the mainstream media in the West and by some academics. I began to believe that this is inevitable and unavoidable due to personal experiences. The book either explicitly or implicitly reflects these misgivings.

The writing was done on the basis of personal recollections,

---

[1] By "the West" I mean the English-speaking countries. I have to declare my ignorance of non-English-speaking countries. Therefore, throughout the book the term "West" is limited to this specific sense.

memories and experience. During the process I searched past diaries and private correspondence. I also visited and revisited the villagers and conducted many informal interviews. I tried to dig out anything written about the place and its people, including production team and brigade accounting books. In the past five years, through letters to my brother Gao Changxian, I have asked hundreds of questions about the past and the present circumstances of the village and its people, questions that I could not have thought of when I was growing up there. Gao Changxian, in turn, asked the relevant villagers and kept sending me any answers he could find. It is based on such material that the story of Gao Village unfolds.

Acknowledgements

No one can write a book without contributions from other people. As the author of a book about actual people whom I know intimately I owe even more acknowledgements. Gao villagers' superhuman resilience, their credulous kind-heartedness and sometimes stupendous passivism, their sense of humility and their under-used unexplored intelligence are the ultimate source of inspiration for the present book. This book owes its existence to Gao villagers.

Of the friends who have contributed to the production of the present book David Lloyd read the book draft twice under heavy pressure of work commitments. As a person who has studied and worked across three continents, and whose intellectual interest ranges from political sciences to literature, and from Japanese language to Asian culture and religion, David's suggestions and opinions are always valuable.

Other friends and colleagues include Peter Lisowski who, as a keen observer of China and things Chinese, always provides me with insights and encouragement; Jon Unger whose expertise both in the field of China studies and in editing academic work is a treasure house that should be sought by every author; Colin Mackerras whose genuine understanding of China, matched only by his sympathy for its people, is a valuable source of professional suggestions and comments; Wim Wertheim, and Maria Flutsch who also read the book draft, corrected mistakes of one kind or another and made valuable comments. However, the remaining mistakes are all my own. Last but not least, Robin Trew and Adrienne Petty helped with the proofreading.

Christopher Hurst deserves more than the usual acknowledgement as a publisher. After having met me only once, a virtually unknown lecturer, he decided to trust me with a contract. Since then he and Michael Dwyer have been a constant encouragement.

Hobart, Tasmania   MOBO C.F. GAO
September 1998

1

THE STUDY OF RURAL CHINA AND THE CASE OF GAO VILLAGE

There are many reasons for us to seek a better understanding of rural life in China. Some are historical or academic. One is that rural support of the Chinese Communist Party (CCP) is recognised as a major factor contributing to the success of the 1949 Communist victory. Another is that the largest social engineering project in human history, that is, the establishment and practice of what was called the People's Commune, occurred in rural China. Other reasons are contemporary and will have implications for years to come. First, even after nearly half a century of Chinese industrialisation, more than 70 per cent of the population remains rural. Second, the dismantling of the commune system in post-Mao China is assumed by many to have promoted the success of China's economic reforms since the 1980s. Thirdly, increasing township enterprises in rural areas have became an important industrial force in China since the 1980s. And finally, with allegedly only 7 per cent of the world's arable land, China has managed to feed more that 20 per cent of the world's population.

Of course, not all of the above are foregone conclusions. For instance, for some scholars at least, it is far from certain that the CCP victory over the Nationalists (KMT) in 1949 was due to rural support.[1] Equally, some people may argue that the rise of township enterprises since the 1980s was not just a post-Mao reform success but had its roots in what happened in Mao's China. However, the issues are important and the continued debate only emphasises their importance.

More important are issues that are not debated, issues that concern our future. Will urbanisation embrace most of China's

---

[1] For the most recent debate on this issue see Philip Huang, Mark Selden and Joseph Esherick in *Modern China*, vol. 21, no. 1, January 1995.

1

700 million rural people? If it does, how and at what speed? Will China be able to feed its population? China has already started to be a net importer of grain. If the trend accelerates, the impact on the world grain market will be felt in every corner of the world. Whatever happens to the rural people in China over the next fifty years, the economic and environmental implications are of an enormity beyond imagination.

It is not surprising, therefore, that a formidable literature on Chinese rural life has been built up by China specialists. A number of these are good macro-studies.[2] Some of these rural studies are sociological or anthropological while others focus on rural political economy and development. Studies on Chinese rural politics, economy and development are numerous. There are also excellent micro-studies of individual villages which cross over area disciplines.

So there is a plenty of information, analysis and discussion on rural China. Why is there a need for another study, the case of Gao Village? First, the area where Gao Village is located has never been studied before. Most of the studies of rural life have been on the areas of north or north-east China such as Shandong, Henan, Shaanxi, or coastal China such as the Yangzi Delta and the Pearl River Delta, or south-west China such as Sichuan and Yunnan. While no area can be said to be typical, Jiangxi, where Gao Village is located, is neither as developed as the coastal south, nor as underdeveloped as the north-west.

Secondly, as already noted, the approach taken by the present study combines academic discussion with personal experience. While some, such as Unger and Chan, base their approach on interviews, others such as Friedman *et al.* and Potter and Potter base theirs on documentary sources combined with interviews. In both cases, they were neither participants nor direct observers. Only a few, such as Hinton and Greene, were direct observers and, to a certain extent, participants. The present author, however, was born and brought up in the environment under study. The starting points of observation and participation are different. I was an observer and participant before I had any inkling of mainstream "Western" cultural and theoretical assumptions. I knew of these only after I had witnessed the events, whereas writers such as

---

[2] This is not a comprehensive survey of the literature in the field. A short bibliography of relevant work in English is given in Appendix 1, pp. 265ff.

Hinton and Greene or Unger and Chan had their theoretical assumptions intact before they approached the subject.

Thirdly, while the present study covers a small area, a village of no more than a few hundred people, its time-scale is very large. It covers a period of more than forty years including four important stages: the stage immediately before and after the land reform; the commune system; the dismantling of the commune system and immediately after; and the new development from the late 1980s to the mid 1990s.

In a word, the present study covers two contrasting periods in one volume: the period of what is called socialist revolution from 1949 to 1978 and the period of post-Mao reforms from the late 1970s to the mid 1990s. China is now at a crossroads: should it continue the hesitant path towards full-fledged capitalism or retain some socialist elements in a market economy through the so-called "socialism with Chinese characteristics"? To return to a Maoist version of socialism does not seem possible now. However, "socialism with Chinese characteristics" is an elusive concept and difficult in practice. Given the international climate and how far China has already moved towards full-fledged capitalism, it is the easiest and therefore most likely road to be taken. Because China is at such a crossroads there has been a lot of debate over what has been achieved and what has gone wrong in both the socialist and post-Mao reform eras. The present study aims to provide evidence and arguments relevant to such debates.

Finally, the present study takes a critical stand with respect to official communist propaganda and the views of the establishment intellectuals in China. It is my belief, as reflected throughout the book, that the political institutions, the economic system, the legal framework and cultural values of the People's Republic of China have discriminated against rural residents who are generically referred to as "peasants". The book attempts to demonstrate that radical policies such as those during the Cultural Revolution brought about visible improvements in areas such as education and health care for the villagers. The establishment intellectuals, however, choose to ignore evidence of this kind. It is because of my sympathy and identification with the villagers that I am critical of blanket condemnation of the Cultural Revolution and of the praises heaped on the post-Mao reforms since the late 1970s.

2

THE SETTING

Gao Village is located on the mid-west border of Boyang County, Jiangxi province. 300 metres to the north-west is its neighbouring village, Lai Village, which is under the administration of Duchang County. 300 metres to the north-east is Wang Village. About one kilometre to the southwest is Jiang Village. About six hundred metres to the south is Xu Village and 400 metres further south is Cao Village. About 100 kilometres away to the north-west is the city of Jiujiang, one of the ports open to foreigners before 1949, not far from the famous Lushan mountain.[1] Less than 100 kilometres away to the east is Jingdezhen, which used to be the porcelain capital of China. About 50 kilometres to the south and west is the largest fresh water lake in China, Poyang Lake.[2] The county centre, Boyang Town, is about a little more than 100 kilometres away. In the 1990s, Boyang County Town had a population of around 65,000, and Boyang County about 1 million.

Currently three villages, Gao Village, Xu Village and Cao Village, form an administrative unit called Guantian *cun weihui* ("village committee"). This committee is the lowest administrative

[1] Lushan was a favourite holiday resort for the rich and foreigners before 1949. After 1949 it became an exclusive area preserved for the high-ranking CCP officials who occupy all the Western-style buildings built before 1949. One of the most important events of PRC history took place in Lushan in 1959 when the outspoken Minister of Defence Peng Dehuai confronted Mao for the Great Leap Forward policies.

[2] The lake is 170 kilometres long from south to north and 74 kilometres wide from east to west. It has an area of 3,841 square kilometres. Its deepest level is 23.7 metres. There are 118 kinds of fish in the lake. There are eight counties bordering the lake, of which Boyang County alone has a population or more than one million. See Liu Hanyan *et al.*, eds., *Boyang xianzhi* (Annuals of Boyang County), Nanchang, 1989, p. 90. The data and statistics on Boyang County in this chapter are all from Liu Hanyan).

unit in rural China and its size is roughly the same as that of a production brigade in the commune system in Mao's China. All village committee officials are local villagers who do not earn a government salary. Their work is paid for by levies on the local villagers. Guantian village committee has a population of about 1,500. Above the village committee is Yinbaohu *xiang*. A *xiang* (a township, or a district), is the lowest rural administration unit where government appointed officials earn salaries from the government. The size of a *xiang* is equivalent to that of a commune in Mao's China. Yinbaohu *xiang* presently has a population of 20,000.

Gao Village is the smallest village of the three in Guantian village committee. In 1997 Gao Village had a population of 351, including those who had left the village as migrant workers.[3] All the villagers are named Gao except the women who have married into the village who usually retain their surnames. In some cases, men from outside Gao Village who become *zhaozhui* (sons-in-law who live in the home of their wives' parents) are required to change their surname to Gao.[4] All children born in Gao Village must invariably be named Gao.

Gao Village does not have a long history by Chinese standards. Its genealogy book traces its roots back only about 200 years. Despite China's turbulent and often violent modern history, Gao Village has never experienced any war and nobody has ever died in battle. The old villagers have heard of *Chang Mao* ("The Long Haired", referring to the Taiping Rebels of the mid-nineteenth century, presumably because they grew their hair long), but no one was said to have seen one. The Japanese invasion did not penetrate this area. Nor did the civil war between the Red Army and the KMT in the 1930s and again in the late 1940s affect

---

[3] Though migrant workers do not live or work in the village any more, they are still considered as belonging to Gao Village because of the *hukou* (household registration) system. Since they are still registered as Gao villagers, those migrant workers do not have permanent residence status in the cities where they work. The subject will be dealt with in later chapters.

[4] *Zhaozhui* happens when a family has no son to continue the genealogy line. *Zhaozhui* has a very bad social stigma, and usually men agree to do this because of their extremely desperate situation such as being too poor to get married or being social outcasts. Men, especially those from the same village may also agree to *zhaozhui* if the woman in question is extremely attractive or if her family is well off.

Group of Gao Village children, posing for the author, 1996.

Gao Village.[5] The only thing they knew about the Communist People's Liberation Army was through a brief encounter with more than 200 soldiers in the early summer of 1949. That summer witnessed the worst flood in anyone's memory. One night when the soldiers passed by the village, one of them drowned in a river nearby. The soldiers stayed in the village for that night only and then went away without leaving a trace.

Gao Village is one of those places idealised in traditional Chinese landscapes: self-sufficient and idyllic. Although the two nearest cities, Jiujiang and Jingdezhen, were once important in their own right, they had little impact on places like Gao Village. One important reason is that Gao Village was not connected with any means of modern transport. Only since the late 1980s has a gravel road, dusty when dry and muddy when wet, passed through Gao Village. Nowadays, there is a regular bus passing Gao village to the county town, and to Jingdezhen.

Even as late as the 1970s, very few people from Gao Village ever travelled more than a few kilometres away from their home. During the Great Leap Forward in the late 1950s, industrial and economic development in Jiujiang and Jingdezhen did have a visible impact on Gao Village. That was when six men were enrolled as factory workers, settled down and had families there.

Until the late 1970s the village had been almost completely self-sufficient. It produced enough food for itself, and villagers wove their own clothes. Until 1977, when I left China for the UK, no villager except the village doctor could afford a watch, or a bicycle. Apart from loudspeakers installed at the production team headquarters which broadcasted government news through official wires and radios, there was no other electricity in the village until 1988. The villagers arranged their work and daily life according to natural light.

Boyang County has a subtropical climate, with an average temperature of 21°C. The coldest weather recorded was 8°C below zero and the hottest 40°C. The average annual rainfall is about

---

[5] The Taiping Rebels took Boyang County Town in July 1853 and killed the head official of the county. In June 1942, Japanese soldiers occupied Boyang County Town and then left after nineteen days. In April 1949, a regiment under General Chen Geng of the Second Field Army of the People's Liberation Army took over Boyang without fighting.

1,600 millimetres. It has four clear-cut seasons: warm and wet in spring, warm and dry in autumn, hot with frequent storms in summer and cold with occasional snow in winter. Because of plentiful rainfall and fertile land it is an ideal place to grow rice. Surrounding Poyang Lake are numerous lakes and tributary rivers. Apart from Poyang Lake itself, there are more than 120 lakes and 225 rivers in Boyang County. Everywhere around the rivers and lakes are paddy fields, green in spring and golden in summer.

The main crops in the area include rice, wheat, barley, sweet potatoes, soya beans, broad beans, peas, cotton, tea, tobacco, peanuts, sesame seeds, rape seeds, sugar cane, gunny and ramie, buckwheat, millet, and a variety of vegetables and melons. Because of the rivers and lakes, the fishing industry is an important part of the economy in Boyang County. In 1985, for instance, the population involved in fishing reached 20,000 and harvested fish were recorded at 10,000 tons.

Gao Village is located in this well-endowed area. In front of the village stand two hills, one belonging to Gao Village and the other to Lai Village, under the administration of Duchang County. On the eastern border of Gao Village a river runs southwards into a lake which itself is connected with a larger river, which in turn runs into Poyang Lake. Surrounding Gao Village are small ponds and streams. The hills used to provide firewood for the villagers, and the streams, ponds, the river and the lake used to provide the villagers with an irrigation system as well as fish and water plants. The paddy fields are terraced for rice and some of the hilly land can be used to produce economic crops such as cotton, sesame seeds, gunny and ramie, peanuts as well as sweet potatoes.

Water plants are a good source of food for raising pigs, which are one of the main sources of protein for the villagers. From the river, the lake and numerous streams and ponds the villagers can catch shrimps, prawns, soft-shelled turtle, crabs, carp, trout, grass carp, silver carp, finless eels, field snails, snake-head fish, catfish, loach, mandarin fish, bream and a variety of freshwater mussels. Most of the different kinds of fish are from Poyang Lake, and every spring they migrate upwards to the tributary rivers and further up to thousands of lakes and streams to breed and lay eggs. Then they swim further up to millions of brooks and ponds to seek food. Some of the fish end up in the rice fields where villagers can catch them very easily. Another good source of food for the villagers are the dozen kinds of frogs which are at the same time natural enemies of insects. These frogs breed and live around ponds and rice fields and keep the harmful insects under control.

All in all, Gao Village can function economically and socially as an independent entity without any connection with the outside world, as it had in fact been doing until the late 1970s. Yet Gao Village is not a remote mountainous place where there are hardly any people. There are numerous surrounding villages, most of them much bigger, and some with more than 1,000 households. In most cases, it is only half a kilometre from one village to another. However, they do not interact economically and one village does not in any sense depend on another. There are no commercial transactions between them, nor is there much cultural or social interaction. The population mass and intensive agricultural activities in the area have not led to any significant commercialisation or qualitative change of lifestyle. Even today, the nearest markets are several kilometres away from Gao Village. The villages remain cellular, to use Viviene Shue's insightful concept,[6] in that each village is a separate entity and the reach of the state is now extremely limited, although the brutality of the local officials is intensely felt.

The concept of "natural village" refers to a group of people living together in one location. They have the same surname, they are housed together and they interact with each other in ways that they do not interact with people from other villagers. Excluding government control and interference, each village is an entity in itself: it has its own governing body and distinct territory.

However, one exception to the generalisation of village independence on the basis of territory is that there could be two villagers of the same surname but from distinct communities who might have a close relationship. About 10 kilometres away from Gao Village there is another Gao Village which has 3,000 households. The villagers of both the big and small Gao villages are from the same ancestral line. When the first generation of Gao villagers

[6] V. Shue, *The Reach of the State: Sketches of the China Body Politic*, Stanford, CA, 1988.

migrated from the north to Jiangxi, some went to settle down in one area while the rest moved to settle down in another. From then on they have maintained a genealogical affinity. As later chapters in the book will show, the ways in which the two Gao villages interact demonstrate how lineage tradition and local politics interact in rural life.

The cellular nature of rural life is also reflected linguistically. The whole of Jiangxi Province is supposed to speak a distinctive dialect called Gan, which is one of the ten major dialects in China.[7] However, the Gan dialect itself is not undifferentiated. The people in Boyang County speak Gan with one accent, while those in Duchang County speak with another. The residents in Boyang County Town speak a variety of Gan that Gao villagers find hard to understand. A Gao villager who goes to Boyang County Town is looked down upon as an uneducated peasant simply because he or she cannot speak the town's dialect. In fact, people in the major cities of Jiangxi Province such as Nanchang, Jiujiang and Jingdezhen all speak distinctive varieties of Gan. Wherever you come from, you betray your identity as "outsider" as soon as you start to speak.

---

[7] The other nine are Mandarin, Jin, Xiang, Wu, Yue (Cantonese), Min, Hakka, Hui and Pinghua. See Li Rong, S.A. Wurm *et al.,* eds, *Language Atlas of China,* Hong Kong, 1987.

3

LAND, WATER AND LOCAL POLITICS

When the first generation of Gao villagers settled down where Gao Village is now, the place was waste land and up for grabs. There is no record of how and when the borders between Gao Village and the neighbouring villages were finally established. What is most likely to have happened is that the first generation of Gao villagers moved to the area on their own and started to open up land for rice plantation as soon as they arrived. They either claimed all the land that was left unclaimed as soon as they arrived, or opened up as much land for plantation as they could physically manage. As the village grew, arable land surrounding it also expanded until the claims of the neighbouring villages prevented it from expanding any further.

Although the boundaries between Gao Village and its neighbouring villages are clearly understood by all villagers in the region, no written record exists. Well before 1949, the territorial borders between Gao Village and its neighbouring Xu Village, Jiang Village, Wang Village and Lai Village had been clearly drawn, including paddy fields, hills, waste land and water resources. If a river or a lake is shared between two or more villages, then they share the water resources. The most common practice is that all parties have the right to fish and use the water for irrigation.

All male and some female adults know their own village's boundaries with neighbouring villages. There has never been a map or a village plan of Gao Village. Every detail is defined orally and passed on by memory from generation to generation. What is remarkable is that this lack of explicitness and official records does not concern the government. What the state, past or present, needs is the official statistics of the arable land each village has so that corresponding land taxes can be collected. Most villages manage to co-exist for generations. However, border disputes have been the most frequent source of village fighting in the area, both before and since the Communist revolution in 1949.

11

Territorial disputes, clan solidarity and residual traditions

The residues of Chinese tradition die hard in this area. These are reflected in the ways territorial disputes are played out and by clan solidarity. When an inter-village dispute arises, a village always acts as one to defend its interest and territory. Furthermore, as shown below in descriptions of the relationship between the big and small Gao villages, different villages of the same clan tend to identify with each other and show clan solidarity in territorial disputes. Residual traditions are also demonstrated by the fact that in territorial disputes the outcome is dependent on the number of *quantou* (fists), that is, the number of adult males that can be called upon in a fight.

Dispute with Lai Village. Gao village shares water resources with Xu, Lai and Wang villages and disputes with these three villages break out from time to time. One of the border lines between Gao Village and Lai Village is a small narrow ditch which channels rain water from higher places to a lower paddy field which belongs to Gao Village. This had been the practice for generations. However, in 1970 Lai Village attempted to block the ditch so that rain water would flow in the opposite direction to its own paddy fields. Each time this happened Gao villagers would clear away the blockage. This went on for some time until finally the two villages had a battle, fighting with fists, shoulder poles and shovels, with a dozen villagers on both sides wounded. It took a long time for government arbitration to take effect because the two villages belong to two different counties. As a result, any solution below the county level was not valid. Eventually each village paid its own medical expenses and the ditch in question remained as it always had been.

In that dispute Gao Village won, largely because Lai Village had accepted the solution that past practice regarding the ditch should remain. That Lai Village decided to accept the arbitration might well have to do with the fact that Gao Village is larger and Lai Village was likely to lose in another fight. When it comes to the disputes with Xu and Wang villages, Gao Village has to concede what it considers to be its rights, simply because Xu Village is twice its size and Wang Village is four times larger. Usually, the larger village will not accept any solution that it does not like and will initiate more disputes and feuds which the smaller village cannot combat.

Dispute with Xu Village. This was the case in the dispute between Xu Village and Gao Village, which arose only in the Maoist period. However, the way of resolving the dispute was very traditional. A reservoir was built in 1958 during the Great Leap Forward, occupying low marshland that both Xu and Gao villages shared. Gao villagers participated in the construction of the reservoir dam, and it was understood that both villages could use the water to irrigate their paddy fields. Some years later Xu Village claimed that Gao village did not have the right to use water from the reservoir when the water level was high since the hills from which rain water flowed into the reservoir did not belong to Gao Village. Xu Village would allow Gao Village to use water from the reservoir only when the water levels became very low. However, when the water level is low, the culvert through which reservoir water normally flows into Gao Village paddy fields is higher than the water level. For all practical purposes, therefore, Gao Village was not allowed to use the reservoir water. What Gao villagers did occasionally when the water level was high enough was to open the culvert at night and close it before dawn so that Xu Village would not know what had happened. If Xu Village knew of it, and this happened from time to time, they would simply destroy the culvert and block the ditch. Gao Village could not afford to have a fight with Xu Village.

The local authorities do not do much to settle disputes of this nature for a number of good reasons. First, to settle a dispute in favour of a smaller village could mean more trouble because the larger village usually will not end the feud until it is satisfied. Secondly, it is in the local authorities' interest to favour the larger village since it contains a larger portion of their power base. Finally, increasingly since the late 1960s, the powerholders among the local authorities are from the larger villages. All this will be discussed further in later chapters.

Dispute with Wang Village. Gao Village used to share a river with Wang Village which also forms the border between them. The two villages have a long history of fighting over water resources from the river. Disputes usually broke out during two seasons.

During the spring season farmers from both villages would harvest grass on the river banks for buffalo fodder and for organic fertiliser. Wang villagers would be reluctant even to let Gao villagers harvest grass on their own side of the river bank. In winter when the water level in the river was low, villagers would drain the river to catch fish. Again, Wang villagers would be very aggressive as they wanted to deprive Gao villagers of this cheap and considerable source of income.

The dispute between Gao Village and Wang Village has a long history. In 1947, both sides prepared for battle with guns and locally-made cannons. Wang village backed off before the fighting actually took place because the big Gao Village 10 kilometres away, which is twice its size came to the small Gao Village's help with a machine-gun, which frightened the Wang villagers. However, the dispute erupted again in Mao's China. During the early 1970s, Wang villagers built a dam on Gao Village's side of the territory and the whole river was included inside the dam as part of Wang Village's territory and was reclaimed as Wang Village's paddy fields. A new river was created outside the dam and Wang Village still claims ownership of most of the river. Largely because of the suppression of clan power in Mao's China, the two Gao villages could not organise a joint fight with Wang Village. As a result, Gao Village has to live with its loss of territory.

Clan solidarity. Even so, the two Gao villages have retained a close relationship. In 1981, when I returned to Gao Village from England, the small Gao Village killed two huge pigs and held a banquet for more than one hundred people to celebrate my homecoming. The most distinguished guests for the occasion, apart from the local government officials, were about twenty village elders and powerholders from the big Gao Village. The clan authorities considered the fact that I was the only person in the whole county who had gone to England as a kind of glory for the two Gao Villages. The occasion was used as a demonstration of solidarity and strength.

However, times have changed. In the days of traditional China, the status of Gao Village would have risen considerably if a village youth had passed the imperial examination at the provincial level. The successful candidate would most likely be appointed as head of a county. Even if the successful candidate was not given an official position but stayed in the village he (always a male) could have been a decisive factor in determining the outcome of local disputes. In post-1949 China, however, a scholar has little influence in local politics. But the villagers seem slow to realise this change.

Land and political economy

At the Communist takeover in 1949 the village had 280 *mu*[1] of arable land distributed among twenty households. When land reform started, Gao Tianqiang's household was classified as that of a landlord and Gao Jingxiang's as that of a rich peasant. Twelve households were classified as middle peasant and six as poor peasant.[2] The average poor peasant household had about 6 *mu* of land and the average middle peasant 13.8 *mu*. The landlord had 45 *mu* and the rich peasant had 33 *mu*. Gao Tianqiang was apparently classified as a landlord because he did not work on the land he owned. He rented the land to some poor peasants while he worked as the village *sishu* teacher.[3] Gao Jingxiang was classified as a rich

---

[1] One *mu* of land equals 0.0667 hectares. *Mu* is the basic land measure unit throughout China and it is also the unit for measuring productivity.

[2] In fact the category of middle peasants is further subcategorised into upper middle, middle and lower middle peasants. Poor peasants also have two sub-categories: farm labourer and poor peasant. The former subcategory includes those who had no land whatsoever. In the political terms of Mao's China, peasants from lower middle categories downwards were classified as basic revolutionary forces to be relied on. Those classified as middle and upper middle peasants were to be united into the revolutionary rank, whereas the landlords and rich peasants were class enemies to be struggled against. In Gao Village, there was only one farm labourer who, during the later 1960s and early 1970s when agrarian radicalism was at its highest, was promoted to be one of the production team leaders.

[3] A *sishu* teacher used to work at his (not her) own home and gave informal tuition to village pupils and in return was paid by whatever kind of produce the pupil's family could afford. The teaching materials were of course classic Confucian textbooks such as *sishu wujing* (the *Four Books* and *Five Classics*). The teacher would never explain anything. He would simply teach the pupil how to say the words and then ask the pupil to read aloud until the pupil could recite the texts. The practice of *sishu* is supposed to have been started by Confucius himself and had continued until late in the nineteenth century. Gao Tianqiang did not work with his hands to produce grain and therefore was considered to be an exploiter.

peasant firstly because he owned more land than the average and
secondly because he rented his land to poor peasants while he
himself worked as a tailor. Had he not had any land to rent he
would have been classified as a handicraftsman, with semi-
proletarian status.

During the land reform carried out in 1951,[4] the land belonging
to Gao Tianqiang and Gao Jingxiang was confiscated. Land in
Gao Village was redistributed equally on a per capita basis. Some
land was taken away from the middle peasants and the poor
peasants were given some land. Gao Tianqiang's brick house was
confiscated and he was given a mud house instead. Only land
was confiscated from Gao Jingxiang, the rich peasant.

There was not enough time for the land reform's impact to
emerge since the equal ownership of land was soon overtaken
by the CCP's desire to push towards socialism, which meant
collective ownership of the means of production in the countryside.
Land reform in Gao Village was soon followed by the mutual
aid teams in 1953, the cooperatives in 1955 and finally the commune
system in 1958, as in the rest of the county. The Chinese Communists were so impatient that they pushed the Chinese peasants
from one change to another until the Great Leap Forward, after
which a modified commune system was stabilised.

The 1959 commune system lasted until 1981 in Boyang County.
Under this system, Gao Village was divided into two production
teams, each with equal population and land. Each team was led
by a team leader and was responsible for its own production,
income and distribution. Any resources that could not be divided,
such as the river, lake and streams, were managed together and
the income divided equally. In the team, no individual owned
any substantial means of production except farm tools such as
hoes, sickles, shoulder poles and wheelbarrows.

Each member of the team was assessed annually for the value
of his or her labour in terms of points. For instance, the best
male peasant might get ten points for one day's work and the
best female might get eight points, while a child labourer might

---

[4] The land reform in Boyang County did not start until June 1950 when a
small scale experiment was carried out. By March 1951 land reform was completed
all over the county. Beginning in April 1951, until March 1952, a countywide
re-examination of land distribution was carried out to reinforce the outcome
of land reform.

get four points for a day. At an assessment meeting every year, every aspect of an individual would be discussed to finalise the assessment. Every evening the team accountant would record every member's points in the presence of the whole team.

Important produce such as grain was always distributed per capita with reference to age differences whereas some sideline produce, usually of small quantity, might be distributed only among adult labourers. In the latter case, how a particular item should be distributed was usually decided by the team leader, who might consult with the team accountant or any other powerholders. At the end of every year, each family's work points were added together as the family's contribution to the team. The value of each family's contribution varied from year to year as did the value of the total wealth created by the whole team. After deducting the value of produce distributed throughout the year, a family was either in the black or in the red. Usually, those families with more children and fewer labourers would be in the red whereas families with strong labourers and few young children would be in the black.

Theoretically, those who were in the red had to pay their debts to the team either in cash or in kind and those who were in the black had to be paid by then team. Practically, however, this was seldom carried out, for various good reasons. First, those who were in the red were among the poorest in the village. They had to make great efforts just to survive and therefore had nothing in the family except the goods distributed from the team, which were never enough. Secondly, the production team leaders' own household, such as Gao Changyao's and Gao Changliang's, were very often in the red. Gao Changyao was the team leader for many years because he was one of the only two Communist Party members in the village. He also gained this status because he was the only person of farm labourer class background who owned no land at all before 1949. Being in the red themselves, the team leaders were not in a good position to push those families into the red to pay their debts unless they paid their own debts first. Finally, a more fundamental reason for the failure of the team to settle the accounts was the sense of clan obligation between villagers. It would violate their sense of propriety to push a family too far in this situation.

As a result, very little could be done to settle the team's annual account. In a good year when the team had some surplus, the families in the black would be given some cash for the Spring Festival. Usually debts and credits were carried over from one year to another until a turn of fortune came to the families in the village. This could occur, for example, when a family in the black might have a member who was ill for a long time; or when the children of a family which had been in the red for many years grew up to be strong labourers.

Though a production team leader could derive some economic benefit for the family and could wield power in the village, it was otherwise a thankless task. He had to balance not only the interests among the villagers but also between the village and higher local authorities. Besides, every detail of the team activities was closely monitored by the villagers simply because everyone's life was involved. The position was performance-related, and leadership quality would have an immediate impact on the well-being of every villager. A comparison between the two teams in the village was inescapable and performance could be seen instantly. Everyone wanted the team to do well, but no one wanted to be too hard on unfortunate households.

Immediately above the production team was the production brigade which usually consisted of between ten and thirty teams, depending on the political climate. When CCP agrarian policies became more radical, for instance during the Cultural Revolution period of the late 1960s and early 1970s, the production brigade became bigger. When the production brigades were small, Gao Village belonged to Guantian brigade along with Xu Village and Cao Village. When the production brigades were larger, Gao Village belonged to Qinglin brigade which consisted of ten villages. The production brigade authorities had the right to appoint production team leaders and accountants, and to levy the teams to raise funds for projects such as education, health and roads. They were also responsible for collecting taxes for the state, for introducing and implementing government policies and new technology and for distributing funds from the government if there were any. The brigade was also responsible for raising funds and for organising brigade enterprises such as rice mills, oil mills and credit cooperatives. There might be Communist Party members in the production teams, but only a production brigade had a Communist Party branch headed by a Party secretary.

GRASSROOTS ADMINISTRATION STRUCTURE IN RURAL CHINA

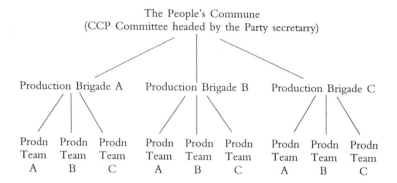

The People's Commune
(CCP Committee headed by the Party secretarry)

Production Brigade A   Production Brigade B   Production Brigade C

Prodn   Prodn   Prodn   Prodn   Prodn   Prodn   Prodn   Prodn   Prodn
Team   Team   Team   Team   Team   Team   Team   Team   Team
A   B   C   A   B   C   A   B   C

Immediately above the brigades sat the commune authorities. Normally a commune would consist of about ten brigades, with a population roughly in the range of 10–20,000. Again during the most radical period of the Cultural Revolution, a commune could be as large as sixty brigades. In 1968, Gao Village belonged to Youdunjie commune which had a population of around 60,000. However, for most of the time, Gao Village belonged to Yinbaohu commune, which had a population of around 20,000. Commune authorities had the right to appoint brigade leaders and Party secretaries. The commune administration was the interface between the higher levels of government and local powerholders. A commune would have a Communist Party Committee headed by a Party secretary and a couple of deputies. All the commune leaders were directly appointed by, and were responsible only to, the state government. Unlike production team and brigade leaders, whose earnings varied from year to year depending on the income created by the farmers with whom they worked and lived, commune leaders had secure and regular salaries from the state government.

While all brigade and team leaders were locals, the main commune leaders were from outside the area. Commune authorities were responsible for maintaining public health and education such as commune hospitals and high schools, public roads, and law and order. Throughout the late 1950s until the late 1970s the commune was responsible for organising and coordinating massive irrigation projects such as reservoirs, reclamation of marsh land and above all dams and dykes. The commune was also responsible for raising funds for commune enterprises such as machine repair shops, agricultural tool workshops, brick and tile kilns, and elementary food processing shops.

In 1981 when the commune system was dismantled, Yinbaohu commune was changed into Yinbaohu *xiang* (township). Although the names changed, the sizes of the administrative units remained the same. So did the administrative responsibilities. However, the change of names was also a change of substance. "commune" and "brigade" meant collectivisation and regimentation of life whereas *xiang* and "committee" do not have such political implications. The village committee at present consists of five people, the Party secretary, two deputies (one of whom is a woman: as a stipulated policy there usually must be at least one woman member on the committee), one accountant and one local militia leader. Each of the three villages has a village head and an accountant. They and the five people of the village committee are paid by the locals and their salaries are drawn from the levies imposed on the peasants. Like the former commune cadres, the *xiang* officials are paid by the government.

As far as land is concerned, the dismantling of the commune system in 1981 brought the peasants back to 1951, that is, when land was equally distributed to households on a per capita basis. The 308 *mu* of land in Gao Village at present has been distributed equally among the villagers according to the number of people in each household, though in theory the collective, that is the village, owns the land. Presently, the household that has the biggest share of land has about 15 *mu* while the smallest share per household is about 3 *mu*.

In relative terms, the present distribution of land is more equal than before 1949. However, in absolute terms, the average household is worse off than before 1949. Each household now has an average of 6.2 *mu* and each person has 0.96 *mu* of land whereas before 1949 the poorest household had 6 *mu* of land and each person had an average of 1.7 *mu* of land. This is because in 1949 there were only 160 people and twenty households in the village whereas in the early 1990s there are 318 people and fifty-one households. Before 1949, of all the household, 60 per cent were middle peasants, with an average of 13.8 *mu* of land, which was only a little below the biggest "land-owner" today who has about 15 *mu* of land. The simple logic is that land in the village cannot be expanded any further to accommodate population growth. In order to understand what this means it is worth pointing out that while the average arable land *per capita* in Gao Village is less than 0.066 hectares, by 1979, the average arable area per head in China was 0.1 hectares, compared with Japan (0.04 ha.), India (0.26 ha.), the United States (0.86 ha.) and the USSR (0.89 ha.).[5]

Water, development and local politics

Rapid expansion of the population has not only exhausted land but also water resources. Water has always been the life blood of rice agriculture and an important source of food and sustenance for domestic animals like pigs and ducks. Gao Village has no way to expand its water catchment. In fact, as discussed previously, Gao village's water territory has shrunk, due to the area taken over by Wang Village. On top of the increasing demand on water resources as a result of population increase and the shrinkage of water catchment there is also the damage incurred by more frequent floods and the gradual destruction of aquatic culture.

Floods have been prevalent for centuries in Boyang County. From AD 381 to 1989 there were 252 recorded cases of flood and drought, of which 158 were floods, averaging one every 10.11 years.[6] Gao Village, like other areas surrounding Poyang Lake, is prone to flooding. The reason is clear: the area is fertile and good for rice growing precisely because it is low and on the edge of Poyang Lake. There is also plenty of rainfall in spring and early summer. When it rains, water flows from the mountains, hills and fields into the streams and rivers, and in turn into Poyang Lake, and from there into the Changjiang (Yangtze River). However, the outlet into the Yangtze is only a very narrow bottle neck. When it rains too much in the areas surrounding Poyang Lake the water level in the lake keeps on rising because the bottle neck is not wide enough for the water to flow out quickly enough.

---

[5] Quoted by Peter Nolan and Robert Ash, 'China's Economy on the Eve of Reform", *China Quarterly*, vol. 144, December 1995, pp. 980-98.

[6] Zhen Canhong *et al.*, *Boyang Xian Shuili Zhi* (The Irrigation Annuals of Boyang County), Shanghai, 1992, pp. 45-51.

As a result, the water in Poyang Lake swallows up the surrounding areas of paddy fields. Often when it rains heavily in other areas of South China along the banks of the Yangtze, the water level in Poyang Lake rises even faster, because no water can flow out of Poyang Lake, and water from the Yangtze also flows back into Poyang Lake. Because the catchment areas surrounding Poyang Lake are so large, there are often areas that have too much rain even though there is no rain in other areas. Thus, Gao Village is sometimes caught in a very strange situation: when it has not rained for months the higher land is in drought, and yet at the same time the paddy fields in lower areas have been swallowed up by floods.

The situation is getting worse for the areas surrounding Poyang Lake, but more so for Gao Village. From the official records of Boyang County, during the thirty-six years between 1912 and 1948 of the Republican period, there was one flood every three years. During the forty years between 1949 to 1989 in the PRC period, there was one flood every two years.[7] The reason, again, is not hard to find. Because of the growing population China is in constant need of more grain. On the one hand, every effort has been made to explore and open up waste land for grain production. On the other hand, bushland and forests disappeared rapidly, either consumed as firewood or as a result of reclamation. The inevitable consequence has been widespread soil erosion.

Soil erosion has led to two developments, both of which have had grave ecological consequences. First, without a green belt, the land surrounding Poyang Lake has less capacity to hold water. Secondly, the river bed of the Yangtze is getting higher and higher. The amount of water that can flow out from Poyang Lake into the Yangtze is diminishing. Again, because of the increasing demand for rice in the entire region surrounding Poyang Lake, peasants have built dams and dykes along its edges to enclose more paddy fields. Poyang Lake's capacity to store water has become smaller and smaller. As a consequence there are more frequent severe floods in the surrounding areas.

For Gao Village nowadays, there is no year without a flood. Here local politics have placed Gao Village in a situation from which it cannot escape. During the commune period of the 1960s

---

[7] Zhen Chaojing *et al.*, *ibid.*, p. 51.

and 1970s when massive irrigation projects were organised, Gao villagers were ordered every year during the slack season to participate in irrigation projects, mostly building up dykes and dams that benefited other production teams and brigades. However, no project was ever carried out that benefited Gao Village.

For a long time, Gao villagers wanted to build a dam to enclose the lake on its south border so that some paddy fields could be opened up in the enclosure and at the same time the village could be protected from flood. However, despite Gao Village's persistent request and the villagers' many years of contribution to other projects without any compensation, the commune and brigade authorities refused to organise people from other villages to participate in the project. The official reason given to Gao Village was that the land enclosed inside the supposed dam was not large enough to warrant such a huge project. In other words, it was not considered to be economically viable. The authorities insisted that if Gao villagers wanted to carry out such a project they could do it on their own, which would take twenty years. So the project was never carried out and as the result Gao Village is the only village in Yinbaohu commune that did not benefit from the Communist infrastructural frenzy in the PRC's first forty years.

From Gao Village's point of view, its exclusion from these massive irrigation projects has little to do with economics. It is just too small to have any say in local politics. More important, none of the local powerholders such as brigade and commune officials were from Gao Village. They were all from the large villages. The paradox of rural politics in the area is the result of the cellular nature of the clan village structures. The more power is decentralised, the more likely it is that large clan villages will hold the balance of power, creating less chance of justice and fair play prevailing in local politics.

During the 1950s and early 1960s when policies were directly imposed by the government, and when not only commune but also some brigade cadres were appointed from outside the area, clan politics were somehow suppressed and the larger villages were restrained from bullying the smaller villages. However, since the late 1960s, right through the Cultural Revolution, rural power was more decentralised and all the brigade officials and some commune officials were appointed locally and more local feedback was sought from the villagers. As large villages had the numbers, local officials came mainly from these. When conflicts surfaced, large villages exercised their strength as power players for their own interest. Individuals from small villages could not be appointed to be brigade or commune cadres because their power bases were too weak. Since the Cultural Revolution, even an appointee from outside the area could not afford to ignore the opinion of a large village because it was in a better position to make trouble. As a consequence, local politics is closely tied up with clan conflict, and when a conflict arises involving two villages of different size, the advantage usually goes to the large village. Because the two neighbouring villages with which Gao Village has had disputes are larger, no settlement could have been made in its favour.

In conclusion, two points must be reiterated. One is that the population increased rapidly in the area since the Communist victory in 1949, while land and water resources on which the livelihood of the local people depended were over-exploited. The second point is that clan structures very often dominated local politics when villagers competed for land and water resources. In the years since 1949 the population in Gao Village has doubled while the land and water resources have been reduced, either as a result of village disputes or of environmental damage.

4

POPULATION AND POLITICS

Mao Zedong once said: "People and people alone are the locomotive of history." By locomotive, Mao, a self-proclaimed Marxist, meant that the people were the driving force that pushed history forward progressively, from a primitive age to the present. However, the excessive number of people in China seems to be one of the main factors which have dragged Chinese history to a standstill for many hundreds of years.

Chinese civilisation was well ahead of European civilisation technically, economically, commercially and socially at least until the Middle Ages. Why is it then that industrialisation and with it capitalism did not spring up in China? Scholars and historians have debated this issue for decades.[1] One argument is that there were simply too many Chinese. For instance, one could argue that too many people meant abundant cheap labour which in turn negated any rationale for making use of technical innovations. Philip Huang's sophisticated and influential thesis of involutionary development in traditional China relies fundamentally on China's problem of population.[2] According to Huang, China's economic and social history until the late 1980s was involutionary. Whatever was developed technically and economically was absorbed and cancelled by the growth of population and hence there was no significant breakthrough of efficiency and productivity.

The population in Gao Village hardly enters this debate over China's failure in bringing about industrialisation and capitalism. However, reference to the larger picture presents us with a back-

---

[1] See, for instance, Joseph Needham, *The Grand Titration: Science and Society in East and West*, London, 2nd impression, 1979 and his monumental volumes of *Science and Civilisation in China*, Cambridge University Press, 1954 onwards; Mark Elvin, *The Patterns of the Chinese Past*, Stanford, CA, 1973.

[2] P. Huang, *The Peasant Family and Rural Development in the Yangzi Delta 1350-1988*, Stanford, CA 1990.

ground for understanding developments. Up to 1949, there were only 160 people in Gao Village. By 1997 the population had doubled to 351. Meanwhile, Gao Village's territory, that is land and water, could not have been further expanded. Therefore, in the forty years since 1949, either there had to be technical innovations to increase production and feed a growing population, or Gao villagers would have to cease their complete dependence on the land and water.

The gap between the rural and urban

When we talk about China we have to be specific about which China we are referring to: the rural or the urban. The urban working class benefited most from the Communist revolution in 1949, an event supposedly brought about with the support of the peasantry. In Mao's China, the urban citizens enjoyed a range of welfare benefits including free education for all, free medical care, virtually free housing because rent was nominal, more or less assured lifetime employment, and a subsidised regular food supply.[3] With few exceptions,[4] the rural population did not enjoy such benefits. There was some free education for a while. For most there was no medical service, and when available, it was certainly not free. On top of this, the peasants had to pay agricultural taxes to the government and to sell grain to the state at the government-controlled price so that it could accumulate the capital for industrialisation. According to one estimate, in 1952–79, by way of agricultural taxes and differential pricing on agricultural and

---

[3] The Chinese government continues to subsidise the urban residents, obviously for political reasons. In 1985 alone, grain subsidies to urban residents reached 27.5 billion *yuan*, about one-quarter of the total wages of all the employees in China that year! See Zhu Ling, *Rural Reform and Peasant Income in China: The Impact of China's Post-Mao Reforms in Selected Regions*, London, 1991.

[4] One exception was what was called the "Five Guaranteed" households. These were childless families of good class backgrounds who were supposed to be guaranteed enough government support for "food, clothing, shelter, medical care and burial expenses". The support was very unsystematic and very often abused by local powerholders. In any case, it was largely financed by the local peasants themselves through a special levy. The levy on this item has been recorded in the brigade account books every year. In Gao Village there was not one Five Guaranteed household.

industrial goods, the state extracted a total of 600 billion *yuan*[5] from the peasantry. Subtracting government investment in agriculture, the state has netted 434 billion *yuan* from the peasants, 24 per cent of the total agriculture sector GNP in that period.[6] According to two Chinese rural economy specialists, the percentages of government financial income exploited from the peasantry by way of differential pricing system in 1957, 1965, 1971 and 1979 were respectively 71, 75.7, 51.6 and 39.4.[7]

The foundation stone for building up these discriminatory policies was the *hukou* system (household registration), by which every household in China was registered either as a rural or urban resident. The *hukou* system virtually wiped out any possibility for a rural peasant to move to an urban area. To eat in a restaurant, one had to present rice coupons, which peasants usually did not possess. Every factory or enterprise in urban areas was an enclosed unit in which each person was registered. Everyone belonged to a unit and the movement or transfer from one unit to another required a whole range of bureaucratic approvals. Therefore, even today, urban life is the envy of peasants.

Throughout the late 1980s and early 1990s some county authorities tried to raise income by selling urban household registration to some rural individual entrepreneurs who had made some money. In some counties, the price for one household registration was as much as 10,000 *yuan*, which was about two years' gross salary for an average wage-earner in China in the early 1990s.

In Mao's China there were usually three paths by which a rural person could become an urban citizen. One was to be enlisted into the army. After completing army service, the ex-soldier, or officer, would usually be assigned work in an urban area. If they were sent back to their rural area, a government official job would be assigned to them. In the entire forty years of Mao's China, six males from Gao Village were enlisted into the army. After they retired from their service, one was assigned

---

[5] *Yuan* is a basic Chinese currency unit. Currently (1996), one US dollar equals about 8 *yuan*.

[6] Wang Guichen and Xiao Dechang, *Zhongguo Nongye Chanye Jiegou* (Production Structure in Chinese Agriculture), Beijing, 1991, p. 54.

[7] Lai Ruihua and Jiang Xiexin, *Zhongguo Nongye Jijin Wenti Yanjiu* (The Problems of Funding Agriculture in China), Beijing, 1991.

to a state farm in which he earned a regular salary. Another was sent to work in a mining factory. Two were given work in the city of Jingdezhen, and two are still serving as officers.

During the 1950s Gao villagers were not keen on joining the army, for both traditional and practical reasons. Until the Communist revolution in 1949 it was a Chinese tradition to look down upon soldiers. A well-known saying states that good men were not to be soldiers, just as good iron was not to be made into nails. At that time Gao villagers did not know whether the Communist regime was stable or for how long it would last, and they did not want to fight in a war. Thus when the government called on villagers to volunteer to join the army to fight in Korea in the early 1950s, only Gao Changan was prepared to go. Gao Changan's parents had died when he was five, and he was adopted into Gao village. He felt an outsider and became a bit of a rebel. That was why he was the only Gao villager willing to join the army.

During the 1960s and '70s, however, Gao villagers' attitudes changed dramatically. Indeed, it was every youngster's dream to be enlisted into the army. It became clear to the Gao villagers that the Communist government was firmly in power and there was no perceived risk of war. Moreover, the army would educate young village boys who would be assigned to "prestigious" jobs after their service. Gao Changqin, the youngest of five brothers, said later that his biggest regret in life was not having joined the army when he was urged to during the Korean War.

It was very difficult for a villager to join the army. First of all, one had to come from a good family background. Those from landlord and rich peasant family backgrounds were excluded. Only since the 1980s when the class labels of landlord and rich peasant were removed did three grandsons of Gao Tianqiang, the village landlord, join the army. Secondly, one had to pass very stringent physical examinations. Few rural youths could meet the criteria. Gao Changshan, who was one of the two production team accountants, tried for several years, but every time he was excluded because he had flat feet. I myself tried for a number of years, but failed every time because of an ear infection.

The second path by which a Gao villager could escape being condemned to rural life was to become a worker. Again, this was very difficult. One did not have the freedom just to go and look for a job. Opportunities arose only when the government permitted a state-owned factory to enrol rural people, in which case a quota would be allocated, from county to commune, from commune to brigades and then down to Gao Village. State factories usually did not allocate a quota to rural areas because they wanted to employ urban youths first. Only during the 1950s and during one specific year of the Cultural Revolution when there was a great wave of decentralisation did the opportunity come to Gao Village. In 1958, four Gao Village males were enrolled as workers. Three went to Jingdezhen as porcelain makers and one left for Jiujiang as a painter. In 1970, two Gao Village males were enrolled to work in Nanchang, the capital of Jiangxi Province. These people married and settled in those cities. They were just ordinary workers, but they were the envy of Gao villagers. Every few years, when they came back to Gao Village to visit their parents and relatives, with small gifts and urban outfits, they attracted special attention because even their clothes were made of types of cloth that were never seen in the village. Villagers wondered how urban residents maintained their youthful looks.

Finally there was an even more difficult path for the villagers to leave the countryside. This was to pass the national tertiary education entrance examination. Once enrolled to study at a university or college a villager could leave the hard life behind forever. However, this path, as the villagers used to say, was as difficult as "climbing up to heaven without a ladder". To start with, too many aspirants competed for too few places. Even today, following a great expansion of tertiary education since the 1980s in which universities and colleges have increased from several hundreds to more than a thousand, there are only enough tertiary places for fewer than three people out of every hundred. By 1995 there were just 25 million tertiary students in China, compared with 1.8 million in Britain and 2.2. million in France.[8] Moreover, it is virtually impossible for rural youth to compete with urban youth for these places. The latter have better teachers and resources. They can afford to buy books and other study tools and have grown up in better educated families.

In the entire history of the PRC, Gao Village produced only

---

[8] Quoted in Sir John Maddox, 'The Case for Basic Research", *Campus Review*, vol. 6, no. 2 January 1996, p. 8.

one university student, and that was myself. I became a university student in 1973 not because I worked harder or because I was extremely clever, but because there was no national tertiary entrance examination. In 1973, after the extraordinary years of the Cultural Revolution, China again started to enrol tertiary students on a large scale.[9] I was lucky that there was an affirmative policy to enrol students from worker, peasant and soldier backgrounds.[10]

In the forty odd years since 1949, twelve males have left Gao Village to become urban residents. As for females born in Gao Village, they would be married away, usually into neighbouring villages where they would remain as rural residents. Only three women from Gao Village became urban residents through marriage. One was my sister who married a mechanic in the county town. Another was married to an army officer in a neighbouring village who later retired to the county town. The third was married to a man from another neighbouring village who later became a porcelain maker in Jingdezhen.

Population, resources and technologies

The rest of the Gao villagers had to stay in the village, relying on its territory of land and water to survive. The villagers did manage to increase the amount of arable land from 280 *mu* in 1949 to 308 *mu* by the 1990s, by opening up some hill land; but this was the limit. To feed the villagers the only alternative was more intensive work and technological improvements to increase grain production.

New technologies were introduced and the villagers did work harder. This was how they managed to feed a population which had doubled in a land of shrinking resources. However, it was

[9] It is often claimed by the current Chinese authorities as well as some scholars in and outside China that schools were closed during the Cultural Revolution. In fact, primary and secondary schools were closed only for a short period, some for one year in 1967, and some for about two years from 1967 to 1968. In the Gao Village area, primary schools were never closed. Some universities started to enrol students on a small "experimental" scale as early as 1971.

[10] Jung Chang, the author of *Wild Swans: Three Daughters of China*, a widely read book in the West, was also enrolled as a student in 1973, through connections that her high-ranking Party official parents had. Jung Chang claims in her book that Mao's radical affirmative policy was aimed at destroying China's education.

not the technology of tractors and combine harvesters; Gao Villagers could never afford that kind of machinery. In any case, terraced paddy fields and the abundant supply of labour combined to make mechanisation an economically unattractive option. The villagers still use buffaloes to pull the plough as the Chinese have been doing for thousands of years; they still use shoulder poles and wheelbarrows to transport goods; they still plant rice by hand, one bunch at a time; and they still thresh rice by hitting the crop against a wooden board. In this respect, nothing has changed.

Instead, new technology was introduced with respect to the variety of crops. One important new crop was short stock rice, introduced in 1963. This has two advantages. Firstly it does not fall over. The traditional long stock rice tends to bend to the ground in windy weather just when it is about to be harvested. When it does, it can become rotten or even sprout in muddy fields. Secondly, short stock rice needs a shorter time to grow. This is especially important for Gao villagers because the shorter life span of the rice crop makes it possible to grow two crops a year in the same field: once in early spring and again in summer. By planting rice twice a year, Gao villagers managed to increase the output of rice[11] from 250 to 300 kilos per *mu* to 500 to 800 kilos per *mu*. This also means that the villagers had to work twice as hard. It was this kind of intensification of soil exploitation that absorbed the ever increasing surplus labour force on the one hand and provided enough food for the ever increasing population on the other.

The different variety of sweet potato introduced in the early 1960s also had a great impact on Gao Village. Sweet potato had been a traditional main crop in the area, but there was only one variety, with a red skin and white flesh. This variety is very sweet, especially if eaten half dry and raw, when it can taste just like fruit. The variety newly introduced to Gao Village has a yellowish skin and egg-yolk like flesh. It is not as sweet as the white potato but it has more starch and the output is much higher. Moreover, it can grow almost anywhere. Therefore, when

---

[11] Throughout the book, rice output refers to *paddy* rice threshed but unmilled, two-thirds of the weight of which become available for consumption as decorticated rice.

the rice crop is not good or when the paddy fields are flooded, sweet potatoes become the staple food.

The other area of new technology is chemical fertilisers and insecticides. Traditionally, Gao villagers use organic fertilisers such as animal and human manure, grass and rice stock used by pigs and buffaloes, and ashes from firewood burned for cooking. There were no insecticides, and the villagers relied on birds and frogs to keep pests under control. Nowadays, chemical fertilisers and insecticides are indispensable. Gao villagers still make use of animal and human manure, but since they need to plant rice twice a year, traditional ways are insufficient. Chemical fertilisers and insecticides can produce quick results. When they were first introduced in the early 1960s, they were very scarce and the villagers could only obtain very limited supplies through a quota system arranged by the commune. Gradually, through the 1970s and the 1980s, more and more have become available. They are like drugs and Gao villagers are now hooked on them.

One serious consequence of the gradual increase in the application of chemical fertilisers and insecticides is that valuable aquatic resources have been gradually wiped out in the area. Even during the 1960s and early 1970s there were plenty of frogs in the ponds and paddy fields. During the extremely hot summer nights in July and August, Gao villagers would cool themselves by sleeping on bamboo beds outside their houses at night, accompanied by the pleasant and soothing songs of the frogs. By the 1980s, there were almost no frogs in the fields. Similarly, to swim and to fish in the ponds dotted around the paddy fields was a routine greatly enjoyed by children. The villagers could catch fish even when working in the paddy. Nowadays, there are no fish in the streams, or in the ponds. There are no prawns, shrimps, or shellfish in the river or the lake. If the villagers want to eat fish and if they can afford it, they have to buy it from a fish farm.

To recapitulate, over the past four decades the relationship between the people of Gao Village and the land has been governed by three factors. First, there has been an absolute physical limitation on land and water resources. Second, the population has grown steadily. Third, in order to feed the ever increasing population, the villagers have had to work harder and introduce new technologies. However, any advantages from increased production, which has led to the destruction of valuable aquatic resources, have been absorbed by the increased population. Thus the already limited natural resources have been further reduced by environmental destruction. As a result, Gao villagers remain poor, trapped by their efforts for immediate survival.

There are few options open to Gao villagers in trying to escape this poverty trap. That of expanding Gao Village's territory is not available. Another option, introducing new technologies that would increase production output dramatically, is not likely to be possible in the near future. By the standard of technologies available today, Gao Village's production output has reached its peak. Yet another option is to check the rate of population increase, and this is the Chinese government's current approach. Finally, there is the option of relocating the villagers through migration into industry, and this has been taking place since the late 1980s.

Population growth and its contributing factors

As already seen, the population in Gao Village doubled in the forty years since 1949. The pattern of increase can be categorised into three periods: 1949-63, 1963-78, and 1978 to the 1990s. These divisions relate to different child mortality rates, health care and population control policies.

Child mortality rate. In 1949-63 sixty babies were born, of which twenty-four died when they were children. The mortality rate was 40 per cent. In 1963-78 there were also sixty babies of which four died when they were children. The mortality rate was 6 per cent. In 1978-91 seventy-six babies were born and six of them died when they were children. The mortality rate was 7 per cent.

From 1949 to 1963 the child mortality rate was high largely due to the lack of modern medical services. Though the Great Leap Forward in 1958 had devastating consequences, it did not last very long, and in Gao Village the Great Leap Forward policies were put to a stop in 1959. Therefore, it is very hard to establish a direct link between the Great Leap Forward and child mortality rates in this period. What is clear, however, is that until 1962 there had not been a single doctor with any qualification in modern medicine within 50 kilometres. As in the years before 1949, no medical treatment was available for simple illnesses such as pertussis, malaria, diarrhoea, and certainly not for pneumonia or hepatitis. If a child fell ill, the parents had only two options: pray to the Buddha or seek a doctor of Chinese medicine who was usually self-trained with few resources other than herbal medicine. The choice for sick children was to build up their own resistance to disease, or to wait for death.

My mother was married when she was sixteen and gave birth to thirteen children. All of the children were born before 1963, and only four survive today. Of those who did not survive, only one died as an adult; the rest died as children. My mother used to say that her tears had been dried up by crying over the death of her children one after another. Every time one of her children fell ill she would go to a temple to pray before the Bodhisattvas to let her child survive. When she found that prayers to Bodhisattvas in a temple near Gao Village did not save her children she would travel tens of kilometres on her small bound feet to find the Bodhisattvas which were said to have the power to cure. However, it never worked. As her children died one after another, my mother lost her belief in the Buddha.

The situation improved dramatically after 1963. In that year two doctors, qualified in both Western and Chinese medicine, were temporarily stationed in Gao Village. Since then vaccination for common diseases such as cholera, measles, smallpox, mumps and encephalitis were carried out regularly. The two doctors also trained a village boy, Gao Shihua, who, when they left in 1970, took over the practice and worked as a "barefoot doctor" until the dismantling of the commune system in 1981.

Traditional values. The reduction of the child mortality rate is not the only factor contributing to the rapid population increase in Gao Village. Another important factor is the desire to have more children, especially boys. This desire derives from a number of causes, some traditional and cultural, some economic and pragmatic. The traditional ideology of Confucian culture dictates that a family needs a male to continue the lineage. According to this ideology, the worst crime anyone can commit is *duanzi juesun* (to die without sons and be the last of your line).[12] When there was a quarrel

---

[12] It is worth noting that Mao Zedong, arguably the greatest revolutionary and

or fight among the villagers, the worst condemnation and insult one could ever make to an opponent was to wish him or her *duanzi juesun*. Villagers who do not have sons feel inferior, and women who do not give birth to sons are considered to be inadequate and incomplete. This is also the reason why four families who did not have sons had adopted sons in Gao Village. Another aspect of this tradition is manifested by the saying *duozi duofu* (the more children you have the worthier your life is), which is taken for granted by everyone in the village.

Economic and sociological reasons. The traditional values which underpin this practice are not without a rational and pragmatic basis. To start with, given the economic and sociological structure of Gao Village before or after 1949, children are the only social security for old age, especially sons, as daughters are to be married away. Given the lack of medical facilities and lower living standards, there is no guarantee that a child will survive. Therefore, more sons are required as a security measure.

There are other pragmatic reasons connected with the clan structure of villages in the area. Everyone wants his or her own village to have more males in order to fight better with neighbouring villages. A villager from a large village feels superior, speaks louder and moves more boldly. If a brawl breaks out in a market place involving people from two villages, the villagers from the small village, knowing their place, will usually withdraw and thus loses face by avoiding a fight.

Even within a village, the sphere of influence and power is based on the number of male fists. The proportion of power and

---

rebel in contemporary Chinese history, did not seem to be able to break away from this traditional ideology. During the fatally important Lushan Conference in 1959, Mao repeatedly said to the audience of high ranking CCP officials that he should take the responsibility for initiating the disastrous Great Leap Forward policies and that he would die without sons and be the last of his family line. Mao's two brothers died for the revolution and his favourite eldest son died in the Korean War when he was sent by Mao to Korea under the guardianship of Peng Dehuai. Mao was in fact not without children. His daughter Li Min with one of his wives, He Zhizhen, and his daughter with Jiang Qing both survived. One of his sons with He Zhizhen, Mao Anlong, also survived. However, Mao Anlong was psychologically unstable. Mao apparently did not consider him and his daughters worthy to carry forward his line.

influence of a family parallels the number of males who can fight. A family of many brothers is always respected and feared. The family with the greatest number of adult males would have the greatest say in village affairs and it could intimidate the village leader. The only exception to adult male numbers as the basis of power politics was having the background of a landlord or rich peasant in Mao's China. At that time, these families were utterly suppressed and they never dared to enter local politics and power games. However, since the 1980s when their class labels were taken away this exception has disappeared.

There are also always a number of genealogical branches and offshoots in a clan village. In Gao Village, there are five branches. Very often, tensions exist among different branches and sometimes conflicts break out. Again, adult male numbers take political precedence. The branch with the greatest number of adult males will usually intimidate and bully the small branches.

My father was the only son of two who survived childhood. When I was about ten years old and my two surviving younger brothers were still very small, my father was one of the weakest figures in the village. The status of my family was only slightly better than those labelled as landlord and rich peasant families. Children of other families always bullied and teased me and called me names. Sometimes I would escape from their bullying and run home. Sometimes, even my home could not be a hiding place. They would throw stones on to our roof which was made of very thin tiles, which my family could not afford to replace. When it rained the roof leaked everywhere in the house. Therefore, having our roof stoned was not only an insult to the family, but also had grave economic consequences. Nonetheless, my parents would not dare to confront the parents of these children. In any case, they would simply have ignored my parents or would have insulted them further. Once I had a fight with a boy whose family was one of the most feared in the village. His father, one of several brothers who in turn had many sons, dashed to my house and slapped my face without asking questions. My parents' response was "Put up with it and grow up quickly".

There are other reasons why Gao villagers have wanted to have more children both during and since Mao's time. During the commune period, the socialist idea of equality was manifested in the equal distribution of grain and other staple food to each

family on a per capita basis. Since distribution of food was not
related to how much a family contributed to producing food,
those families who had more labourers and less children were in
fact subsidising those families who had few labourers but many
children. Therefore, the upbringing of more children did not
require much extra cost, as the cost of food, which was the main
item in the family budget in village life, was absorbed by the
system of "all eating from a big pot".

In post-Mao China the commune system has been dismantled,
and the "big pot" no longer exists. However, with regard to the
system of land distribution, it is still economically sensible to have
more children. In 1981 when the two production teams in Gao
village were disbanded, territory was divided and allocated to
households on a per capita basis. Each person, irrespective of sex
or age, was allocated an equal amount of land. Each family was
said to have contracted with the government to work the land
that had been allocated. This contract prevented the allocated
land from being sold or rented. Apart from this each family could
do whatever it wanted with the allocated land, as long as the
designated taxes and levies were paid.

This system also promised that every five years the land of the
whole territory would be re-allocated so as to accommodate population change. Therefore the more children a family has the more
land would be allocated to the family. From the point of view
of the whole village, the larger the population the smaller each
share of land becomes. However, from the point of view of each
family, the more children it has the bigger its share of the pool.
The original rationale for stipulating conditions such as equal distribution on a per capita basis, re-allocation of land every five
years and prohibition of sale and renting of land was probably to
maintain a degree of equality. However, after many years of practice,
the government realised that these polices counteracted its policy
of population control. Thus in November 1993, the CCP and
the State Council jointly issued a document in which it decreed
that from then on, there would be no land distribution in cases
where there was an increase in the number of household members,
and secondly no reduction for fewer household members.[13]

---

[13] The document is called *zhonggong zhognyang guowuyuan guanyu nongye he
nogncun jingji fazhan luogan zhengce cuoshi* (Several policy measures by the CCP

Government population control policies

It is clear that traditional ideology, cultural values, the social structure of village clans, the economic structure and the government's social and political policies have all combined to influence Gao Village's population development. But what about the government's family planning and population control policies? What effects do those sometimes brutal and still very controversial policies have on population development in Gao Village? In general, until the 1990s family planning and population control policies had little impact on Gao Village. Though the policies were talked about for many years since the early 1970s in the area, no serious measures were taken until 1979 when Jiangxi provincial authorities issued very clear guidelines.

According to these policy guidelines, a mother who had two male children or one male and one female child had to have oviduct ligation. A mother who had daughters but no sons could be allowed to become pregnant again. If any mother violated these guidelines, the family would be fined. The amount of the fine was not clearly stipulated in the guidelines. In other words, local authorities had to decide what fine would be appropriate on the basis of local conditions.

Even those guidelines were difficult to implement because grassroots officials either went slow by pretending not to know, or blatantly resisted. There was no way in which superior authorities could monitor the implementation of the guidelines. As a solution, Boyang County authorities worked out a scheme of allocating quotas to the local authorities. Every commune was given a quota of the number of women to be operated on. The commune authorities further allocated the numbers to various brigades, who in turn would decide how many women should be operated on and in which village. The village authorities would decide which particular individual should be operated on. If any of those who were ordered to have the operation refused, a fine would be imposed. In Gao Village this was 100 to 200 *yuan* for each violation. In 1980, five families in Gao Village were found to have violated the guidelines and each was fined 100 *yuan*, which at that time

and the State Council Concerning Agricultural and Rural Economic Development).

was a very big sum for the villagers. However, no villager would hesitate to spend money in order to have an additional baby.

With a quota system, the higher authorities had a way of monitoring the implementation of the family planning guidelines, since operation numbers could be checked easily in hospital records. However, the villagers soon found a way to beat the authorities. Since the quota system only requires operation numbers, old infertile women were sent to hospitals to have the operation to fulfil the quota while young women went on getting pregnant. The village authorities cooperated with the villagers to fool their superior authorities. After all, apart from the fact that village officials themselves wanted to have more children, it would have been very difficult to implement a policy that is resisted so widely.

By 1983, the county authorities had to further stipulate that any women below the age of forty-five who had had two children had to undergo this operation. Since 1990, the provincial policy is that any woman who has had one child has to have an IUD and any woman who has had two children has to undergo ligation. If the first child is a girl, another pregnancy will be allowed after five years. If the first child is a boy, no more pregnancies are allowed. Any woman who violates the policy is apprehended and taken to the operating room by force. If she is pregnant an abortion is carried out immediately, regardless of the maturity of the pregnancy.

In order to carry out such a brutal policy, a very effective monitoring system has to be developed. In fact there is no such system in force. All that the county authorities can do is to fix a target population increase rate for each *xiang*. In 1994, the target rate of population increase was 0.8%, with flexibility to a maximum of 1.5%. The local authorities are required to fulfil the target as one of their primary performance indicators. After every annual review, if any village fails to fulfil the target, the responsible officials will either be demoted, fined, or dismissed according to the extent of their failure.

What effects did these policies have on Gao Village? By 1995, thirty-five women in Gao Village had had the ligation operation and twelve women had an IUD. Another three families were fined, not for having violated the policy by having more children but for their failure to have ligation or an IUD. This is the most visible impact of the population control policy in the 1990s.

Some Gao villagers, like villagers all over the country, have found another way of coping with the authorities. Before their pregnancy is visible, the mother disappears from the village and hides in another village, usually in her mother's or a friend's home. The woman does not come back until after the baby is born. The most the local authorities can do is to fine the family, who will usually pay if it is not too much. The trouble is that the authorities cannot afford to impose a fine that is excessive because to do that would be self-defeating if the family cannot pay. However eager they are to please their superiors, they cannot take away the guilty family's primitive shelter and limited amount of grain which is just enough for survival. For many villagers that is all they have.

Since 1991, when these population control measures began to be most brutally enforced, four Gao Village women hid themselves during their pregnancy and came back with new born babies. One of them was one of Gao Changshan's daughters-in-law. Gao Changshan has five sons and three daughters, all grown-up and strong and now his is one of the most powerful families in the village. The families of the other three women all had some influence in the village, either because of political clout, like Gao Chouyin who was the village head, or because of strong adult male power, like Gao Dongshen who has three brothers and a dozen nephews. Usually, it is the officials of the village committee who have to implement the population control policies. However, village committee officials want to get involved with a village's internal affairs as little as possible. The only reason they are brutal to villagers with respect to population control is because they are pressurised by the township and county authorities.

One important way Boyang County authorities try to monitor and pressurise the village committee is by routine and sometimes unexpected inspections. Once violation is found to have occurred, a whole year's bonuses of all the officials of the village committee are forfeited. However, how can inspections work if the power-holders in every natural village do not cooperate? The answer is that inspections generally uncover nothing. Only those families who are not protected by village powerholders, or those who are easily intimidated tend to comply with the brutal population control measures.

Several general points can be made to conclude this chapter.

First, there was little population mobility in the forty years' history of the People's Republic of China. With the introduction of the *hukou* system there was strictly no freedom of movement, and a great wall had been built to divide the rural from the urban. This division did not break down until the late 1980s when migrant work was allowed to take place.

Secondly, with the introduction of basic health care and the resultant reduction of child mortality, the rural population increased rapidly in forty years. In the case of Gao Village the number of people doubled. Thirdly, the increase in production as a result of hard work and new technology did not have a visible impact on the living standards of Gao villagers. The benefit from the increase in output was cancelled out by the increase in population. Gao villagers have been kept in a poverty trap by what can be called an involutionary development.

Fourthly, although population control has been a declared policy since the 1970s, the effect of the policy was very limited until the 1990s. One reason is local resistance. Another is that some other government policies actually motivated population growth. During the commune years, the egalitarian distribution system motivated Gao villagers to have more children, as did the allocation of land on a per capita basis during the 1980s. Other reasons for population growth include cultural values, the need for social security, and local clan and genealogical politics.

Finally, the population control policies since the 1990s have been very effective largely because of their coerciveness and brutality. These polices, or the measures taken to implement them, can be seen as a serious violation of human rights. However, for the Chinese government and its policy makers, population control in China is a strategic priority, considered as a matter of national survival and requires war-time efforts.

5

LIVING STANDARDS

Living standards are difficult to quantify, especially when there is a lack of hard statistics at the village level. Even the most comprehensive record, *Dadui Taizhang 1949-1978* (The Basic Brigade Statistics Record 1949-1978)[1] is incomplete. In it, more than half the items are left blank. For the item "Income of the Commune", there are only statistics from 1969 to 1978 while from 1949 to 1968 the pages are all blank. As for health and education, the book only has records from 1972 to 1978. Another difficulty is that these statistics are total figures for the brigade and no breakdown figures are provided for each production team.

The production team's own records are even less complete because for many crucial items, and for many years, records simply no longer exist. The production team accountant was supposed to keep these records. However, over four decades, the position had been occupied by several accountants, and there was no requirement for one to hand over the records to the next accountant. Paper is scarce in rural China and most of the record papers were used for other purposes, or simply as toilet paper by the accountant's family.

The other complication is that over a period of forty years, production team organisation changed five times. When agrarian policies were radical, the government wanted the peasants to form larger production teams. When the policies were less radical, the peasants were ordered to form smaller teams. The rationale was

---

[1] *Dadui Taizhang* is classified as "state secret". It includes the class backgrounds of all the households, memberships of the Communist Party and the Communist Youth League, statistics of the local militia, the amount of state government taxes and levies each year, annual production output, local government financial income and expenditures, peasants' income, crop distribution and unit yield, development of mechanisation and development of production team and brigade enterprises.

that the larger a production unit was, the higher the degree of public ownership became, and public ownership was automatically assumed to be more socialist. Thus, during the Great Leap Forward the two production teams in Gao Village were disbanded to form one team. In 1960, the team was again divided into two teams. They were thus alternately combined and divided in 1969, 1972, 1974 and 1977. Every time there was a change, land and agricultural tools would have to be re-divided and new account books would have to be established.

Despite a lack of satisfactory official records, other sources of information on the living standards of Gao Village are available. In this chapter, housing, consumption of staple foods, the value of one day's work by a villager in terms of cash at that time, composition of diets, unit yields in the village, state taxes and local levies, consumer goods and so on are discussed.

Housing

Before 1949, there were twelve houses: eight large brick houses, two small brick houses and two mud houses. One of the small brick houses belonged to the landlord Gao Tianqiang and the other belonged to the rich peasant Gao Jingxiang. Each of the large brick houses belonged to a lineage group of families who were either middle peasants or poor peasants. In 1951 the land reform team confiscated the landlord's brick house and the landlord was moved to a mud house. Apart from that, housing ownership remained unchanged.

The seven large brick houses were all of the same pattern, with very thick brick walls: cool in summer and warm in winter. The builders managed to achieve this effect by means of an ingenious technology. Each brick is of rectangular shape, 25 centimetres long and 15 centimetres wide. Unlike bricks made nowadays, these bricks are very thin, only 1.5 centimetres wide. They are all of a dark grey colour. The bricks are not laid one on top of another, but are put together in fives to form a box, one at the bottom and one on each of the four sides. Then the box is filled with dry soil before the next box is formed on top of it. So the walls are formed by thousands of small boxes. Each box is glued to the next with white lime. Those little boxes form a very effective insulation system. They are also inexpensive since the

filling is soil and dust from the building site. The white lime is
not only cheap because it is local, but it is also good for decoration,
with its long-lasting white colour.

The houses all face south to avoid the bitter northerly wind
in winter and take in the cool breeze in summer. There are two
spacious rooms on both the east and west sides and a rectangular
room at the back. The four main rooms all have a wooden floor
made of oak. In the middle of each house there is a big hall, so
big in fact that it is divided into two parts by a huge skylight in
the middle of the roof, through which rain falls into a pool inside
the house. Each of the four main rooms has two wooden windows,
on which human figures and flowers are carved by the finest
craftsman in the area. The pool is built with elegant large scale
stones under which water is channelled away. Attached to each
of these houses is a small cottage used as a kitchen, usually by
two or three families of the same lineage group.

The walls of the mud houses are made of clay that is not
baked in a brick kiln. Because soil on the river bank is very
sticky, villagers can use it to make solid clay bricks 20 centimetres
long and 10 centimetres wide and thick. The soil is first pressed
hard on the ground and then made smooth with water. When
the clay is half dry, the villagers cut it into pieces. When the
pieces are completely dry they become hard bricks. Finally, these
bricks are then laid one on top of the other to form a wall.
These are cheaper than baked bricks because the villagers can
make them themselves. They do not last as long because after
some years they tend to erode under the rain. Usually, to prevent
erosion, villagers string rice stalks together into pieces to cover
the clay walls.

What I disliked about the smaller houses which did not have
a skylight in the middle of the hall was that the rooms were very
dark. There are no windows except two little holes on the front
wall of the house. In some houses there were one or two glass
tiles, each the size of a brick, that provide some light for the
rooms. However, ever since I could remember, I had never seen
that kind of glass tile on sale in the area, and nobody in the
village had ever bought one. Out of desperation, I once dug a
hole in the middle of a brick wall in my house and made a
window with two pieces of wooden board, so that I could read
in my room. The villagers were horrified, and rightly so though

I did not realise it at the time, at my destruction of a wall that had lasted for more than two hundred years.

There are good reasons for the villagers not to have windows to let in light. To start with, for hundreds of years, the pattern of village life has been to get up at dawn and not to return home until after dark. Daylight is hardly ever needed in the house. Secondly, windows need glass and other kinds of technology that Gao villagers cannot afford. Without this technology, windows let in rain and wind in winter and mosquitoes in summer. I can still remember the bitterly cold winter days when the wind and rain were howling and beating against the "modern" windows that I made by damaging a wall of "historical" value. Finally, houses with windows are a higher security risk. In the days before 1949, like other parts of China, there were bandits visiting the area. Even in Mao's China, there were thieves from other villages. In post-Mao China, security is certainly not any better.

To all intents and purposes, the traditional houses were good enough for Gao villagers for more than a couple of hundred years. However, with the increase of population since the 1960s, the existing houses have become inadequate. More housing was needed to accommodate newly-weds and new families. Yet, since 1949 most of the families could not afford to build new houses. Throughout the 1960s and 1970s, a moderate house with a wooden frame structure and mud clay walls would cost somewhere around 3,000 *yuan* to build. On average, a full day's work would earn an adult male in Gao Village less than 1 *yuan*. Suppose the best adult male villager worked 300 days a year at 1 *yuan* a day, it would take him ten years to earn 3,000 *yuan*. In fact, for the entire period of Mao's rule no one in Gao Village could have earned enough work points in a year to the value of 300 *yuan*. To expect Gao Villagers to build new houses on their earnings from farming was unrealistic.

There was no government support in this respect. What happened as a solution to the housing problem was that the villagers dismantled those ingeniously built large houses and used the materials to construct smaller houses for more families. By the 1990s, five of the six large brick houses had been dismantled to build smaller houses to accommodate more people.

The rationale for the destruction of those large brick houses was not just economic. It also has something to do with the tradition of inheritance. In a family of many sons, all the members could live together when only the oldest son is married with children. However, when the other sons grow up and get married, more space is needed, and relationships inside the family can also become too complicated for living together under one roof. The process of *fen jia* ("separation of the family") has to take place. When *fen jia* takes place, everything is equally divided among the male children. How else are they going to divide the house if it is not dismantled?

If a family has four or less male children, it can still manage to live under the same roof, because each male child ran occupy one room. The parents are usually pushed to live in the rectangular room at the back of the house. Gao villagers managed in this way until the 1970s. However, when any one of the four sons' children start to have a family, problems arise. The son in question needs a house with more rooms, and yet he cannot afford to build a new one. He needs the materials, his share of the large house, to help with the building of a smaller house with more rooms. Thus the dismantling of the large house has to take place.

By the early 1990s, more than half of the households in Gao Village had built "new houses", albeit small and primitive ones. The houses are lower, and it is usually one house to a family. There are no more skylights in the middle of the house. Nor can they afford the luxury of a wooden floor. They have a mud floor instead, and the internal walls are made of mud clay instead of wood as they used to be. Some internal walls are made of newspaper and other waste paper glued together. In order to save costs, some families only have the front wall and back wall of the house made of baked bricks, the former for appearance and the latter for weather conditions. The two side walls are built with unbaked clay bricks.

The bricks and wood taken from dismantling the old brick houses, once shared out among its former residents, were not enough for each family to build a new house. Thus each family had to save for years for the additional cost. They would have to plan many years ahead by buying one piece of wood this year, another tree trunk next year, and some tiles the year after until finally they had saved enough resources to launch the biggest project in their lives: building a house for the family. Loans from banks or the government for housing construction were never available, so most of them had to borrow from relatives and friends, sometimes up to ten or twenty *yuan* from each source.

There were other ways in which the villagers helped each other to lessen the cost burden. One was for friends and relatives to come and work at the building site. Apart from a master builder and a bricklayer – local professionals who in the 1960s and 1970s were paid roughly one to two *yuan* a day plus three meals – most of the other work was carried out by the family and relatives or friends without payment. Of course, help is mutual; but reciprocal favours may not be offered for many years, since the building of a house is a once in a lifetime project.

Another important way of helping is through the loan of tools. It is essential for villagers to borrow from each other as a way of pooling resources for a single project. Tools are lent without charge. Villagers even tend, albeit reluctantly, to lend their tools to families they do not like. This is because everyone is more or less related, and therefore has a sense of obligation to everyone else. Moreover, the custom of helping each other has been practised for so long that not to lend what you have is considered morally unacceptable. Of course, there is also the practical consideration: you may in future have to borrow something from the very family to which you fail to render your generosity.

Still another important way of helping is again derived from a long standing tradition. When a family builds a house, there is usually a celebration. During the celebration each family of the whole village is invited to send one member to join a banquet. The banquet is held on the day when the roof beam right under the roof ridge is set in place. This roof beam is the highest and most central in position and is considered to be the most crucial and oracular part of the house. Therefore, a banquet is held, red paper couplets written with lucky and good wish characters are pinned up, and firecrackers are set off. Friends, relatives, respected village elders and all those who have helped attend the banquet. Clan powerholders and village officials whose presence is meant to give "face" to the family are also invited. Apart from the village officials and clan powerholders, villagers who attend the banquet have to give the family some cash as a gift, usually wrapped in red paper. This gift can be just two, three or five *yuan*. In the 1960s and 1970s 10-20 *yuan* was considered generous.

The amount of money given on such an occasion rests on

many considerations. One concerns the amount received from the family in question in the past, as if to repay a historical debt that can date as far back as a couple of generations. Another important consideration is the current prestige, power and prospects of the family in question. It obviously pays to invest more in a powerful or potentially "wealthy" family. Sometimes, a family has to borrow money to fulfil the obligation of giving a gift. At the time when they have to give, villagers find this practice of gift giving extremely stressful and burdensome, and so they call it *renqing zhai* ("human relationship debts"). However, when they receive the favour, it is a great help. It could amount to as much as several hundred *yuan* for some families, which was a considerable income in the 1960s and 1970s. Economically, the practice is a sort of investment, or reverse mortgage: the villagers pay an instalment on the mortgage before the loan is made. For some villagers, their payment may not yield anything until many years later or indeed their investment may never be realised.

Despite all the factors discussed above such as building materials inherited from the large old brick houses, long term investment in the form of gifts, many years of saving and help from the villagers at no cost, other sources of funding are required for Gao villagers to build a house. Until the later 1970s only three families managed to build their own small houses. One was built by Gao Couyin, who worked as an accountant for a commune rice mill enterprise, and the second by Gao Shihua, who was the village's "barefoot doctor". The third was built by Gao Yunfei, the landlord Gao Tianqiang's son by his former wife, who was a primary school teacher. All three had regular cash income from sources other than farming.

During the 1960s and '70s there was little money around and for those who worked in agriculture there was no cash for many years in succession. When I was small, the only cash I had ever seen was at each New Year's Eve when I was given some bank notes as a gift. It was always something like 0.1, or 0.2, or 0.5 *yuan*, at most 1 *yuan*, and it was given to me by my mother's lover. My father would never have been able to give it to me. I could only keep the money for a few days before I had to give it to my mother for urgent family use. As peasants, we were supposed to be content as long as we had enough to eat. We never did have enough.

From 1980 to 1995, however, nine more houses were built in Gao Village. How did this happen? Where did the villagers get the cash from? Two important developments since the late 1970s in China have had a great impact on Gao Village, and the most visible aspect of the impact was the villager's ability to build those houses. One occurred in the early 1980s, not long after the end of the Mao era. From the early 1950s to the late 1970s, the Chinese government, as part of the push for industrialisation, imposed a differential pricing system by which Chinese industrial products had always been priced higher than similar products on the world market while agricultural produce had been "consistently priced at a third of the US price and a fifth of Japanese and European prices".[2] Furthermore the peasants were not allowed to sell their produce at local markets. They had to sell to the state at a designated price. Since 1979, however, the Chinese government changed its policy in this respect. The price of agricultural produce was raised by 25 to 40 per cent and compulsory purchase of grain by the state was also reduced.[3] These reform policies from 1979 to 1984 brought a substantial increase in income to Gao villagers who were then able to save some cash for house construction.

Since 1985, however, the situation began to deteriorate and Gao villagers would have descended further into poverty had not another new development occurred. The industrial expansion in the Special Economic Zones such as Shenzhen and other coastal areas in southern China led many young people to leave Gao village as migrant workers. The cash income from these migrant workers not only helped sustain life in Gao Village, but also provided funding for housing construction. More attention will be paid to these two developments shortly.

These new houses are built in a traditional style. There are two small rooms on either side of a hall which is also the main entrance. At the back of the house is a rectangular room, a part of which is used for storage and another as a kitchen. There is usually a small pigsty hut connected with the kitchen. The

[2] Zheng Yi, 'The Perils faced by Chinese Peasants", *China Focus*, vol. 1, no. 3, April 1993, p. 1.

[3] Zhu Ling, *Rural Reform and Peasant Income in China: The Impact of China's Post Mao Reforms in Selected Regions*, London, 1991.

framework of the house is made of timber and the whole structure consists of twenty tree trunk poles in four columns, connected by beams. The structure can stand alone without walls and the four walls can be constructed of anything: bricks, timber, fence-like bamboo screens, or just a partition made of rice straw for those who cannot afford anything else. No iron or steel of any kind is used in these traditional houses.

In Gao Village, however, there is one house that is made of concrete and iron and steel. It is three-storeyed with large glass windows and twelve rooms. The owner is Gao Hanzheng who was not born in Gao Village. He arrived with his mother, who married a Gao villager after her first husband died. As a boy, Gao Hanzheng was not good at school work and sometimes fought with teachers. It happened that his maternal uncle worked in the building industry in Jingdezhen, and as industrial expansion occurred in the 1980s, he was able, through his uncle's connections, to contract a number of construction works, and made a fortune by making full use of cheap village labour and became the village's only rich man.

By examining the remaining eight households that have built new houses since 1980 we will see how changes in agricultural income had little impact on Gao villagers even in the post-Mao reform period. Of the eight households, one house was built by the village doctor Gao Shihua who had already had one house built during Mao's time. Another two houses were built by Gao Chaojin and Gao Guoneng, who are carpenters. These two made some money by using their carpentry skills and by working as migrant workers far away from the Gao Village area. Another household was that of Gao Renzhu, one of the sons of the former rich peasant in Gao Village. This is the only household that was able to build a house with savings from agricultural income, as a result of the early 1980s price rise in agricultural produce. The remaining four households were able to build their own houses principally because they had inherited and used the building materials from the two large brick houses which were dismantled.

Food and diet

There is a Chinese saying which goes: *min yi shi wei tian* ("food is the most important thing in the whole world"). *Tian* "heaven" or "sky" is the biggest and most sacred thing in the world and *min*, the ordinary people, take *shi*, which is food, as *tian*, that is, as the biggest and therefore the most important thing in the whole world. This is because many Chinese farmers have never been far away from starvation, so much so that the Chinese take hunger for granted.

My personal experience serves as an illustration. From 1965 to 1966 I was boarding at a high school which was about 10 kilometres away from Gao Village. I would go home every Saturday and return to school every Sunday, carrying a week's food and firewood on my shoulders. I had no shoes to wear and I would have to walk barefoot on a very rough gravel road back home and to school once a week, with a shoulder-pole on one end of which I carried something like 8 *jin*[4] of rice and a bowl of pickled vegetables with a few pieces of fat pork or salted bean curd thrown in. On the other end of the shoulder-pole was a week's supply of firewood to give to the school.

The school had a kitchen and two cooks for more than 1,200 students and about thirty teaching staff. The kitchen cooked full meals for teachers but only rice for the students. There were fifty students in each class, and for each of the three meals we ate a single huge bucket would be brought into the classroom to serve us all; rice porridge for breakfast, steamed rice for lunch and supper. A ladle was used to distribute the rice and we would eat in the classroom, mixing it with whatever we brought from home. I would have pickled vegetables for every meal. I would have 0.3 *jin* of rice porridge for breakfast, 0.5 *jin* of rice for lunch and the same amount for supper. There was never anything fresh or meaty and anything that was not picked or salted would become rotten.

When I was at university from 1973 to 1976 in Xiamen, the food was much better. Nonetheless, I was hungry all the time. For instance, sugar was rationed, 0.4 *jin* per month for every student. Once a month I would go to the shop with the ration coupon, and as soon as I bought that 0.4 *jin* of sugar I would gobble it up in a couple of mouthfuls. Not until I arrived in the UK in 1977 did I realise that I had been hungry for more than twenty years of my life. The first time I cooked for myself in a

---

[4] *Jin* is a basic Chinese weight unit which is exactly 0.5 kilos.

student flat in Cardiff, I used oil as if it was water, two litres a week, I put on weight quickly and I then understood what it meant to have enough in my stomach.

The staple food in Gao Village, as in other villages in the area, is rice. In the Chinese language, to say "to have a meal" literally means "to have rice". When harvests are good, the villagers are happy to have steamed rice every day. When harvests are bad, the villagers have to eat rice porridge and other replacement food such as green vegetables and sweet potatoes. Sweet potato is easier to grow and its unit yield is higher than that of any other crop. There is no dairy food whatsoever. The villagers have never heard of butter or cheese. The three most important domestic animals are pigs, chickens and water buffaloes. Buffalo are considered the main means of production because they pull the ploughs. Female buffalo are well looked after for their calves. A good buffalo can cost as much as one third of a medium house.

Every household raises pigs, which are kept in a pigsty. Until the 1980s, pigs were the only source of cash income for the villagers and pigs are also the main source of oil and protein. Usually it takes a year to raise a piglet until it weighs somewhere between 50-100 kilos, when it is either killed for domestic consumption or sold to the government. A few well-to-do families are able to raise two pigs a year, selling one to the state for cash and killing the other for the Spring Festival. Throughout the 1960s and 1970s, a pig of about 100 kilos could fetch an income of a little more than 100 *yuan*. My family could never raise a pig over 150 kilograms. As we did not have enough grain for ourselves we simply could not waste good grain to raise pigs. During extremely difficult times when we had to consume a large quantity of vegetables for survival, my mother would send me out to pick wild vegetables and grass to feed our pigs. Our pigs were always thin and never grew. At that time, the best judgement of whether a household was doing well was to look at its pigsty.

Killing a pig therefore for the Spring Festival was a big event in a household. I can remember only a couple of times in my twenty years in Gao Village that my family was able to kill a pig for our own consumption. Even then, most of the pork was either sold or used to repay debts. We usually kept only the head, the legs, the tail, the internal organs and a quarter of the meat. A portion of the meat kept at home was to be consumed during the Spring Festival. The rest would be preserved with salt and was to last for the whole year. When there was a special occasion, such as having a local craftsman invited home to make tools, or a festival such as the Dragon Boat Festival, or the Moon Festival, a few pieces of pork would be cooked. The pig fat would be fried until it melted into oil which was precious for cooking. Every bit of the pig was useful and even the body hair was washed and packed to be sold to the state shop for something like 0.5 *yuan*.

Ideally, chickens and eggs would be a good source of food. However, free range chicks and hens would eat up the grain from nearby fields, and the villagers never found confined hens and chicks profitable. Chicks and hens were banned on and off for most of the commune period. In 1994 when I went to Gao Village, chicks and hens were again banned and my brother and friends had to buy eggs from the market to treat me.

The villagers do not grow much wheat or barley because the unit yield is found not to be as high as rice. Besides, flour products are less filling. While half a kilogram of rice is filling enough, half a kilogram of flour does not go very far in any form of food. The villagers like to have flour products such as noodles and bread. However, they can afford such food only on special occasions, such as the Dragon Boat Festival. There are local flour mills that make noodles, but they were only cooked on occasions such as birthdays or to honour a guest. My usual birthday present was a bowl of noodles, sometimes with an egg or two. When women give birth to a child, friends and relatives also cook noodles for the woman, as flour products are believed to produce milk.

The villagers grew their own vegetables on their private plots. Despite political campaigns, private plots have never been taken away from Gao villagers since the 1960s. In the commune years, every piece of land was supposed to be owned by the collective. However, every household was allocated, on a *per capita* basis, some land to produce anything it wanted for its own consumption. These allocations of land were called "private plots". The precise amount of land allocated to households as private plots is not known officially. In Qinglin brigade, of 3,484 *mu* of land on record, 224 *mu* was recorded as being allocated as private plots in 1961, about 0.06 per cent of the total land. According to official records, the percentage was kept more or less within this range until 1978. In Gao Village, however, every villager was allocated at least 0.1 *mu* per head. The total amount of land allocated as private plots was never less than 10 per cent of the total land from 1961 to the end of the commune era.

During the commune period Gao villagers mostly used the private plots to grow cotton for weaving cloth and vegetables for their own consumption. All the year round we had different kinds of green vegetables for feeding the pigs and for ourselves. Whenever there was not enough rice and grain for the family, we would eat a lot of vegetables. For people living in an affluent society, fresh, green vegetables are considered important for a healthy diet. For us, however, they were unpalatable and unappealing. Sometimes, we ate so many vegetables that we were disgusted with them. It was very difficult to swallow vegetables every meal every day without other foods to go with them.

Around once every two years when an old buffalo died the villagers would have some beef. However, the best meat would be sold at the market for cash income for the production team. The remainder would be distributed among the villagers, something like 5 kilograms per household. There was no goat, or lamb in the area. During the years when chickens were not banned, each household might kill one or two chickens for the Spring Festival at the end of the year.[5] For Gao villagers, there was very little other meat in their diet. There are no official statistics on meat consumption for Gao Village, and from what I can remember, an average annual consumption of pork in my family never exceeded 5 kilograms per person. According to official statistics, the average annual per capita consumption of fish was merely 1.35 kilos and that of meat was 6.35 kilos by the rural residents in 1985 in Boyang County, compared with an average annual per capita consumption of 15 kilos of fish, 15 kilos of meat, 1 kilo of chicken and 1.5 kilos of eggs by the town residents in Boyang in the same year. If and when there were eggs, my family would need to sell them to the state shop to earn some cash income. The average annual consumption of eggs in my family would be no more than fifteen per person.

From before 1949 and till the early 1970s the Gao villagers'

---

[5] For the villagers, birthdays and ages are still calculated on the basis of the lunar calendar, according to which a year ends sometime in February.

poor diet was compensated for by aquatic products. As there were so many ponds and streams leading to the river to the east of Gao Village, which in turn led to a lake which is in turn connected with Poyang Lake, there used to be plenty of fish and other water life in great variety. In spring, all kinds of fish swam up from the Poyang Lake to breed. Fish then could be caught easily, and every one of them was full of eggs. These were a great delicacy. In summer, when the villagers channelled water from the ponds and streams to irrigate their paddies, the ponds and streams would be dried up and there would be live fish to be picked up at the bottom. Sometimes, the villagers would be able to get 10 or 20 kilos of fish from a small pond. In winter, the villagers would work the river and the lake into many segments and each segment would be dried up in turn to catch fish. In front of the village there is a large pond, which again would be dried up to catch fish for the Spring Festival. Every household would have a variety of fishing implements, some as many as ten different kinds. There were other kinds of aquatic life such as eel, shrimps, prawns, shellfish and several kinds of snails. By putting a special net along the edges of the river and lake under the water grass and weeds, the villagers were able to catch shrimps. With luck, one catch could weigh as much as 1 kilo.

I use the past tense in the above paragraph because this rich and cheap source of healthy food is no longer available to Gao villagers. In the 1990s there are no more fishing activities and there are no fishing tools in the households. This is not only the case in Gao Village; the depletion of aquatic resources has taken place all over the area. Even in the great Poyang Lake fish have become scarce. For instance, in 1965, 6,222 tons of fish were harvested from Poyang Lake. In 1979, the amount was reduced to 3,316 tonnes, a 56.6 per cent reduction.[6]

As discussed previously, the most important factor for this environmental destruction is the ever increasing application of chemical fertilisers and insecticides. According to official statistics, chemical fertiliser use rose from 0.4 to 8.8 million tonnes between 1957 and 1978.[7] Increasing demand for grain production on the

---

[6] Liu Hanyan, *The Annuals of Boyang County*, p. 337.

[7] *Zhongguo Tongji Nianjian, 1993* (China Statistical Year Book 1993), Beijing, 1993, p. 349.

same amount of land meant more intensive labour and more chemical products for quick results. Chemicals killed the organic system on which fish depended.

Another factor is related to the campaign to wipe out the epidemic of schistosomiasis. This disease, also called snail fever, is known in China as the "blood-sucking disease" and has plagued the people around the Poyang Lake for many years. The disease is caused by a parasite which lives on snails only and will get into the human blood if infected. The infection is only carried by water containing parasitical snails. Since the Great Leap Forward, the county authorities surrounding Poyang Lake did two things which put an effective end to the epidemic of schistosomiasis, but also destroyed much marine life. One was to use aeroplanes to spread parasiticide to kill the snails, and the other was to mobilise masses of people to change the course of many streams and rivers. Both methods not only killed the snails and therefore the parasite, but also devastated other marine life in the water system.

The main remaining source of protein is *tofu*.[8] When one household made one load of *tofu*, it would be cut into identical small pieces and other households would either borrow several pieces for their own consumption or they would give the household some soya beans in exchange for some pieces. Those who borrowed would give the household the same amount back when they themselves made it.

My mother used to make *tofu* once every month as a kind of business. She would grind soya beans first with water on a family mill, then she would use a cloth net to extract the liquid. The liquid would then be heated in a huge wok with baked gypsum until it boiled. It would then be left to cool until it became jelly-like. Finally, my mother would put the jelly into a cloth which would be placed under a mill stone, and had the water squeezed out until she had solid *tofu*. She would have to spend several hours in the evening grinding the soya beans. Then she would spend the whole of the next day finishing the rest of the work. It was an agonising process for a woman with bound feet. When other villagers came to get some *tofu*, they would give my mother the amount of soya beans required to make the same amount of *tofu*. All my mother would get in return for her labour

---

[8] *Tofu* is from Japanese which is a loan from the Chinese *doufu*.

was enough raw materials for the next load of *tofu* as well as the soya bean residue which was good food for the family's pigs.

The ever increasing population in Gao Village has finally put a stop to this source of protein as well. When people are hungry they do not choose food on the basis of quality or benefit to health. The rational approach is to choose whatever has the greatest bulk so that the stomach is satisfied. In Gao Village, the rational choice was to grow more rice since it can be planted twice a year, and thus the unit yield in terms of quantity is much higher than the soya bean yield or any other crops. More and more land has been turned into paddy fields. 1 *mu* of land may yield 1,000-2,000 *jin* of rice if planted twice a year, but the same amount of land can only yield something like 1.50 *jin* of soya beans. Before 1949, roughly half of the land in Gao Village was used to grow cotton, soya beans and other kinds of economic crops. By the end of the Mao era, apart from the private plots and some land for growing cotton, almost all the land in Gao Village had been turned into rice fields. According to official records, the area of Qinglin brigade had 800 *mu* of land for growing soya beans in 1949. However, by 1978, this had been reduced to only 327 *mu*.

It is sometimes argued that it was left-wing agrarian radicalism that forced peasants to give up economic crops, with a dramatic reduction of income.[9] It is true that the rhetoric of agrarian radicalism during the Cultural Revolution was that cash crops should be suppressed. The argument was that they would lead to commercialism which in turn would breed capitalism. However, what happened in Gao Village shows that the reduction of cash crops has been a long process and was largely the result of the villagers' own choice. The market and commercialism would have meant little to Gao villagers unless there was a surplus over and above the grain that was required for basic survival. This leads us to the period since the late 1980s in post-Mao China.

The picture in Gao Village in the 1990s is radically different. With the degradation of the environment and exhaustion of natural resources, life in Gao Village would have been impossible had

---

[9] David Zweig, *Agrarian Radicalism*.

there not been another development, i.e., industrial expansion
along the south coast of China. Industrial expansion several hundred
kilometres away has had a great impact on Gao villagers. Foreign
and private enterprises along the coastal south required cheap
labour and Gao villagers were eager to take up the opportunity.
Since the late 1980s, more and more Gao villagers have become
migrant workers. By 1996, about 30 per cent of Gao villagers,
all of them young and most of them male, had left the village.
The fact that so many Gao villagers leave the village to become
wage earners is significant in two ways. First the population burden
on limited resources has been reduced. The same amount of grain
can be distributed among fewer people. Secondly, the remittance
sent by the young migrant workers means additional cash income
for the villagers. Only in this situation do the market and commercialism makes sense.

Nowadays, the villagers go to the markets more often and they
purchase more goods, ranging from television sets to food. As a
result, households specialising in sideline production have sprung
up in the area. Gao villagers do not make *tofu* any more. Instead,
they buy it from the market. They still grow whatever they can;
but what they cannot, they can afford to purchase from others.
In 1994 when I visited the village, it was a discovery as well as
a shock for me to find that my brother the village shop owner
had bought agricultural produce such as sugar cane, cabbage and
garlic from the market at the Boyang County Town 100 kilometres
away to sell to Gao villagers.

Boyang County Town is urban, and one would have imagined
that agricultural produce would be taken from Gao Village to be
sold there. What actually happened was that surrounding Boyang
County Town, there were many specialised vegetable farmers
who sold their produce at the town markets. I asked Gao villagers
why they did not produce these things themselves. They said
growing vegetables profitably required specialised knowledge and
technology. Moreover, I was told, if one household produced
something, it might be stolen before it was ready for consumption.
The most important point of course was that the villagers could
now afford to purchase some produce whereas previously they
would have had to go without if they could not grow it.

Clothing

The degree of self-sufficiency in Gao Village can be seen most clearly in the villagers' clothing. The villagers had a tradition of making their own clothes. They grew cotton which would be fluffed by a local craftsperson who would work from household to household. During winter evenings, women and girls would spin the fluffed cotton into yarn by using a traditional spinning wheel. The villagers would then invite another craftsperson to weave the yarn into cloth. During the 1960s and 70s there was a craftsman in the village who fluffed the cotton and a craftswoman who wove. They would work at the client's house and eat with the family. They would also be paid something like one *yuan* a day. Mostly, it was just one or two days work. When the cloth was made, a village tailor would be invited to the house to make clothes.

My father used to be a tailor, as was the rich peasant Gao Jingxiang. They did not have a sewing machine and everything was hand-made. Even buttons were hand-made, out of cloth. The villagers had a traditional way of dyeing their cloth by using leaves from a local tree.

It was an essential job for the women in the village to make shoes. Soles were made of many layers of cloth that had been left over from cuttings of clothes. These layers of cloth would be glued together with rice glue and then stitched hundreds of times with strong hemp thread, which was again made by the village women. This kind of sole was warm, comfortable and could last for a long time. The villagers also wove wheat and barley straw to make hats for summer and bamboo leaf hats to wear when it rained. Palm coir was used to make rain capes which were everlasting and easily adjusted for working in rice fields. Every man was expected to make his own working shoes out of rice straw. These shoes would not last more than a few days, but a capable man could make a pair in half an hour, without any special tools.

A bed mattress would be made of rice straw. The villagers would also make their own mosquito nets and quilts. Pillows were made of buckwheat husks. Throughout the 1960s and 70s, the villagers hardly ever bought any clothes from a shop. At most they would buy some cloth which was referred to as *yang bu* ("cloth coming from the oceans far away"), meaning cloth of foreign origin. They liked this foreign cloth because it was shiny and looked smart. But it was too expensive. In any case, it was rationed, and each person was given only less than 2 metres of cloth coupons per year. Every villager would have one suit made of *yang bu*, worn for special occasions such as the Spring Festival or visiting a relative or friend.

Every household would also have to save the rationed *yang bu* for sons and daughters who were going to get married. Only the bride would have several outfits made of colourful *yang bu*. Until I went to university in 1973, I never dreamed of having clothes made of *yang bu*. My greatest desire, as far as clothing was concerned, was to wear white home-made shirts instead of black or blue shirts. However, my mother would not allow me to wear white shirts because they needed to be washed more frequently and would not last long. In any case, soap was rationed and was used very sparingly.

Since the late 1980s, again, the picture has been different. No household fluffs cotton or spins yarn any more. The craft has died out. People will laugh at you if you wear a pair of rice-straw shoes, or home-made clothing. The young villagers now wear leather shoes, rubber shoes or boots. Even the old villagers wear sneakers. They still make cloth shoes, but only occasionally, and with *yang bu* materials. They have woollen sweaters, windcheaters, proper raincoats, overcoats, and other clothes made of all kinds of synthetic fibres. Some of them even wear Western style jackets brought home by migrant workers, and with a tie.

Income

It is very difficult to talk about income in a language that is understood in the "West". Throughout the Mao era, a more or less barter economy existed in Gao Village. Secondly, the frame of reference does not make much sense. For instance, nowadays, the rough exchange rate between Chinese money and the US dollar is that 1 *yuan* equals US$0.125. An average migrant worker from Gao Village working in Shenzhen Special Economic Zone could earn about 400 *yuan* a month, which is about US$50. After deducting all the expenses, the migrant worker may be able to send 100 *yuan* a month back to Gao Village, which is US$12.50.

What does this amount mean as income for the Gao villagers? It is difficult to see the significance of this amount of income without listing the price and cost of living indexes in Gao Village.

As this is not a textbook or a monograph on economics, I will avoid a comprehensive price comparison. In any case there are no official statistics on Gao Village. However, I will list the prices of certain items of daily necessity in the 1970s before I discuss the income of Gao villagers at that time. It has to be pointed out that inflation was very low from the 1960s to 1970s.

A box of matches cost 2 cents in Chinese currency.[10] 1 *jin* (half a kilo) of sugar cost 60 cents, 1 *jin* of pork 69 cents, 1 *jin* of soya sauce 13 cents, 1 *jin* of salt 7 cents, a bar of soap 16 cents, 1 *jin* of fish 40 cents, 1 *jin* of shrimps 30 cents. A school textbook cost about 50 cents, a pair of sneakers 3 *yuan*, a pencil 5 cents, an average package of cigarettes 20 cents. While a watch or a bike cost 120 *yuan*, a meal in a factory or university canteen cost less than 50 cents. A transistor radio in the early 1970s cost more than 100 *yuan*, but 100 *jin* of un-husked rice had to be sold to the state at the price of only 9.8 *yuan*.

Before we proceed with a discussion of the villagers' income we need a brief introduction of how the commune system recorded and evaluated its members' contributions. Every farmer belonged to a production team of about ten to twenty households. The way of recording and evaluating a member's contribution to the team was the calculation of work points. Every day, the production team leader would assign different kinds of work that needed to be done on that day to each individual member. Most of the time, in order to simplify the task of work assignment and to monitor the team members' work effectively, several work groups would be formed, each of which was headed by a group leader. The production team leader would assign a specific task to each group leader the night before and the group leaders would assign specific tasks to its members the next morning.

In the evening, the group leaders and the production team accountant would work together to record each member's work points. Any member who worked for a full day from dawn to dusk would be recorded as having earned ten work points. Half a day's work would be given five work points and so on. However,

---

[10] 1 *yuan* has 100 cents.

these work points were only gross points which recorded the team member's labour time, but not labour value because the team members' ability varied from individual to individual. Some were stronger than others and some were more skilful.

A way of distinguishing between the labour time and labour value of each team member was the annual evaluation of each member's labour value. This was again measured in terms of points, on a scale from three to ten. The labour value point was called the base point, as opposed to the gross point. If the best labourer was evaluated as having ten base points he would earn ten points for a full day's work. In other words, his or her gross points and base points would be the same. In this system, the gross points recorded the team members' labour time while the base points recorded labour value. If person A had a base point of five and person B had a base point of ten, then the labour value of person A's full day's work would be only half of that of person B. If person B worked for half a day, his or her gross point on record would be five which would give a base point of 2.5.

The best woman labourer in Gao Village, according to the official record of 1964, scored only 5.6 base points and the best male labourer scored 9.6 base points. In other words, the best woman labourer's full day's work was worth only a little more than half of the best male labourer. During the Cultural Revolution in the early 1970s, because of radical policies, the best woman labourer could earn as much as eight base points. For the villagers, the rationale for gender inequality was that men and women were often, but not always, assigned different tasks. A child labourer might earn three or four base points. An elderly man might earn six or seven base points for a full day's work. One can imagine how important the annual evaluation of base points was for the villagers. My experience was that the system worked quite well and did more or less reflect the true contribution each member made to the team, gender inequality aside.

Finally, it has to be noted that each member's base points only reflected his or her contribution. The true value of each member's contribution depended on the total income of the production team, and this varied from year to year. Suppose the total income of the production team in a particular year was 700 *yuan* and the total base points of the all the team members was 10,000, then every ten base points would be worth 0.7 *yuan*. Accordingly, the best labourer, evaluated as having ten base points, would earn 0.7 *yuan* for a full day's work. A woman who was evaluated as having five base points would only earn 0.35 *yuan* for a full day's work.

To bring the system to life it will help to discuss the income of one family in the years 1963, 1972 and 1992, each being representative of a different political period: 1963 and 1964 were claimed by the Chinese authorities to be the best years after the Great Leap Forward and before the Cultural Revolution, 1972 was in the middle of the Cultural Revolution period, and 1992 was in the middle of the post-Mao reform years of Deng Xiaoping's era. In 1964, my family consisted of five people: my father Gao Renfa, my mother Gao Yuanrong, my two younger brothers Gao Changxian aged ten and Gao Changwen aged four, and myself aged thirteen. I worked during school holidays, and my mother worked occasionally. My father was very weak and therefore was assigned to look after the production team's buffaloes as a special concession. The whole household together earned 1,886 base work points. In 1964 every ten base points was worth 0.72 *yuan*. The total value of my family's work points was 131.50 *yuan*. In that year, my family also contributed some household fertiliser to the team which was worth 3.77 *yuan*. The total value of my family's contribution to the team was therefore 135.27 *yuan*. In the same year, grains and other agricultural produce distributed to my family by the production team were valued at 215.40 *yuan*. Thus my family was 80.13 *yuan* in debt.

100 *jin* of un-husked rice was valued at 7.9 *yuan* in 1964 and my family received about 2,600 *jin* of un-husked rice plus about ten *yuan*'s worth of other agricultural produce. The rice distributed to my family was hardly enough for us to survive for the year. To put rural income at that time in context, as my father's base point was above average at seven, he was required to work for 244 days to buy a bicycle. A top labourer could just about earn enough in one day to buy 1 *jin* of pork, or fish, or sugar. In that year, fourteen households were in the black and twenty-three households were in the red. Gao Renkai, who was ill most of the year, incurred the greatest debts and his family ended the year owing the team 191.82 *yuan*. Gao Changniao, the best male labourer, was 113.04 *yuan* in the black.

The income described here did not include the income each household received from working on their private plots. My family had in some years had as much as 2.5 *mu* of land as a private allotment to grow vegetables, cotton and other economic crops. As I said before, we never lacked vegetables and those were entirely grown on private allotments. Also excluded was income from fishing, raising pigs and chickens when possible. However, it is impossible to establish a statistical basis for these sources of income. An annual income of 100-200 *yuan* per household would not be an over-estimate.

Having examined the income of one family, we next review the income of one production team in 1963.[11] The total income of one production team (there were two teams in Gao Village at that time) was 7,317.90 *yuan*, of which 93.8 per cent was agricultural income and 6.2 per cent was from sideline production income such as raising ducks and selling fish. Production costs totalled 1,712.29 *yuan*, of which 1,576.22 *yuan*, 21.5 per cent of the total income, was spent on agricultural input; 75.98 *yuan*, 1.03 per cent of the total income, was spent on sideline production; and other management costs amounted to 60.09 *yuan*, 0.8 per cent of the total income. 9.88 per cent of the total income, i.e., 724.24 *yuan* was paid to the state as agricultural tax. Taking away the production cost of 1,712.29 *yuan* and the state tax of 724.24 *yuan*, the rest was considered to be the team's net income. However, a further 195.25 *yuan* (4 per cent of the total net income) for the Public Accumulation Fund and another 146.25 *yuan* (3 per cent of the total net income) for the Public Welfare Fund had to be paid to the production brigade. Another 90.80 *yuan* was taken away as salary for the brigade officials. Eventually, only 4,384.87 *yuan* (60 per cent of the total income) was distributed to the households, with a resulting average household income of 292.31 *yuan* and per capita income of 56.86 *yuan*. This was a 4.5 per cent increase on the per capita income in 1961. As stated in the preface to the production team record sheet, 1962 was a year when the government stressed that production team income

[11] The figures of 1963 are shown here because official figures for 1964 were not available. To the best of my knowledge, there might be some variations, but the differences between 1963 and 1964 would be small enough for our purposes.

should be distributed to its members as much as possible and Public Accumulation and Welfare Funds should be kept at a minimum.

By 1972, my father had been dead for a number of years and I was the main labourer in the household. In 1972 my family earned a total of 1,099.4 base points, which was valued at 89.05 *yuan*. The "unit labour value", i.e. the value of every ten base points, was roughly 0.81 *yuan*. I also earned another 197.36 *yuan* as a "barefoot teacher". The value of agricultural produce distributed to my family in 1972 was calculated to be 381.33 *yuan*. My family was again in the red, owing the team 94.92 *yuan*. In 1972 I was teaching grade seven students mathematics and Chinese and my salary for the whole year was only 197.36 *yuan*. My colleagues at the school who had similar responsibilities but were appointed by the government and had urban resident status earned five times as much as I did.

A month's salary for an experienced lecturer at university level was almost as much as I earned from all sources during a whole year. It took only two months for an average porcelain factory worker in Jingdezhen to earn as much as I earned for the year as a rural teacher. The cost of living in urban areas was no higher than in rural areas because prices were fixed nationally at the same level by the government. It is true that rural residents did not have to buy vegetables from the market since they were allowed to grow them on their private plots. However, vegetables did not cost urban residents much because of the price cap and government subsidies. For instance, it cost only 5 cents in Chinese currency to buy a *jin* of Chinese cabbage in the 1970s. Yet although my earnings were meagre compared with my colleagues who had urban resident status, my position as a "barefoot teacher" was the envy of every villager.

Gao villagers, like other villagers in the area, had a brief honeymoon with the post-Mao reform policies during the early 1980s when the price of agricultural produce rose dramatically, and when the prices of industrial goods did not follow the increase and the local authorities had not yet introduced various kinds of taxes and levies. After 1984, however, the situation deteriorated rapidly, for two main reasons. The first was that following a quiet period immediately after the death of Mao, the cost of chemical fertilisers and insecticides and other industrial goods rose quickly.[12] On top of this, various kinds of taxes and levies imposed by the local authorities over and above the government agricultural tax were too much for the villagers to bear. In 1991, Gao villagers had to pay various levies on twenty-nine items. In 1992, this was reduced to twenty-six items. All the levies were imposed on a *per capita* basis.

Although the price of agricultural produce rose dramatically after the reforms started in 1979, by the early 1990s the price increase became nominal. For instance in 1992, 100 *jin* of un-husked rice could be sold to the state at more than 40 *yuan*, which was more than three times the price in 1972. However, if input costs and other payments are taken into consideration, this price increase for agricultural produce did not mean an increase in income. The family of my brother Gao Changxian is an example. Gao Changxian is married with three children, two daughters and one son. With my mother living with him there were six people in the family. In 1992, he had 4 *mu* of paddy fields and 2 *mu* of dry land on which he grew cotton and rape seed. 4 *mu* of rice yielded 2,000 kilograms which gave him 832 *yuan*; 2 *mu* of dry land yielded 50 kilograms of ginned cotton which gave him an income of 300 *yuan*; and 300 kilograms of rape seed gave him 360 *yuan*. The total yearly income was therefore 1,500 *yuan*. Production costs were 80 *yuan* for seeds and 648 *yuan* for various chemicals. The taxes and levies in 1992 totalled 80 *yuan* per person, which for Gao Changxian's family came to 480 *yuan*. The family's net income was 292 *yuan*. Gao Changxian and his wife each spent about 180 days in the field, which means that they each earned 0.8 yuan a day, which is about US$0.4 at the present exchange rate.[13]

In spite of an aggregate 200 per cent inflation since 1972, Gao Changxian and his wife each earned 0.8 *yuan* a day, which is

[12] As for how and why the cost is so high see Chen Feng, "Huafei Shengchan Gongying He Xiaoshou de Genben Wenti he chulu" (The Fundamental problems underlying the production, supply and sales of chemical fertilisers and the Way Out), in *Gaige Sikao* (Contemplating the Reform), Rural Development Centre, ed. Beijing, 1992.

[13] The example of Gao Changxian is based on information obtained through personal interviews with him at the end of 1992. The example is also cited in David Schak, ed., *Entrepreneurship, Economic Growth and Social Change: The Transformation of Southern China*, Queensland, 1994.

more or less the same amount at face value as the best village labourer could earn back in 1972! In 1992, 0.8 *yuan* was only a little short of being enough to buy two and a half of the popular Kent or Three Fives cigarettes. However, for most of the villagers in the 1990s there was a noticeable improvement in the quality of life, reflected in things such as clothing, housing space and other consumer goods. The key to the improvement in the 1990s does not lie in income from growing agricultural produce, but in income from young Gao villagers who have become migrant workers thousands of kilometres away from Gao Village.

Consumer goods

Throughout the 1960s and 70s Gao villagers used very few consumer goods that they could not make themselves. Even a washbasin was made of wooden boards strung together with bamboo strings. In 1962 my father managed to buy an enamel washbasin at the cost of something like 3 *yuan*. He said it was for me to use at high school when I had to board there. No one was allowed to use the basin and it was safely put away for three years until 1965 when I took it to high school. My father, an avowed Buddhist, never spent a cent on buying something for himself except matches and incense. He used these not to burn joss sticks before the Buddha but to light his tobacco. He grew his own tobacco and he smoked heavily. Very often, he would use a wooden stick instead of incense in order to save money. My elder sister's favourite story of how my father scrimped and saved was his refusal to use an umbrella. He would explain that every time an umbrella was used its life got shorter. Usually, Gao villagers could only afford paper umbrellas painted with tung oil, made by a local craftworker. Only the well-to-do could afford a cloth umbrella.

There was very little that Gao Village would buy from the shops, the nearest shop being some 3 kilometres away. They would have to buy matches, salt, soap, kerosene for lamps, joss sticks, some red paper for writing couplets for the Spring Festival, and rationed sugar if they could afford it. But Gao villagers would make their own soya sauce from soya beans. They would make sugar from sugar cane or from sweet potatoes, or even from rice. They would also make their own wine from rice, a spirit called *sake* in Japanese. Before my sister was married in 1960 my family could not afford kerosene, so we continued to use an oil lamp, a very dim light, but economical. After my sister's marriage, light improved dramatically because my brother-in-law, an engine mechanic on a ship, was able to supply my family regularly with used engine oil. I always looked forward eagerly to my brother-in-law's visit. Once every two months he would bring several apples or some sweeties and biscuits, a great luxury for the family. My mother would cook two eggs for him while we children looked on with our mouths watering. She would only let us have a taste of my brother-in-law's presents and put them away for more important use such as treating a guest or giving gifts to the right people on the right occasion.

Until the late 1970s no Gao villagers could afford a watch, a bike, or a radio. One of the doctors stationed in Gao Village from 1962 to 1970 had a radio. Every night, groups of Gao villagers would go to the clinic to listen to this radio. Before the late 1970s only two people in Gao Village had a watch. One was Gao Yunfei the landlord's son, a school teacher, and the other was Gao Shihua, a "barefoot doctor". I managed to buy a watch for 120 *yuan* only in 1977, when I was sent by the government to study in Britain. The government paid for it as part of the scholarship allowance. In order to have a presentable image, all of us who were going abroad were given a huge amount of money, something like 950 *yuan*, to smarten ourselves up. When I wrote back from Beijing to tell my brother about this, he could not believe that so much money had been given to me for nothing. To the Gao villagers it was like the *Arabian Nights*. Since I was small I had always wanted three things: a knife that could be folded, a torchlight, and a pair of rubber boots. I had none of them until I left the village.

In the whole of Qinglin brigade, with 593 households and a population of 3,610, there were only thirty-six watches, twelve bicycles, twenty-five sewing machines and thirty radios by 1978. Nowadays, however, small consumer items such as gloves and socks, or a torchlight, a hat or a scarf are no longer thought a major consideration in the family budget. There were only two bicycles in Gao village in the early 1980s. Now there are forty-two. There are also a couple of colour, and twenty black and white television sets.

Six years after I left the village in 1973, the fortunes of my family changed for the better. One reason is that all my brothers have grown up. However, the main reason was the extra cash income that I started to send home. When I graduated from Xiamen University in 1976, I was assigned to teach English there. At that time, the salary of those employed by government institutions, as opposed to those employed by government enterprises which had a salary system of eight grades, were scaled in twenty-four grades. My salary was at the lowest grade, which was 38.5 *yuan* a month.[14] Then in 1977, because of my poor family background and "good performance" and after I successfully passed three tests in English, one oral, one aural and one written, I was sent by the Chinese government to Britain to study English. I was there for three years, and my salary of 38.5 *yuan* a month was continuously paid back in China. Since every aspect of my expenses was taken care of by the Chinese government, plus £3.08 a month pocket money, I could afford to let my mother and brothers have all my Chinese salary. As a result, my family was the first in the village, after the "barefoot doctor" Gao Shihua, to have a bicycle. They were also the first to have a colour television, because I bought it for them in 1992.

Because of the "consumer boom" in the area since the late 1990s, many villagers have set up small stands selling a variety of goods. A typical stand is made of a small shelter with one opening facing the road where the traffic comes and goes. These can be locked up at night and they are just big enough to store all the goods on sale, which are displayed on three sides. There is a counter at the front, usually with a family member sitting behind it who serves customers. They cannot be called street corner shops because there are no streets in the villages. There is only one road running through the villages to the Boyang County Town and all the shops are installed along this road. A kilometre away to the east of Gao Village, there are now half a dozen shops along the road. About 2 kilometres to the west of Gao Village there are another half dozen shops set up along the road.

Gao Village has had one such shop since the late 1980s. It

---

[14] It was rumoured among the Chinese that when the twenty-four-grade system was originally conceived, the first grade was designed for Chairman Mao, who, however, only agreed to accept a grade three salary which was something like 500 *yuan* a month.

was owned by a Gao villager's son-in-law, who used to be an army officer and who had lost his job at the county government. In 1991, however, with 6,000 Australian dollars that I had given him, my brother Gao Changxian had a house 3 metres wide and 7 metres long built along the road and set up a shop. Soon afterwards the son-in-law's shop disappeared because it could not compete with Gao Changxian's shop. Gao villagers were very pleased about the affair. One village powerholder said to me in 1992 that Gao Changxian's shop had saved face for Gao Village because it was actually owned by a Gao villager. The son-in-law was not a Gao villager and his surname was not Gao. To Gao villagers, to have a non-Gao shop in Gao Village indicated the weakness of Gao Village since nobody was wealthy enough to open up a shop. Gao Changxian's shop in 1994 had a turnover of around 30,000 *yuan*, with a very small profit margin, of around 200 *yuan* a month.

A number of factors contributed to the consumer boom in Gao Village, but an increase in agricultural income is not one of them. The principal factor is the cash income from young Gao villagers working as migrant workers. To the present day, around 30 per cent of the people in the area have left as migrant workers. If each migrant worker sends an average of 100 *yuan* a month back to Gao Village (which they in fact do, as we will see in a later chapter), the cash income from ninety-eight Gao Village migrant workers in 1995 would amount to 117,600 *yuan*. This is a huge amount of money for Gao villagers, on top of which the absence of these migrant workers alleviates a substantial burden on village resources.

Another important factor is that some consumer goods are simply much cheaper now than, say, ten years ago, thanks to the industrial boost since the 1980s. An ordinary watch costs around 50 *yuan*, or even less, nowadays, whereas its cost was at least 100 *yuan* before 1978. Today's prices are such that if inflation is taken into account a villager should be able to buy a watch at a cost equivalent to 12 *yuan* fifteen years ago, whereas the actual price at that time was set at 120 *yuan*! This is just one example of how the government fixed the price of industrial goods to the disadvantage of rural residents. This price change applies to other consumer goods as well, such as bicycles, radios, rubber boots, garments and television sets.

The general picture at brigade level

Table 1 (see Appendix 2) provides a general picture of income at the brigade level. It shows important indicators of income: *per capita* consumption of grains, "unit labour value" as defined above and annual *per capita* income in Chinese currency. The statistics in the table are not complete in that it only contains the figures from 1969 to 1978. The record book that I had access to leaves the year 1968 blank. The reasons for the incompleteness of records were discussed at the beginning of this chapter. 1971 and 1972 were the best years of all during Mao's reign. 1973 was a year of disaster because of a serious flood in spring and a serious drought in summer. The villagers had to live on *fan xiao liang*, i.e., the grain collected from the peasants but stored locally and resold to the peasants by the state to avoid famine. The chart also shows that towards the late 1970s though grain production output kept steady (steady level of *per capita* grain consumption), unit labour value kept on declining and *per capita* annual income remained flat. This was the case because of the pricing system which suppressed the value of agricultural produce.

Towards the end of the 1970s the rural situation was indeed deteriorating. This was not just the fault of the collective system. It was the result of a number of combined factors. One was the continuous increase of population. Another was the gradual environmental degradation. Yet another was the detrimental pricing system. During the 1980s, further deterioration of the farmer's situation was checked by the reforms, among which the increase in prices of agricultural produce had the most important impact.

By and large, living standards in forty years had hardly improved though production output increased. The gains from the increase in output were partly taken away by the exploitative nature of the pricing system and the state's compulsory purchase of grain, and partly cancelled out by the increase in population. In terms of material well-being, development in Gao Village during these forty years was involutionary and Gao villagers were kept in a poverty trap by the state policies, environmental degradation and population increase.

6

RURAL HEALTH

If we are to single out the area in which Gao villagers benefited most in Mao's time, it was health. The child mortality rate has been reduced impressively since the 1960s. It was during the Mao period that Gao villagers, for the first time in the history of the village, had access to modern medical services on their doorstep. It was also during this period that vaccination and immunisation were introduced and carried out regularly, and the epidemic of schistosomiasis was brought under control.

It has to be pointed out at the outset, however, that the reduction of child mortality and the improvement of health in Gao Village was not so much a result of an improvement in economic circumstances. As I have shown in the previous chapter, Gao villagers' economic circumstances improved very little in Mao's China. It would also be quite wrong to assume, however, that modern technologies such as vaccination alone were responsible for the general improvement in health in Gao Village.

The existence of modern technology does not necessarily mean that it will be available to people like Gao villagers. It requires political will, government resources and effective administration to make modern medical technology available to villagers. Whether anything short of the Communist government in Mao's China would have been able to deliver what has been delivered to Gao villagers in terms of health care is now a hypothetical question, nonetheless worth asking because its implications are very relevant. In the 1990s economic circumstances improved considerably in Gao Village as a result of remittances from migrant workers, and modern medical technology should have been more prevalent now in the 1990s than in the 1960s and '70s. However, all indications in post-Mao China are that the health care situation in Gao Village has recently deteriorated because of the government's lack of effort.

Before the 1960s

Until the 1960s Gao villagers had never known what penicillin, or streptomycin, analgen, antibiotics and many other drugs looked like, or how they worked. They never in fact took tablets. All they were prescribed by traditional Chinese doctors were herbs, dried insects and animal parts in their original forms. These were then either ground into powder or boiled to produce a liquid to be drunk. It is hard to know in what sense traditional Chinese remedies were effective as a treatment. Some practices appear dubious, at least to some. For instance, a patient believed to have lung trouble is often told to eat pig's lungs. If you have a weak spleen you are asked to eat more pig's spleens. If you feel dizzy and weak, you are supposed to have anaemia, and you will be told to have pig's blood and any kind of fruit that has a red colour such as dates. It may well be true that insects such as cicadas, centipedes, beetles and natural objects such as orange skin and honeysuckle have substances that are medically useful. However, there are diseases that cannot be dealt with effectively by Chinese medicine. Diseases such as measles or those causing fever respond better to treatment by Western medicine.

This is not to denigrate Chinese medicine, which has a fine tradition and sometimes proves useful to patients. I personally benefited from Chinese herbal medicine. Ever since I was small I have had a chronic ear infection in my right ear, which still recurs from time to time. Gradually my ear developed a kind of ringing that I could hear constantly. In 1985 my father-in-law mentioned this to an acquaintance of his who was one of the most prestigious traditional Chinese medicine doctors in China. The doctor, without having ever seen me, sent me a prescription from more than 200 kilometres away in Fuzhou. I then went to a traditional Chinese pharmacist in downtown Xiamen and brought back several packages of dry herbs of more than twenty kinds. Xiamen University where I worked at that time still had an elderly woman who was paid to brew herbal medicine for the staff and students. I had to go to her three times a day to pick up the herbal juice, and drink a good bowl of it every time. The course took me two months to finish. It worked, and the kind of ringing that I used to endure never returned. But then the doctor who gave me this prescription was a well-qualified professional. Moreover,

Chinese medicine may be effective for illnesses that are chronic or long term. An acute disease may come to its conclusion before the herbs can have any effect.

Effective or not, Gao villagers usually do not go to the doctor anyway. Illnesses such as otitis, rhinitis, periodontitis and malaria are very common and so taken for granted that the villagers do not bother about them. Discharges such as pus running from children's noses, ears and eyes are a normal scene in the village; as normal as meals, the toilet and sleep. When I had ear infections as a child nobody cared about it, so I did not care either because I thought it was a normal part of life.

Other common diseases that Gao villagers suffer from are colds, influenza, diarrhoea, asthma, arthritis, furuncle, carbuncle, abscess, bronchitis, pneumonia and TB. My father died of bronchitis and my mother suffered from emphysema. Every man and half the women over sixty years old in Gao Village suffer from a cough of one kind or another. The reason why fewer women suffer from it is probably that fewer of them smoke. Again, coughing for the elderly is considered a normal part of life and they do not see the doctor unless they have a fever. It was like this before 1949, it was like this during Mao's China and it was still like this when I visited the village in the 1990s. When I asked Gao Renwei, the eighty-year-old who used to personify the Buddha, to go to see a doctor for his cough, his reply was "What for? An old man like me does not have many days left. It is a waste of money. It is too expensive."

But it is not just a matter of money. I certainly could afford to pay for my mother to a see a doctor. But where and how? There is no rural hospital, and no urban hospital would admit her because hers would not be considered to be an emergency case. All a hospital would do was give her an injection and then send her home. My mother's emphysema was never cured and the disease kept reccurring whenever the weather was cold. In early February 1997 she fell so ill that my brothers and sisters in China were just waiting hopelessly for her to pass away. After my intervention a physician in a military hospital at Jiujiang, whom I know of as one of the best doctors in the area, drove more than 100 kilometres to Gao Village to give my mother treatment. She survived only another ten days.

Since Gao villagers eat plenty of fresh vegetables there are no symptoms of vitamin deficiency. Some lack of vitamins is also compensated for by sunshine and fresh air. Though hunger constantly haunts Gao villagers, I do not recall any serious famine except for a brief period during the Great Leap Forward. Because of the variety of food resources from grain to aquatic products, malnutrition was not usually a serious problem for Gao villagers. The worst time in anybody's memory was in 1960 soon after the Great Leap Forward when Gao villagers had to make food out of ground rice husks. The elderly villagers said to me that never before the Great Leap Forward, including before 1949, did the villagers have to eat rice husks. Even during the worst years they just had to eat a lot of vegetables instead of rice to survive.

The most serious causes of child mortality before the 1960s in Gao Village were measles, rubella, chicken-pox and smallpox. Vaccination and immunisation since the 1960s has thus reduced the child mortality rate in Gao Village from 40 per cent during the period 1949-63 to 6.6 per cent during 1963-78 and 7 per cent during 1978-91. The single most serious cause of disease for the elderly was and still is infections of the respiratory system. Heart trouble, heart failure, hypertension and other cardiovascular diseases are rare. Bronchitis, bronchial asthma and emphysema are the most common. Before 1949 and even during the early years of the PRC until the 1960s, very few people lived beyond sixty years of age. My father died in 1963 at the age of fifty-eight. My mother would not have survived until the age of seventy-eight had she not had constant medical attention since the early 1980s. When I visited Gao Village in 1994, the villagers kept on telling me that my mother was fortunate to be able to afford to live on medicine. When my father was ill, the family could not afford any treatment for him. For her last ten or so years my mother lived on powdered milk and eggs and countless medicine bottles, things that my father could not afford in the 1950s and '60s.

The golden period in Gao Village

In the 1960s great efforts were made by the Chinese government to make medical technologies available to rural residents, including the re-organisation of medical resources so that some staff were sent to rural areas, and other measures such as the massive vaccination and immunisation programs. Gao Village benefited greatly from these efforts not only because fatal diseases such as measles and small pox were to disappear completely, but also because two properly qualified doctors, Dr Li, a general medical practitioner and Dr Hu, a pharmacist, were sent by the county authorities to be stationed in Gao Village. Gao Village was chosen because it happened to be located at the centre of the four brigades which the clinic was to serve. Dr Li and Dr Hu were paid by the government, each with a salary of around 60 *yuan* a month.

The two doctors, who provided services to Gao villagers on their door step, therefore not only did not place any financial burden on the villagers but actually added to their income. Both of them, especially Dr Li who did not have a big family to support, would regularly buy seasonal vegetables as well as aquatic products such as fish and prawns from the villagers. Dr Li was the biggest money-spender in the village and his consumption provided valuable cash for the villagers. As the community was so close and the two doctors knew the circumstances of the villagers so personally, they never refused to treat any Gao village patient because of their inability to pay. Sometimes, Gao villagers could only afford to pay the doctors with produce from their private plots such as cucumber, beans, pumpkins, cabbage, or more valuable items such as peanuts, or foodstuffs such as noodles, bread and rice cakes. For a quick treatment such as applying a plaster to a furuncle, Dr Li would not request payment. If a child had a fever Dr Li would know what to do. If he could not treat a complex case, he would refer it to a hospital.

For some reason, the most prevalent disease for children during the summer season was and still is impetigo which appears on the body, face, arms, legs, back and elsewhere. Almost every child in Gao Village has suffered from the disease at least once. One boy's head was so badly covered that he was simply referred to as "Rotten Head". After he grew up he still had dozens of scars all over his head. He is still called "Rotten Head" today and hardly anyone knows his real name. Dr Li was very effective and resolute in treating the disease. He would cut a hole in the middle of the infected area and then squeeze the infected discharge before he put on a plaster which he had made himself. The disease would disappear in a few days. The magic plaster was made of a rubberised fabric and medical extracts. Dr Li would extract medical elements from several Chinese herbs. These medical extracts were then made into a jelly-like substance, black and very sticky, which was painted on to the rubberised fabric.

The clinic was also a cultural centre for the villagers. The two doctors were the only people who had a radio and a newspaper in the village. They were both over fifty, and their families lived in other villages. They therefore liked to have villagers around in the evenings. No appointment needed to be made and anyone could just walk to the clinic and have a chat any time they liked. It was from the clinic that the villagers learned about the spaceships and sputnik, about nuclear weapons, and about the Vietnam War. Later during the Cultural Revolution it was also through the clinic and Dr Li's radio that the villagers came to know what had happened in Beijing and also learned to sing the eight model Peking Operas that were broadcast again and again over the radio. Both doctors, especially Dr Li, were treated as more than members of the village; they were admired, respected and loved. For Gao villagers the clinic was a God-sent gift: cultural and medical services at very little cost, plus extra cash income from the two doctors' consumption.

The two doctors of course could not solve all medical problems. After all they had very primitive facilities and were not trained to treat very complex illnesses. One case figures prominently in my memory. In 1963, one of the best labourers and one of the most intelligent young villagers, Gao Changxin who was about to be the next production team leader suddenly fell ill. The two doctors could not find the cause of the disease and did not know what to do. The nearest hospital was 125 kilometres away and there was no ambulance. In fact there was no motor vehicle of any kind in the area. As a last resort, the family asked the village god Wang *Taigong* ("Grand Wang Buddha") to do something about it. The tiny wooden statue of Wang *Taigong*, half a metre tall and draped in red cloth was placed on a long altar. Joss sticks were then burned in front of the statue. Amidst the upward curling grey smoke from the incense burning before the Buddha, two women held a bamboo basket pan on which they had put rice. Another woman held a chopstick which was used as a divining rod. Gradually the chopstick started moving and scripts were made on the rice. It was interpreted by another elderly woman that Wang *Taigong* himself would like to make a prescription for the patient and would like to pick the Chinese herbs from Dr Hu's pharmacy.

Gao Renwei, who usually acted as Wang *Taigong's* embodiment, was again asked to dance in a trance. He was then put in charge and acted as Wang *Taigong* himself. Gao Renwei asked another villager to hold one side of his usual tool, a wooden fork made of a tree branch, while he himself held the other side. The two then started shaking the fork left and right until finally Gao Renwei started to murmur some unintelligible sounds and white froth appeared at the corners of his mouth. The other villager let go of the fork and Gao Renwei rushed towards Dr Hu's pharmacy. Dr Li and Dr Hu were shocked and would not let Gao Renwei enter the pharmacy. Gao Renwei kept on uttering strange sounds while the villagers negotiated with the two doctors. Finally, Dr Hu gave in. Gao Renwei then entered the pharmacy and used the fork to point at the medicine drawers one after another. Dr Hu followed his instruction by opening these drawers and taking some herbs from each of them. Gao Renwei did not say how much because he was not supposed to speak any human language in this state of trance. So Dr Hu had to decide the quantity of each herb by his own instinct and experience. After more than a dozen drawers were pointed at by Gao Renwei and opened by Dr Hu, the prescription was duly made. The family then took the herbs and cooked them for Gao Changxin to take.

Gao Changxin died soon after, but the legend of Wang *Taigong* was still kept alive. Gao Renwei was said to be able to swallow pieces of chinaware without damaging his stomach when in a trance, a feat no ordinary human could accomplish. Although I have never seen Gao Renwei swallowing even one piece of a broken bowl the scene of him picking up Chinese herbs in Dr Hu's pharmacy haunts me to this day. In 1994 when I visited Gao Village I went to see Gao Renwei and asked him about the event and his ability to swallow chinaware. He responded only with giggles.

As the causes of health problems in Gao Village are many, tackling them on all fronts would have spectacular results, and this has happened since 1960s. There was a campaign by the government to educate rural residents in basic hygiene. School children, for instance, were told about germs and viruses and the benefits of washing hands and drinking only boiled water. A well was dug in the village to provide cleaner water for cooking and drinking. The villagers used to wash clothes, vegetables and other things including babies' nappies in the same pond in front of the village. Gradually, they came to know that to let light and air into the house was not just good for vision but also got rid of dampness and was therefore good for health. As more and more children were educated, habits in the village became more hygienic. It used to be the case that a simple fever suffered by a child might lead to all kinds of complications, but now Dr Li could keep the situation under control.

Other diseases such as favus of the scalp just disappeared due to personal hygiene. Favus used to be very common in Gao Village. Seven villagers used to suffer from the disease, and they all had the nickname *lati* which is a local dialect term for the Mandarin *laizi*, indicating a person affected with favus on the head. The main character of Lu Xun's widely read *The Story of Ah Q* has this disease. A serious case of the disease would destroy all the hair on the head and produce a disgusting yellow discharge which, when dry, would stick to the scalp. Since the 1960s, however, no one has suffered from this disease. Ascariasis also used to be common. Those who suffered this disease were usually children who would not wash their hands, or would eat unwashed vegetables and fruit. As more and more children went to school and were told about the basic habits of hygiene, those affected by ascariasis became fewer and fewer.

The "barefoot doctor" system[1]

In 1972 when Dr Li and Dr Hu retired and went back to their own villages, they had already trained the villager Gao Shihua, who became a "barefoot doctor". By 1972 there were three "barefoot doctors" in Qinglin brigade, with Gao Shihua stationed in Gao Village.

The policy was that village doctors had to be locals. Moreover, they were not to be paid by the state government but by the

---

[1] The system has drawn much attention all over the world. For a professional discussion see Peter Lisowski, "The Emergency and Development of the Barefoot Doctor in China", *Journal of the Japanese Society of Medical History*, 1979, 25: 339-92.

local community. In order to reduce the cost and to make sure that doctors had good personal relations with the locals they had to work like other villagers in the field when there were no patients to treat. If the villagers did not wear shoes when they worked then neither should the doctor. Hence the term "barefoot doctor". The idea was that only by knowing the financial hardship (without regular salary) and physical hard work (working in the field) of the villagers would the doctor understand their health problems and needs.

However, as a matter of fact the three "barefoot doctors" in Qinglin brigade hardly worked in the field. For one thing, with only three doctors covering a population of more than 3,000 they were truly very busy with patients. Moreover, the three doctors were not financially compelled to work in the field like the villagers. Only when the brigade leadership was prepared to follow the sometimes radical policies imposed from above did the three doctors work in the field during the very busy season of July. This only happened a couple of times during the entire period of the "barefoot doctor" system from 1972-81. Otherwise, the three "barefoot doctors" only worked on their families' private plots. During the last few years of the system, they even stopped doing this. Instead, they would ask their relatives or friends or other villagers to do the work for them. In return, they were given free medical services. Thus, the "barefoot doctors" put on their socks and shoes.

The system worked like this: any villager was entitled to seek treatment. For each visit to the doctor, the villagers had to pay a registration fee and the prescription cost. The prescription was made up and dispensed by the doctor at the time of the visit. Registration fees varied. It was 0.05 *yuan* to 0.10 *yuan* when the system was first set up. During the late 1970s the fees were increased to 0.5 *yuan*. The cost of medicine was supposed to be the actual purchase price which only the doctor who had prescribed it knew. The villagers had to pay the doctor upon treatment. With the receipt, the villagers could then claim back the money from their production team accountant. At the end of each financial year, all the costs of the medical services of the production brigade, including the three doctors' salary payments and purchase of medicine and equipment, were put together to decide how much each production team should pay on a per capita basis. If the amount of money reimbursed by one production team to its members was more than its due, the team would be in the black, and this amount would be kept to offset the next year's due. If however, the amount that a production team reimbursed to its members was less than its due, the team had to pay the difference to the brigade. Therefore, in theory at least, every villager had access to free medical services, and the cost was paid by the whole community, the production brigade.

Some statistics will help to show how the system worked, and to indicate its cost. Again, I do not have comprehensive data for all the years from 1972–81. However, the figures available here are enough for our purpose. In the financial year 1973/74, the cost of the system in terms of levy on each villager was 0.87 *yuan*. In 1977 it was 1.06 *yuan* and 1.89 *yuan* in 1981. In 1973/4, Gao Village's due was 203.45 *yuan*, and the two production teams in Gao Village reimbursed its members by 243.73 *yuan*. Gao Village was 14.33 *yuan* in the black from the previous financial year. Therefore, altogether in the financial year 1973/74 the village was 54.61 *yuan* in the black. In 1981, Gao Village had to pay a total cost of 481.95 *yuan* and it actually reimbursed its members 509.36 *yuan*. Gao Village was 27.41 *yuan* in the black.

In 1972, the highest number of visits to the doctor by one household was eight and the lowest, one. Three households visited the doctor only once and six households visited the doctor eight times in the whole year. The household of Gao Changyao incurred the highest cost which was 8 *yuan*, including registration fees and prescription costs. The lowest was only 1 *yuan*. In 1977 the highest number of visits to the doctors in Gao Village by one household was eighteen, with a cost of 4.24 *yuan*. Also in 1977, Gao Jingzhang, who happened to be the father of Gao Shihua, the village "barefoot doctor", was referred to hospital once and as a result he incurred the cost of 25.6 *yuan*.

In 1972 Gao Shihua and the other two "barefoot doctors" worked together in a clinic in the production brigade administration building. This was built at the centre of Qinglin production brigade, which had around three thousand people in the 1970s. Gao Shihua's family was of course in Gao Village. Dr Xu was from Xu Village and Dr Jiang's family was in Jiang Village. The three doctors went to work at the clinic in the daytime and came back to their own village to sleep at night. Each of them had an office in which there was also a bed. They would sleep in the office when they preferred. Theoretically at least, one of them had to sleep in the office in case there was an emergency.

The original idea of the "barefoot doctor" system was that a village doctor was not to be paid a regular salary in cash. Instead, his income had to come from work points like any other villager, and be directly related to the annual wealth created by the community. Since a "barefoot doctor" did not have urban residence status and the family lived in a production team, the household would receive the same amount of grain and other agricultural produce as other households in the team.

However, each of the three doctors served the whole brigade, not just the team they happened to belong to. This situation gave rise to three problems. The first was how to make the other production teams share the cost of paying the three doctors. The second problem arose from the fact that the income of the production teams, and therefore the income of its households, varied from one team to another. Income varied because of factors such as production team leadership, planning, the quality and quantity of land and team members' work efforts. If the three doctors' payments was directly related to the teams they belonged to, a "barefoot doctor" whose family happened to live in a poorer team would earn less than his colleagues who might not have necessarily worked harder. The third problem was that although the three doctors served the whole brigade, the three production teams to which they belonged had to distribute grain and other agricultural produce to their families. In theory at least, the three doctors would have to pay back the three production teams. However, they did not actually contribute to the production of the crops from which they received a share and they therefore had to take away a share of the already limited resources from their teams while they served members of the other teams.

The solution was that the three doctors received their payments directly from the brigade instead of the teams they belonged to. Their level of payment varied from year to year, depending on the average income of the brigade. The formula was 365 days multiplied by the average brigade "unit labour value". In 1976, the average brigade "unit labour value" was 0.7 *yuan* and Gao Shihua's payment in that year would have been 255.5 *yuan*, which was much higher than the best labourer. The best labourer would not be able to earn that much because even if he earned ten base points a day, which would be extremely rare, he would not be able to work 365 days a year. The three doctors' payments were therefore part of the cost of the brigade clinic which was shared by all the teams on a per capita basis. Therefore the problem of sharing the cost of the payments to the three doctors and that of different levels of income among the thirty production teams was solved. However, the third problem was never solved because grain and other agricultural produce distribution had to come from a production team. Therefore, at the end of each financial year the doctors would be paid in cash by the brigade administration and they in turn would pay their own production teams for the grain and other goods which had been given to the household for the whole year.

Of course, the three doctors could not wait until the end of each year to get cash to spend on themselves and their families. Therefore, throughout the year, they could borrow cash from the clinic to spend. For the amount of cash they borrowed they would write a slip, stating the date and amount of money borrowed and sometimes the purpose of the loan. Again at the end of each financial year, each doctor's loan slips were added up to be deducted from that year's total payment. The clinic did not have a secretary, let alone an accountant. The doctors themselves had to run their own accounts. They saw the patients, made prescriptions, sold drugs and received the money. They were not supposed to make a profit and all they were required to do was to charge the right amount for the drugs so that there was enough money to pay for replacements. Registration fees were fixed by the brigade authorities, and the fees each doctor received from the villagers were supposed to be part of the clinic's income.

But none of the doctors kept a record of either the patients or the payment for each session. They could indeed charge the villagers more than the purchase price for the drugs so as to make profit. The only way the villagers could monitor whether they were charged more than the purchase price was through comparison and/or experience. They might question the doctor as to why an item cost more than before. This monitoring was possible because there was little inflation in Mao's China. The other checking mechanism was the close community. Almost everyone knew everyone else and nothing could be hidden. If, for instance, a doctor lived a life that was outrageously different and indicative of great wealth, a review of the clinic would be called for and the doctor would be in serious trouble. In China at least at that time, suspicion alone could cause one's downfall.

Under this system the three "barefoot doctors" not only did not have to bare their feet, but also ate better and wore better clothing. They earned more, though how much more no one knew. They had cash to spend. The villagers, however, accepted this as a fact of life. In fact the three doctors were hardworking and were not suspected of much wrongdoing. Still, they had a good life by local standards. Gao Shihua was able to build a house in the 1970s and he was the only one from Gao Village who had a watch and a bicycle before 1977.

The villagers were not doing too badly under the system either. It was a more or less free medical care system with virtually no support from the state government. One reason why the cost of such a system was not too high was that there was a political check on the doctors, which prevented them from accumulating conspicuous wealth. Coupled with this was the very low level of consumption and expectations of material life. Secondly the villagers did not usually visit the doctor much. They took many diseases for granted, and therefore would not bother to see the doctor. The third important reason was that complicated diseases that involved more than standard treatment were not covered by the system. For instance, one single surgery in a hospital would have been enough to bankrupt the entire Qinglin brigade clinic.

The case of schistosomiasis

It is not known how schistosomiasis originated in the area. Gao villagers cannot recall a single serious case before the 1940s. Perhaps it is because they did not recognise the disease until they were made aware of it by the Communist government. According to the *Boyang County Annuals*, the first case of the disease in Boyang County was discovered by an American, Faust E. C. Moleney, in 1924. By 1956, 107 communes in the Boyang region, with a total population of 211,788 were known to be infected. The consequences of this disease were so serious that a village could be completely wiped out by it. One village in Zhagang commune had 110 households and a population of 1,500 by the end of

Qing Dynasty. By 1953 only twelve households were left, since most of the villagers had died of schistosomiasis. In one village in Lianhu 3,000 villagers died of the disease and sixty households were wiped out between 1939 and 1949.

Schistosomiasis was a disease that plagued South China for a long time. By the mid 1950s, the disease had infested more than 350 counties of twelve provinces. Ten million people were discovered to have the disease and the areas affected by this plague covered a population of 100 million. In 1955 Mao raised the idea of completely exterminating the plague. In 1956, a task force was set up by the State Council to coordinate the work. By 1958, one of the worst infested areas, Yugan County, was reported to have eliminated the disease. Mao was so pleased to hear the news that he spent a sleepless night writing a poem, the title of which was "Seeing off the God of Plague".

Schistosomiasis is caused by flukes of the species *schistosoma japonicum*, which live on tiny freshwater snails. The parasite will enter a human body through contact with water in which there are snails. The parasites will penetrate the skin and reach the bladder and intestines, from where they may spread to other parts of the body. The severity of the disease depends on the number of parasites that enter the body.[2] In the most serious cases, if untreated, the patient will have a swollen abdomen due to ascites and die within a few years. The local people called it "the big belly disease". Sufferers develop an enlarged abdomen and women become infertile. In other cases, the flukes will travel through the blood vessel to the spleen and liver, which will gradually be destroyed, thus causing death. Even in less severe cases, the disease is extremely nasty because it can lead to liver and spleen tumour formation in ten or twenty years. Before the disease is fully developed the patient may look perfectly normal. It is almost impossible to get rid of the disease without medical treatment because the body is not able to develop a defence system against this kind of parasite.

The Chinese government did two main things to control the plague. One was to identify the infested population and treat them with parasite-killing drugs. The other was to eliminate the

[2] Dr Tony Smith, *The New Macmillan Guide to Family Health*, London, reprint, 1989, p. 855.

cause of the disease. The most effective way of getting to the cause is to wipe out the snails in which schistosomes multiply, because without their snail hosts the parasites will die. Boyang County established its first Station for Prevention and Treating of Schistosomiasis in 1955. In 1956, the county administration set up a task force to coordinate the work throughout the county and four sub-stations were set up. In 1958, a schistosomiasis hospital was set up for treating schistosomiasis sufferers. Several similar regional clinics were also set up in the county. Regular physical check-ups were carried out every three years and everyone aged seven and above was encouraged to go for a check. Doctors were sent out to rural villages to oversee this. In the 1970s, the technique used to identify sufferers was simplified. A drop of blood from an ear lobe was all that was needed. Once identified as having the disease, the patient would be hospitalised and treated with parasite-killing drugs. Usually a course of treatment would last one to two weeks. Half a year after the treatment, a follow-up check had to be made to see if any trace of the disease could be found. If it was, a second course of treatment would be embarked on. During the period of treatment in hospital, patients had to pay nothing aside from their own food. During the 1960s and '70s, in order to encourage the poor to participate in this treatment, every day spent by the patient in hospital for schistosomiasis treatment was rewarded with the same amount of work points they would have earned working in the field.

In order to wipe out the snails, many thousands of villagers were mobilised from time to time in campaigns, almost once every year, to dry streams, brooks and ponds. Old ones were levelled and new ones were dug. Even some rivers were made to change their course to dry out the old rivers and wipe out the snails. The other way of wiping out the snails was to spray chemical onto the infested marshes and water areas. In 1971, for instance, two planes flew over the county for forty-six days and sprayed over 110,000 *mu* of water areas. These measures, though very effective in wiping out the infested snails, were very destructive to the environment. Hundreds of aquatic species were lost along with the snails. Table 2 of Appendix 2 shows the amount of work and effort by the government to deal with the plague of schistosomiasis in Boyang County.

As can be seen in the table, it was during the two most radical periods, the Great Leap Forward in 1958 and in 1970 during the Cultural Revolution in Mao's China, that most people were checked and treated. This cannot be a coincidence. In almost every political campaign, Mao's intention was to target the privileged and powerholders such as intellectuals and Communist Party cadres, and to favour the most disadvantaged such as rural dwellers and the poor. However, results did not always parallel these intentions, and the Great Leap Forward was a disastrous example of this. In the case of schistosomiasis, the villagers did benefit from the government's efforts in Mao's China. Yet the environmental effects were and still are very bad for the villagers. Strong political will, effective administration and mass mobilisation were required to carry out a task such as dealing with the schistosomiasis plague on such a huge scale. Up to 1978, i.e., the end of Mao's regime, fifty Gao villagers, one-sixth of the population, were treated for schistosomiasis.

I myself was treated twice, once in the County Station hospital and once in the regional station hospital. My brother Gao Changxian was also treated twice. A friend of mine Dr Xiong Peikang is one of the foremost specialists in treating schistosomiasis in China. He also carried out more than 800 successful operations removing infected spleens from schistosomiasis patients. All this was done at the government's cost. Without this the villagers could in no way have afforded the operation.

The post-Mao period

When I visited Dr Xiong in 1992 his protests and complaints came up again and again over dinner. Dr Xiong is now retired in a comfortable house and spends his time listening to Peking Operas. He still does some occasional consultancy work. He complained that the present government did not do enough for rural people and that what everyone cared about was money. As Table 2 shows, not much has been done by the county authorities since 1980. The regional sub-stations built to prevent and treat schistosomiasis have all been dismantled. The county station was badly run and seriously short of funds. In 1992 when I visited the hospital where I had received my treatment I could find hardly any patients; the place looked deserted. One should not be surprised that the disease rate in 1985 shot up to 13.63 per cent from 5.6

per cent in 1979. Not many could afford to be treated in hospital any more, because it was not free. In 1996 there were ten Gao villagers known to suffer from schistosomiasis. The *xiang* clinic gives them medicine to take at their own home, and each course of treatment costs more than 20 *yuan*. The real danger of re-emergence of the plague has already alarmed the local community. In 1994, I saw a line of huge characters written on a wall in Jiang Village. In a reference to the poem Mao wrote in 1958 it read "We shall see off the God of plague again!"

Early 1997 when I went to attend my mother's funeral there was a doctor on tour in Gao Village checking the villagers for schistosomiasis. Both my brother and sister were diagnosed as having the disease. I urged them to be treated as soon as possible. Their response, however, shocked me. They wanted to have another check up in Boyang County Town because they did not trust the local doctor. They claimed that the doctor might have given them a false diagnosis to make them buy medicine from him! Either both my brother and sister had the disease, which means the plague is on the verge of coming back, or the doctor gave them a false diagnosis. Either case is a bad sign of the current development in the area.

The "barefoot doctor" cooperative medical system was abandoned in 1981. The three doctors all set up their own private practices. While the villagers are more and more disinclined to see the doctors because they have to pay and they do not know how much the cost will be each time, the doctors have all become very rich by local standards. Gao Shihua built another house in the 1980s, this time from brick rather than mud. Unfortunately he died soon after the house was completed, leaving a widow and three children. Dr Jiang built a huge house of ten rooms, with a backyard enclosing a pond and the front yard as huge as a car park, all smoothly concreted. There is also a separate kitchen and Dr Jiang is one of the few in the area who possesses a motorbike. Dr Xu also built a house which is like a castle, with a well inside a huge kitchen. The well has an electrically operated pump; when a button is pressed water comes out automatically. Dr Xu is the only person in Qinglin who has pressurised running water, which is more convenient than gravitational tap water. His share of land is rented to tenants, and the villagers keep on giving him everything that is available in return for his services.

He once boasted that people gave him so many watermelons that his family had to feed the pigs with them.

Meanwhile, praying before the Buddha for good health and treatment has once again became fashionable. By the late 1970s the practice had almost completely disappeared. Now it has re-emerged, like many old Chinese traditions. The temple half a kilometre away from Gao Village has been restored. When I visited it in 1994, three grotesque statues were sitting on the altar, with hundreds of joss sticks burning in front of them. There were two men in the temple, looking after the place and living on donations from the pilgrims. Donations ranged from rice, bread and cloth to money. The poor, the helpless and hopeless would save hard to donate in return for the Buddha's well wishes, like my mother used to do before the 1960s. Whether this is religion or superstition depends on one's perspective. In 1995 when I took two of my Australian colleagues to visit Gao Village, the temple was destroyed by a fire. The statues, however, were not burned and were placed outside for the villagers to pray. When we visited the site we were asked to donate 20 *yuan* for the reconstruction of the temple.

I was also surprised to find that there were Christians in the area. This is the first time in history that any villagers have converted to Christianity. Not a single Christian believer had been recorded in the area before 1949. After 1949 it was not possible for anyone to preach Christianity in the area until the late 1980s. I myself had never heard of the term before I went to university. There are now said to be more than fifty among the population of around three and a half thousand. They meet regularly once a month or so and more frequently during slack seasons. They sing Christian tunes with Chinese words and pray to Jesus Christ. In 1992 when I visited them in the house in the neighbouring Wang Village where they usually gather together, I saw the character of "love" in huge strokes on the wall behind the altar, each of which was built up from smaller characters composed of several sayings. These included "Love is eternal tolerance", "Love means not to be jealous", "Love means not to boast", "Love means not to be arrogant", "Love means to like truth only", "Love means to forgive the evil of others", "Don't be selfish" and "Don't do shameful things". On the altar, supported by two hot water flasks and a tea mug, stood two copies of the Bible in Chinese and a poster of the Virgin Mary and child with the angels.

None of the villagers currently living in Gao Village has become a Christian. I encountered a Christian woman who was born in Gao Village but now lives in Jiang Village. I asked her how she had become a Christian. She said that those people were nice and they helped each other in many ways. In times of difficulties such as illness and debts, the Christians would help each other by lending farm hands, cash and other things. Whether they are Christians in the Western sense is another question, but clearly a lack of organised support of any kind encouraged them to form a cooperative group as a means to help each other.

During my interview with a group of self-proclaimed Christians I discovered that it was a spontaneous development and the local authorities so far have not intervened. There is no church in any sense of the word. The villagers hold their religious gatherings in one of their own houses. There is no father or priest, but only a coordinator, who was an acquaintance of mine and very active politically in Mao's time. His name is Wang Biaogui. I was interested to know whether anyone from outside the area had come to preach Christianity. Wang Biaogui said that there was no external involvement and that the idea came to him after he had heard about Christianity from other areas.

In the Boyang County Town around 100 kilometres away from Gao Village there used to be a Christian church which had been set up by foreign missionaries and paid for by the indemnity demanded from the foreign powers after China was defeated in 1890. The church was located near the County Schistosomiasis Prevention and Treatment Station. The missionaries left the county in the 1940s before the Communist revolution in 1949. Throughout the 1960s and '70s, the church was used as Boyang County's Party school where Communist Party officials from all over the county studied Communist ideology. Since the 1980s the building has been deserted, with broken windows and rubble everywhere. The County Town people are not as desperate as the rural villagers in Yinbaohu, at least not yet. If Gandhi was right that "to a hungry man, God is bread", the church in Boyang County Town may yet see its revival.

By and large rural health has improved greatly since 1949. As a result of health care technology such as immunisation introduced by the government, the child mortality rate has fallen sharply in Gao Village. Hygiene education has also helped Gao villagers in preventing many common diseases that used to plague them. Government efforts have also brought the fatal plague of "snail fever" under control. The most distinctive feature of health care improvement during Mao's reign was that the poorest and the socially most disadvantaged benefited from the government's efforts. The reform policies since the 1980s, however, have began to abandon the most disadvantaged. Despite many faults, the "barefoot doctor" system appears to have worked quite well for Gao villagers. Now this system has been abandoned. The lack of an organised health care system means that those who cannot afford it tend to resort to other means such as praying to the Buddha for protection. A small number of people have opted for their version of Christianity and the social support this brings with it.

7

RURAL EDUCATION

Education is another area in which Gao villagers benefited greatly in Mao's China. Before 1949, not a single woman in Gao Village was really literate. My mother Jiang Yuanrong was the only woman who could read her own name and a score of other characters. My mother had two years of *sishu*[1] education when she was a child. Later after she was married and moved to Gao Village she forgot most of what she had learned. As an indication of the change since 1949, the number of women in Gao Village who have had some education has grown significantly. By 1996 there were forty women in Gao Village who had had education of three years or more. By 1949 only six Gao villagers were literate, all of whom were men. Two were from the landlord family: Gao Tianqiang, the landlord himself and his son Gao Yunfei. Gao Tianqiang was a *sishu* teacher and Gao Yunfei finished a college education diploma and later became a primary school teacher. The other four were Gao Renyun, Gao Changyu, Gao Changcai and Gao Renyu. All of them were from upper middle class backgrounds. Gao Changyu later was chosen to be one of the two production team leaders in Gao Village for some years in the commune period. Gao Renyu and Gao Changcai were each accountants for the two production teams in Gao Village. Only Gao Renyun did not take up any public position, but he nevertheless remained one of the powerholders in village affairs and clan activities.

Except for Gao Yunfei, all five went to *sishu* where the students

---

[1] *Sishu* is a traditional way of teaching children in China. For lengthy and in-depth discussion on the subject see Colin Mackerras, "Education in the Guomindang Period 1928-1949" in E. Fung and D. Pong, eds, *Ideal and Reality: Social and Political Change in Modern China, 1860-1949*, University Press of America, Lanham, NY, and London, 1985, pp. 153-83, and works referred to there. See also page 15, n. 3.

were only taught to read Confucian classics. The class was conducted at the teacher's home. There was no grading of students, and everyone was taught individually. The student was taught only how to read the characters and no explanations were given. They would then go away to read the text aloud until they could recite it. The teacher would then teach the next text, and the student would go away to read aloud and to recite. This process would continue. The faster the student, the more texts he or she would be given to recite.

The Western approach to learning was introduced long before 1949 in urban China and some parts of rural China. In Boyang County one Western style school was opened in 1902. In 1935 Boyang County government decided to abolish all *sishu* schools in the county. However, in the Gao Village area there was no change until the days of the Communist revolution. There were no subjects such as mathematics, chemistry, geology, music or painting for the students. Even important skills such as using the abacus were not taught at a *sishu*, but rather were learned through apprenticeship.

Education in Gao Village since 1949 can be segmented into four periods. The first period covered the years 1950-5 during which "literacy crash classes" were carried out for the villager and villager cadres. The second stage, 1956-65, was when primary education for Gao villagers started for the first time in its history. The third was the Cultural Revolution period, 1966-81. Finally the fourth period dates from 1981 to the present in post-Mao China. In each period there was a distinctive impact on Gao Village brought about by government policies in education.

1952-1955

In 1952, the Boyang County government launched a literacy campaign. There were two kinds of "literacy crash classes" organised for the villagers in the early 1950s. One was called "winter class", conducted in December and January when there was not much farm work to do, and the other was the evening class. The class was conducted by a member of the land reform work teams who were sent by the government from the cities or towns. The classes were as much for political propaganda as for improving literacy. The villagers were first taught how to read and write their own names. Then they were to learn terms such as "Communist Party", "class struggle", "landlord", "poor peasants". Mostly, there were no standard textbooks and the teacher would invent things as he (there were no female teachers) went along. The villagers were curious and somewhat enthusiastic at the beginning. However, after one or two classes, they were no longer interested. They did not see the relevance of their lessons and found them too hard. During the evening classes, most of them would fall asleep after a few minutes. Many of them regarded it as amusement. Women would often not go. They had to do the housework and look after children. The work teams would go from door to door to urge people to go to the classes, but without much success.

Most male villagers only managed to recognise their own names. Only three young males in Gao Village who were either restless or intellectually curious managed to carry on for some time. They were Gao Changming, Gao Changyao and Gao Changyin. Gao Changming eventually left Gao Village and went to Jingdezhen as a worker in a porcelain workshop. Gao Changyao was later selected to the position of a production team leader in the commune period. Gao Changyin went even further and eventually became a Brigade Party secretary until he was brought down during the Cultural Revolution.

Interestingly, the three were all from poor peasant backgrounds. Whether their determination to learn resulted from their desire to change their status or from special encouragement from the work team is not clear. It is perhaps no coincidence that the three were the most active in class struggle against the landlord Gao Tianqiang. In 1994, Gao Renyun, the most articulate of the village elders and one of the powerholders in the village, revealed during an interview that Gao Tianqiang was not classified as a landlord during the land reform in 1951. He was re-classified as a landlord during the "re-check of classes" in 1953.

The main cause for the change had something to do with Gao Changming. After the land reform in 1951, every household had an equal amount of land on a *per capita* basis, including Gao Tianqiang. Gao Tianqiang then loaned a piece of land to Gao Changming free of charge. Later, probably in 1953, when Gao Tianqiang asked Gao Changming to return that piece of land, the latter not only refused, but also accused Gao Tianqiang of being "a class enemy who was counterattacking to settle old scores", meaning that he wanted to take back the land confiscated during the land reform. It happened that in 1953 the county Communists started the "re-check of classes" campaign which was aimed exactly at the so-called "counterattack". The work team believed Gao Changming's version of events and the label of landlord was firmly attached to Gao Tianqiang. He suffered from this stigma until his death in 1978.

In order to train local villagers who would be loyal, and who would be able to carry out Party policies, the Communist authorities also organised special literacy classes for the chosen few. These were young activists who showed some ability to learn. Gao Changyin was one of them, and the only one from Gao Village. Gao Changyin was an ambitious young man and in many ways a far-sighted person. When the Poor Peasant Association first started my father was chosen as the representative from Gao Village. He was chosen for two reasons. First, he was very poor by the time the Communists took power (a story to be told in later chapters). The second reason had something to do with the incident in 1949 when a batch of Communist People's Liberation Army soldiers passed through Gao Village. There was the worst flood in anyone's memory at that time and one of the soldiers was drowned when the troop waded through the river to the east of Gao Village. So the troop stopped at Gao Village and knocked at the villagers' doors for help. Everyone was so scared that they would not open the doors. It was my father who first came out to see the soldiers and then persuaded other villagers to give them some help.

The soldiers apparently took note of this and passed the information on to the work team. Thus, when the clan elders urged my father to represent Gao Village, he was accepted by the Poor Peasant Association. However, about half a year later, by which time Gao Changyin was very active and apparently knew what he was doing, he told my father to go home and not to come to the Association any more, since my father could not read and write, and so did not know what to do at meetings. My father went home without saying a word, not so much relieved or disappointed as not knowing exactly what was happening. Thereafter, Gao Changyin became one of the most active villagers. He became more and more active because, according to Gao Renyun's account, he wanted to protect himself. Gao Changyin in 1949 was said to have joined the Ninth Road Army, a local bandit force of several hundred which happened to support the Nationalists. The Ninth Road Army was eventually wiped out by the Communist force in 1950. As there was no proof that Gao Changyin did join the Ninth Route Army, his active participation in class struggle helped and he was promoted.

Because of Gao Changyin's active involvement in supporting land reform, he was chosen to attend a special literacy crash class organised for local activists. The class was held in Boyang Town for a couple of months and all costs were covered by the government. Gao Changyin joined the Communist Party in 1954 and was finally promoted to brigade Party secretary. The indoctrination of notions such as class struggle and the history of the Communist Party were an essential part of these crash classes for the villagers. They were also taught such things as how to maintain public and personal hygiene, and how to write a receipt.

I have a copy of a textbook printed in 1950 which was used by one of the activists who later became the brigade accountant. There are forty-three lessons in a book of fifty pages. The first lesson is about personal hygiene, and the students are told to wash and keep their fingernails, nose and neck clean. The second lesson tells of the importance of eating slowly, the third of how to avoid dysentery, the fourth explains the necessity of wiping out mosquitoes and the fifth talks about benefits to be gained from the sun. The next lesson tells of the history of the People's Liberation Army, and this is followed by two lessons on how the Chinese fought the Japanese invasion. There are also a couple of lessons on how, i.e. according to communism, people could live a better life.

1956-1966

In 1952, the first primary school was set up in Qinglin, covering a population of about 1,500 villagers. There were only classes for first year to start with. Gradually, the Qinglin School was developed and in 1958 it became a full scale primary school from years one to six. I do not have comprehensive statistics on the scale of the school and number of students, and the *Basic Brigade Statistics Record* has left the years 1949–71 blank.

According to the *Boyang Annuals*, the percentage of school children attending school in Boyang County in 1953, 1958, 1965,

1979, 1984 and 1985 are 48.85, 80.6, 68.3, 84.13, 93.79 and 94.8 respectively. There is no way one can check the reliability of these figures and it is quite safe to say they are not very accurate. However, the general trend shown by these figures none-theless reflects what really happened. It is certainly true that the rate of children attending school had increased dramatically by the late 1950s; it is also true that the rate increased again in the period from the late 1960s to the late 70s.

Significantly, despite the current Chinese authorities' claim of great calamities caused by Mao's radical policies during the Great Leap Forward and the Cultural Revolution it was during these two periods that the attendance rate of children at school increased greatly. It rose from 48.8 per cent in 1953 to 80.6 per cent in 1958, the year of the Great Leap Forward. Again, the rate increased from 68.3 per cent in 1965, the year before the Cultural Revolution started, to 84.13 per cent in 1979, three years after the Cultural Revolution was officially declared to have ended. The figures also reveal the fact that during the early 1960s, the years when China's education was dominated by Liu Shaoqi and Deng Xiaoping's policies which were accused of representing "capitalist restoration" by Mao and his radical followers, the rate of rural school children at school dropped from 80.6 per cent in 1958 to 68.3 per cent in 1965. The situation in Gao Village seems to correspond to the general trend reflected by these figures.

From 1956 to 1959, twenty-five school children from Gao Village went to Qinglin School, of which there were only three girls. By 1962, fifteen out of the twenty-five had dropped out. Only ten of those remained to finish a six-year education in primary school, of whom only one was a girl, my sister. By 1965, only three went on to secondary school, one to senior high and two to junior high in 1966 when the Cultural Revolution started. The one who went to senior high is now working as a technician in Nanchang, the capital city of Jiangxi Province; the one who went to junior high is now a school teacher in Qinglin; and I was the third. In 1959-65 only nine children went to school, of whom only one was a girl. Three managed to finish six years of education, of whom two went on to finish senior high during the years of the Cultural Revolution.

There were many reasons why fewer children went to school in the early 1960s than in the 1950s. One was that the number of school children was smaller. When Qinglin School expanded in 1956, because it was the first time, those children who never had any opportunity before now all wanted to go to school. It was also a year when the Chinese government and the people were most confident of what they were doing and most optimistic about their future. Even those who had already passed the school age went to school. Two Gao villagers were already sixteen years old when they became year four students. By the early 1960s the number of school children had dropped because of the previous years' large intake.

The other reason was that in the 1960s China's education system became more formal, and a standard nationwide examination system was imposed. No leeway, less affirmative action, was given to socially disadvantaged rural residents. It was difficult for most of the village children to cope with the work, let alone pass the strictly imposed examinations. Almost all of them had to help the family with work such as gathering firewood, catching fish for the family diet, looking after the younger ones while parents were out in the field and picking wild vegetables for family pigs. They did not have a light or even a table, to do their homework. In any case, their parents would not be able to help with their homework. They began to hate school and their parents did not see the point of sending them there. The third reason was that for the first two years after the Great Leap Forward, life was difficult, not in an ordinary sense, but in unusual circumstances. During the most difficult time in 1959, the villagers were actually starving and they could hardly walk let alone go to school.

Even a daily school routine was daunting for the children. Until 1970, there was no school in the village. The nearest school, which was Qinglin Primary School, was 1.5 kilometres away. School would start at 7 a.m. and children were required to be in the classroom to read Chinese texts for an hour before breakfast. It was called "Morning Reading", apparently a methodological residue from the *sishu* practice. After breakfast, school would start again from 8.30 a.m. until 12.30 p.m. Then after lunch school resumed from 2.30 until 6.30 p.m. Therefore, the children had to walk to and from school six times a day. Imagine a seven year old child walking 9 kilometres a day, in boiling hot weather in summer and bitterly cold weather in winter. Most families could not afford a pair of rubber shoes and some children just walked barefoot all year. One could hardly blame the parents who withdrew their children from school, especially those who did not show they could do well academically. One can also understand why the villagers were reluctant to send girls to school.

Still, the villagers liked to have their children educated. They respected and admired those who could read and write. My parents were among those who would do anything to get their children educated. My sister was the only girl who finished six years of education in Gao Village until the 1960s. My parents insisted on sending my sister and myself to school when my family was in the most difficult of circumstances. We were always in the red and owed the production team debts every year. Every time my family went to get the grain as it was being distributed, those villagers who were in the black would, understandably, show my parents either by saying something or by their facial expression that we owed them our living. Still, my parents persisted and my mother would go to work in the field despite her bound feet. My father's last words on his death-bed in 1964 were that my education should be continued. There were others, though in a much better situation, who struggled to have their children educated. By the 1970s, there was one university graduate, four senior high school graduates and seven junior high school graduates in Gao Village.

1966-1981

When the Cultural Revolution first started in 1966 in Beijing, it had very little impact on rural China. By then, there were three high school students from Gao Village. Gao Chaojiang and I were boarding at Youdunjie Junior High, which was 10 kilometres away from Gao Village. Gao Chaodong was a senior high school student boarding at Number One High School in Boyang County Town, which was 100 kilometres away. Gao Chaodong, the only senior high school student from Gao Village, was the son of Gao Changyin, the Party secretary of Guantian brigade. Youdunjie Junior High was the only high school at that time for a population of 80,000 in the Youdunjie region. The school was set up in 1958, the year of the Great Leap Forward, with only two classes to start with. By 1966 when I was there, the school had expanded to nine classes, with an enrolment of around 450 students and a teaching staff of thirty. There were no senior high classes in the school, so any one going to senior high had to be enrolled in a school in the County Town.

Gao Chaodong was of course the envy of the village. The villagers hardly saw him because he came home only twice a year at the most. He wore different clothing and spoke a different language. He learned to speak Mandarin, considered by Gao villagers to be the language of government officials. They did not consider him to belong to Gao Village any more because they could not understand his language. Gao villagers speak a variety of Gan, which is one of the nine major dialects in China. They feel alienated whenever Mandarin is spoken to them. They found it amazing when I spoke Gan to them after many years of absence.

In the late 1960s while Gao Chaodong was looked upon as privileged and above the reach of the villagers, I had to remain a humble country bumpkin. Every Saturday I had to walk home and every Sunday I had to walk back to school with a week's rice, food and firewood on my shoulder-pole. Youdunjie School was a school of solid programs and good teachers. It was there that I came to know something about algebra, geometry, biology, chemistry, physics and the ABC of English. However, solid and stimulating learning lasted for only one year. By the second half of 1966, the Cultural Revolution had begun to have its impact on rural China. Classes were stopped and students were encouraged to rebel and to "struggle" against their teachers. From then on until 1968 when I "graduated" from Youdunjie Junior High, not much academic learning had been accomplished. I returned home and became a regular peasant.

In China, it is now fashionable to claim that the Cultural Revolution was a ten year disaster which destroyed China's educational system. Like all other generalisations, the claims about the Cultural Revolution, especially those enthusiastically initiated and maintained by the Chinese government, must be taken with caution. To start with, the Cultural Revolution was not one, discrete, ten-year-long event. During the course of ten years, many events took place, some of which were destructive and others constructive. What happened to China's higher education was most disruptive and destructive. Most universities did not start to enrol students again until 1972. Postgraduate courses were completely stopped and did not start again until 1978. With some exceptions, China also stopped sending students to study abroad until 1972.

However, in primary and secondary, especially in primary education, the disruption was not so damaging. It is true that classes were stopped for some time, and in some cases for as long as two or three years. It is also sadly true that some teachers were unjustly and pointlessly victimised, on some occasions with terrifying brutality by the students. As for myself, it was a painful experience to have my education interrupted. Being one of the top students in the school, I certainly hoped to go on to senior high school education. My hope was dashed by the events of the Cultural Revolution.

However, these unsavoury facts should not blind us from seeing that the Cultural Revolution was also constructive in primary and secondary education, at least for the rural residents. In fact, as early as 1967, about half a year after the initial interruption and turmoil, the Chinese government called for all primary school students to "start class again to make revolution", though in reality some rural schools did not start "normal" teaching until 1969. Qinglin School was never actually closed down. There were classes throughout 1967 and 1968, with Chairman Mao's quotations, mathematics, literacy and other science subjects being taught to children in years one to four. However, for year five and year six students, only Chairman Mao's quotations and his three essays were taught. The three essays were "To Serve the People", "The Foolish Old Man Who Removes the Mountain" and "In Memory of Dr Berthune".[2]

After a short time of disruption, primary and secondary education greatly expanded during the Cultural Revolution years in rural China. From 1969-71, the radical policies encouraged communes to establish senior high schools and brigades to set up junior high schools. Before the Cultural Revolution, many communes did not have high schools and village children had to board in high schools far away from home if they wanted to continue their education. Many of them could not go to high school because of the distance and cost of boarding.

Some statistics will indicate how the Cultural Revolution was constructive in education for rural people. In 1955, there were

[2] The last of the three essays was written by Mao to commemorate the death of Dr Berthune, a Canadian doctor who served the Communist troops during the war of resistance against Japan.

two secondary schools in Boyang County. In 1956 there were three, and in 1957, five. In 1958 there were three more and by 1962 the number of secondary schools had increased to sixteen. By 1966 there were eighteen secondary schools in Boyang County, mostly located in the County Town and regional centres like Youdunjie. There were just 6,500 secondary school students for a population of roughly 70,000. For the first twenty-seven years since 1949, secondary schools had increased from two to eighteen, an average increase of 1.38 secondary schools a year. In the ten years from 1969 to 1979 as a result of radical policies during the Cultural Revolution, senior secondary schools increased to forty-one and junior secondary schools shot up to 265 in Boyang County, with an average annual increase of 3.06 schools. Even if we take the two disruptive years of 1967 and 1968 into consideration, the annual increase of secondary schools in Boyang County would still be 2.5 schools. By 1979 the number of secondary school students reached 29,238, which was 4.48 times the number in 1966.

One of the charges against this radical expansion of education in rural China put forward by the current Chinese authorities and élitist intellectuals and scholars since the death of Mao is that it was at the expense of the lower standard of education. In 1980, in the name of raising educational standards, the number of senior high schools in Boyang County was reduced from forty-one in 1979 to eleven, and the number of junior high schools was reduced from 265 to fifty-two. Qualified teachers were withdrawn from rural areas and were placed again in a small number of privileged schools in the County Town. For the rural Chinese who constitute 80 per cent of China's population, such an accusation against the expansion of education in rural China during the Cultural Revolution period and subsequent reverse of policies could hardly be justified.

During the early 1960s, and again since the late 1980s, resources have been more and more concentrated on a small number of privileged schools, mostly located in the urban sector of China, all in the name of quality management and improvement. The contents and methodology were oriented towards urban society, and in fact were a copy of the Soviet Union system. The Cultural Revolution policies in education were precisely aimed at stopping this trend, which was accused of being anti-socialist – indeed capitalist and revisionist – with the latter referring to the copying of the Soviet Union. For Gao villagers, the so-called "quality policy" in the 1960s meant very little except for Gao Chaodong, the son of the brigade Party secretary, who was educated to leave Gao Village. For the villagers, classes catering for more children to learn literacy skills, elementary sciences and basic calculating skills were more important and relevant.

During the so-called Cultural Revolution period, in order to pursue the goal of education reform so that education would be more accessible to the underprivileged, textbooks were changed to be more practical and less academic. The length of primary school education was shortened from six to five years, secondary school from six to four years. In order to make teachers available for the fast expansion of schools, two very dramatic measures were also taken at the same time after 1969. One measure was that a large number of qualified teachers were sent from the urban sector to the rural areas to teach in rural schools. The other was that educated local villagers were recruited as "barefoot teachers". The rationale behind the "barefoot teachers" scheme was the same as that behind the "barefoot doctors" in that the teachers were not formally educated for the profession, nor paid by the state government with a regular salary. Instead, they were supposed to work in the fields like the local villagers during busy seasons, and were to live "barefoot" like the local villagers.

Primary and secondary education

It was in this atmosphere of radical reform that a primary school catering for students from years one to three was set up in Gao Village in 1969, and I was appointed as the school's only teacher, a "barefoot teacher". I had to teach three classes at the same time. I would ask students of year one and two to do some exercises while I was teaching year three students. Then I would turn to year two students while the others were doing exercises. Subjects taught were: calligraphy, Chinese language, arithmetic, music, arts, sports and farming skills. Every weekday including Saturday, there was the "morning reading" before breakfast, during which time I would sit there to supervise the students. The Chinese since *sishu* school tradition place great importance on reading aloud to memorise textbooks.

The first class in the morning after breakfast was calligraphy. The Chinese consider calligraphy not only a form of art but also one of the primary indicators of educational accomplishment. If one's handwriting of characters looks good one is automatically considered to be well educated. That is why Communist Party officials in China like to write something in calligraphy, because they want to show they are persons of learning and educational accomplishment. So every weekday, half an hour was given to calligraphy practice. While supervising the students I would practice the art myself. There were three periods lasting forty-five minutes for sports, and one hour for farming skills every week. There was also one period for music and one period for arts every week. The rest of the time was spent on Chinese language and arithmetic.

The children, of course, liked sports. However, sports facilities were next to non-existent. There were only table tennis and basketball games. There was no table tennis table, much less a basketball court. The children had to use their class tables to play table tennis. Most of the time, they just ran around. I was also supposed to teach the children a set of freestanding exercises and some para-military drills such as forming a line and turning left and right in a line. The parents cared little for sports and thought it was a waste of time. This was understandable from their point of view, because their physical strength was always so stretched to the limit by farm work that they considered non-productive physical activities a waste of energy. As for farming skills, they appreciated these even less because nobody needed to learn them from me. However, it was a required part of the curriculum, which might be worthwhile for urban children who would other- wise never have had the chance to see how anything was grown. This shows how rigid Chinese uniformity has always been: what might be done somewhere must be done everywhere.

As a "barefoot teacher" I received, like other Gao villagers, whatever there was to be distributed from the production team and my contribution was recorded in the form of work points. In busy seasons when farm work was the most arduous I worked in the fields like other villagers. In this way, the villagers had few expenses with regard to the teaching staff. However, they had to pay for the cost of textbooks and stationary such as pencils, exercise books, Chinese brushes and ink. Again because of deliberate government policy, the cost of textbooks was kept at the lowest level, from 0.2 *yuan* to 0.5 *yuan* a textbook. Altogether, a student had to pay an average 3 to 5 *yuan* annually for the textbooks and stationary. Such a low cost nonetheless constituted a very substantial amount for some households. All boys and most of the girls of school age in Gao Village at that time attended school when I was teaching there. This was unprecedented and would not have been possible had there not been a school set up in Gao Village.

From 1969 to 1972 I taught thirty-six Gao Village children, of whom twenty-one were boys and fifteen were girls. Of the thirty-six children, twenty-one finished three years of schooling, but only three of them were girls. There were four girls of school age at that time who did not go to school at all. Of the four, three of them were daughters of the only two Communist Party members in Gao Village, Gao Changyin and Gao Changyao. Gao Changyin used to be the brigade Party secretary, but was in disgrace by 1969. Gao Changyao was one of the two production team leaders at the time.

Clearly, even at the most radical time of Mao's China, females were discriminated against due to a combination of factors. Cost was still one factor, even though by the standards of the urban and town sector in China the cost of 3 to 5 *yuan* a year was next to nothing. We have to remember that for the villagers even 10 cents in Chinese currency had an important value, a fact the urban Chinese were never really able to appreciate. Secondly, girls were the first to suffer when domestic help was required. Child labour in the form of domestic help ranged from looking after the younger ones while adults were at work in the field and keeping the firewood burning in the stove while mother was cooking, to picking wild vegetables for pigs and spinning yarn for the family. Some of that work, such as spinning, was traditionally done by females, but other work was not.

The ultimate cause for discrimination was that girls were less valued in the family (although not less loved by their parents). Given that there was not any form of social security and the elderly had to rely on the family to be looked after, girls were considered to have less value because they had to be married off and a security investment had to be made on the son or sons for old age. Just as before 1949, the economic and social structures in Mao's China were such that individuals were not valued in their own right. Their values were assessed as part of the household in which they lived. What symbolically and substantially demonstrated this collective household value was the production team accountancy book: contribution and distribution were not recorded individually but altogether under the single name of the "master of the household", usually a male in the family.

Notwithstanding the gender discrimination, the number of children attending school increased rapidly in those years, largely as a result of the establishment of the village school which made access more obtainable; and this was done at no cost to the state government. Before 1952 there was not a single modern school in the area that had a population of 1,673 in 1949 and 2,229 in 1958. Since 1952 until 1969, there was only one school for students from years one to six in an area that had a population of 3,048 in 1969. By 1972, there were ten village schools set up to cater for students of years one to three for a population of 3,160.

Although there are no statistics available for the number of students attending school during 1958-69 to compare with later years, the fact that the number of "barefoot teachers" in the Qinglin area increased from zero in 1968 to twenty-three in 1972 and twenty-four in 1978 is a clear indication that the number of children attending schools increased dramatically since 1969. By 1972, there were 378 children at primary school and seventy-one children at secondary school in the area. By 1978 when the population reached 3,610 in Qinglin, there were 153 children at secondary school and 600 at primary school.

By 1972, every village had a school for year one to year three students. After they had finished year three in a village school, children had to attend year four and five at Qinglin School to finish their primary education. In 1972, because of the great expansion of primary education, Qinglin School was expanded to include a secondary school establishment in which education for year six and year seven students was offered. As no funding could be expected from the government, the solution of 'barefoot teachers" was the only choice. I was appointed by the Qinglin brigade authority as one of the "barefoot teachers" to teach secondary school children at Qinglin School. My position in Gao Village was filled by a female "barefoot teacher" who had had only three years education. As for myself I had only one year of secondary education. I was asked to teach some subjects which I had not learned. Every time I had to work hard to learn the subject before I entered the classroom to face the students, some of whom were older than me. This situation was probably one of the reasons why the post-Mao authorities and the Chinese intellectual élite accused the Cultural Revolution educational policies of lowering the standards. By the same logic, the secondary school component at Qinglin School was closed down in 1980.

The issue of quality is not something that can be debated here. However, for the villagers the Cultural Revolution policies appeared to be more relevant and practical. In any case, the more urgent issue for people like Gao villagers was how to make education even at elementary level available. What sort of quality are we talking about when most villagers had no access to even rudimentary education? The Cultural Revolution policies did boost access and therefore more people became educated. Compared with one senior secondary school graduate and two junior school graduates in the entire pre-Cultural Revolution period of eighteen years in Gao Village, there were four senior secondary school graduates, eight junior secondary school graduates, one college graduate and one university graduate from Gao Village in the ten year Cultural Revolution period.

Tertiary education and my own case

Tertiary education is a case in point. Without some affirmative action to favour disadvantaged rural residents it is not possible for village children to compete with children from the urban areas, let alone those from the élite backgrounds of the intelligentsia and Party officials. Apart from better teaching facilities and better resources, children from an urban and town background can get help from their parents for their homework because their parents are in general more educated than rural parents. Urban parents can afford to provide most of what is needed for their children's education such as books, reading materials, field trips, private music and art lessons, which most village children have never seen or heard of.

It is not that rural people are not trying. Some have tried very hard, but without success. Take the case of my second younger brother. He was lucky in that he went to secondary school in the 1980s when I could afford to help him. He took the national college entrance examination four times, but he failed on each occasion, at one time by just four marks. Every time he failed he was encouraged to repeat year twelve, which is the final year of secondary education. By rural standards, it was very costly to repeat year twelve for three years and few villagers could afford that without external help. Moreover, I had to make the arrangement through the "back door", i.e. personal connections, for my brother to repeat year twelve and to repeatedly re-sit the national examination. I had also arranged private tuition for my brother. All these could not possibly be done by any villager in normal circumstances. Despite all his efforts my brother failed to pass the entrance examinations.

Of course, all this could simply mean that my brother is not intelligent enough. However, he is certainly not as stupid as the Chinese élite assume all rural people to be. My brother has been quite successful since he gave up further attempts at college entrance examinations. He first went to Xiamen as a migrant worker in the late 1980s. By 1995, he had become a foreign businessman's assistant manager, the workshop supervisor and chairman of the trade union in a cutlery factory in Xiamen.

The Chinese intellectual élite always stigmatise rural people, the peasants, as by nature stupid. As Suzanne Pepper observes, for the Chinese intellectual élite "someone with a particularly slow manner of speech is not mentally or physically handicapped but 'just a typical peasant' ", and the basis for the saying that 'the peasants work like animals" is that they "must be born to that kind of life to be able to accept it".[3] Jung Chang, author of the widely-read book *Wild Swans*, took the same patronising attitude when she bitterly attacked all the policies of the Cultural Revolution.

In any case, thanks to radical policies, there were two university students in the Qinglin area in 1973, one from Xu Village and

[3] Suzanne Pepper, *China's Universities, Post-Mao Enrolment Policies and Their Impact on the Structure of Secondary Education, A Research Report*, Centre for Chinese Studies, University of Michigan, Ann Arbor, 1984, p. 115.

one from Gao Village. Xu Xianqi from Xu Village went to Shanghai Jiaotong University and later became a railway engineer. I myself went to Xiamen University to study English. Both Shanghai Jiaotong and Xiamen universities are national universities of good reputation, as opposed to regional universities in Jiangxi Province. There were only two university students from the Qinglin area who graduated from provincial universities before 1973.

Without the disruption caused by the Cultural Revolution, I could have finished my three years of formal junior school education at Youdunjie School. Being one of the top students at the school I might have been able to pass the examinations to qualify for senior high school education in the County Town. With possible support from my sister who was married and lived in the County Town, I might even have been able to complete three years of senior high education. However, the chance of my entering a university through the competitive national entrance examination would have been very slight.

There were many reasons why I, a peasant who had not even completed junior high school education, was enrolled to Xiamen University. First, the national entrance examination was abolished. However, examinations were set up by regional education authorities to streamline the candidates in 1973. In Jiangxi Province two examination papers were set, one involving writing an essay, one testing mathematical ability, to exclude many aspiring candidates. In fact, examination papers in some provinces were quite tough and in Liaoning Province, for instance, the papers caused a political incident.[4] I did not know how well I had done in the examinations. It is likely that I had done better than others but worse than some. In any case my papers did not show that I was completely hopeless and that was enough as far as the academic aspect was concerned.

---

[4] That was when one of the candidates, Zhang Tiesheng, refused to answer the examination questions. Instead he wrote a few lines of protest, complaining that it was not fair to expect people like him (he was a production team leader in a village at that time) to compete with those who stayed in the cities and who had experts to coach them for the examinations. Zhang Tiesheng's protest was conveniently picked up by Mao Yuanxin, Chairman Mao's nephew, who was one of the provincial officials in Liaoning Province at the time, and other radical left politicians to launch another attack against the conservative faction within the Communist Party.

Second, the political aspect was even more important. According to the ideology at that time, the policy was that the candidates should and must be only those recommended by the grassroot masses, and in this case, from the villagers. However, in reality only the local powerholders could decide who was to be a candidate. Therefore, whom to recommend as a candidate was a hotly fought issue in local politics. The candidate had to come from a good family background, thus excluding those from landlord, rich peasant or even middle peasant background; They had to have some recognised level of literacy such as a secondary school education; finally the candidate had to have an impeccable record of political performance. This criteria embraced everything ranging from being politically correct in every political campaign to not having stolen anything and being unconnected with sexual scandals (such as having sex with your partner before marriage).

I was from a poor peasant background, and I had a reputation for having the "highest level of education" in the area because I was already teaching secondary school students. I was almost perfect except for my political record. In 1971 I was accused of wanting to preserve the feudalist genealogical record of Gao Village. This is an issue that I discuss in Chapter 9. However, in spite of this I was recommended as one of the three candidates to take part in the academic examinations and the issue of my political crime in 1971 was not even raised.

To understand this, the enrolment policies and the intricacies of local politics need to be discussed. First of all, the number of candidates was dependent on the quota given from the top levels down. The Central Ministry of Education decided how many students were to be enrolled according to the number of places available in all the universities in China allowed for by the resources. The total number was then allocated to different provinces and cities. Each province in turn allocated the number of enrolments to different counties. Each county then allocated the enrolment number to various communes. By the time it got to Yinbaohu commune in 1973, the quota was 0.46 of a candidacy. In other words, less than one student was allowed to be enrolled from Yinbaohu commune.

At the same time, the number of enrolments was also allocated to different universities. For instance, if Xiamen University was given to enrol four thousand students, it had to be told by the

Beijing authorities how many should be enrolled from Fujian Province where it is located and how many from other provinces. According to this quota, Xiamen University would send a staff member to these different provinces to select its own candidates. First rate institutions such as Beijing University would be given the first chance to select and then second rate universities and so on. Obviously, university staff members could not go to all of the different communes to select candidates. What happened instead was that each commune recommended its candidates to the county authorities, which had the responsibility of providing the university enrolment staff with the names and files of all those recommended.

In this whole process of planning and selection, each level of the bureaucracy had some power to influence the final outcome. The central and provincial authorities had some power to decide who got what quota. University enrolment staff had the power to select from the candidates provided. The county authority had even more vital power because it could not only decide what quota to give to which commune but also had the freedom to decide whose names and files were presented to which university. Meanwhile at the commune level, because there are so many villages in a commune, the authority had to make sure that a balance was seen to be achieved. In Yinbaohu commune, three candidates were recommended to the county authority to create a balance. Once someone was chosen by a university the other two were out of the race as the quota was less than one.

In the process of selecting the three candidates, the commune authority decided that the Education Department of the Commune Committee should take charge of the whole affair. Since the expansion of schools took up most of the young talent this arrangement was the only logical possibility because most of the candidates would have to come from the teaching staff in the commune. It so happened that the man in charge of the Commune Education Department was from the nearby big Gao Village which was supposed to have genealogical connections with my Gao Village. This man's name happened to be Gao Changyan, which could be taken as the name of my brother because the first two characters of his name were the same as mine. The naming system in the village works like this. Everyone born in the village has the same surname, which is one's first name. Every male of the same generation has the same second name. Only the last name belongs to the individual alone.

There were two teachers in Qinglin School where I was working at the time who would have objected to me as a candidate had Gao Changyan not been the head of the Commune Education Department. They all thought that I had a special relationship with Gao Changyan and therefore dared not challenge their superior. It also so happened that the then Party secretary of the commune was someone from outside the area, who had a very good relationship with Gao Changyan. Because Gao Changyan recommended me strongly all the brigade and commune officials thought that to object to me being recommended would risk a fight not only with the head of the Commune Education Department but also the Commune Party secretary who held supreme power in the commune. So they went along with it.

But that was only half the battle won. After the examination there was the hurdle of passing the physical check-ups. Before the departure from Yinbaohu to Tianfanjie, about 70 kilometres away where the physical check-up took place, I told Gao Changyan about my worries. As a result of chronic ear infections my right ear was already partly deaf and I was bound to fail the hearing ability test. Gao Changyan told the person who took the three of us to Tianfanjie to look after me in this respect. However, there was not much that he could do about it. All the way to Tianfanjie and the whole night before the check-up took place, I was worried and anxious, not knowing what to do.

Next morning the process duly started and I had all the other check-ups completed except the ENT (ears, nose and throat) session, which I had kept until the last. When I saw that one of my former classmates from Youdunjie School, nicknamed "Yellow Buffalo" because of his physical strength, was also there, I had an idea. He agreed to stand in for me at the ENT check-up, and with great relief I passed the test.

However, that was not the end of my ordeal. After all was done we waited and waited to hear the news. I was then told that Xu Xianqi was chosen by Shanghai Jiaotong University, we were both out of the race. No one was surprised that Xu Xianqi was chosen. He had had the best credentials of the three of us: he was a member of the Communist Party while we were not;

he had served in the army for three years, considered to be one of the primary indicators of political loyalty and reliability; he was also already a member of the Brigade Committee. On top of that, he was good-looking and very presentable (among the files there was a photo of each candidate). I had to give up and forget about it. Then, just about one month before the school term started, I received a notice from Xiamen University saying that I was enrolled to study English. It hit me like a thunderbolt. I had never wanted to study English and could not even pronounce the alphabet correctly.

I never found out exactly why I was chosen by Xiamen University. It was rumoured that the teacher from there who went to Boyang County to select candidates had liked what he read about me. But I could never confirm this because the teacher said to be responsible had left for Hong Kong soon after I arrived at Xiamen University. However, in 1992 when Gao Changyan wanted me to help him find a better job assignment for his daughter who was graduating that year, he told me that it was his help that made my going to Xiamen University possible.

After having heard that I was out of the race Gao Changyan rang up a Mr Huang, one of the key people in charge of providing names and files to various universities, and asked him to recommend me on the strongest possible terms. Mr Huang, Gao Changyan told me, happened to be his close classmate in college. When Mr Huang asked Gao Changyan whether the person in question was his own brother, Gao Changyan avoided the question by telling Mr Huang that it did not matter whether the person was a brother or not; he should just do as he was requested. Mr Huang did so and so there I was at Xiamen, a student of English.

However, I was unable to help Gao Changyan to get a better job assignment for his daughter. Like many Gao villagers, Gao Changyan overestimated the importance of scholars in contemporary China. In any case, I was not living in China any more and what I could do was extremely limited. Apart from the fact that I respect Gao Changyan as a person and feel grateful for his help, whatever the real nature of it, I have also been pressured by Gao villagers to be obliged to Gao Changyan. Every time I go back to China I have to bring him a present. I am certainly made aware that I owe him a debt that has not been fulfilled. By saying this and giving the detailed account of what happened regarding my enrolment in the university I intend to give an intimate account of how local actors, social customs and state government policies interact with each other in local politics in the area.

The post-Mao period

A brief examination of what happened at the national level provides a good background for what happened in the area where Gao Village is located. In 1965 the total number of students at China's secondary schools was 14.4 million, whereas the number for the academic year 1977-8 was 68.9 million, plus another million in specialised schools. Since 1979, when the post-Mao Chinese authorities started to reverse the Cultural Revolution policies, student numbers in China's secondary schools began to decline. The decline in 1980 alone amounted to nearly 14 million. During this year 23,700 secondary schools were closed down in China.[5] Why did the post-Mao Chinese government do this? Again I quote Suzanne Pepper:

> The reversal of the Cultural Revolution decade's emphasis on expanding general secondary education has been rationalised in terms of the very limited numbers that can be accommodated in college, as though that were the chief aim of such schooling. Moreover, the rapid development of secondary schooling during the Cultural Revolution decade was said to have "spread financial resources very thinly and aggravated the shortage of qualified teachers".[6]

However, the "barefoot teacher" system did not cost the state government much. In the case of Qinglin area, the expansion of Qinglin School to include a junior secondary school component did not cost the state government anything extra because it was all paid for by the brigade, which received its income from the villagers. The only evidence supporting the post-Mao Chinese government's claim is that some qualified teachers were sent down from the cities to town areas or rural regional centres to teach.

[5] These are Chinese official figures quoted in Suzanne Pepper, *China's Universities*, p. 14.

[6] Suzanne Pepper, *ibid.*, p. 13.

For instance when Youdunjie Junior School was expanded to include a senior component, a number of teachers sent down form Boyang County Town were appointed to teach there. When the policy was reversed by the post-Mao Chinese government, those teachers went back to Boyang County Town. In other words, the urban and town sector lost some qualified teachers to the rural sector during the Cultural Revolution.

However, no teacher from the urban sector was ever sent to Qinglin School when it expanded. Therefore, the closure of the junior school component of Qinglin School had no financial justification whatsoever. The closure of a large number of secondary schools in rural areas was driven by an ideological strategy to re-create privilege for a few and to continue to keep the rural residents as an underclass. "So firm is the commitment to this strategy at present that no effort is being made to counteract or even camouflage the aura of special privilege that has been re-created – particularly for the children of intellectuals – in the matter of access to schooling."[7]

In the entire history of Gao Village up to the 1990s, there have been only six senior school graduates, of which one graduated before the Cultural Revolution, three during the Cultural Revolution and only two since. In 1994, there was only one student at senior secondary school. To date, there has only been one technical college student and one university student, both of whom completed their studies during the Cultural Revolution. In January 1996 there were four students at junior secondary school and none at senior high. Some children could not pass the examinations that were required to progress from primary to secondary school. Some simply could not afford to go.

The village teacher Gao Chaozhen's two sons, for instance, failed to continue secondary school education because of family hardship. Gao Chaozhen's wife had to have a gallstone operation in a city hospital in Jingdezhen. The family had to save every cent to pay the debts resulting from medical bills and the two boys had to forgo their education. Instead, one, aged fourteen, left for Fujian and the other, aged sixteen, left for Guangdong as migrant workers.

The fact that Gao Village children have to travel 7 kilometres

[7] *Ibid.* p. 116.

every Sunday to board at the only secondary school in Yinbaohu *xiang* also makes some give up education. The Yinbaohu secondary school is the only school set up by the brigades during the Cultural Revolution that was not closed down. This is because it is located at Jin Village, where the commune administration used to be located and where the *xiang* government now sits. Gao Village children, like myself in the past, now have to travel back home every Saturday and to the school every Sunday, carrying with them food for a week. Apart from the distance and boarding costs involved, Gao Village children have other problems that I did not even have to contemplate in the late 1960s.

With the dismantling of the commune system, the already cellular villages became even more out of the reach of the state government. A good indication of the weakening of state power is the almost total lack of coordination to maintain irrigation projects. Massive irrigation projects like the ones carried out during the 1960s and '70s are almost impossible nowadays. Even the existing ones are out of repair. Every village is left to care for itself. Clan powers which had re-emerged with greater strength since the early 1980s began to overwhelm local politics. Historical village feuds erupt from time to time over which the state government remains helpless.

A telling example is a feud between Jin Village, the biggest village in Yinbaohu *xiang*, which has 1,000 households and its neighbouring village which is much smaller. In a large scale battle involving locally made cannons and guns which took place in 1991, seventeen people from the small village were killed by Jin Villagers. When the county authorities and police came to investigate the affair, they were unable to proceed because nobody dared to come forward with the truth. A crippled man from Jin Village claimed that he was the sole initiator and organizer of the fight and that he was ready to take responsibility for the death of seventeen people. What was astonishing was that the county authorities and the police could do nothing other than to accept this version of events. The crippled man was taken away and put into jail and the affair was considered to be settled. Everyone knew, including the police and the county authorities, that it was arranged by the clan authority in Jin Village that the crippled man come forward and claim responsibility. In return for his service the crippled man's family would be looked after by the village for as long as he was in jail. The *xiang* government, which was largely dominated by Jin Villagers, pretended not to know anything about the fight that took place in its own backyard. During the height of the feud, there were Jin Village guards on duty everywhere and any outsider passing through Jin Village even on a public road was questioned and searched.

Yinbaohu *xiang* is on a longish territory, at the southern end of which is Jin Village and some other small villages. At the north end of the territory there are Gao Village, Xu Village, Jiang Village and a number of other small villages. There are also some small villages in the middle. During the commune period, the commune government was located at Jin Village for no apparent reason other than the fact that Jin Village was the largest. Without Jin village's support, no local government could function properly. When the commune system was dismantled and the name of the local government was changed to *xiang*, the *xiang* government had to remain in Jin Village for the same reason. The main difference is that during the commune period, the most important commune officials were appointed by the county authority and were often communist cadres from outside whereas during the post-Mao period the *xiang* government officials were supposed to be elected locally, as a result of which the *xiang* government came to be dominated by Jin villagers. Therefore, the balance of power and leverage that the state government used to enjoy during the commune period was lost after Mao. The result was an almost complete breakdown of state control.

By the same logic, the only junior secondary school in Yinbaohu *xiang* had to be located in Jin Village. Children from other villages have to travel to and board in Jin Village if they want to continue their education. In order to frighten off children from the north of the Yinbaohu *xiang* so that the only government supported secondary school could be theirs alone, Jin villagers employ all kinds of tactics to harass students from the north. These tactics include sexual harassment of girl students and blatant robberies. Children from Jin Village openly bully children from the north by teasing and beating them up. A girl from Jiang Village was once seized by a group of Jin villagers and fondled all over her body. From time to time a group of Jin villagers would simply surround a classroom and start shouting: "So and so come out! We want to f–k you!" It has become so bad recently that children

from the north dare not go out at night. It may be true that all
these acts are not necessarily organized by the Jin Village clan,
but it is a fact that all acts are committed against children from
the north. Teachers dare not interfere. Once a teacher tried to
confront the Jin villagers. He was badly beaten and told that they
would kill him if he dared to interfere again.

When I visited Gao Village in 1994, the villagers, the village
committee officials and some teaching staff from the north gave
me detailed accounts of this horrifying situation. They want to
start a separate secondary school in the north at their own cost
to put an end to it. However, it is now very difficult to attempt
to establish a school. The original school building for the secondary
school component has been dismantled, and there are no teaching
staff. It is impossible to organise concerted resources to employ
local talent, such as the "barefoot teacher" of Mao's time, without
government support, which of course is now not available. In
any case, there is such hostility between the village committee
and the villagers that any attempt to raise funds from the villagers
is seen as corrupt village committee officials hoping to enrich
themselves. As we shall see in later chapters, given what has been
happening, it is entirely logical for the villagers to be suspicious
of those village officials. Instead these teachers, the village officials
and villagers all came to me for help when I was there in 1994.
Seeing that I was now an overseas Chinese, they thought I could
just donate $10,000 from my pocket there and then. In their
world view, all overseas Chinese are rich.

Primary education was less affected by the policies brought in
after Mao's time. The school set up in 1969 in Gao Village was
not disbanded. It has carried on teaching year one and year two
students. Unlike the Cultural Revolution period, year three students
have to travel to Qinglin School. The original school house has
been sold. Before the commune system was dismantled in 1981,
all agricultural tools and other property had belonged to the two
production teams, but subsequently on dismantling the commune
system they were distributed to households, and so the school
house also went. From then on, anybody who taught had to do
so at his or her own house, just like the traditional *sishu* teacher.
For the first few years the classes were taught by Gao Chaojiang,
my school mate at Youdunjie and one of the two junior secondary
students in the late 1960s. Then it was taken over by Gao Chaozhen,

one of the senior high school graduates during the Cultural Revolution. The hall of Gao Chaozhen's house is used as a classroom, in which there are a dozen stools and two taller longish stools as tables. In front of these there is a blackboard, the very one I used when I was a teacher. At the back of this "classroom" there is a kitchen for the teacher's family. On the right-hand side there is a room partitioned by a screen made of bamboo which is the bedroom for the teacher and his wife. This arrangement looked less chaotic because Gao Chaozhen's two sons had left home to be migrant workers far away in coastal China.

In the 1990s, Gao Chaozhen is paid around 90 *yuan* a month, a total of 1,080 *yuan* a year, of which 540 *yuan* is paid by the state government. The remaining 540 *yuan* has to be paid by the village committee, which derives its income from levies on the villagers and from students' tuition fees. A year one or year two student has had to pay a total annual fee of around 60 *yuan* since the beginning of the 1990s. By 1995, the fee had gone up to more than 70 *yuan*. A year five student now has to pay an annual fee of around 150 *yuan*, and a junior secondary school student has to pay up to 250 *yuan* a year. The fee is collected at the beginning of every year and is handed to the village committee. It is broken down into a dozen items to cover registration, textbooks, exercise books, insurance, examinations and the county, *xiang* and village education funds. It is worth pointing out at this stage that the so-called education funds at three levels are also raised through local taxes from every villager. In other words, payments to these funds are levied twice, once on every villager and again on the students.

During the late 1980s and early 1990s, many Gao Village children failed to attend schools; most of them were girls. In 1994, for instance, eight children who had already passed the school age for years one and two did not have a single day of schooling, and most of these too were girls. During the early 1970s when I was a teacher, most children, including girls, had at least one or two years' education. During the late 1980s and early 1990s girls were left out of school because when the cost was too prohibitive and when a preference had to be made, the villagers would prefer to send boys to school for social security reasons.

According to Gao Chaozhen, however, by 1994, all children

at the school age of year one and year two were at school in Gao Village, seven boys and six girls for year one and three boys and five girls for year two. The reason Gao Chaozhen gave was that since the 1990s, the villagers had begun to see the importance of literacy for all their children, including the girls, when they leave to become migrant workers. All the feedback from Gao Village migrant workers has been that the better educated you are, the better chance you have of finding a job with better pay. Another important motivation for migrant workers to be literate is that they can write home. As we shall see in Chapter 11 it is traumatic for children at the age of fourteen to sixteen to leave home and work as migrant workers far away from their village. Writing letters is an important way to maintain the emotional balance between parents and children. Above all, it is the remittances from migrant workers that enable the villagers to pay for the cost.

In order to manage what is called quality control, the county educational authorities impose county-wide examinations from time to time. The results are compared and the teachers of those schools who have good examination results are given some financial bonus. Because only three subjects are examined – ideology, Chinese language and arithmetic – all other subjects are neglected by most school teachers. In Gao Village school, for instance, there are no arts, music or sports classes. Even at Qinglin School, which is the Centre Primary School in the area, there are no such facilities. When I was teaching at Qinglin School in the 1970s there were two basketball courts and one table for table tennis. In 1994 when I visited the school there was none. The teachers told me that even if you had the funds to put up a basketball court, for instance, the basketball framework would be stolen within no time. For the villagers, sport is a silly pastime anyway.

What the state government does spend money on, which can be positive for the rural areas, is a system of training for those teachers who used to be "barefoot teachers" and who do not have urban resident status. There is a regular examination available for those teachers who want to change their status. Any teacher who has more than five years teaching experience can take the examination. Having passed, the teacher is given a certificate as well as urban resident status and is paid a regular government salary. The subjects that are examined are History of Social Development,

Dialectical Materialism, Teaching Methodology, Classroom Psychology, plus Chinese language and mathematics. The examinations are extremely difficult to pass, according to Gao Chaozhen who failed several times and has now given up hope. Through this process of promotion and since some teachers who used to be "barefoot teachers" in the 1970s were dismissed in the 1980s, there are now twelve teachers paid by the state government, and nine teachers paid by the village committee in the Qinglin area.

To conclude this chapter, it is worth emphasising that in the first years of the Communist regime genuine efforts were made by the government to improve education and raise literacy standards in the Gao Village area. Development in education in rural areas was most visible during the two most radical periods of the People's Republic, i.e. the Great Leap Forward and the Cultural Revolution. It was during these two otherwise destructive and chaotic periods that education in the Qinglin area became more accessible to rural residents. On the other hand, during the early period of reform in the 1980s many rural schools were closed down and the number of children attending school fell sharply in rural areas, all in the name of streamlining and quality improvement. The situation improved again in the 1990s only because of income from migrant workers.

8

THE GREAT LEAP FORWARD

Much has already been written on the subject of the Chinese Great Leap Forward.[1] The ideology of collectivisation, the enthusiasm for building a socialist new China and the impatience for speed and scale, which had finally led to the Great Leap Forward, can be traced back to the mid 1950s. However, the Great Leap Forward itself was in full swing only from 1958 to 1959 and did not last much longer than a year before Mao himself started to call for adjustments.

The pressure for fast development had been building up for quite some time. As early as July 1955 in a speech addressed to provincial Party secretaries, Mao expressed his dissatisfaction with Deng Zihui, the man in charge of agriculture, for his "right wing opportunism" and "right wing conservatism", which actually meant a cautious development of collectivisation. On 20 June 1956, the *People's Daily* published an editorial at the suggestion of Liu Shaoqi, Zhou Enlai and Chen Yun which advocated being on guard against both right-wing conservatism and left-wing impatience.

---

[1] See, for instance, Byung-Joon Ahn, "Adjustments in the Great Leap Forward and their Ideology and Legacy" in Chalmers Johnson, ed., *Ideology and Politics in Contemporary China*, Seattle and London, 1973, pp. 257-300; Roderick Mac-Farquhar, *Origins of the Cultural Revolution*, vol. 2: *The Great Leap Forward, 1958-60*, New York, 1983; Joseph Williams "A Tragedy of Good Intentions: Post-Mao View of the Great Leap Forward", *Modern China*, Oct. 1986, no. 12, pp. 419-58; Alfred Chan, "The Dynamics of Policy-making in China: The Case of the Great Leap Forward, 1958", unpubl. Ph.D. diss. University of Toronto, 1988; Felix Greene, *A Curtain of Ignorance*, London, 1965; Isabel and David Crook, *The First Years of Yangyi Commune*, London, 1966; Carl Riskin, *China's Political Economy: the Quest for Development since 1949*, 1987; Jean-Luc Domenach, *The Origins of the Great Leap Forward: The Case of One Chinese Province*, Boulder, CO, 1995; Jasper Becker, *Hungry Ghosts: China's Secret Famine*, London, 1996.

Mao was reported to have said, "I don't read this kind of stuff".[2] Moreover, the Anti-Rightist Movement in 1957 paved the way for the radicalism of the Great Leap Forward because everyone was intimidated by the wide scale attack against intellectuals and no one dared to criticise the impulsive policies of the Great Leap Forward.

Ironically, most of the ideas of the Great Leap Forward did not come from Mao himself. According to one version of events, the idea of overtaking Britain in fifteen years in steel and iron production and other major industrial goods was inspired by Krushchev's slogan of the Soviet Union overtaking the United States in fifteen years.[3] On December 20, 1957, Liu Shaoqi revealed Mao's idea in his address to the Eighth Congress of the National Trade Union in Beijing. Liu Shaoqi, the man who had a reputation for being practical and cautious, went as far as saying on 5 July 1958 that it would only take China two or three years to overtake Britain. He said to the workers at Shijingshan that they would be able to see communism realised in China in their lifetime.[4] Communism here meant full realisation of the principle of 'from each according to one's ability and to each according to one's needs".

The term "Leap Forward" which best indicated China's impatience with development was actually an invention of a cautious man, who in 1957 changed his attitude completely after he was criticised by Mao for his conservatism – none other than Zhou Enlai himself.[5] The idea of the People's Commune was first implemented by Chayashan local authorities in Suiping County of Henan Province in April 1958. When Mao visited Shandong Province and was told by the then Shandong Provincial Party secretary Tan Qilong about the practice of the People's Commune in August 1958, Mao made an offhand remark "People's Commune, that's good". A journalist picked up the remark and a headline "People's Commune Is Good, Chairman Mao's Instruction" appeared

---

[2] Xie Chuntao, *Dayuejin De Kuanglan* (The Raging Waves of the Great Leap Forward), Zhengzhou, 1990, p. 270.

[3] Wen Lu, *Zhongguo Zuohuo* (Misfortunes Caused by Leftism in China), Beijing, 1993, p. 281.

[4] Ma Qibing *et al.*, *Zhongguo Gongchandang Zhizheng Si Shi Nian (1949-1989), Zengding Ben* (The Communist Party of China in Power, 1949-1989), edn with supplement, Beijing, 1991, p. 148.

[5] Xie Chuntao, *Dayuejin De Kuanglan*, p. 12.

on the *People's Daily* several days later. Thereafter, local authorities everywhere competed to set up People's Communes.

The idea of every one eating together in a public canteen was again a kind of experiment originating from the local authorities. On 8 July 1958, the *People's Daily* published a report advocating the establishment of public canteens in the People's Communes by arguing that there were eight advantages for having a public canteen, including the promotion of efficiency in work because everyone could eat and go to work at the same time; the liberation of women from the kitchen; provision for the elderly and the disabled, and the reduction in family quarrels and public hygiene. The idea of the public canteen was also supported by Liu Shaoqi who, when visiting Shandong on 14-18 July 1958, praised the practice and suggested that every factory should make their own iron and steel instead of relying on supplies from outside.[6]

In July 1958, Li Fuchun and Li Xiannian, two of the main Party leaders in charge of central planning, in their *di er ge wu nian jihua yao dian* (Outlines for the Second Five Year Plan) stated that it would take no more than three years for China to overtake Britain in industry and that the rate of agricultural increase would be as high as 35 per cent. Bo Yibo, another main player in central planning, gave a report entitled *liang nian chaoguo yingguo* (Overtaking the UK in two years) on 17 June 1958.

The fairy tale reports of 10,000 *jin* (1 *jin* equals 0.5 kilos) yield of rice per *mu* (0.0667 hectares) again were cooked up by local authorities. The Guangdong Party secretary, Tao Zhu, for instance, published an article in the Communist Party's theoretical journal the *Red Flag* on 15 July 1958 entitled *bo liangshi zengchan youxian lun* (Refuting the theory that there is a limit to the increase of grain production), in which he said it was possible to produce 3,000-10,000 *jin* of grain on 1 *mu* of land in Guangdong. The impulsive Foreign Minister and Vice Premier Chen Yi said that he had seen with his own eyes the "fact" that in Fanyu County of Guangdong Province the yield of sweet potatoes was 1 million *jin* per *mu*, 600,000 *jin* of sugar cane per *mu* and 50,000 *jin* of rice per *mu*.[7] Tan Zhenglin, was another radical communist leader

---

[6] Ma Qibing *et al., ibid.,* p. 148.

[7] Chen Yi, "Guangdong Fanyu Xian Fangwen Ji" (Travel notes from Fanyu County in Guangdong Province), *People's Daily*, 26 September 1958.

who was reported to have said that the amount of grain that could be produced was only limited by one's imagination.[8]

When Mao was later asked by Li Rui whether he was not suspicious of such incredible figures of grain production, he replied that his gullibility was influenced by an article written by the well-known scientist Qian Xueseng who said that it was possible to produce 10,000 *jin* of rice on 1 *mu* of land if enough light was given.[9] Led by this misguided faith in a pseudo-scientific approach, in some places, farmers were told to install equipment to light the fields at night and to use air-blowers to ventilate the extremely closely planted rice plants.

Driven by a frenzied desire and enthusiasm to transform a poor and backward China into a wealthy socialist nation, the Chinese leadership from top to bottom were out of their mind carrying out all kinds of experiments, the results of which sometimes even shocked themselves. When Zhou Enlai, the man who invented the term 'Leap Forward", visited his adopted daughter from Thailand in a school, he found the sight of school children making iron and steel in the school backyard beyond belief.[10]

The degree of enthusiasm varied from province to province and from county to county, but fanaticism was the rule of day, so much so that from very early on the Communist Party central government had to warn the local authorities not to be over-enthusiastic. On 3 August 1958, the CCP Central Committee issued a circular, warning the various leaders to be cautious.[11] On 29 August 1958, the CCP Politburo Conference at Beidaihe passed a resolution concerning the People's Commune, in which local

---

[8] Dong Cunbao, *Tan Zhenglin Waizhuan* (An unofficial biography of Tan Zhenglin), Beijing, 1992, p. 160.

[9] Li Rui, *Mao Zedong De Gongguo Shifei* (The Merits, Demerits, Right and Wrong of Mao Zedong), Hong Kong, 1993, p. 158. Qian probably meant that it was theoretically possible if planting was close enough and if the problems of ventilation and light could be solved. This version of the story was also reported by Cai Yongmei, "Zhang Yangfu Chi Qian Xueseng" (Zhang Yangfu denounces Qian Xueseng), *Kaifang Zazhi* (The Open Journal), no. 11, 1992, pp. 68-70.

[10] Sirin Phathannuthai, with James, Peck, *The Dragon Pearl*, New York, London and Toronto, 1994.

[11] Ma Qibing *et al.*, op. cit., p. 149.

authorities were warned of "rashness, haste and compulsion", asked not to expect miracles from collectivisation, and told that collectivisation could only be carried out step by step.[12]

However, there was competition in being seen to be radical. The more radical and in a way the more imaginative the provincial leadership, the crazier and more irrational the experiments. From the information available, the Provinces of Shandong, Henan, Hebei, Anhui and Guangdong were among the most daring and enthusiastic. Therefore, the consequences were the most serious in these places. Jiangxi Province was one of the least affected. During the most difficult years of 1960-1 when famine was prevailing in China, groups and groups of Anhui rural residents left their home and travelled to Jiangxi Province to beg for food in order to survive. Some actually travelled to Gao Village. For Gao villagers, Anhui people became another name for famine refugees.

Famine and Death Toll

Famine was undoubtedly prevalent during the years 1959-61 in China, and a large number of people died as a result. It is claimed by both Chinese and Western scholars that the death toll could have been as high as 30-50 million.[13] However, as long as the Communist Party, which was responsible for the famine, remains in power, it will be very difficult to obtain hard evidence to support a relatively exact number of deaths. The estimate of 30 million or more is largely based on the normal rate of population increase in China at that time, which appears to indicate that this number of Chinese went missing between 1959 and 1962.

With the present state of knowledge, we have to be cautious in reaching conclusive figures for several reasons. First, during the famine, the fertility rate and therefore the birth rate must have been low. For instance, more than 700,000 babies were

---

[12] Geoffrey Hudson, A.V. Sherman and A. Zauberman, *The Chinese Communes, A Documentary Review and Analysis of the "Great Leap Forward"*, London, 1959.

[13] Edward Friedman *et al.*, *Chinese Village Socialist State*, New Haven and London, 1991; Barry Naughton, in Kenneth Liberthal *et al.*, *Perspectives on Modern China, Fortieth Anniversary*, 1991; Andrew Nathan, *China's Crisis*, 1990; and Jasper Becker, *Hungry Ghosts: China's Secret Famine*.

born in Jiangxi province in 1957 whereas the number in 1961 was only a little more than 420,000.[14] Nationally, the annual average birth rate was more than 30 per cent during the 1950s and 1960s whereas it was only 20.86 per cent in 1960 and 18.02 per cent in 1961.[15] Because of the magnitude both in terms of length of time and population base, the lower birth rate must have contributed significantly to the population shrinkage. Therefore, the missing people in this respect could not all be counted towards the death-toll.

Second, we cannot be certain that the figures published by the Chinese authorities are accurate. There was no census during the period and data collection both in terms of technology and administration was chaotic.[16] Apart from a 1953 census, there was not even a sampling before 1957. "China's statistical system began to disintegrate in the early 1958 and did not fully recover until over two decades later."[17] Beginning with the Great Leap Forward, there was a breakdown in the statistical system, and "the Great Leap Forward caused such confusion in population reporting that the official national total for year end 1960 is a somewhat arbitrary 10 million less than the estimate for the previous year end".[18]

Thirdly, even the census carried out in 1953 can be questioned for its accuracy. According to Wertheim, Chen Ta (or Chen Da), an outstanding demographer in China who had organised censuses before, was criticised by the Chinese authorities in 1957 because he attacked the 1953 official census which claimed that China's population had risen from 450 million in 1947 to 600 million in 1953. According to Chen, the 1953 census was unscientific and was largely an assessment based on regional random samples.[19]

[14] Ma Juxian, Shi Yuan and Yi Yiqu, *Zhongguo Renkou: Jiangxi Fence* (China's population: Jiangxi Province), Beijing: Zhongguo Caizheng Jingji Chubanshe, 1989, p. 78.

[15] *China Statistical Yearbook 1984*, Beijing: China Statistical Publishing House, 1984, p. 83.

[16] In this respect see Ruo Lin Jingzi, (Chinese translation of the name of a Japanese author), and translated by Zhou Jianming, *Zhongguo Renkou Wenti* (Problems of Chinese Population), Beijing: Zhongguo Renmin Chubanshe, 1994.

[17] Judith Banister, *China's Changing Population*, Stanford, CA, 1987, p. 13.

[18] *Ibid.*, p. 41.

[19] Wim F. Wertheim, "'Wild Swans' and Mao's Agrarian Strategy", *Australian*

An expert in Chinese demography, Dr Ping-ti Ho, Professor of History at the University of Chicago, in his book *Studies on the Population of China, 1368-1953*, also questions the 1953 census for not being a census in the "technical definition of the term". According to the 1953 census, the increase in China's population in the period 1947-53, including the years of nationwide wars between the Communists and the Nationalists involving millions of soldiers, was an astonishing 30 per cent. Some of the so-called missing people might never have existed.

Finally, as an indication of the difficulties experienced in monitoring population figures, during the Great Leap Forward years there was an enormous migration movement. From 1957-60, because of industrial expansion and decentralisation, the number of industrial workers doubled, resulting in a massive rural to urban migration. As a result of policy adjustment imposed by the Chinese government, from 1960 to 1963, nearly 30 million people moved back from the urban to rural areas. It is possible that when rural residents migrated to the urban areas, some were double-counted, by registers in both the urban areas and their places of origin. But when they moved back to their places of origin, they had been struck from the registers in their work place.

Hardship in the Gao Village area

Though the Jiangxi provincial leadership was not among the most fanatically radical, the people in Jiangxi and the Gao villagers also suffered the consequences of the Great Leap Forward which brought serious hardship to the latter. In the history of Gao Village since 1949 it was only during the Great Leap Forward that a suicide occurred. A woman hanged herself because of family hardship. The Great Leap Forward years were the only time in anybody's memory that Gao villagers had to pick wild vegetables and to grind rice husks into powder to make food. The elderly villagers did not remember ever eating rice husks before 1949. These are in fact difficult to digest and can damage the intestine. What was most common and very often talked about by the villages in later years was that after having consumed rice husks it was very difficult

China Review, August 1995, pp. 7-9.

to evacuate the bowels. Many people could only do so with the help of a spoon.

Throughout my twenty years in Gao village, I do not remember any particular time when my family really had enough to eat. After my sister went to live in Boyang County following her marriage in 1962, some of my happiest times were spent visiting her. An ordinary meal in her house was always a banquet for me and I would eat so much that every time I visited her I would have stomach problems. It was not that my sister was well off or that she would treat me specially. Her family was just an ordinary town family with urban resident status and with my brother-in-laws's regular salary. As a rural resident, life was *always* a matter of survival. However, the Great Leap Forward made life even more difficult than usual. The most unforgettable single event in my memory about these difficult years was when once my mother brought home one sweet potato for us to quench our hunger. We had not had much to eat for days and my mother went to Jiang Village to see a friend, hoping to get some help. Her friend offered two sweet potatoes. My mother ate one and brought the other one back home for me and my brother to share.

I was only seven at that time, but because of the famine, I had to go to the hillside, river banks, field edges and marsh land to pick wild vegetables to eat. The woman who hanged herself was one of my next door neighbours. There were always quarrels in that family, particularly between the woman and her mother-in-law. In 1960, life was getting extremely difficult and the mother-in-law kept insisting that the younger woman eat the least and worst food in the family. The mother-in-law forced the woman to eat tree bark and *guanyin tu* ("Bodhisattva earth" a kind of local soil that was supposed to be edible as if the Bodhisattva's kindness made it possible for human consumption) until eventually the latter could bear it no longer. She hung herself in the family toilet. Apart from this death and another in Jiang Village, we never heard of any other death caused by the hunger or famine during those years in our neighbouring villages. For what it is worth, Table 3 in Appendix 2 does not show any abnormality because of the Great Leap Forward.

According to this table, the rate of increase in 1958 and 1959 was very low and the number of people in 1959 and 1960 was the same; there appears to be some abnormality here. According to these figures, the female population increased by twenty-two from 1959 to 1960 while there was a decrease of twenty-two in the male population. However, there was an unusual increase of population by 203 in 1961, supposedly the most difficult year during the Great Leap Forward. There are two plausible explanations. One is that the figures in 1960 were not accurate and the 1961 figures had to compensate for errors recorded in 1960. The other explanation, which is more likely, is that since 1958, a significant number of rural young from the area were enrolled as workers in Jingdezhen, Jiujiang, and Boyang County Town as local industry was expanding fast under Great Leap Forward policies. Five families left Gao Village during the Great Leap Forward —one moved to Jiujiang, three to Jingdezhen and one to Shishan State Farm. However, when the Chinese authorities started to make adjustments to the radical policies, many of these people were ordered back. One Gao Village family returned.

Nor did the *Boyang Annals* record or even mention any death from starvation because of the Great Leap Forward in Boyang County. Only some statistics are available for the county, and only for selected years. Therefore, it is hard to tell whether there were any deaths from starvation.

Expansion of local industry and its consequences

One of the primary aims of the Great Leap Forward was to decentralise industry and to boost local initiative. This had a twofold rationale. First, by mobilising the broad masses, the Chinese leadership hoped that industry would expand faster. This was the well-known Maoist Mass Line which was thought to be the magic weapon which the Communists had used to defeat the Nationalists. The second aspect of the rationale was the utopian vision of transforming the Chinese peasantry into industrial workers without having to go through the process of urbanisation and dislocation of rural residents. These two aspects of Maoist ideology re-appeared during the Cultural Revolution. There is some solid evidence that the decentralisation of industry and the promotion of local initiatives, started during the Great Leap Forward and further promoted during the Cultural Revolution, had some beneficial effects for China's economy. For example, the economy of township enterprises since the 1980s is considered one of the pillars of the success of post-Mao reforms. Research shows that many successful township enterprises were direct descendants of initiatives from these two periods.[20]

In 1958, Boyang County was designated as one of ten "experimental counties" by the Central Ministry of Light Industry to carry out "commune enterprises". The process started in February 1958, and within the space of a few months, 3,623 local industrial enterprises were set up in Boyang County. These enterprises ranged from porcelain making, cement factories, coal and charcoal production to glass and paper making and iron and steel production. My sister, for instance, was enrolled in a porcelain factory and became an artist, making drawings on bowls and plates. Some of these enterprises survived whilst many of them were later closed down due to their being considered impractical or simply a waste of resources. The porcelain factory, for instance, was closed down within two years. Because of over-enthusiasm and a lack of rational coordination, hasty local initiatives caused environmental destruction. The speed with which trees were cut down was so fast that on 14 October 1958 the county authorities took measures to stop the alarming process. However, the initiative did boost the county's local industry and by 1965, 149 of these enterprises were still running.

In order to fulfil the quotas of iron and steel production imposed

---

[20] See for instance, Peng Kunlun, "Guangdong Xiangzhen Qiye Yunxing Jizhi De Tuantao" (Discussion on the Operating Mechanism of Township Enterprises in Guangdong), *Zhongshan Daxue Xuebao* (University Journal of Zhongshan University), no. 4, 1992, pp. 8-14; Bo Yibo, *Ruogan Zhongda Juece Ji Shijian De Huigu* (Recollections on Several Important Decisions and Events), vols I and II, Beijing, 1993; Edward Friedman *et al.*, *Chinese Village, Socialist State*, New Haven and London, 1991; Huang Daoxia, Dao Zhou and Yu Zhan, *Jidang De Nongcun Biange* (Turbulent Transformation in Rural China), Beijing, 1988; Samuel P.S. Ho, *Rural China in Transition, Non-Agricultural Development in Rural Jiangsu, 1978-1990*, Oxford, 1994; Zhong Pengrong and Yang Qingbing, "Hengdian Zhi Mi" (The riddle of Hengdian), *Ban Yue Tan* (The Fortnightly Forum), no. 19, 1994, pp. 46-7; *Zhongguo Tongji Nianjian* (China Statistics Year Book), Beijing, 1991; Christine Wong, "The Maoist Model Reconsidered: Local Self-Relances and the Financing of Rural Industrialisation" in William Joseph *et al.*, eds, *New Perspectives on the Cultural Revolution*, Cambridge, MA, and London, 1991, pp. 183-96; and Kristen Parris, "Local Initiative and National Reform: The Wenzhou Model of Development", *China Quarterly*, no. 134, June 1993, pp. 242-63.

by central government planning, various authorities from the provincial down to the commune level were urged to make iron and steel through local initiatives and unconventional methods. Backyard furnaces making iron and steel was one of the absurd and unforgettable scenes of the Great Leap Forward. However, it would be mistaken to assume that such things took place everywhere in China. It did not take place in Yinbaohu commune. Boyang County did make an attempt to set up a furnace at Lianhuashan, a mountainous area about 70 kilometres away from Gao Village. More than twenty Gao villagers were involved in the initiative in Lianhuashan; most went for a couple of months and then returned. Some worked there longer, but for five months at most. Their work was to transport firewood and charcoal for the furnaces. There is no reliable information, let alone statistics, available on the scale of iron and steel making in Lianhuashan. However, since more than twenty people from Gao Village alone were involved, we can assume that the futile exercise in Lianhuashan must have been on a huge scale and therefore wasted a lot of resources and energy.

Having failed to produce enough iron and steel, even including useless scraps, the county authorities ordered the commune and brigade authorities to collect iron and steel objects from village households to make up the required amount. I can still remember the scene vividly. A group of stern faced men from outside the village guided by village activists such as Gao Changyin searched from house to house. Woks and *dings*, another kind of cooking vessel of ancient style, were smashed; any metal objects in the house except hoes and ploughs were taken away as iron and steel to fulfil the quotas. Nails, spoons, slicers and shovels were confiscated and even door bolts were pulled off. It was extraordinary and the villagers were speechless and terrified. Tons of those objects were handed over from villages to the brigade, from brigades to the commune and from communes to the county authorities. In 1994 none of the villagers I asked knew where their household objects finally ended up and what had become of them. It was typical of how the rural residents were brutally treated by the authorities, past or present.

Public canteen and communism

The confiscation of cooking facilities was made possible, at least theoretically, by the fact that the households did not have to cook at that time. In Gao Village, a public canteen was set up in May 1958 but disbanded at the end of 1959. There were three cooks who worked full time to make food for the villagers, three times a day, every day for one and a half years. Gao villagers never actually ate together sharing tables with other families in the public canteen, as was the case in some parts of China. The public canteen only cooked rice and Gao Village households still prepared their own dishes, so each household was allowed keep one wok for this purpose.

Each meal time, following the shouted instructions of the village leader, each household would send a representative with a bucket in hand to line up, waiting for the food to be dished into it by one of the cooks. Then the food would be taken home and shared by everyone in the family. The amount of food given to each household was dependent on the number of people in the household. Of course, the cooks knew the figures very well. If they did not, they were reminded by the person who was holding the bucket. In my family, it was usually my duty to fetch the food from the public canteen. At the beginning there was enough food for everyone and we children thought it was great fun. Gradually, however, food became scarce and the amounts dished out became smaller and smaller. I remember that at one stage the public canteen could only afford to make rice porridge which was so thin and watery that we used to joke about using it as a mirror. Because of the lack of food the villagers did not have the strength to carry out their work. In their language they would say two bowls of porridge like that would only provide enough strength to pass water once in the toilet.

It was true that women were liberated from the kitchen, children were looked after together in a group, and the elderly and disabled did not have to do anything other than sit in groups whiling away their time chatting. Before the commune system, women only did occasional work in the fields apart from housework. In the commune, women started to work in the fields like men for the first time in Gao Village. Before the commune was set up and when there were still cooperatives, households used to have their own farming tools and private plots growing anything from fruit trees to vegetables. During the Great Leap Forward, everything was pooled together in the commune, except the family homes. In some parts of China, the grain and properties of the better off villages were taken away to give to the worse off villages so that everyone was equal. Radicalism did not go that far in the Qinglin area presumably because the leadership was not fast enough to follow the trend before the policies were called to a halt. For instance the villagers had private crops even during the Great Leap Forward (see Table 5 in Appendix 2).

Again, these figures may not be accurate in the technical definition of the term as that kind of accuracy is not possible in rural China. There may also be other problems with the statistics in the *Brigade Basic Statistics Record*. For instance, it is not clear what is meant by private run crops in the years before the Great Leap Forward. Land reform was not carried out in Qingling until 1950 and even for some time after that there was private ownership of land before the cooperatives were launched. What makes matters more confusing is that in the *Brigade Basic Statistics Record*, the villagers are recorded as having started to own private plots in 1961. The total amount of land allocated as private plots in the whole Brigade was 224 *mu* from 1961-70, reduced to 149 *mu* in 1971, increased to 305 *mu* from 1972-4 and then reduced again to 241 *mu*, and remaining more or less the same until the late 1970s. The land for private run crops does not include the land allocated as private plots since the latter were recorded in a separate table in the *Brigade Basic Statistics Record*, which did not start until 1961. Moreover, I know for certain that vegetables were produced and consumed by the villagers themselves and were never produced collectively in Qinglin. Apart from the so-called private plots, therefore, the villagers had kept others plots of land to produce things for themselves. Even these records may not have recorded all the land that was actually kept by the villagers for private use. According to these official records, the two categories of land for private use put together was only about 0.36 *mu* per person. However, I know from my own experience in Gao Village that for most of the time in Mao's China 0.5 *mu* of land per person was kept by Gao villagers for private use. In other words, at least in Qinglin, agrarian radicalism was never as radical as was claimed officially or assumed by some scholars.

While the villagers were pushed to do this and that without knowing what was going on, the village activists were full of energy, busy at meetings and passing on messages from their superiors. Everything was happening so quickly that nobody, including the village activists, was able to interpret what was going on, or predict future events with any certainty. Gao Changyin, the foremost village leader, kept on parroting what he just heard from his meeting in the County Town that communism would arrive soon in China and everyone would live in paradise. Asked what communism meant, Gao Changyin said something that the villagers joked about in later years. He said communism was when everyone could live in a foreign style house of several storeys with electricity and telephone upstairs and downstairs. I still remember his Chinese words: "*lou shang lou xia, dian deng dian hua* (literally meaning "storey up and storey down, electric lamp and electric speech"). The Chinese always think that foreign style houses of several storeys are comfortable and modern. For the villagers who could not afford to light an oil lamp, electricity for lighting was clearly a good symbol for paradise on earth.

It is worth noting that both in the former Soviet Union and in China, wrapped in communist ideological rhetoric, there was always the desire for modernisation and material improvement. In order for ordinary Russians to understand his vision, Lenin was reported to have said that communism meant collectivisation plus electrification. However, for the Gao villagers, Gao Changyin's promise of telephone and electricity upstairs and downstairs just meant *wang mei zhi ke* ("imagine seeing red bayberries to quench your thirst") and *hua bing chong ji* ("draw a pie to satisfy your desire for food").

Production

There is no information available, let alone reliable statistics, on the production output and grain distribution in Gao Village for the years during the Great Leap Forward. However, the *Brigade Basic Statistics Record* has a record of production output from 1949-78 though the reliability of the statistics cannot be ascertained without further investigation. According to these statistics, there was a reduction of production output in the brigade.

It is highly unlikely that in any given two years the actual output could be the same. However, in Table 6 the same figure was given for four years consecutively from 1961-4. The statistics shown here, therefore, cannot be interpreted technically. However, they can be interpreted as indicative of production output in Qinglin brigade. The production output figures do suggest a drop in 1958, compared with the figure in 1957. Then there were two years of stagnation until 1961, which showed a slight increase. However, the total production output in 1964 was still less than that of 1950. In 1950 the total population of the brigade was 1,723 whereas by 1964, the population had reached 2,678. It is not difficult to imagine that there was a serious shortage of food for the villagers in those years.

However, a slight decrease, or even a considerable decrease in production output alone might not necessarily have led to famine if other factors had not conspired against the villagers. The three worst years in terms of production were 1949, 1954 and 1973 because natural disasters struck in these three years mostly seriously (see Table 7). According to the official record of the brigade, the amount of land affected by floods in 1949, 1954 and 1973 was 3,963 *mu*, 4,088 *mu*, and 3,954 *mu* respectively. The effect of natural disasters in those three years therefore was very serious indeed. Nonetheless, the villagers did not experience famine in 1949, 1954 and 1973.

One of the reasons for this was that at least in 1949 and 1954, the population was comparatively smaller. But there were other factors. At the time immediately before 1949 the Nationalist authorities were collapsing and the Communist authorities had not yet firmly established themselves. It is therefore reasonable to assume, though I do not have any statistics to back this up, that the burden of taxes and levies imposed on the villagers was not detrimental enough. In 1954 and 1973, the Chinese government was able to and did help the villagers. Again, I do not have any reliable statistics to support this. However, my own experience in 1973 and 1974 was that Gao villagers received government help to avoid famine. We were able to purchase grain reserved by the government at a local storage house at government controlled prices. I personally purchased some grain in this way and transported it home by pushing a wheelbarrow. During the Great Leap Forward years, however, there was no grain for Gao villagers to purchase from the government because there was a shortage everywhere and by 1961 grain reserves in government storehouses had all been used up. The Chinese government had to extract as much grain as possible from the rural residents to meet the demands of urban residents.

Causes of disaster

Still, the cause of reduction in production output during the Great Leap Forward somehow remains to be debated. Several reasons were offered by the Chinese authorities and Chinese scholars. One was that there were three consecutive years of natural disasters all over China from 1959-61. According to one source, the amount of arable land affected by natural disasters in 1959, 1960, and 1961 was 206.82 million *mu*, 344.95 million *mu* and 400.38 *mu* respectively.[21] However, the Chinese themselves do not agree that natural disasters were the main cause. Liu Shaoqi, for instance, declared that natural disasters bore only 30 per cent of the blame.

Another reason often put forward was the withdrawal of technological and capital support by the Soviet Union at the most critical time of China's construction. The Soviet Union's sudden withdrawal of aid to China at that time certainly had a debilitating effect on China's economy. However, it is unlikely that this had a direct and immediate effect on China's grain production and therefore the extent of famine as a consequence.

Other reasons were offered on the basis of anecdotal evidence, such as food wastage caused by everyone eating together, crops left to rot in the fields because everyone was ordered to make iron and steel, and time and energy wasted by digging fields three feet deep – the method of "deep ploughing". This might have happened in isolated cases, and would not have continue for long. It is inconceivable that villagers, including the local authorities, would let crops rot while they were starving.

Other reasons suggested include the argument that because local authorities all boasted of their production output, the state government therefore took away more grain from the peasantry.[22]

[21] Zhao Feng, *Tian Tong Wange* (The Paradise Elegy), Beijing, 1993, p. 242.

[22] Ding Shu, "Cong Dayuejin Dao Dajihuang" (From the Great Leap Forward to the Great Famine), *Hua Xia Wen Zhai, Dayuejin Lishi Zhuanji, Shang Xia* (Supplements 1 and 2 to *China News Digest*), CND-CMO, nos 75 and 76, June 1996.

This is hardly convincing. If the state government had extracted too much grain from the peasantry the question remains as where the grain had gone, why there was a grain shortage everywhere and why the Chinese government had to import 4 billion kilos of grain in 1961 and even more in 1962. There are no statistics available to show how much grain was extracted from the Qinglin area during those years. When I put the question to the villagers whom I interviewed they all denied that they had to hand over more grain to the state in those years.

None of the things that were said to be causes of reduction of grain production happened in Qinglin brigade. No crop was left to rot and no food was wasted as a result of everyone eating together. Even during the public canteen period no one was allowed to eat to his or her full just to waste food. There was no backyard furnace in the Qinglin area and no one was foolish enough to dig the land three feet deep. Even nationally, many of the absurd practices such as the backyard furnaces were quickly stopped and fanaticism such as boasting of outrageous production outputs and the so-called "Communist Wind" of sharing everything with everyone else had faded in 1959, long before the nationwide famine started. There must therefore be some structural causes for the famine rather than one or two isolated phenomena.

One structural problem was that because of the decentralisation of industry and expansion of local industries, industrial population expanded rapidly. In 1957, the total number of industrial workers was 24.5 million. By 1960, the number increased to 50.2 million.[23] Industrial expansion had two immediate effects on food production and food consumption. One was that agricultural resources were reduced. This was because industrial expansion on the one hand took away arable land which could be used for grain production and on the other hand reduced the labour force input in agriculture. The second effect was that the increase in number of industrial workers meant an increase of urban consumption of grain, requiring more grain transfer from the rural to the urban sector. In 1958, industrial workers increased by 29.9 million of whom 10 million were from the rural areas. On 30 April 1959, Chen Yun, the most cautious planner among CCP leaders, complained that too much grain had to be collected to be sold to the urban residents.

[23] Ma Qibing *et al.*, p. 193.

He said that compared with 1958, 9 billion kilograms more grain was required in 1959 to meet urban demand. Liu Shaoqi admitted at a central government work conference on 31 May 1960 that all the problems have come down to one problem, namely food, for which the urban sector competed with the rural sector. He said that there was too much expansion of industry, transport infrastructure and education and the peasantry could not produce enough to feed the non-agriculture sector.[24]

It was for this reason that, from 1960, the Chinese government sent millions and millions of urban residents back to the rural areas, in order to lessen the burden of grain demand. By 1963 nearly 30 million residents were moved from the urban to rural areas. The household of Gao Renchang was forced from the city of Jingdezhen to settle down in Gao Village. Gao Renchang went to Jingdezhen in 1958 and worked in a porcelain factory and his whole family went with him. He could not have resisted this forceful repatriation because he was accused of having once joined the anti-Communist Ninth Route Army in 1948. Thus, Gao Village alone took over the burden of feeding four people from the Chinese government.

Other structural problems arose when the economic system was changed from cooperatives to communes in 1958. In the cooperatives, the production and distribution units were smaller, and therefore, work efforts and individual contributions were better monitored. As a result, individual rewards corresponded more closely to individual efforts. Being suddenly pushed into a commune system in which production and distribution units were larger, the villagers were understandably confused, if not outright resentful. Coordination was difficult and the monitoring of individual efforts became extremely complicated. In this confusing process of transformation, a system of rewards that corresponded closely to contributions had yet to be worked out. It should not be surprising therefore that sufficient efforts were not channelled into production.

These problems were noticed by Wang Shaofei, who was working at the Economic Research Institute of the Chinese Academy of Sciences. On 2 May 1959 Wang Shaofei submitted a report in which he stated these structural problems.[25] They could not

[24] Ma Qibing *et al.*, p. 200.

[25] *Ibid*, p. 164.

be solved easily. Some were not solved until a couple of years later when the villagers got used to the commune system and when a comprehensive system of coordinating team efforts, monitoring individual contribution and distribution according to work efforts was finally established.

According to Gao villagers, one type of command did affect grain production, that is close planting. As pointed out by Becker, presumably being inspired by pseudo-scientific ideas of Soviet Academician Lysenko, local officials, ordered by their superiors, forced Gao villagers to plant rice shoots too closely. The practice, according to the villagers, was not only more labour consuming but also led to a reduction in rice output.

During the Great Leap Forward, due to impatience for development, enthusiasm for innovations and zeal for radicalism, plus ignorance and personal ambition, the Chinese leadership at various levels carried out all kinds of outrageous experiments in their efforts to modernise China. Though the impact of the Great Leap Forward varied from place to place, depending on many intricate factors, the Chinese peasantry paid a terrible price for its consequences. The Great Leap Forward might not be a product of outright irrationality, or madness, as it is often claimed, and might have its own logic and rationality. However, the terrible lesson learnt is that China is so huge and when it is uniformly ruled, follies or wrong policies will have grave implications of tremendous magnitude.

To conclude, it is worth reiterating that there was a famine in Gao Village as a consequence of the Great Leap Forward; but no one actually died of starvation. Follies such as local furnaces making iron and steel and public canteens did take place in the county; but not in the Qinglin area. When pressed during my interviews the villagers admitted that the government had not actually extracted more gran from them because the local officials reported inflated output statistics. However the state government did not allow them to hand over less grain either. There was a shortage of food for Gao villagers because there was a decrease in production output. The main reason for the decrease was that the villagers were not prepared for so many sudden and fundamental changes – political, economic, social and technical – at the same time. As a result there was no effective management and production activity was disrupted. As the same thing happened all over China no government aid was possible to help with the shortage. They should have obtained some help to avoid famine, as they did in 1973; but they did not because there was a shortage everywhere in China. The situation was made worse as a result of the rapid expansion of urban population. The government wanted to guarantee a regular supply of food for the urban sector, however meagre the supply might have been, because urban famine would have been more visible and therefore more threatening to the country's stability. The end-result of all this was that the rural residents were left to starve.

9

THE CULTURAL REVOLUTION

The subject of the Cultural Revolution has been dealt with extensively in the field of China studies.[1] Since the 1980s, the Cultural Revolution has been referred to as the ten-year period 1966-76 and condemned by the post-Mao Chinese authorities as "ten years of chaos and disaster". Volumes of books in Chinese and other languages are published every year denouncing the Cultural Revolution. Biographies and memoirs have been written telling of horrendous nightmares and incredible personal suffering. Personal accounts are usually written by the educated élite who were either severely victimised, sent down to rural areas for years, or deprived of the normal lifestyle they felt they deserved. For Party powerholders and intellectuals, the Cultural Revolution was more destructive than the Great Leap Forward. If there is one thing that the Chinese Communist Party powerholders and Chinese intellectuals have in common regarding Mao's China, it is that they unreservedly denounce the Cultural Revolution.

There is a very good reason for this. Both types of people were the main targets of criticism and victims of class struggle during the Cultural Revolution. For the very same reason, rural China was the least affected by it. For some parts of rural China, and for a limited period of time, agrarian radicalism did have an adverse effect on production output and hence peasants' income.

However, this does not seem to have been the case in Qinglin brigade. In 1967 and 1968, two of the Cultural Revolution years

[1] So much has been written on the subject of the Cultural Revolution that even a partial list of the references will be too much for our purpose. For a quite comprehensive survey and evaluation of the literature see Mobo C.F. Gao, "Maoist Discourse and Critique of the Present Assessment of the Cultural Revolution", *Bulletin of Concerned Asian Scholars*, vol. 26, no. 3, 1994, pp. 3-21; and "Memoirs and the History of the Cultural Revolution", *Bulletin of Concerned Asian Scholars*, vol. 27, no. 1, 1995, pp. 49-57.

considered to have been the most destructive, grain production in Qinglin brigade new steadily, as shown in Table 6. In 1972, grain output was the highest ever in Qinglin brigade. There was a dramatic decrease of grain production output in 1973 when there was a devastating flood. The floods in 1974, 1975, 1977 and 1978 were also destructive, though not as bad as that in 1973. Only in 1976, when flooding was not very serious, grain production increased markedly – the third highest in the history Qinglin brigade. The more frequent and serious floods in the late 1970s only confirm the detrimental environmental consequences discussed in Chapters 2 and 3.

Production

It is often argued, for instance in the most authoritative account by Zweig cited above, that it was economic crops that were most severely hit by the agrarian radicalism of the Cultural Revolution. Two aspects of the Cultural Revolution's radicalism are said to have affected economic crops adversely. One was the advocacy of Mao's philosophy of Self-Reliance. In order to feed such a large population without having to rely on imports, the peasantry was urged to grow grain at the expense of economic crops. The other aspect was more ideological. As economic crops were market and commercially-orientated, they were to be suppressed. According to this version of radicalism, marketisation and commercialism would breed capitalism which was exactly what the Cultural Revolution was fighting against. Whilst these two aspects of agrarian radicalism were openly declared policies during the Cultural Revolution, how much influence they had in places like Qinglin is far from clear.

Table 8 shows that though there had been some reduction in cotton, rape seed and sesame production since 1973, peanut production actually went up in these years until 1978. As for economic crops grown by the villagers themselves, whilst cotton, rape seed and sesame seed production went down since the mid 1970s, peanut and vegetable production increased during the same period (see Table 5). Moreover, tobacco production by the villagers themselves increased from an average of 9 *dan* annually from 1949 to 1972 to 12 *dan* in 1973, and rose to 15 *dan* in subsequent years until 1978 when the output dropped again to 12 *dan.*

As discussed in previous chapters there was a gradual decline of cash crops in the area. However, as a general trend this took place both before and after the Cultural Revolution. It was not so much caused by agrarian radicalism as by the immediate need to feed the increasing population.

Power struggle and village clan connections

Before the Cultural Revolution started in 1966 there were three production brigades in Qinglin area. They were Qinglin brigade, Xifen brigade and Guantian brigade, the last of which consisted of Xu Village, Cao Village and Gao Village. Gao Changyin was the Party secretary of Guantian Brigade. Cao Village was located in the south, Gao Village in the north and both were of similar size. In between there was Xu Village which was as big as Gao and Cao Villages put together.

There were four important brigade officials: the brigade Party secretary, Gao Changyin from Gao Village; the brigade accountant Xu Congxian from Xu Village; the deputy head of the brigade Cao Dajiang from Cao Village; and the head of the brigade Wang Biaohua from Wang Village. Only Wang Biaohua was from outside the brigade. His role was obviously to balance the power influences of the three villages. In theory, the brigade Party secretary held the most powerful position in the brigade, followed by the head of the brigade and the brigade accountant. In practice, Wang Biaohua held more power than his position had prescribed and most of the time Gao Changyin had to fall in line with Wang in order to exercise his power. The reason was that since Gao Village was only half the size of Xu Village, Gao Changyin had a weak power base. He had to rely on Wang to shield him from any possible attack from Xu villagers. To remain in power Gao Changyin worked very hard to please the Xu villagers, so much so that Gao villagers often complained that he had never done anything good for Gao Village. Still Gao Changyin could fall off his tight-rope at any time. He remained in power only because the commune authorities protected him. The beginning of the Cultural Revolution, which removed protection from above, was the end of Gao Changyin's career.

The two "rebels" who rose up to criticise Gao Changyin were Xu Conggui and Gao Renkai, both of whom had personal grudges against him. Xu Conggui used to be a production team accountant in Xu Village. From 1963 there was a Socialist Education Movement in rural China. During this movement the "Four Clean-up" measures were carried out, targeting grass-roots officials for corruption. The "Four Clean-up" aimed to clean up corruption in the four areas of "work points, finance, accountancy and storage". In 1964 when the movement reached Guantian brigade, Xu Conggui was discovered to have been corrupt. As a result Xu Conggui was fined a small amount and was subsequently dismissed. The fact that it was under Gao Changyin's leadership that Xu Conggui fell led the latter to have a personal grudge against him.

Gao Renkai had a different cause for personal grievance. He was a craftsman making bamboo tools such as baskets. He often travelled from village to village, working for households, and sometimes stayed overnight in the household he was working for. Presumably because of his being away from home much too often, his wife became Gao Changyin's mistress. The worst part of this affair was that it was an open secret known by everyone in Qinglin, and an incredible amount of face was lost because others knew of the affair. Thus Gao Changyin became Gao Renkai's life-long enemy, though there was little the latter could do until the Cultural Revolution which gave him a perfect opportunity.

Xu Conggui and Gao Renkai became comrades-in-arms as soon as the Cultural Revolution started. The fact that a Party secretary had had a mistress could itself have serious political implications for Gao Changyin since a Communist was not supposed to be dissolute in this way. However, Gao Renkai and Xu Conggui chose a different strategy. For one thing, Gao Renkai did not want to be made a laughing stock by letting people poke fun at his wife's affair. In any case, it would have been no good for this to be seen as personal revenge. They also held a more powerful weapon against Gao Changyin. This was the fact that Gao Changyin had supposedly been a member of the anti-Communist Ninth Route Army. This crime alone, if proved, was enough to finish Gao Changyin. According to Gao Renyun, one of the clan power-holders in Gao Village, Gao Changyin became a Communist activist as soon as the land reform started because he wanted to save his own skin. He actively supported the Communists to prove his loyalty to the new regime. Gao Changyin's strategy had worked. Not only was he forgiven for the supposed affiliation with the local bandit force, he was rewarded with Communist Party membership and eventually the position of brigade Party secretary.

As the Cultural Revolution started in 1966, Gao Renkai and Xu Conggui began to attack Gao Changyin on the issue. By writing big posters stuck up on the walls of the brigade administration building, Gao Renkai and Xu Conggui not only accused Gao Changyin of having joined the Ninth Route Army; they also accused him of trying to run down underground Communists. With funds made available to "rebels" of the Cultural Revolution and daily allowances, Gao Renkai and Xu Conggui travelled around to Jiujiang, Jingdezhen and Boyang County Town to collect evidence that Gao Changyin was not just an ordinary member of the anti-Communist Ninth Route Army, but also an active participant.

Specifically, they accused Gao Changyin of trying to shoot down two underground Communists who passed Gao Village when they were trying to escape the pursuit of the Ninth Route Army. In the posters Xu Conggui and Gao Renkai stated that when the two Communists were running away from Youdunjie and disappeared into the hill in front of Gao Village, Gao Changyin picked up a gun and shot at them from behind. Gao Changyin naturally denied all this and there was no witness to be found to support Gao Renkai and Xu Conggui's allegation. However, the accusation alone was enough to end Gao Changyin's career as a Communist official. In 1969 when the three production brigades of Guantian, Xifen and Qinglin were amalgamated into one Qinglin brigade, Gao Changyin was pushed aside and told to work as an ordinary peasant to earn work points in Gao Village. Since Gao Renkai and Xu Conggui were unable to provide evidence, or to find witnesses, to prove that Gao Changyin had a gun and had opened fire at the two Communists who were eventually caught and executed by the Ninth Route Army, Gao Changyin was able to keep his membership of the Communist party. However, he never recovered his official position.

Cultural Revolution at Youdunjie school

When the heatwave of the Cultural Revolution reached Youdunjie
School in 1967, I became one of the first batch of Red Guards
because of my credentials. I came from a poor peasant family
background and I had good academic records. The Red Guards'
first activity was to write posters to criticise the teachers. I was
frustrated that I could not write anything because, being at the
school for only a year, I did not know anything about the teachers.
All I could think of was that these teachers were a bit strange
because they did not behave like the rural people I knew. For
instance, I found it very strange that a woman teacher wore high
heeled shoes. I also found it strange that of the five teachers who
taught us, three were not married, including a woman aged fifty
and our mathematics teacher, a tall and attractive woman of thirty-five. I kept on asking myself what problems these people might
have. It was also incredible for me that the Academic Dean of
our school could be so fat. Every time he passed my way, I
would observe him stealthily, and watch him until he disappeared
into the distance, wandering how anyone could have such a big
belly. The subject of English was even more incredible to me.
The letter "w" was pronounced as "*dabuliu*" for which I gave three
Chinese characters to transliterate the sounds that meant "beat",
"not" and "six". I wondered what the hell this could mean.

I was shocked to read in posters that whenever he washed,
our geography teacher would check that his bath water was exactly
37°C. Another teacher was revealed to have disliked the school
toilet so much that every time he wanted to relieve himself he
would go to the nearby forest. Some senior students raided the
geography teacher's office-home (as he had no family he lived
in his office) and confiscated his diaries. In one of the diary entries
the poor bachelor recorded how he was once sexually attracted
to a woman whom he was sitting with on a bus. A poster accused
the teacher of "having dirty thoughts". I admired the senior students
at the school who knew enough and were sharp enough to
denounce this kind of behaviour as "bourgeois". However, I found
the way some students savagely hit the teachers very distressing
and incomprehensible. I also discovered that those who beat the
teachers were the ones who could not perform well academically.

In August 1967 I was chosen as one of the student representatives

to go to Beijing to see Chairman Mao. It was the first time I
had an opportunity to travel on a train. We had to carry our
own bedding all the way to Beijing, and mine was home-made
and had many stitched up patches. For the four days spent on
and off the trains we had nothing to eat but biscuits. But I enjoyed
the biscuits very much because they tasted so sweet. The return
trip to Beijing lasted for about a month and I enjoyed it enormously.
Everything was new, exciting and fascinating: the length of the
train, the rhythm of the marching sound, the levelness and the
enormity of the northern plain, the wide and symmetrical streets
in Beijing, the scale and magnitude of the Great Hall of the
People and History Museum, and the vastness of Tiananmen Square.
For some reason I was not very impressed with the Forbidden
City. Looking back now I think that this was because to me it
represented the old and backward China.

In Beijing we slept on the floor at the Agricultural Museum.
As a group we were highly organised and strictly disciplined like
soldiers. Our organisation was military: we were formed into
squads, platoons and companies. Everywhere we went we carried
Chairman Mao's *Little Red Book*. When we were on a bus going
to visit a place we would sing revolutionary songs and recite
Chairman Mao's quotations. As our main aim was to learn from
the revolutionary experience of the Beijing Red Guards, we spent
most of our time at Beijing and Qinghua Universities reading
their posters, and so I did not even get the chance to see the
Great Wall. I devoured the posters and copied them without
really knowing what they were all about. By the end of the trip
I had three thick notebooks full of notes taken from these posters.
One of these notes that left a deep impression on me was a
report of a speech made by Tao Zhu who said that except for
Chairman Mao and Vice-Chairman Lin Biao there was no one
who could not be criticised and "struggled against". Still, I could
not get the message and every thing seemed too remote from
my life and concerns.

One day we were taken to the Tiananmen Square to see Chairman Mao. We got up at five in the morning and sat on the
square to wait for the Chairman to appear. We were warned
again and again to sit still and not to move an inch. We waited
for hours on the square, with millions of other Red Guards. We
kept on singing songs and reading Chairman Mao's quotations

and shouting slogans. We were too young and too excited to be bored or tired. Finally at about noon, some open carriage cars appeared, carrying Chairman Mao and other leaders. The cars ran so fast that before I even caught a glimpse of the Great Leader it was all finished. Some screamed and screamed until their voices cracked. Some cried like babies. I did not feel much about seeing Chairman Mao. To me it was too quick and too uneventful.

Back home at the village, however, it was different. Every Gao villager was proud that I went to Beijing to see Chairman Mao. They kept on asking me how he looked. I was too ashamed to admit that I did not really see him clearly, so I gave elaborate descriptions of the Chairman, inventing things out of my impression of his portraits. The villagers thought that I was no ordinary person, being chosen to be taken to the capital to see Chairman Mao. Even friends of my sister and brother-in-law, urban residents who were supposed to be more sophisticated, saw me in a different light after the Beijing trip. One of them actually came to examine my features to find out what was so special about me. They thought I must have been born with an extraordinarily lucky and fortunate fate.

Cultural Revolution at Guantian Brigade

My fate, however, did not take a turn for the better. After the Beijing trip, as schooling stopped, my education discontinued. Besides, I did not really know what the Cultural Revolution was about. Some senior students, who had not been chosen to go to Beijing to see Chairman Mao, seemed to know. They "bombarded the headquarters" of the Youdunjie District government and took over power. They rewarded themselves with new army uniforms which everyone wanted to have, and other things including new bikes. Because they appeared so smart, the boy "rebel" students had the attention of the most beautiful girls in the school.

I found all these were beyond my reach. I did not even think that if I did the same thing I could obtain the same reward and prestige. At the end of 1967 when I packed my luggage and went back to Gao Village as a Red Guard, I became a "loyalist" instead of a "rebel". Though I plunged directly into the power struggle surrounding the case of Gao Changyin I judged the situation with a conventional sense of what was "right" and what was "wrong".

From my point of view, there was no solid evidence that Gao
Changyin took part in anti-Communist activities. All Gao Renkai
and Xu Conggui wanted was personal revenge. I was naive enough
not to have realised the intricate clan connections behind the
dispute. I wrote hundreds of posters defending Gao Changyin
and thus established myself as a formidable "writer" in the area.
At that time the thought that I could be seen as defending Gao
Changyin because he was a Gao villager did not occur to me.

It was many years later that I realised I had in some way been
used by some Gao villagers such as Gao Shihua, the village doctor,
to defend another Gao villager. As a matter of fact, most Gao
villagers had nothing good to say about Gao Changyin. He was
seen as arrogant and ruthless by his fellow villagers and only knew
how to curry favour with his superiors to advance his career.
The way he treated my father and the brutality and fabrication
with which he and Gao Changming used to participate in class
struggle against the landlord Gao Tianqiang were typical of Gao
Changyin's behaviour. However, there was no doubt that dis-
crediting Gao Changyin had harmed the prestige of Gao Village.
Though nobody else openly came forward to defend him, very
few Gao villagers actually wanted to see Gao Changyin fall. The
fact that I was actively involved was largely a result of encouragement by Gao Shihua, who provided me with all the information
I needed.

Again it was many years later that I realised that Gao Shihua
had had a personal interest in encouraging me to defend Gao
Changyin. Gao Shihua and Gao Renkai's father were brothers
and the two families had been sharing a house. The two brothers
agreed not to dismantle the house to share building materials and
the younger brother let the elder occupy one room more. However,
when the two families were getting bigger, the younger generation
did not get on well with each other largely because of the dispute
over one room. The quarrels between the two families were so
serious that they were not on speaking terms even though they
lived under the same roof. Gao Shihua began to hate Gao Renkai
and did not want him to succeed politically.

Another important reason for Gao Shihua to defend Gao Changyin was that by 1967 Xu Conggui's brother Xu Congchun began
to study medicine. Gao Shihua's keen sense of local politics told
him that if Xu Conggui succeeded in his political aim either Xu

Conggui himself or someone from Xu Village would be put in charge of Guantian brigade. The end result of this would be the promotion of Xu Congchun as the brigade doctor who would then have a chance to change from rural to urban resident status.

Gao Shihua's political awareness was confirmed later. As soon as Gao Changyin was pushed aside Xu Conggui became the director of the Guantian Revolutionary Committee. Xu Conggui failed in his bid for further advancement only when the three brigades amalgamated into one Qinglin brigade in 1969. When amalgamation took place, people from Jiang Village became the dominant brigade officials simply because Jiang Village was three times larger than Xu Village. Jiang village people remained dominant in Qinglin brigade until 1981 when the brigade was dismantled and when Gao Village, Cao Village and Xu Village were again asked to form a unit, this time called the Village Committee. Since 1981, the main powerholders in Guantian Village Committee have been Xu villagers.

At that time in 1967, however, I was absolutely ignorant of these local political intricacies. I just acted as I thought was right to defend Gao Changyin. Gao Changyin had never spoken to me about the case, nor had any Gao villager. I, as a Red Guard, was at the front while Gao Shihua stayed back. Despite my Red Guard efforts, Gao Changyin was overthrown. Gao Chaodong, Gao Changyin's son who was a senior high school Red Guard, could not help either. In any case, he seldom came home as he was busy fighting factional battles in Boyang County Town.

"Class enemies" and village clan connections

The next thing that happened to Guantian brigade and Gao Village during the Cultural Revolution was the struggle against the existing landlords and rich peasants. The way the struggle started and how it was carried out also owed something to clan connections. In order to understand how genealogy and the clan system played a part in this, there is a need to discuss further the niceties of genealogical relations at the village level.

Though all Gao villagers were offspring of one family, they considered themselves to come from five different branches in the genealogical tree because they were different descendants of the five brothers of the second generation in the family. The members of each branch felt closer to each other and they tended to present a single identity in relation to the other branches. In times of difficulty, for instance, the household would ask the member families of its own branch for help first. Even when children fought in the playground, those of the same genealogical branch would tend to stick together.

There was always an issue which would make the villagers identify themselves with their own branch. The case involving the marriage of Gao Shuilan, a daughter of the rich peasant Gao Jiangxiang, is a good example. Gao Shuilan was not only the prettiest but also the most intelligent girl in Gao Village at that time. She had only three years of education, but taught herself to read and became a good actress by acting as the main character in two Peking Operas when Gao Village formed a theatre troupe during the Cultural Revolution. Gao Shuilan belonged to one of the smaller genealogical branches. A boy from another small genealogical branch, Gao Changquan, wanted to marry Gao Shuilan. However, the boys from the largest of the five branches in Gao Village wanted to block the marriage. They wanted to do this because they hated Gao Changquan, who was strong, able and ready to confront any bullying from the big branch. These boys were also very jealous of the fact that Gao Shuilan was to marry Gao Changquan. The scheme to block the marriage was headed by Gao Chaodong, one of the sons of the former brigade Party secretary Gao Changyin, who was the only senior high school graduate in the village at that time. Eventually, on the advice of a senior member of the branch, Gao Changyu, Gao Chaodong and the other boys withdrew their scheme and the marriage went ahead. The scheme was withdrawn only because none of the boys other than Gao Chaodong was a good enough match for Gao Shuilan. Gao Chaodong himself could have married Gao Shuilan, but he did not want to because she was the daughter of a rich peasant, and thus categorised as a class enemy.

In village affairs, especially in selecting production team leaders and accountants, particular care had to be taken to maintain a power balance among the different genealogical branches. In Gao Village, the largest among the five genealogical branches happened to include Gao Changyin. After his downfall, the two production teams were amalgamated into one, and one of the two production team accountants, Gao Changcai was consequently dismissed, largely because he was Gao Changyin's brother. Since 1969 the brigade authorities had always been careful to appoint people from branches other than that of Gao Changyin as production team leader for fear that Gao Changyin would monopolise power in Gao Village.

The only exception was Gao Changyu who also belonged to Gao Changyin's branch. Gao Changyu was appointed as production team leader for a couple of terms. He was chosen because he was not only a very able leader who was hardworking, fair and skilful but also known to be personally on bad terms with Gao Changyin. Gao Changyu did not like Gao Changyin largely because he disliked the way Gao Changyin treated the landlord Gao Tianqiang unfairly and brutally for his own career purposes. However, Gao Changyu was never completely trusted by the brigade authorities because, as a nephew of Gao Tianqiang, he never concealed his sympathy towards the landlord. Whenever the production team was in a bad shape and needed a good leader. Gao Changyu was appointed to clear up the mess. But whenever the policy of class struggle was emphasised, Gao Changyu would be dismissed again.

After Gao Changyin was dismissed, the Cultural Revolution in Qinglin reached a stage when landlords and rich peasants became the main targets. There were no official guidelines, directives or orders, from above or from anyone regarding which landlords and rich peasants were to be "struggled against" and in what way and by whom. But the political climate at that time was such that anyone could pick on any landlord or rich peasant for a "class struggle" session. Usually no villager would have a personal grudge against a landlord or rich peasant. This was the case because for a long time since 1949 they had been treated as non-human. It was nearly twenty years since the categories of landlord and rich peasant had been labelled class enemies. They had been brutally victimised, humiliated and unjustly treated, so much so that they had no right to defend their interests whatsoever. They could not say no to anyone and they dared not offend any villager. They did the dirtiest work and they got the least reward for it.

Even if a poor villager had any personal grievance before 1949, by now there was no real cause for any villager to have any personal grievance against this class of people. So when the climate was created to turn the Cultural Revolution's attention towards them, Gao villagers did not take any action against the landlord Gao Tianqiang and the rich peasant Gao Jingxiang. Only one

villager, Gao Chouyin, who was chosen as a member of the
Guantian brigade Revolutionary Committee largely because he
belonged to one of the small genealogical branches in Gao Village,
went to Gao Tianqiang and asked him to hand over any books
that he had. Gao Tianqiang obediently gave Gao Chouyin all he
had, which was a box of books, most of which were on Chinese
medicine. Gao Chouyin, however, handed the books to the Guantian brigade Revolutionary Committee headed by Xu Conggui
who in turn gave all the medical books to his brother for professional
study.

Meanwhile the "small Red Guards" at Qinglin School were
looking for targets of class struggle and they turned their attention
to the category of landlords and rich peasants. Constrained by
their parents and brought up amongst intricate genealogical relationships, they could not and would not pick on landlords and rich
peasants from their own villages; instead, they turned their eyes
towards other villages. Thus, school boys aged seven to twelve
from Gao Changyin's genealogical branch chose Xu Tianyun in
Xu Village who was classified as a counter-revolutionary as their
victim. They searched Xu Tianyun's house and took him to
"struggle meetings". They beat him up and had him paraded from
village to village. In return, school children from Xu Village did
the same things with Gao Tianqiang. As the struggle against class
enemies was sanctioned by official policy, nobody from either
village could do anything to protect their own fellow villagers.
The household of the other class enemy in Gao Village did not
suffer this time for two reasons. One reason was that the rich
peasant Gao Jingxiang died in 1960 and family members were
usually not targets of the struggle. The other was that Gao Jingxiang
did not belong to Gao Changyin's genealogical branch whereas
Gao Tianqiang did. It is clear that official policy, genealogical
structure and clan differences all worked together to make this
category of people hapless victims of the Cultural Revolution.

The commune and brigade authorities were well aware of the
fact that village clans and genealogical branches tended to protect
their own members, and so were sympathetic towards the categories
of landlords and rich peasants who belonged to their own clans
or genealogical branches. As a solution to promote the atmosphere
of class struggle and to strengthen the surveillance of the supposed
"class enemies", the commune authorities ordered all landlords,

rich peasants and counter-revolutionaries to move away from their own villages. In September 1969, Gao Tianqiang's family was ordered to settle in Jiang Village and the rich peasant household of Gao Jingxiang was moved to live in Xu Village. In return, one rich peasant household and one landlord household from Jiang Village were moved to live in Gao Village. These households did not move back to their own villages until February 1979.

Paradoxically, the removal of these people from their own villages proved to have the opposite effect from that intended by the commune authorities. Away from intricate genealogical niceties, with which they had not wanted to be involved, these people were detached from internal genealogical conflicts and tensions. They worked hard to earn work points and were not involved in any local genealogical complications. As disinterested outsiders, they were left to themselves. Other villagers were nice to them because there was no longer any cause to accuse the villagers of being nice to the "class enemies" on the basis of clan connections. The two households from Jiang Village were treated with politeness by Gao villagers, as was always the case with guests, and even with respect. In 1994 I talked to the two Gao families that had moved out and the two Jiang families that had moved in. All of them said that the ten years from 1969 to 1979 were the best years in their lives. They looked back over them with nostalgia and kept returning to the villages that had been their homes for ten years.

Another victim of village clan connections

Another twist in the case of Gao Changyin in 1971 led me to become another victim of the Cultural Revolution. Again it had something to do with genealogical tensions in Gao Village. The cause of the incident was my searching for paper to practise calligraphy. By 1971 I was a "barefoot teacher" in Gao Village school. As a result of writing posters and the fact that I had to teach it to children, I had developed a keen interest in practising calligraphy. I would usually practise for at least half an hour every day. However, I could not practise as much as I would have wanted to because there was a lack of paper. Paper was very scarce in rural China and the villagers could not afford large quantities. In Gao Village, the villagers could not even afford paper for the toilet. Instead, they would use a bamboo slice or tree twigs. I used to search everywhere for paper for calligraphy practice. I would write on old newspapers if I could get hold of any. Very often I had to write on the same piece of paper again and again until it was completely black.

It happened that one day at the production team storage house, I discovered a pile of paper, the record books of the Gao Village genealogical tree. I was so pleased to see what I considered to be a pile of waste paper that I took some pages home to practise calligraphy. These genealogy record books had been preserved in Gao Village for a long time. They were made of very fine classic Chinese paper and had recorded the birth of every child born in Gao Village since the first generation. Every genealogical branch was meticulously documented. When I took the paper I was not alone in the storehouse. Gao Changyin's brother Gao Changcai as well as my classmate in Youdunjie school, Gao Chaojiang, who belonged to another small genealogical branch to which Gao Chouyin also belonged, were also there. My family happened to belong to Gao Changyin's branch.

At that time there was a conflict between Gao Changyin's branch and Gao Chaojiang's branch simply because Gao Couyin had been selected to represent Gao Village as a member of the brigade Revolutionary Committee in place of Gao Changyin, who had fallen at the beginning of the Cultural Revolution. The rationale for this was that the brigade Revolutionary Committee should consist of at least one member from each village. Gao Changyin's downfall meant Gao Couyin's promotion, hence the hostility between the two branches.

In 1973 there had been another wave of Cultural Revolution activities in the Qinglin area. A two member work team was sent to Gao Village to supervise these activities. The two members were actually village officials from Jiang Village whom I knew personally. One of their activities was to wipe out what had been termed the "feudalist" practice of preserving the records of genealogical trees. Therefore, all the genealogical record books were confiscated and were meant to be burned. Now, without realising the full implications of the genealogical conflicts existing at that time, and having thought very little about the business of genealogical records, I took those pages without a second thought.

Actually my thinking was in line with the official policy. I too thought that to preserve the village genealogical records was "feudalistic". But it would surely be better to make some use of that nice paper by practising calligraphy on it than to just burn it. I was a bit scared at that time and that was why I had not taken the whole lot. However, I was not scared of being accused of preserving "feudalist" records. Instead, I was afraid of the uncertainly over what might happen to me for taking things without permission. Yet I knew that if I asked I would not be given any. So I took some, hoping that the work team would not notice the missing pages. My trouble was that I never gave any serious thought to what was happening in Gao Village because I always felt detached and wanted to get away from the place. I took those "earthly" things so lightly that I did not for a moment suspect that Gao Chaojiang would report me to the work team. But he did.

There was another small incident that also got me into trouble. At that time I was isolated intellectually and spiritually; there was nothing in the village that could stimulate me. By then the two doctors had left Gao village and there was not even a newspaper for me to read. Of course I could not afford to buy a radio. There were no books to read. I had already read Chairman Mao's four volumes of selected works a couple of times. I even bought Marx's *Communist Manifesto* and *Wages, Prices and Profits*, Engels's *Anti-Dühring,* and Lenin's *Materialism and Empirio-Criticism, State and Revolution,* and *Imperialism is the Highest Stage of Capitalism.* I spent a great deal of time on these dry books. After a while they became terribly boring and I started to read the Chinese classics again. One late afternoon when I was sitting on my doorstep reading the classical novel *The Water Margin,* one of the two members of the work team was passing by. He greeted me and asked what I was reading. I showed him the book. He then said that he wanted to have a look at it. I let him take the book without saying a word. Later, I was accused of reading "feudalist yellow" books.

I had therefore committed two crimes. One was to preserve "feudalist genealogical tree records" and the other was to read "feudalist yellow books". I was suspended from my teaching and taken away to Qinglin School to be "struggled against". I was put under house arrest at Qinglin School apparently because my profession was teaching and "the masses" who were to criticise me should also be teachers. The "struggle sessions" went on for two weeks. Every evening, I would be ordered to sit on a bench surrounded by all the teachers from Qingling who were supposed to question and criticise me. During the day when the teachers had to teach I was ordered to write confessions. I was not allowed to go home and I had to eat at Qinglin School. My mother was allowed to visit me once. She could not say anything articulate but just cried. At the "struggle meetings" all but two of the teachers had nothing to say. They just sat there, watching the two who were conducting the show.

Of the latter one was Jiang Jinghuan, the principal of Qinglin School, and the other was Xu Xiandeng. These two people, especially Xu Xiandeng, would scream at me and bang the table, demanding that I confess. Jiang Jinghuan was a typical petty official who would do whatever he was told to do by his superiors. That was how he kept his position as a principal. He had urban resident status and earned a state government salary. Jiang had changed schools several times before being assigned to Qinglin. At every school he had attended he had problems with other teaching staff. However, he always kept his position because he scrupulously obeyed his superiors.

The case of Xu Xiandeng was different. It only dawned on me later that the whole idea of having me "struggled against" in Qinglin School was for his benefit. Xu Xiandeng was married to the sister of Xu Conggui, and the whole incident was a plot to continue Xu Conggui's crusade against Gao Changyin. By 1971 the latter was still a potential threat, who might stage a comeback. Although he did not hold any official position, he was not completely down. Firm evidence could not be established that he had actually shot the two underground Communists in 1948. He had not only managed to retain his Communist Party membership but had also maintained considerable power in Gao Village because of the power-base of his genealogical branch. For any major decisions in Gao Village, Gao Chouyin had to consult with Gao Changyin, or else he ran the risk of not being able to implement them.

All Xu Conggui wanted was to extract a confession from me that it was Gao Changyin who had instructed me to hide the genealogical records. So he entrusted his brother-in-law Xu Xiandeng to do the job. This was officially proper and organisationally convenient, since I was a teacher. However, Xu Xiandeng did not have the courage to say explicitly that all he wanted was that I would name Gao Changyin. Naturally, I insisted that I did not want to preserve feudalist genealogical records. I protested again and again that all I had intended to do was to get some paper to practise calligraphy. Xu Xiandeng knew what I said was true, but he persisted until finally he wrote up a version in which Gao Changyin was named as the person behind the idea. I refused to sign it. I was released eventually after I signed another version in which I admitted that I had made two serious mistakes: reading *The Water Margin* and taking away the genealogical record pages.

Innovations of the Cultural Revolution

However, there was more to the climate of the Cultural Revolution than political fallouts and genealogical intrigues. For the Qinglin people at least, there was a cultural revolution in a narrower sense. Compared with Party officials and the intelligentsia in China, the villagers were the least adversely affected by the Cultural Revolution politically. Culturally they mostly gained from it. The positive influence of the Cultural Revolution was reflected in four general areas: the rise of educational standards; unprecedented cultural and sports activities; paradoxically, a partial breakdown of genealogical tensions; and finally a healthy extension of the role of the state in rural life.

Education. Thanks to innovative approaches to education such as the "barefoot teacher" system there was a great boost in literacy among Gao villagers. A school catering for students from years one to three was set up in Gao village in 1969. The success of village schools was such that even the post-Mao Chinese authorities could not dismantle them. It is extremely unlikely that there would have been a village school in Gao Village without the Cultural Revolution initiative. Owing to the existence of the village school almost all children in Gao Village have had at least two years' education. During the Cultural Revolution period almost all children including girls had an elementary education of three years. This was made possible not only because the village school had made going to school more convenient, but also because of the very low cost. Like the other villagers, the "barefoot teacher" earned only work points. Moreover, the cost of books was deliberately kept low by the state government.

The other fundamental reason why parents were willing to send their children to school during the Cultural Revolution was the fact that agrarian radicalism was so egalitarian that there was no rationale whatsoever for the parents not to send their children to school. In the extreme version of the commune system, the distribution of agricultural produce (which was all the villagers had) was carried out on an absolutely equal per capita basis. As a result, those households with more labourers and fewer children were actually subsidising those households with fewer labourers and more children. In other words, there was virtually no difference in terms of income between those households that were in the red and those that were in the black. The difference in income had to come from family management and better output from private plots. Individual household contributions to the commune, that is, labour input to the production team, was not correspondingly rewarded with distribution. Debts and credits were in the accounting books only and settlements were delayed indefinitely.

Indeed, this was the fundamental rationale for the post-Mao Chinese authorities to scrap the commune system. It could be argued that as individual efforts were not rewarded there was no motivation to work hard. Hence, the argument has been put forward by Chinese and foreign scholars alike, that the commune system encouraged laziness and rewarded those who did not want to work. However, both my personal experience and the production statistics of Qinglin brigade do not support this argument. The villagers did work hard, but not because they were all selfless people who were striving for a utopian society, as portrayed by the official propaganda. They were every bit as economically rational as any other human being on earth. The reason they worked hard in spite of the lack of an effective system that could grant immediate rewards was that they had a long term point of view.

Family fortunes were unpredictable and any family could be in serious trouble at any time. Those households that had fewer children now might have more children some years later. A strong labourer might suddenly fall ill. From a long-term point of view the system took care of everyone. More importantly, there was an intricate and intimate monitoring system including measures such as the annual evaluation of base work points. Every villager knew everything about everyone else, and deliberate laziness could hardly escape the other villagers' notice. Because the community was so small and intimate there was also a very strong sense of obligation. When the villagers worked in a team or a group an individual could not but make similar efforts unless there was a genuine reason for not doing so. If one individual did not make enough effort he or she would be singled out and criticised openly, sometimes quite harshly. Furthermore, it was not completely without immediate rewards. For instance, when the income of the production team was good, those households that were in the black would be paid some cash at the end of year. In times of emergency, those households that were in the black could also borrow some cash from the production team. Sometimes at the end of the year, when a household that was in the red killed a pig for the Spring Festival, a portion of the pork might be given to a household that was in the black to offset debts.

Notwithstanding all the shortcomings of this system, the end result was that there was no rationale for a household to make use of child labour to boost family income. Therefore, as the cost was also kept very low parents sent their children to school. Only in some cases where an older child had to look after a toddler when both parents were out in the field would problems possibly arise for a child of school age. The convenience and flexibility of a village school could solve precisely this kind of problem.

When the post-Mao Chinese authorities abolished the commune system in 1981 in Gao Village, the situation changed dramatically. First of all, those who sent children to school had to bear, at least partially, the cost of employing a teacher since they had to pay a tuition fee. Secondly, a household might be compelled to use child labour to help the family since each household was on its own. Third, the village teacher could not afford the flexibility of allowing an older child to look after a toddler because of the quality improvement drive discussed in Chapter 7.

There was evidence of deterioration in education in Gao Village after the Cultural Revolution during the early 1980s, as is also discussed in Chapter 7. This deterioration was halted not by government input into rural education but as a result of industrial development far away from Gao Village which sparked a wave of working migrants. This is discussed in Chapter 11.

Cultural activities. It is often claimed by the Chinese intelligentsia and some foreign scholars alike that the Cultural Revolution, by burning books and attacking other aspects of traditional Chinese culture, made China into a cultural desert. Whether this is true for urban residents and the élite intelligentsia is not the point of discussion here. For the rural residents of Qinglin this kind of generalisation is somewhat out of proportion. To start with, there were no books to be burned. The landlord Gao Tianqiang's books were confiscated but not burned; and the rest of the villagers had hardly even seen paper. As for other aspects of traditional Chinese culture, some would have been thrown out anyway by the process of modernisation, with or without the Cultural Revolution. I cannot see any positive impact on the well-being of Gao villagers from carrying on practices such as Wang Taigong's impersonation to make a prescription discussed in Chapter 6, and the continuation of genealogical records. As for other aspects of traditional Chinese culture such as the celebration of the Spring Festival, the Dragon Boat Race Festival, the Qingming Festival to commemorate the dead and ancestors, and the Moon Festival, all these went on as usual during the Cultural Revolution, as is discussed in Chapter 12, only sometimes covertly.

There had not been a cinema, nor had there been a theatre in the Qinglin area before the Cultural Revolution. Before and during the Cultural Revolution there was one theatre which put on folk plays in the Boyang County Town and another in the Youdunjie region. However, these shows were only for urban and town residents and Party officials. The villagers in Qinglin never had a chance to see these shows. Gao Village had a music band before the Cultural Revolution, formed of volunteers. There was a drum, a few gongs, a couple of horns and trumpets owned by the village. There was always someone who could play the Chinese two-stringed violin. Whenever there was a wedding or a funeral ceremony, the villagers would sit together and put on a performance of folk songs and tunes. There were no books of words or of music; the songs and tunes were passed down by mouth and memory. The band was still in existence during the Cultural Revolution and performances were put on from time to time for occasions such as weddings and funeral ceremonies. Only in 1971 when the work team was in Gao Village did the band not put on any performance at all. In 1980 when I went back there from Britain, the village band put on a show in my house to celebrate my homecoming.

Other cultural activities like temple fairs had never taken place in the area. Only two things ceased during the Cultural Revolution in Gao Village; the practice of Wang Taigong and the continuation of genealogical tree records. Since the 1980s, the practice of keeping genealogical trees has re-emerged whereas no member of the younger generation really believes in Wang Taigong any more. Wang Taigong Buddha is no longer to be found in the village.

On the other hand, there were other cultural activities during the Cultural Revolution that were never in existence before and will never reappear in future. From 1968-73, there was a great surge of theatre troupes in Qinglin, boosted by the eight Model Peking Operas which were pushed by Mao's wife Jiang Qing and widely broadcast on radio and in films. Qinglin brigade, Qinglin School and even Gao Village had a troupe. All the young people from Gao Village took part in the enterprise, including the rich peasant's daughters and sons and the landlord's son. The older ones performed in the band and the younger ones were actors and actresses. There was no professional director and every one was part-time and amateur. The directing and acting were made easier because the villagers had heard and seen so much of these operas broadcast over the radio and in films. They could more or less recite many of the famous lines. All they had to do was to turn the words into folk tunes which everyone knew by heart. As they had seen so much in films the villagers just copied the actions.

Over a period of three years Gao villagers performed four Peking Operas: *Taking Tiger Mountain by Strategy, Shajiabang, The Red Lantern* and *The Red Regiment of Women Soldiers.* Gao villagers were invited to perform far away in other villages. The villagers improved their literacy by reading and reciting the scripts, and at the same time enriched their cultural life. It was unprecedented in Gao Village and it was a high point of their cultural life, both before the Cultural Revolution and after.

These cultural activities could only take place during the Cultural Revolution for two main reasons. The first was that the Cultural Revolution created an atmosphere for cultural innovation and local initiative. It was very innovative because though the scripts and actions were copied from the Peking Operas, the music was taken from local folk tunes. There was a cultural optimism and a spirit of collective effort. The performances were made easier because of repeated exposure from the government propaganda machine. The other was a more fundamental economic reason. Though the theatre troupe had most of its rehearsals during the evenings and on rainy days, their activities were subsidised by the production team. They were given full-time work points when they went out to perform and bonuses were given for the time they spent on rehearsals. Costumes and other costs were also paid for by the production team. Without the support of a collective system the whole enterprise could not even have been imagined.

Sport. The other activity that some Gao villages now remember with nostalgia was sport. Usually rural people, and especially the elderly do not care much about sport. They tend to think it is a waste of time and energy. However, when the brigade authorities organised races among the villages, the young villagers responded not only because they had to but also because they wanted to win honours for their village. In any case it was great fun for the youngsters who took part in the races. Again, when they took part in races, they were given work points, despite complaints by some old villagers. In fact, the villagers only had basketball matches because the game was easier to learn and could involve more people than, say, a game of table tennis. Gao Village once even set up a basketball court, to the great excitement of the young. During the slack seasons and the Spring Festivals, this court was the centre for outdoor activities. Apart from the fun and excitement for the young, basketball games and races increased the village team spirit and promoted exchanges between different villages. In post-Mao China, the organisation of such races was inconceivable for the villagers. Even schools do not have sports any more since all time and energy has to be devoted to academic competition. The collapse of the collective spirit is such that even Qinglin School could not install a basketball court. In 1994 when I asked the Principal of the school for an explanation, his reply was simply that basketball facilities would have been stolen by the villagers.

Intra-village marriages. As has always been the case, local politics was closely intertwined with the village clan structure during the Cultural Revolution in the Qinglin area. At the village level, village politics was equally intertwined with genealogical structures in Gao Village. This was clearly illustrated by the case of Gao Changyin at the beginning of the Cultural Revolution. However, by the end of the Cultural Revolution, paradoxically, almost miraculously genealogical tensions and conflicts were greatly reduced. Superficially, this subtle change could be attributed to official anti-tradition rhetoric and propaganda during the Cultural Revolution. However, a closer examination of the composition of households reveals that the cause is more structural; the expansion of marriage relationships among the villagers of different branches. Once a marriage is established between two different branches, the differentiation between the two and genealogical identification with one branch is instantly blurred.

Before 1949 there had not been a single intra-village marriage in Gao Village. Marriages were always arranged by a go-between. Before the Cultural Revolution there was only one intra-village marriage, a *zhaozhui* marriage, in which the man had to live with and be part of the woman's family. *Zhaozhui* used to carry, and still does carry, a social stigma for the man. It is thought that only the parentless, the extremely poor, the hopeless and helpless would have a *zhaozhui* marriage. In this particular case, there were a number of reasons for the marriage having taken place. First, the woman Gao Meihua was not only very attractive, a great asset anywhere, but also the best female labourer. Her base work points were the highest of all the women in the village. Secondly, Gao Meihua's family was quite well off, with a big house. But the family had four daughters, and no male to inherit. Thirdly, the man Gao Changqin had four brothers, three of whom were married with children. The family had a big house, but it was packed with people. Gao Changqin was of marriageable age and the family could not allocate even one room for him to live in when married. Therefore, *zhaozhui* was the best solution for both Gao Changqin and Gao Meihua's households. Even so, Gao Changqin was too proud to like the idea and he was extremely unhappy with his parents and his elder brothers for forcing him into the marriage.

Since the Cultural Revolution there have been eight intra-village marriages. Moreover, these marriages had not been forced as a result of family circumstances. In fact, most parents had been against them: it is the young people themselves who have insisted on them. The reason is not hard to find. First of all, the younger generation of Gao villagers are better educated and therefore less likely to accept an arranged marriage. More important, however, it was the collective system and cultural activities during the Cultural Revolution which provided the conditions for young people to establish intimate relationships. At least two marriages were the direct result of couples performing Peking Operas together. One of them was between the rich peasant's daughter Gao Shuilan and Gao Changquan, who was later to become a production team leader.

The collective system of working was also a catalyst for romance. There were always humour and jokes when a group of people worked together. The young people would work together in a team in the daytime and in the evenings they would all gather at the production team house to record their work points. All this gave them an opportunity to follow personal pursuits. It is true that even in traditional China the rural poor of both sexes were never as sexually restrained as the educated élite. But the participation in public life by women and their liberation in terms of self-expression and self-fulfilment were never as extensive and obvious as in the period of the Cultural Revolution in Qinglin, and Gao Village. For example, it was through local militia training sessions that Gao Chaoxin and Jiang Tonger fell in love with each other and got married.

State machinery. Before 1949, rural villages in Qinglin had always remained cellular in that each village was an independent and self-sufficient unit. The state had almost no role to play. The commune system established in Mao's China made it possible for the state to make some inroads into the cells. However, the reach of the state until the early 1970s was still limited in that the economy was completely agricultural and self-sufficient. The structures of the production team and production brigade had not in any sense broken down the clan and genealogical structures of the villages. Therefore, rural Qinglin was still cellular. By the early 1970s some Cultural Revolution policies did bring the state and the villagers into a closer relationship.

Paradoxically, this was not done by brute state interference, like the post-Mao family planning policy, but through the encouragement of local initiatives. To start with, the expansion of education, the establishment of village schools and the creation of "barefoot teachers" had brought more local people within the reach of state modernisation. There was a more direct connection and structural linkage between the state and local authorities. For instance, before the Cultural Revolution, neither the commune nor the brigade, let alone the production team, had a role in local education. What number of teachers were to be appointed, and where to set up which schools were all part of a plan drawn up by the authorities from above. The villagers and local authorities were completely at the mercy of the government, which chose to give or not to give resources as it saw fit, and there was no interaction between the two. This has changed because of the Cultural Revolution's encouragement of local initiatives. The same applies with regard to health and medicine. That is why there are no statistics on education and health in the *Basic Brigade Statistics Record* before 1972. The local authorities had no access to these statistics before then.

It was also during the Cultural Revolution that the villagers were mobilised to carry out irrigation projects, some of which involved hundreds of thousands of people. Mobilisation for such projects, work undertaken by villagers without any pay, is not possible in China today. Another example was the local militia. Local militias existed before and after the Cultural Revolution in Qinglin. But it was during the Cultural Revolution that young local militia men and women were organised efficiently, comprehensively and with a great sense of achievement. These men and women were organised for training, for brigade infrastructure projects and for cultural and sports activities. The militia in Qinglin were not indoctrinated, as is sometimes believed to have generally been the case in China, to be aggressive against class enemies or foreigners. The training was practical and organisational, and cultivated a team spirit, a sense of purpose and discipline.

The linkage between the state and the local village authorities was also reflected by formal structures both physical and organisational. In the centre of Qinglin a block of three houses was built to house the brigade administration centre. In one of the blocks was the medical clinic, a shop and a canteen. In another block were brigade offices, and finally there was the conference block.

There were five permanent brigade staff: the Party secretary, the head of the brigade, the women head of the brigade, the brigade accountant and the head of the local militia. They were all paid by the villagers and worked full-time to run the affairs of the brigade. There was a line of communication between the brigade and the commune and between the commune and the county authority.

In post-Mao China, Qinglin brigade has been organised into three village committees and the buildings at the brigade administration centre have been dismantled, the materials shared by the villages. Each village committee has a staff of five, altogether three times the number of staff they had during the Cultural Revolution. All of them are paid as full-time officials by the villagers and yet none works full-time. There is no village committee building and there is not even an office for the three village committees. There is no direct line of communication, physical or organisational, between the village committees and the *xiang* government. The village committees do not organise any cultural or sports activities. Nor is their work concerned with local education and health. Like the local authorities before 1949, the village committees are just there to collect taxes for the state and impose levies for themselves. By a single stroke, the state machine that had been built during the Cultural Revolution was scrapped overnight by the post-Mao Chinese authorities, and the social structure of the villages was put back to how it was before 1949. Even the name of *xiang* was the same as that used before 1949. Yet everyone calls this restoration of the past "Deng Xiaoping's reform".

Local enterprises and irrigation projects. There were other initiatives during the Cultural Revolution. For instance, the first brigade enterprise, an oil pressing workshop, was set up in 1973. Another brigade enterprise was set up in 1974. By 1976 there were seven brigade enterprises. Qinglin brigade started to possess machines such as a rice mill, flour mill, cotton gin and diesel engines in 1972. By 1976 there were ten diesel engines, seven rice mills, one flour mill and two cotton gins. In 1973, Qinglin began mechanical irrigation and by 1976 the brigade had twelve water pumps for irrigating the rice fields. Even Gao Village had bought a diesel engine. It used to be the case that all irrigation, if possible, was done by a traditional water wheel. Gradually most irrigation could be done by water pumps driven by diesel engines. There were other initiatives during this period such as fish farms, a forest station, pig farms and an experimental agricultural station. Technical initiatives included plastic covers for rice seedlings to hasten sprouting in early spring. But all these initiatives and projects were insignificant compared with the massive and labour intensive infrastructure build-up of irrigation projects during the Cultural Revolution. In 1967-78, three huge dykes were constructed in Qinglin alone, without any outside or government help. These are the Qinglin, the Xifen and Guantian dykes. The three dykes put together are more than 9 kilometres long, formed by more than 7 million cubic metres of earth, all of which was dug with shovels, spades, and carried with baskets and shoulder poles by the villagers.

A number of general points can be made to conclude this chapter. First, unlike in urban and town areas, there was not that much political and cultural turmoil in rural areas like Gao Village during the Cultural Revolution. This was the case for two main reasons. One was that in rural areas there were few intellectuals and high ranking Party officials who were the main targets and therefore victims of the Cultural Revolution. The other main reason for the absence of horrendous violence was that in rural areas there were very few high school and university students whereas some of the teenagers in urban areas and towns were violently radical. Some grass-roots Party officials in rural areas were victimised, like Gao Changyin. However, what they went through was not nearly as bad as in the cities. The fact that landlord and rich peasant families suffered also was not something unique during the Cultural Revolution. They had suffered since 1949 and the victimisation of this class of people did not end until the 1980s.

The second point is that local clan politics interacted with Cultural Revolution policies. The Cultural Revolution provided the political climate for victimisation; but victimisation was carried out by rival clan villages against each other's villagers, or genealogical rivals against each other in their own village. Xu villagers victimised Gao Tianqiang and Gao villagers victimised Xu Tianyun. The political climate of the Cultural Revolution also provided conditions for rural residents to take revenge on the basis of a personal grudge. Xu Conggui wanted to topple Gao Changyin because he was dismissed and punished during a political campaign when the latter was in charge. Gao Renkai wanted to persecute him because of his affair with Gao Renkai's wife. Gao Chaojiang reported me to the work team because his genealogical branch and mine were rivals.

The third important point is that not only were production activities not disrupted, but also significant advances were made with respect to education, health care and cultural and recreational activities during the Cultural Revolution in rural areas like Gao Village. Improvements in rural education, health care and cultural activities were not made at any cost to the government. They were the results of local efforts, encouraged by the Cultural Revolution's radicalism. In these respects, the Cultural Revolution was a period of positive innovation which benefited the rural population.

10

REFORMS SINCE THE LATE 1970s

The most dramatic aspect of rural reform since the late 1970s has been the dismantling of the commune system. In the commune system, apart from private plots allocated to the villagers, land was in theory owned collectively by the commune and managed by the production brigades and production teams; in practice, however, land was owned by the village and managed by the production teams. After the commune system was dismantled, land was in theory owned by the state and managed by the household; in practice, however, land was still owned by the village while being managed by individual households. For instance, if any land is to be used by the state as a factory site, some compensation has to be paid to the village by the state or the enterprises involved. Equally, if a villager wants a piece of land to build a house, a sum of money has to be paid to the village.

When the commune system was disbanded in 1981, all land in Gao Village was pooled together and allocated to individual households on a per capita basis: that is, each person received an equal distribution of village land. Each household now manages its own land and can grow whatever it sees fits. All the state requires is a certain amount of agricultural tax. In order to avoid the ideological stigma of privatization, the Chinese government first called the program of household land distribution "the Production Responsibility System", indicating that individual households did not own the land but only had the right to manage it. Then in 1984 the villagers were told that this system was to last for fifteen years or more. In order to stabilise the rural situation and to encourage investment the Chinese government later went further to declare that the responsibility system was to last indefinitely. At the beginning, land in Gao Village was to be re-distributed every five years in order to account for the change in the number of people in each household resulting from deaths and births. In 1994, the Chinese government decided to tell the villagers not to re-distribute land. Instead, the present distribution was to remain unchanged irrespective of changes in the number of people in each household.

There was nothing conceptually bold about the dismantling of the commune system and the equal distribution of land to households. Practically, the whole idea meant a restoration of the "land-to-the-tiller" program carried out in the early 1950s. There are several points that need to be made to clear away misunderstandings of this so-called rural reform. First, it was not Deng Xiaoping's idea or policy to start with. The practice was carried out in Sichuan and Anhui Provinces towards the late 1970s, first secretly by the peasants themselves, later with the backing of the Party secretaries of the two provinces – Zhao Ziyang, later China's premier and then General Secretary of the Party; and Wan Li, later to be the Chairman of the People's Congress.[1]

Second, it is not true that the commune system was dismantled all over China in a single year in 1978. In Jiangxi Province, 69.5 per cent of villages had adopted the responsibility system by 1979. By 1981 the figure had risen to 92.6 per cent and by 1982 it was 99.3 per cent.[2] Household distribution of land did not take place until 1981 in Gao Village.

Third, it is not true that the dismantling of the commune system in and of itself led to a dramatic increase of income for the Chinese peasantry.[3] The so-called liberation of productive forces by "privatisation" should not be romanticised. In fact, what played a greater role in boosting rural income was the increase in the price of agricultural produce allowed by the government.

Fourth, it is not true that the commune system was bankrupt all over China, and that all peasants therefore welcomed its destruction without reservation. In terms of the growth in grain production, the commune period was not as bad as has been suggested. In fact, from 1959 to 1977, the growth rate was 2.9 per cent per

---

[1] Lu Xueyi, *Nongcun Chengbao Zerenzhi Yanjiu* (Studies on the Production Responsibility System), Shanghai, 1986.

[2] *Fenjin De Jiangxi, 1949-1988* (Jiangxi in Strife, 1949-1988), Jiangxi Sheng Tongji Ju (The Jiangxi Provincial Statistical Bureau), Nanchang, 1989.

[3] For one of the most recent attempts to analyse the Chinese rural reform see Joseph Fewsmith, *Dilemmas of Reform in China Political Conflict and Economic Debate*, New York and London, 1994, pp. 19-55.

annum, which was not significantly lower than the figure of 3 per cent achieved during the reform period 1978-90.[4] It was therefore not surprising that many communes resisted the change for many years, and that there are still some functioning today because their members do not want to dismantle them.[5]

On the other hand, as well as destroying the commune system, rural reforms since the late 1970s have also done away with some positive initiatives of the previous decades. As was shown in the last chapter, the state machinery which was generally effective and essentially non-corrupt was swept away by the destruction of the commune system. In the Qinglin area, not only was the organization of the production brigade done away with, but also the physical structure of the Brigade administration buildings was dismantled. The structure of local authorities and the running of village affairs was restored almost to pre-1949 levels, as if the Communist revolution in 1949 had not occurred. As for now, corruption and brutality are worse than before 1949 because the local gentry, who had been trained on the basis of Confucian moral codes, was replaced by unrestrained local officials. The effective and low-cost "barefoot teacher" and "barefoot doctor" systems were discarded. The poor and the helpless are left to fend for themselves.

In Gao Village the school house was sold, the production team storage house was demolished, and the remaining building materials were given to the individual households. The former basketball court, the best location in the village, was possessed by Gao Changyao, one of the former production team leaders who was one of the only two Communist Party members in the village; he built a house on it. Following his example, other villagers started to occupy whatever land they could lay their hands on. There used to be two paths running vertically and horizontally across the middle of Gao Village, like a cross. In 1992 when I visited the village the two paths had gone and there

---

[4] John Wong, "Implications of the Growth Trend in Mainland China's Grain Production", *Issues and Studies*, vol. 28, no. 1, January, 1992, pp. 38-41.

[5] For the role and function of the commune system and for how some communes resisted the post-Mao policy change see William Hinton, "The Chinese Revolution: was it necessary? was it successful? Is it still going on?", *Monthly Review*, vol. 43, no. 6, Nov. 1991, pp. 7-8; and *The Great Reversal*, 1991.

had been a complete transformation of Gao Village's physical appearance. There was no proper path any more in the village. Dirty ditches and smelly pigsties were everywhere, blocking every way possible. There is no village centre, nor is there a playground for children. In short, there is no longer any focal point for public life in the village.

The head of the village conducts village affairs from his home. I noticed that one of the levies the villagers were commanded to pay was for a newspaper subscription. So I asked Gao Changquan, the village head, if I could borrow some newspapers to read. His wife managed to find some bits and pieces from a dusty corner; Gao Changquan himself did not read the paper and no one else was allowed access to it. So Gao Changquan's wife used it as wrapping paper.

Another characteristic of post–Mao rural China is the return of clan politics to village life. Even in a suburban county of Nanchang, the capital city of Jiangxi Province, one hundred thousand villagers were reported to have participated in a clan book recording ceremony. In Lin Hu County of Hunan Province, 230 of the 273 administrative villages[6] were reported to have established clan committees; 38 per cent of those in the clan committees were members of the Communist Party or local government officials.[7] It was reported that in Hunan Province a feud between two villages dating back to the 1920s resurfaced in 1993 when a Li Village factory was damaged by villagers from Liu Village. A fight between the two villages involving home-made weapons took place, leaving five people dead and twelve wounded.[8]

In Yinbaohu, Qinglin and Gao Village, more blatant clan politics also returned. The fact that Jing villagers could block a police investigation of the death of seventeen people caused by a village

---

[6] Administrative village, as opposed to natural village, is an administration unit which is a village committee that governs a population roughly the same size as a production brigade in the commune period. A large natural village, like Jing Village in Yinbaohu, may be divided into two administrative villages, that is, two village committees whereas a small village like Gao Village has to be included with Xu Village and Cao Village to form an administrative village.

[7] Jiang Zhenchang, "Dalu Ganqun Guanxi Zhi Yanjiu" (A Study of the Relationship between Masses and Officials), *Zhongguo Dalu Yanjiu* (Mainland China Studies), vol. 35, no. 11, pp. 51–62.

[8] *China Focus*, vol. 1, no. 10, 1993, p. 8.

feud shows the degree to which the state has lost its power in Yinbaohu *xiang*. In Gao Village, a clan committee was formed consisting of nine members. This clan committee has the right to take important decisions concerning Gao Village, such as how much land will be given to whom as building sites. In 1994, for instance, six households were given permission to build houses in the best locations after a lavish banquet was given to clan committee members.

Since the late 1970s, the revival of clan structures and clan power in Yinbaohu villages has gone unchecked. If there is a fight between two clan villages, the likely outcome is, as in international relationships, not decided by justice or fair play, but by a demonstration of force based on village size. As the county authority's inability to do anything about the feud between Jing Village and its neighbouring small village has shown, villages have nothing to do with the state except the payment of agricultural taxes. The reason that there are not many village feuds in Yinbaohu *xiang* is that the large and powerful villages are content while the small and weak villages cannot afford to initiate a fight. Gao villagers will never forget or forgive Wang villagers for enclosing their water territory. They desperately want a fight to settle the account but Gao Village currently does not have the strength to launch such a fight. When I was in Gao Village in 1992, the village elders were talking of purchasing some guns to fight Wang Village.

Like other villages, Gao Village renewed the practice of village genealogical record keeping. The Gao Village clan committee is in charge of organizing the continuation and maintenance of the clan book record. Like christening a child in the tradition of Western Christianity, every child born in Gao Village has to *shang pu* (be entered in the genealogy book). For the boys, *shang pu* is a very solemn occasion: joss sticks have to be burned and a food offering has to be made in a proper ceremony when a name is given and recorded in the book. On every New Year's Day of the Lunar Calender, all the male villagers have to *bai pu* (prostration in front of the genealogy book) in order to keep alive the memory of the ancestral line for the village as a whole.

Genealogical branch conflicts also began to penetrate village life again. Thanks to intra-branch marriages in Gao Village, tensions and conflicts had quietened down significantly in the late 1970s.

However, there are signs that the villagers have started to identify themselves with genealogical branches again. This was clearly shown in 1992 when they used my homecoming as an occasion to demonstrate genealogical identity and unity.

One day a group of male villagers came to pay me a visit. I was a bit surprised that they had all come together, because usually individual villagers would come to see me on their own. We sat together, chatting away while we ate peanuts and so on. I still did not realise what was happening half an hour later when another group of male villagers came to visit me, this time with a music band. They came to my old house and started to sing me some folk songs and play some age old music. About an hour after they had gone, another group came, again male heads of households, this time with some gifts for me. Then another group came. Finally, towards the end of the afternoon, the first group came again, this time with a long piece of cloth as a gift. Only then did I realise that each group represented a genealogical branch! One branch first thought of the idea of paying me a visit in a group. Then other branches followed, each one wanting to outdo the other in ceremony. Not wanting to lose face and to be outdone by the other branches, the first group came again because they did not come with a gift the first time. At the end my old house was full of gifts, with cloths and good fortune calligraphy hanging around everywhere. In return, and urged by my mother, I took five photographs of them, each picture for all the members of one genealogical branch, male, female, adults and children, sitting together.

The Chinese establishment intellectuals like to claim that rural reforms since the late 1970s have liberated the peasants from the shackles of the commune, and that production output increased dramatically as a result. McMillan, Whalley and Zhu attribute 78 per cent and Lin attributes 86.5 per cent of the growth in output per unit of agricultural inputs to the adoption of the Production Responsibility System.[9]

It is reasonable to assume that Chinese peasants would work

[9] John McMillan, John Whalley and Lijing Zhu, 'The Impact of China's Economic Reforms on Agricultural Productivity and Growth", *Journal of Political Economy*, vol. 97, no. 4, 1989 pp. 781-807. Justin Yifu Lin, "Rural Reforms and Agricultural Growth in China", *American Economic Review*, vol. 82, no. 1, 1992, pp. 34-51.

harder on their own land to grow crops for themselves. Since the responsibility system has given them a sense of ownership and the right to grow their own crops, it is natural also to expect that they would work harder than in the commune system. However, it would be wrong to assume that peasants did not have a sense of ownership in the commune system. Under the leadership of a production team leader, and within a production unit of ten to fifteen households, peasants could have a very keen sense of ownership and self-management. Moreover, the elaborate evaluation and monitoring systems of work points and team work were sufficient for coordination and supervision.

The lack of motivation, if such there was, might come partly from the lack of a system of immediate reward since debts and credits could not be settled in any given year. Those who had credits could not be paid by the production team because those who were in debt could not pay the production team. There was no cash around in rural China. This was largely because the government controlled prices and had a monopoly over the procurement of agricultural produce. Therefore, one crucial factor in post-Mao China was the change in the price and procurement systems.

In the commune period, apart from agricultural taxes and local levies paid by the peasants, the government had monopoly control of the grain market, and any surplus grain peasants produced had to be sold to the state at the state-designated price. One post-Mao reform policy which led to an increase in rural income was the rise of prices for agricultural produce and the reduction of the amount of monopoly purchases of grain by the state. Before 1979, the state forbade peasants to sell anything at the market and they were made to sell them to the state at state-controlled prices. This was called monopoly procurement, and by its rules more than 180 items of agricultural produce had to be handed in to the state. In 1979 this was reduced to sixty-two. In 1981 the amount of grain sold to the state through monopoly procurement was only 64 per cent of that in 1978.[10] Not only was this system reduced so that peasants could sell their produce in the

---

[10] An Xi-yi, "The Development and Improvement of Agricultural Marketing in China" in John W. Longworth, ed., *China's Rural Development Miracle with International Comparison*, Brisbane, 1987, pp. 18-25.

market, but prices for different sorts of monopoly procurement rose from 25 per cent to 40 per cent in 1979. It is therefore not unreasonable to assume that if the government had altered the pricing and purchasing policies in the commune period they would have had the same effect on the peasants' income.

That pricing and procurement policies were a crucial factor can be seen from what happened after 1985. Before 1985, after fulfilling the quotas, villagers could sell their produce to the state at the above-quota bonus price (for grain and oil seeds these prices were 50 per cent higher than the quota price; for cotton it was 30 per cent higher). The villagers also had the option to sell their produce at negotiated prices, which were slightly lower than the market prices. Furthermore, sale at negotiated prices was not compulsory, and the villagers had the option to sell their produce in the market.

Grain procured at the above-quota and negotiated prices was sold at considerably lower prices to urban residents, causing substantial financial losses for the government. For instance, in 1994 government subsidies totalled 22 billion *yuan*, equivalent to 14 per cent of total government revenues. Assuming that the Chinese peasantry benefited too much from price increases in agricultural produce, and seeing that subsidies for urban residents were stretching the government's budget, the government responded in 1985 by lowering monopoly purchase prices for agricultural produce and raising the prices of industrial goods. In 1985, the state monopoly purchase price of grain was 28 per cent lower than that in 1984. At the same time, prices for chemical fertilisers were 43 per cent higher than in 1983, and prices for insecticides were 82.8 per cent higher than in 1983.[11] Monopoly procurement was reimposed and grain trade on the free market was prohibited unless quotas had been met. In spite of the government's assurance in 1984 that the Production Responsibility System would remain unchanged for at least fifteen years, agricultural production output at national level dropped in 1985. For instance, national *per capita* output of grain dropped from 392.84 kilos in 1984 to 360.70 kilos in 1985.[12]

[11] An Xi-yi, *ibid.*

[12] *China Statistical Yearbook 1995*, Beijing, 1995, p. 31, Tables 2-9.

Because of price rises and market freedom, villagers' income in Gao Village as a whole increased during the early 1980s. As the production output figures show (see Table 9), the increase in income did not arise significantly from a great boost of grain production, as production output had not been on the increase consistently since reforms were introduced in 1981.

The figures show that there were very good years in 1972 and 1979 before the reform took place. On the other hand, in 1983, two years after the Responsibility System had been implemented, there was a significant drop in production output. The figures for 1982 and 1985 indicate a significant increase, and the 1985 figure does not correspond with the national figures, which show a decline in output. This is so presumably because in the Qinglin area there is a time-lag before the area catches up with government policy changes since the market is little developed there. In any case, because of the change of policy after 1985, the increase in output did not lead to an increase in income.

Therefore, reform policies regarding price and procurement by the post-Mao Chinese government did boost peasants' income in the early 1980s. However, the increase in income as a whole in Gao Village did not come without some cost, specifically an increased polarisation between the well-off and the extremely poor. Whilst the relatively well-off households could afford to purchase chemical fertilisers and insecticides at higher prices in order to increase their production output, poor families had to go without.

There are two families in Gao Village whose members have to beg regularly to survive. One family is that of Gao Changliang who was one of the former production team leaders. When Gao Changliang was alive, the family was already in debt because he had had a respiratory disease. He died in 1986 at the age of fifty-five because the family could not afford medical treatment. Since then, his wife and children have had to beg every spring before new crops have been harvested. Another family that has to go begging is that of Gao Chaodian, who is known for his lack of planning and inept management of the family budget. Regular begging had never been seen in Gao Village either before 1949 or in Mao's China.

While most Gao Village families were better off in the early 1980s as a result of price increases and market freedom, farming cannot make anyone in the area rich. In Gao Village there is only one family that really did well, but not out of farming. That was the family of Gao Hanzheng. Gao Hanzheng was not a born Gao villager. He came to Gao Village with his mother who married a Gao villager in 1967 and hence had to change his surname to Gao. Gao Hanzheng benefited from his uncle by his mother's former marriage. Because of his uncle's connections in the city of Jingdezhen, he got hold of some building contract work. As a building contract agent, he made use of cheap village labour and made a fortune through commissions. He had made enough money to build a three storeyed imposing house in Gao Village in 1991, which cost something like 70,000 *yuan*. The house was built with concrete and iron and steal, with large windows of glass, a huge balcony facing south, which takes in the cooling breeze in summer. It is the first such building in Gao Village's history. Gao villagers are immensely proud of their adopted son who was said to have won face for the village. Gao Hanzheng, a school truant when a boy, who used to be considered as good for nothing except playing tricks, has become one of the most important people in the village and is asked to sit at banquets on all important village occasions.

In Guantian, which consists of Xu Village, Cao Village and Gao Village, the wealthiest households are not engaged in farming. Apart from Dr Xu, the two wealthiest people are Xu Guohua and Xu Xianzhen. Xu Guohua became rich because he ran the local chemical fertiliser and insecticide agency, selling to the villagers for the government. He had the power to sell what he wanted, to whomever he wanted, at whatever prices he wanted. He obtains these precious commodities from the state at one price and can then sell them to the villagers at another. He can do this unchecked not only because Xu Village is the largest among the three, but also because the local powerholders turn a blind eye to his business. He is the son of Xu Xianjiao, the deputy head of the *xiang* government.

Xu Xianzhen made his fortune in a similar way because he runs a cotton purchasing agency for the government. Xu Xianzhen was a cotton inspection expert during the commune period. Since the 1980s, the policy of commercialisation and privatization allowed him to develop a monopoly in the area. When the villagers sell cotton to the state, a grading has to be made as different grades of cotton are sold at different prices. Xu Xianzhen alone has the right to decide the grades of cotton sold by the villagers. He can therefore designate a lower grade for cotton he buys from the villagers, then sell it to the state at a higher grade, and higher price.

The other consequence of reform is a rapid increase in crime, and a sense of insecurity. There were also crimes during the commune period. The most common form of crime was not committed by an individual so much as by clan villages. Very often the small villages were the victims. It happened from time to time during the commune period that a group of villagers would steal things from a nearby village. The property stolen was mostly village trees, grain stored in a village storage house and sometimes water buffalo. Water buffalos were and are still the most important means of production for the villagers because they are used for pulling ploughs. A good buffalo in the 1970s cost as much as 600 *yuan*, one-fifth of the cost for building a good traditional house. Villagers would not usually steal buffalos from a nearby village because they were not something that could be hidden away. Stealing a buffalo from a long distance was not easy because a buffalo could not walk fast and villagers had no way to transport them. Buffalo stealing was therefore rare, although it sometimes happened. Usually the perpetrators were members of a large village which could not be challenged. Gao villagers never dared steal anything because the village was too small. By the late 1970s, all the trees surrounding Gao Village were either cut down by the villagers themselves or stolen by other villagers. The village storage house was also broken into once and several thousand *jin* of rice was stolen.

Another common form of theft during the collective period was stealing vegetables from someone else's private plot. Children especially liked to pick melons and fruit of all kinds. Almost every child did this at some time. Gao Hanzheng, later the self-made rich Gao villager and Gao Chaozuo, son of Gao Changyin, the former Party secretary of Guantian brigade, were notorious for their thefts. Sometimes adults pinched things from the private plots of others. There was not much anyone could do about this. However, one custom was a very strong deterrent. Very often we would hear someone screaming around the village, with a knife in one hand and a chopping board in the other. The owner of the stolen property (often a woman and never a man) would curse the thief by shouting that whoever did the stealing would be chopped to pieces in his or her next life. While screaming like this she would chop the board with her knife. It was very terrifying to be cursed like this even if you did not believe in the next life.

Since the late 1980s, however, theft and crime of a different nature have emerged. There are now life-threatening robberies. Thefts have become more organised and larger in scale. For instance, in 1992 three of the largest buffalos in Xu Village were stolen and transported on a truck, then slaughtered as beef for sale. The police could have arrested the offenders because there were clear indications as to who had done it. However, the police told Xu Village to pay a sum of 4,500 yuan before they would start the investigation. The case was never taken up because Xu Villagers could not pay the sum.

Rural villagers are also the victims of crimes in towns and cities when they travel as migrant workers. One Gao villager was forced to pay 45 yuan for 3 jin of bananas at a Yingtan train station, a price ten times that in the market. Gao Changwen witnessed one of his friends beaten into a coma at Xiamen railway station by a gang who took 500 yuan from him. Gao Zhiming, a boy aged fourteen, went to Guangzhou to find work in 1991. He was beaten up badly by a group of people and was robbed of the 20 yuan that he had with him. Failing to find any work and being penniless Gao Zhiming had to beg for food all the way home from Guangzhou.

In some places it is no longer safe to travel on a bus or in a train. Not only are there robberies and thefts but extortion by government employees is also common. For example, during every Spring Festival when millions of migrant workers from rural China go home for a visit, some state employees of the country's railway service try their best to extort money from the poor villagers who would usually take some cash home. My brother Gao Changwen was a migrant worker in Xiamen. During the Spring Festival of 1992 he took a train from Xiamen to Nanchang to go home for a visit. When he was on the train an attendant insisted that the carton Gao Changwen had with him was too big to put on the luggage shelf even when it was clear to everyone that it was not. Gao Changwen had to pay the attendant 20 *yuan* before the matter was settled.

The above incidents, in addition to those that I either witnessed or experienced during my travels in 1992 and 1994, were good indications of the situation in post-Mao China. Once I was travelling on a ship at night from Nanchang to Boyang County. One of the ship's cabin crew was trying to steal the watch I was wearing on my wrist while I was sleeping. He gave the watch back only because I was awakened by his action. And when I was travelling on a bus from the city of Jingdezhen to Gao Village, a group of youngsters surrounded me suddenly and pushed me around. The next thing I knew my passport was in the hands of one of the boys.

When I was travelling on a train from Nanchang to Xiamen, we were in a sleeping car and an attractive lady sleeping in the berth beneath me was woken up by a middle-aged man who said that she was sleeping in his berth. But the woman had a valid ticket for the berth which she had bought at Nanchang Railway Station. That man also had a valid ticket for the same berth. What happened was that the car attendant had sold the berth twice, and pocketed the 200 *yuan* cash for herself. The woman had to sit all night as she could not fight with the man. The car attendant said that it was not her business to decide who should sleep in the berth.

When the train stopped at Shao Guan Station in Fujian Province the next morning it was early dawn. It was stuffy and one of our neighbours sitting at the window wanted to open it for some fresh morning air. As soon as the window was open and before any of us could realise what was happening, the man's shirt hanging behind him flew out of the window, grabbed by a hand from outside. All his business papers, his identity card and 400 *yuan* were gone. We watched a boy strolling away into the distance with his trophy.

And for the first time in the entire history of more than two hundred years of Gao Village there was a robber from the village. His name was Gao Zhanglin, and he was sixteen when he committed a robbery in 1988 on a bus crowded with passengers. He took out a knife and forced someone who looked like a businessman to give up his combination-lock suitcase, but he did not know how to open the suitcase. So he used an axe and chopped it open. Instead of a suitcase loaded with cash as he had expected, it was packed with sunglasses. Gao Zhanglin was caught within two weeks and sentenced to eight years' imprisonment. In 1994 he had still not been released, but instead had been transferred to a labour camp to do coolie work.

Corruption at the grassroots

There was a saying during the late 1980s which can be translated as "Officials in Mao's time were as clean as air, those in Hua Guofeng's time were seen nowhere, and Deng Xiaoping's officials are millionaires". Though there are many millionaire officials in urban areas as well as along the south coast of China, no officials in Qinglin can be anywhere near as rich. Nonetheless, local Party and village officials are among the wealthiest in the area. A clear indication that the Party officials are getting rich is housing. In any village in Yinbaohu *xiang*, the best houses were mostly built by the Party and village officials. The house owned by the head of Yinbaohu *xiang*, Yu Jisong, from the largest village in the area, is so big that it looks like a castle, surrounded by huge brick fences. The officials smoke the most expensive cigarettes, one cigarette costing 1 *jin* of rice, and they all have motorbikes, some of which were imported from Japan and Taiwan.

One example may indicate the degree of polarisation in the area. During the Spring Festival in 1991, Yu Jisong lost one of his eyes in a festive framework display. He was flown from Nanchang, the capital city of Jiangxi, to Guangzhou to have an operation because he wanted the best treatment, the cost of which exceeded 10,000 *yuan*, an astronomical figure for the villagers. The surgeon who had operated on Yu's eye was said to have been given more than 10,000 *yuan* in cash as a gift. Yu's nominal salary as the head of Yinbaohu *xiang*, where the average annual *per capita* income in 1992 was 400 *yuan* (although for official statistics purposes 600 *yuan* was reported to the county authorities),[13] was roughly 4,000 *yuan* a year. One could well ask: where did he get his money from?

To understand this we need to examine briefly how the workings

---

[13] These figures were obtained from an interview with Xu Xianan, who was from Xu Village but now works at Boyang County Policy Research Office.

of the local fiscal system changed after 1978, the landmark year of reform in China after Mao. Before 1978, it was deemed by the central planning system that income from various sources at various levels must all be handed to the state. In rural China, peasants contributed to state revenue by paying agricultural taxes and by selling surplus grain to the state at state controlled prices. In return, the state was responsible for all expenditures such as local education, health, roads and agricultural investment. The state was also responsible for paying the salaries of government officials at the commune level and above. Production team leaders and accountants were paid by their teams through the work point system, just like other villagers. Production brigade officials were also paid by the villagers themselves through contributions paid to the brigade. Contributions towards such funds from each production team varied from year to year, depending on production output, but at a fixed percentage, normally 2 per cent of the gross income. Apart from the agricultural tax which was an average of 10 per cent of the gross income, production teams also had to pay a fixed rate of what were called Public Accumulation Funds and Public Welfare Funds. Table 10 in Appendix 2 shows the percentage of various items in the years for which statistics are available.

Though figures are not available for enough years to draw any major conclusions, they are at least indicative of the periods before and during the Cultural Revolution and immediately before the disbandment of the commune system. Though Chinese peasants contributed through the Public Accumulation Funds, very little public work was done in rural China except by the villagers' own hard labour. Though Chinese peasants contributed to the so-called Welfare Funds, there was virtually no welfare in rural China aside from a few symbolic Five Guaranteed households.[14] For several decades the Chinese peasantry was thoroughly exploited by the state. The government exploited Chinese peasants by forcing them to sell as much grain as possible to the state at state controlled prices, so that living costs in the urban sector could remain low.

[14] For the elderly in a household that was of good class background and childless the government was supposed to guarantee provision of five essential items for life: shelter, food, clothing, health care and burial. However, in practice government support was very meagre and not nearly enough for the purpose. There has never been a Five Guaranteed household in Gao Village.

The propaganda machinery of the Chinese state termed the state's coercion of monopoly purchase as "encouraging the peasants to sell their surplus grain to the motherland". In fact, Chinese peasants seldom had surplus grain in those years. The producers of grain were ordered to consume no more than a given quota of what they had produced through back breaking labour so that the urban sector could have a cheap supply of grain.

That said it is also clear that in those years the items for taxes and levies were few and the rates were fixed. The villagers knew what to expect and what they contributed appeared to be accountable. It was at least not the case that all their hard work and hunger were for the benefit of local bullies. In the post-Mao reform period, however, and especially since the late 1980s, rural residents have gradually come to be at the mercy of local bullies.

The process started with the state's initiative to give the local authorities more responsibility. In 1978, the central government had launched what was called *caizheng baogan zhi* (Financial Contract System), which basically meant that local authorities could share a certain percentage of the revenue they had raised, instead of handing all of it to the state as used to be the practice. The rationale was that the system would give various local authorities incentives to raise more revenue, since the more they raised the more they could share. What the system also meant was that various local authorities must at the same time share the same percentage of responsibility for expenditure. Theoretically, the system is economically rational. First, the government would face fewer difficulties in collecting revenue. Second, since the local authorities have some funds for expenditure, money could be better spent for the residents under their administration, for it was they, not the central government, who knew local conditions better. Third, it could give the local authorities incentives to develop local enterprises.

In practice, however, in a country where officials are not held accountable, the system could be a recipe for abuse of power and corruption. It is not difficult to see that the Financial Contract System could lead to three developments at the same time. The first is that levies can become extremely arbitrary, so that rural residents are completely at the mercy of local authorities. The second development is that funds raised could be spent on useless, whimsical or ridiculous projects instead of on basic services such as health and education. Third, it is an open door for corruption. Local authorities can pocket whatever amount they want from however much is raised. It is very difficult to prevent local authorities from being corrupted, first because there is no standard by which their finances could be audited, and second because they could bribe their superiors to get out of a messy situation. In those rural areas where there are flourishing local industries, local authorities can raise sufficient revenue from industrial taxes. In those areas, the burden of levies for local revenue does not all fall on the peasantry. In Yinbaohu *xiang* and Boyang County, where there are no local industries of any significance, the burden of levies falls heavily on the helpless peasants.

An example of arbitrary levies for wasteful projects took place in Boyang County in 1991. The new head of county appointed in 1990 wanted to develop industries. So he thought up some wonderful projects. He called the projects by three colours: silver for cotton growing, blue for fish farming around the Poyang Lake, and gold for growing tobacco. As the county had been growing cotton and cultivating fish for ages, there was not much for him to do in these two areas. Therefore the governor focused on the gold colour of tobacco. By his orders, every household of the *xiangs* where it was possible to grow tobacco on a large scale was ordered to build a tobacco roasting house, the cost of which was around 700 *yuan*. Whoever refused to build such a roast house would be fined. Many households did as they were told. Yinbaohu *xiang* was not ordered to do this because it was mainly a rice growing area.

In order to raise enough funds for building a tobacco factory every government employee in the civil service category, such as teachers and *xiang* government officials, was ordered to contribute in instalments a loan of between 500 and 2,000 *yuan*, depending on his or her salary level. The county authorities promised to pay back the loans, if not in cash at least in kind by distributing cigarettes! Those who refused to pay would have it deducted from their salaries.

What happened eventually was that the project was abandoned both because the soil was found not to be good enough to produce superior tobacco to compete in the market, and because the central government would not approve such a project. The county head did not think of seeking the government's approval first, nor of testing the soil before ordering the construction of roasting houses and before ordering civil servants to contribute. So the roasting houses were built for nothing, thousands of them left useless like pillboxes. Those who paid did not know how and when they would get their money back. The conception and implementation of the Gold Project in Boyang County is clearly reminiscent of similar disastrous projects carried out during the Great Leap Forward.

In 1990, the village committee ordered Gao villagers and Xu villagers to plant orange trees to make money. A loan was duly arranged for the purchase of orange trees. Gao villagers were ordered to uproot the trees on the hill in front of the village. The pine trees on the hill were chopped down and each household was given a quota of holes to dig, each measuring 1 cubic metre, for planting orange trees. At the beginning, the villagers were promised 1 *yuan* for each hole they dug. Later, the promise was broken. The villagers not only did not receive a cent for the work they had done but also were fined 17 *yuan* for the death of each orange tree they had planted. In 1992 I could see that most of the orange trees that had been planted had died. The suitability of the soil for growing oranges was never tested, and there was no system by which the orange trees could be irrigated. Now the villagers are left to pay the loan.

In 1994, the same thing happened again. The villagers were ordered to plant mulberry trees on the same hill. This time, the villagers were at least paid for it. A payment was made for every ten trees planted. I saw the villagers plant: they just dug a very shallow hole and inserted a bunch of mulberry trees together to fulfil the quota. Some of them did not even bother to cover the plant roots with soil. I protested by saying that those trees would not grow and that even if they did they should not be planted all together in one hole. The villagers counselled me not to worry because it was all for nothing in any case. None of the mulberry trees survived.

In 1989, the villagers in Qinglin were ordered to pay 5 *yuan* per person for building pavilions in the middle of paddy fields so that when villagers worked in summer they could have a place to rest. It was an excellent idea supported by everyone. The money, a total amount of 40,000 *yuan*, was duly collected. However, by 1994 not a single pavilion had been built. No one in the village committee bothered to give an account of where the money had gone.

In 1990, the villagers were told that the former Qinglin brigade owed the government about 20,000 *yuan*. In order to pay the debt, every villager was ordered to pay 18 *yuan*. According to my informants, one of whom was the village school teacher Gao Chaozhen, the whole thing was a fraud and no account was given as to where the money had gone. This lack of accountability explains how the local officials get their money.

The head of Gao Village, Gao Changquan, who is a member of the Guantian village committee, is a heavy smoker and drinker. He smokes one packet of cigarettes and drinks one bottle of rice wine a day. The daily cost of these two items is around 5 *yuan*. Gao Changquan's nominal salary for the whole year of 1995 was no more than 1,000 *yuan*. He has no other source of income except from his share of land, with which he has to support a family of four. One small consolation for the Gao villagers, who wonder where Gao Changquan gets his money, is that, presumably because of his expensive tastes, he has not built a large house for himself. At least not yet.

One of the most common forms of extravagance funded from the public purse are banquets. When there is a meeting, or when there is a problem household that cannot afford to pay all its taxes and levies, or when a woman violates the family planning policies, the village committee members are called together. The first thing to decide for such an occasion is what and when to eat. Usually one member of the village committee will be assigned specially to organise the purchase of food and drinks for a meal. Banquets are held in different villages in the homes of village committee members. This arrangement not only allows members to keep the occasion to themselves but also allows them to keep the leftovers of each banquet, which can be very substantial. If a banquet is held for a guest the occasion will be even more elaborate.

Because I was a distinguished guest and an overseas Chinese who is expected to be rich enough to donate to local projects, several banquets were arranged for me when I visited. There were always more than a dozen dishes, a lot of spirits and beer, and expensive cigarettes. There is a peculiar custom with cigarettes in the area. Apart from those passed around during every occasion, each person at the table, including the ones who do not smoke, will be given a packet of expensive cigarettes as a gift. The brand of cigarettes varies from occasion to occasion, depending upon who the guest of honour is. The least expensive for such an occasion in the early 1990s was *San Chong Jiu* (Three Nines) sold for 3.7 *yuan* a packet and the most expensive brand was *Hong Ta Shan* (Red Pagoda Mountain) sold for around 10 *yuan* a packet, the cost of 10 *jin* of rice.

The annual total cost of banquets and eating together by the local officials in one village committee is hard to verify. When the cost of some occasion is recorded it is classified in the general category of management costs in the accounts book. One figure will indicate the extent of such extravagance at the villagers' cost. In the Qinglin area there is a lake belonging to all the villages which could not be carved up for distribution in 1981 when the commune system was disbanded. As a solution, the lake was used as a fish farm for all the villages. A lake management committee was formed to manage this fish farm. The annual income from the fish farm was on average more than 30,000 *yuan* in the early 1990s. However, the villagers had not benefited by one cent from the income. The head of the lake management committee told me in 1993 that the amount of money that he had personally approved for banquets for the members of the six village committees and *xiang* and county officials was around 60,000 *yuan* in 1991-3. This is 20,000 *yuan* a year and does not include the banquet costs of the six village committees themselves. The rest of the income from the fish farm was given to local officials in kind: all the village committee members were given fish regularly and free of charge. Jiang Shuigui also admitted that fish was regularly sent to the *xiang* and county officials. The local term for such a practice is *da gou* (literally "beat the dog", meaning "throwing food at the dog so that it will not bark").

While the local officials are eating up public funds, the burden of local levies has become increasingly heavier. The following figures of taxes and levies paid to the state government, the county, *xiang* and village committee show the burden of taxes and levies the villagers had to bear in the the early 1990s. In 1991, Gao Village had to pay the national government (in *yuan*) 4,463.5 for agriculture taxes, 357 for a special agriculture tax, 168.9 for a slaughter tax, and 209 for an education tax, a total of 5,198.4

yuan. To the county, Gao Village had to pay an education levy of 1,686, women and child health insurance levies of 67.44, a family planning levy of 369.21, a broadcast communication levy of 75.87, a *corvée* levy of 683.91, a total of 2,909.43 *yuan.* Also in 1991, Gao Village had to pay the *xiang* government an education levy of 1,405, a *corvée* levy of 421.5, a Five Guaranteed household levy of 112.4, assistance for households with members serving in the army of 182.65, a construction labour levy of 140.5, insurance for households without male labour of 606.96, a domestic animal immunisation levy of 150.88, government bonds and militia training levy of 140.5, a fine for failure to fulfil the 1990 cotton production quota of 2,300, a Jiangxi Province newspaper levy of 28.1, other newspaper levy of 140.5, and stamp duty of 8.43, a total of 5,647.42 *yuan.* Finally, Gao Village had to pay a village committee conference fee levy of 140.5, a levy for the village school of 838, a salary for village committee members levy of 1,459 and a village committee management levy of 281, a total of 2,718.5 *yuan.*

There were 308 people in Gao village in 1991, and *per capita* payment of taxes and levies in that year was 53.48 *yuan.* As the *per capita* gross income was 400 *yuan,* though it was reported to be 600 *yuan* to the county authorities, taxes and levies in 1991 amounted to 13.3 per cent of gross *per capita* income. If the various taxes paid to the government are excluded, the amount of the local levies was 36.6 *yuan,* which is 9.9 per cent of gross *per capita* income.

Compared with the rate of tax on personal income in developed countries, these rates do not seem very high. However, this comparison is not valid. To start with, the tax is regressive. No one is exempt from these taxes and levies in rural China and these are the rates for everyone. Second, the government and local authorities do almost nothing in return for the taxes and levies that the villagers pay. There are no hospitals and no school has been built since the Cultural Revolution. The villagers have to pay for education and medical services anyway. There are no public works and maintenance such as roads and sewerage in the villages. If there is a need for any public works such as roads or irrigation projects the villagers are called to work on them and to pay for them on top of these taxes and levies. In 1990, for instance, grain was collected at the value of 1,670.79 *yuan* from Gao Village to pay for the quota of irrigation work imposed by

General view of Gao Village from the south-west.

The author with his mother, sisters and brothers, and their children, by the house where he was born. He stands at the back, third from right.

Gao Changquan, Gao Village member of the Village Committee.

Above A village kitchen.

Right Christian setting in a villager's house. (The big character is the word for 'love', with sayings on the strokes. These are Christian messages as understood by the villagers.)

A village bed.

The village school classroom. The blackboard is the one the author used in the 1970s when he was a 'barefoot' teacher.

Close-up view of Gao Village.

the county and *xiang* authorities.[15] This contribution from Gao Village was in addition to their contribution to other projects and building material contributions such as gunny-sacks. Third, in contrast, urban residents in China are not only exempt from paying a personal income tax, but also have till recently been enjoying the benefit of virtually free accommodation, free education and free medical care. Their food is subsidised by the government and their per capita income, according to official figures, is on average at least three times more that that of rural residents.

The villagers are taxed four times over, by the state, the county, the *xiang* and the village committee, for education for which they end up paying again, in cash, if their children go to school. They have to pay *corvée* which they are ordered to do anyway; they have to pay for newspapers they do not read and family planning which they hate. Another levy, the so-called woman and child insurance levy, is actually for covering the cost of forced abortion. In 1991, they even had to pay for government bonds that they could not afford to buy! All this on top of the fact that since the late 1980s the villagers have not been allowed to sell any agricultural produce in the market unless the quota imposed on them to sell to the state at the state controlled prices has been fulfilled. It is pure plunder and exploitation by the state. And yet the post-Mao Chinese authorities and its establishment intelligentsia are singing songs about how the post-Mao reform has transformed peasants into masters of their own destiny.

In the early 1960s the figures suggest that the agricultural tax was around 10 per cent of gross income, and Public Accumulation and Public Welfare Funds took 7 per cent. Only around 60-70 per cent of the gross income in Qinglin was returned to the villagers for distribution while the rest was for various funds, taxes and agricultural inputs and management costs. During the period of the Cultural Revolution, the rates of taxes and levies were reduced according to statistics at the national level, though there are no firm figures available for Gao Village.[16]

---

[15] *Yinbaohu Xiang Guantian Cunweihui Gao Jiacun Xian Xiang Shangdian Jilei Ji Lianhu Lianxi Yu Gongkuan Biao*, 1990 (Contribution table by Gao Village for the County and Xiang infrastructure and Lianhu and Lianxi dykes, 1990).

[16] For the reduction of taxes at national level during the Cultural Revolution

In 1991, all the taxes and levies amounted to 13.3 per cent of the villagers' gross income. On the surface, the burden of taxes and levies seems lower in post-Mao China. However, in reality this is not the case if three important factors are taken into account. The first factor is that in Mao's China the 60-70 per cent of gross income for distribution was the percentage after agricultural inputs had been deducted. Since the late 1980s agricultural input costs, such as the cost of chemical fertilisers, rose rapidly. The case of Gao Changxian discussed in Chapter 5 is a good example. In 1992, Gao Changxian's crop income was 1,500 *yuan*, for which he spent 728 *yuan* on chemical fertilisers and insecticides. This input alone was 48 per cent of his gross income.

The second factor which should be taken into consideration in comparing the two periods is that income figures before the commune system was dismantled did not include crops from private plots. Income from crops and vegetables on private plots was at least 10 per cent of the total income in Gao Village since the amount of land allocated as private plots was around 10 per cent.[17] The third factor is that in Mao's China there was either direct investment from the state government in education and health or the villagers did not have to pay individually once collective funds were pooled for such purposes. The Qinglin School which was established through government funds in 1952, was expanded in 1958, and is still the only school in Qinglin apart from village schools run by villagers themselves. In the early 1960s until the end of the decade, two doctors were sent to Gao Village at the government's expense. Now in Qinglin there is not a single doctor paid by the state government. During the Cultural Revolution, a senior high school, a dozen village schools and a "barefoot doctor" clinic were established at the cost paid by the villagers collectively. But those who went to schools and saw the doctor at that time did not have to pay. Since the 1980s, however, the

---

period see Li Hengluo *et al.*, *Zhongguo Nongmin Fudan Shi, Di Si Zhuan* (History of taxes and levies burden of the Chinese peasants), vol. IV, Beijing, 1994, pp. 290-312.

[17] According to Whyte, in some areas, income from private plots and sideline production could be as high as 25 per cent. Martin King Whyte, "The Social Roots of China's Economic Development", *China Quarterly*, no. 144, Dec. 1995, pp. 999-1019. Also see He Liyi, *Mr China's Son: A Villager's Life*, Boulder, CO, 1994.

villagers are levied four times over the education, and yet those who go to school still have to pay.

In 1992, local levies were even more plundering. New items such as insurance for village officials (presumably because of the rising conflict between the villagers and village officials), a household record registration fee, house content insurance, a high-tension electricity network and program-controlled telephones were added. The last two items are purely for the benefit of the urban and town sector since they do not exist in rural areas. All in all, taxes and levies in Gao Village totalled 80 *yuan* per capita, which was 20 per cent of average *per capita* gross income.

Boyang County, indeed all of Jiangxi Province, was not the worst hit in this respect. In Hunan and Anhui Provinces for instance, peasants riots against brutal levies were reported. The situation was so serious that the central government was alarmed. Premier Li Peng and General Secretary of the Party Jiang Zemin both made stern speeches about the needs to curb local authorities. On 19 February 1992, the central office of the CCP and the central office of the State Council jointly issued an urgent circular in an attempt to curb increases in local levies. The Supreme People's Court and the Ministry of Supervision both issued documents prescribing guidelines for control of the local authorities. These documents state that the total local levies (excluding agricultural taxes by the state) should not exceed 5 per cent of the peasants' gross income. However, by 1996 nothing had changed. Gao villagers knew about the government's policy and guidelines concerning local levies, but that made no difference. Levies in 1993 were higher than in 1992, and they kept on increasing.

Local authorities can get away with imposing more levies by simply providing false statistics. For instance, the average per capita income in 1994 was reported to be 800 *yuan* whereas in fact it was no more than 500. According to the village committee accountant, the local authorities were told that Jiangxi provincial authorities would simply not accept their reports if the figures did not show a designated percentage increase in annual income. To give false statistics has of course long been the habit of local authorities in China. The head of the Education Bureau in Boyang County, who was one of my students back in the early 1970s, stated during an interview that all the statistics on education in

Boyang County, as far as he knew, had been inflated by at least 30 per cent.

If the villagers refuse to pay any of the levies, the village committee will instruct the local militia to storm the house and take whatever can be found. Pigs and furniture may be taken away as payment. This happened to two Gao villagers, one of whom was the village school teacher. Because of hospital costs for his wife, he had to withdraw his two sons from school. His two sons aged fourteen and sixteen had to leave Gao Village as migrant workers. Still, Gao Chaozhen could not afford to pay the levies that year. The militia sent by the village committee took away his pig as payment.

One reason village committee members are so aggressive is that their own salary payments are tied to fulfilment of the levy collection. According to *xiang* government policy, if only 70 per cent of levies are collected, they only get 70 per cent of their salaries. In fact, authorities at any level could set their own policies. For instance, in order to push the villagers to pay the levies on time, the Guantian village committee promulgated a policy that 30 per cent interest would be charged on overdue payments. Furthermore, the policy dictated that income from interest charges was to be given to village officials as a bonus.

It is not that the villagers do not resist the local authorities. Gao Renwei, the colourful figure who used to play the Buddha of Wang Taigong, for instance, once quarrelled with village officials and even fought with the militia who stormed into his house to take possession of his furniture. He was arrested and released only after he agreed to pay a fine of more than 2,000 *jin* of rice.

In Xifen Village in 1991, more than forty villagers together signed a letter of complaint and handed it to the county authorities in 1991. The person they complained about was the Party secretary of the Xifen village committee who, among other things, managed to spend money from the public purse to keep three mistresses at the same time. Nothing happened to him and he was still Party secretary in 1994. When I inquired as to the reason for his immunity I was told that the relevant authorities had been bribed by him with regular gifts. The common phrase in Qinglin is *chile zuiruan, nale shouruan* ("Your mouth becomes soft to the person who gives you food and your hands are soft to the person who gives you gifts").

Still, resistance against levies is not uncommon. For some people like Gao Chaodian, there is nothing that a village official can do. There was no worthwhile furniture to take possession of, and his family had to beg to survive when the food ran out. Gao Chaodian owed the Village Committee more than 1,000 *yuan* in 1994. He was charged 30 per cent interest on his debt. But the village committee could not do anything about him because he had nothing to be taken away.

Again, even the structure of debts reflects clan politics. For instance, by 1994, Xu villagers owed more than 40,000 *yuan* to Guantian village committee whereas in Gao Village, apart from Gao Chaodian, no one was allowed to be in debt. This is not because Gao villagers are generally better off than Xu villagers but because Xu village is the largest of the three villages in Guantian. The Party secretary and the accountant of the village committee are from Xu Village. In addition, Xu Village has the only doctor, Xu Congchun in Guantian. The deputy head of the *xiang* government, the only member from the Qinglin area Xu Xianjiao, is a Xu villager. Xu Xianzhen and Xu Guohua (the son of Xu Xianjiao), run the cotton and chemical fertiliser agencies for the *xiang* government. The village committee and the local militia are therefore less aggressive towards Xu villagers. Of course, if a villager like Gao Chaodian is completely broke there is nothing that anyone can do about his debts. However, the Xu Village households that owed the village committee 40,000 *yuan* do not belong to this category. Rather, because of the power that Xu Village has, some Xu villagers can get away with not paying, at least for some time.

In spite of the burden of levies on the villagers and the brutal measures taken against some villagers to extract payment, debts exist and local authorities are short of funds for public works. One of the three deputy heads of Yinbaohu *xiang* informed me during an interview in 1994 that the Yinbaohu *xiang* government budget in 1993 had a deficit of 70,000 *yuan*. While the villagers are crying out that the levies are too many and too much, local authorities think they are insolvent.

Reforms since the late 1970s have, however, had a positive impact on Gao Village in two main respects. One is that by disbanding the commune system Gao villagers are freer, that is, freer in the sense that they can grow crops of their own choice on their share of land, and can arrange their own time of work. The other is that price reforms in the early 1980s boosted Gao villagers' income. However, some qualifications need to be made in both respects.

First, the degree to which Gao villagers can pursue their own interests in terms of crop options is limited. To start with, Gao Village has to produce enough grain to feed its population. Gao villagers cannot opt for cash crops simply because these crops may increase income. Nor can they hope to purchase grain for self-consumption from the market: the transaction cost may not pay and furthermore there is no free market in the true sense of the word. Secondly, local authorities still command what to grow. From time to time, quotas are imposed from the above authorities dictating Gao villagers' crop options. For instance, from 1992-94, Gao villagers had to fulfil quotas of cotton, not because there was money to be made for Gao villagers but because the central government imposed quotas on Jiangxi Province so as to support China's textile industry.

The positive impact as a result of price reforms also has to be qualified. To put it simply, the benefit of price reform was short-lived. There are two reasons for this. One is that since 1985, quotas of state purchase and restrictions on market sale were re-imposed on rural residents. Gao villagers had to fulfil the purchase quotas of the state before they could sell anything at the market. Moreover, there was no market price in a real sense since local authorities had put a ceiling on most types of agricultural produce. Secondly, price increases in industrial goods soon caught up, and the cost of agricultural inputs cancelled out any benefit from the price increases for agricultural output. During my interviews, Gao villagers estimated that by the early 1990s agricultural output per *mu* produced by some households had increased by one-third compared with that during the 1970s. However, I was reassured by Gao villagers and my brother Gao Changxian that the increase was not simply a result of household ownership of land. It was largely a result of more intensive application of effective chemicals.

While reforms since Mao have brought some qualified benefit to Gao villagers the reforms have also destroyed some positive initiatives developed during the Cultural Revolution. The most obvious areas are rural education and health care. In spite of all their faults and problems, local education and health care developed through cooperative effort during the 1970s and had provided basic but essential services to rural residents like Gao villagers. The Chinese élite may not have much time for such cooperatives; but for the rural residents they were effective and affordable. Since the reforms, while more education and health care resources were channelled towards the urban sector and the privileged, rural residents were left to fend for themselves. Village schools in most villages including Gao Village have not been dismantled. They still function, though on a smaller scale, and provide an essential education service to the villagers. But there has been a return to clan culture, a more widespread and higher level of corruption by local officials, an increase in the crime rate, and brutal and arbitrary local levies.

By and large, either during the pre-reform or post-reform period, income from agriculture alone had not fundamentally changed the quality of life and standards of living for Gao villagers. It was an involutionary development of grave environmental consequences through which Gao villagers were kept in a poverty trap. If there was any hope of prosperity brought about by the reforms during the early 1980s, that hope was dashed by the end of the decade. It was the industrial development along the costal south that helped Gao Village look forward to the future.

11

MIGRANT WORKERS[1]

Since the late 1980s, a large number of rural residents have left their homes to work in the fast developing areas in coastal south China. By the mid 1990s, it was estimated that the number of people, mostly rural, constantly on the move, and working away from home had reached 100 million in China at any given time.[2] By 1995, ninety-eight Gao villagers had left as migrant workers, about 30 per cent of the total population of the village. Such a large percentage of people leaving the village not only reduced the ecological and resource pressure on the village territory, but also provided unprecedented cash income for the villagers.

This phenomenon is not isolated to Gao Village. In Jiang Village, the *per capita* net income in 1992 from farming was around 200 *yuan*. This was less than the income from migrant workers' remittances in the same year, a total of 130,000 *yuan*, which gave Jiang Village an extra per capita income of 216 *yuan*. According to the head of the *xiang* government, 20 per cent of the population in Yinbaohu *xiang* had left as migrant workers by 1992. In Youdunjie Region, an area that has a population of 140,000, 40,000 rural people had left as migrant workers by 1994.

There are a number of "push and pull" factors that have worked together and brought about this unprecedented phenomenon of

---

[1] The information and statistics in this chapter are based on two field work research trips made in 1992 and 1994 to Xiamen and Guangdong. Some of the information and statistics are also used in Mobo C.F. Gao, "Migrant Workers from Rural China: Their Conditions and Some Social Implications for Economic Development in South China" in David Schak, ed., *Entrepreneurship Economic Growth and Social Change: The Transformation of Southern China*, Brisbane: Centre for the Studies of Australian and Asian Relations 1994, and "Welfare Needs and Problems of Migrant Workers in South China" in Wing Lo and Joseph Cheng, eds, *Social Welfare Development in China, Constraints and Challenges*, Chicago: Imprint Publications, 1997, pp. 101-20.

[2] Martin King Whyte, 'The Social Roots of China's Economic Development," *China Quarterly*, no. 144, Dec. 1995, pp. 999-1019.

migration in China. One factor has been the government's loosening of controls surrounding household registration. Another is the rapid industrial development which has occurred in the coastal south, providing work opportunities for rural residents. A third factor is the increasing deterioration of the rural situation since the late 1980s. With the rapid rise of input costs in farming and the increase in local levies, the villagers have been forced to leave their villages as migrant workers.

As we saw in Chapter 10, the loosening of state control which lay behind post-Mao reform policies, such as the disbanding of the commune system and the formation of the Financial Contract System, though it did not lead to a breakdown of the state in rural Qinglin, nonetheless gave rise to abuses of power and corruption by local officials. The function and role of grassroots authorities such as the village committee and the *xiang* government are little more than that of extracting taxes and levies from the villagers, who are left as victims of the arbitrary rule by corrupt local officials. Reform since the late 1970s has restored rural life to its clan structure controlled by village powerholders. One could easily imagine that the Communist revolution in 1949 had never taken place. As was the case before 1949, the villagers are left at the mercy of local lords, only such local lords in present-day China can be more unscrupulous because they are not constrained by any sense of moral responsibility as some of the gentry before 1949 had been by the Confucian code of behaviour.

Of course, we must be cautious not to overstate the similarities between the periods before 1949 and that in post-Mao China. For one thing, the clans and Communist local officials have not yet totally merged as one political body. Whilst before 1949 clan power and the gentry were intertwined, in present-day China clan power and the local official authorities still comprise two distinct political entities. Nonetheless there is a great deal of overlap. Furthermore, if the state chooses to, it can still exert power over the local authorities. A clear example of this is the implementation of family planning policies. Since the early 1990s, a large number of abortions and IUD operations have been forcefully carried out in Qinglin and Gao Village, and local clan power has been unable, and in fact has never tried, to stop these brutal measures. The state is also able to impose production and procurement quotas and procurement prices. So far at least, clan power focuses not on organised resistance against state power but on inter-village politics.

Though the dismantling of the commune system and decentralisation of financial responsibilities for revenue and expenditure has not led to a complete breakdown of the state, the result has nevertheless been an increasingly deteriorating situation for the villagers in areas like Qinglin. This has been an important "push factor" for the villagers to leave as migrant workers.

However, in other areas such as Guangdong and Fujian where there has been rapid industrialisation and commercialisation (either as a result of foreign investment and/or the expansion of township enterprises) the situation is more positive. Industrialisation in these areas has turned a large number of villages into towns, and towns into cities. As urbanisation takes place rapidly the economy of self-sufficiency breaks down, and with it disappears the cellular nature of the village structure. Commercialisation has also flourished in these areas.[3] In the most commercially developed provinces, on average one in every seven rural households has been involved in non-agricultural businesses.[4] One likely consequence of such industrial development and commercialisation is that with income from industrial production, local authorities can raise sufficient revenue without having to plunder the villagers for financial income.

Therefore, one positive outcome of the decentralisation of responsibility for revenue and expenditure in post-Mao China has been the push for local authorities to attract external investment, to expand township enterprises, and to initiate local projects, albeit some have been unrealistic and wasteful (like the tobacco project in Boyang).[5] Unfortunately, inland areas like Boyang are not in

---

[3] For the development of commercialisation in these areas see, for instance, William A. Byrd, "The Impact of the Two-Tier Plan/Market System in Chinese Industry", *Journal of Comparative Economics*, vol. 11, no. 3, 1987, pp. 295-380; *China: Internal Market Development and Regulation*, Washington, DC: World Bank, 1994. Jean Oi, *State and Peasant in Contemporary China: the Political Economy of Village Government*, Berkeley, 1989; Andrew Watson, "The Reform of Agricultural Marketing in China since 1978", *China Quarterly*, no. 113, 1988, pp. 1-28.

[4] Barbara Entwisle *et al.*, "Gender and Family Businesses in Rural China", *American Sociological Review*, vol. 60, 1995, pp. 36-57.

[5] For a discussion of how the fiscal reform has positively affected the development of rural industry see Jean C. Oi, "The Role of the Local State in China's Transitional Economy", *China Quarterly*, no. 144, December 1995, pp. 1132-49.

a good position to develop local industries on their own initiative. First of all, because of geographical location and lack of infrastructure, there was little chance that foreign investment would want to locate in places like Boyang. Second, for the same reason, fewer opportunities had existed in these areas for the expansion of locally owned township and village enterprises.

The rapid growth of township and village enterprises has been crucial to China since Mao's time.[6] According to one estimate, their "industrial output grew by nearly 17 per cent a year, and their output of services by 19 per cent a year."[7] By the end of 1991, the total production value by township enterprises had reached 11,000 billion *yuan*, one-third of the total industrial production value of China. These enterprises employed more than 100 million workers and used only 5 per cent of China's total investment capital.[8] In the fastest developing province, Guangdong, township enterprises also played an important role. In 1991, the income from township enterprises was 62 per cent of Guangdong's total production value. Exports made by township enterprises reached a value of US $3.5 billion or about 25 per cent of Guangdong's export value of that year.[9]

This success is often attributed to post-Mao de-collectivisation. In a comment typical of this kind, Vicziany states: "Economic reform in the Chinese case entailed above all else, the de-collectivisation of agriculture. The response to this has been an enormous upsurge of entrepreneurial spirit in the countryside, such that the resulting diversification of economic activity in rural China has created rural industries which are 'the most dynamic sector of the economy'."[10] However, it is worth remembering

[6] Gary Jefferson, "Are China's Rural Enterprises Outperforming State-Owned Enterprises?", Research Paper no. CH-RPS#24, World Bank, 1993.

[7] Christopher Findlay, Andrew Watson and Harry X. Wu, "Economic Liberalization in China: the Impact and Prospects for the 'Out-of-Plan' Sector", *Asian Studies Review*, vol. 17, no. 2, Nov. 1993, pp. 3-29.

[8] *Xinhua Yuebao* (Xinhua Monthly), no. 1, 1993, p. 49.

[9] Pen Kunlun, "Guangdong Xiangzhen Qiye Yunxing Jizhi De Tuantao" (A Discussion on the Mechanism of Township Enterprises in Guangdong), *Zhongshan Daxue Xuebao* (Zhongshan University Journal), no. 4, 1992, pp. 8-14.

[10] Marika Vicziany, "Economic Liberalisation in Asia: Its Meaning and consequences, Introduction", *Asian Studies Review*, vol. 17, no. 2, Nov. 1993, p. 2.

that in principle, the form of ownership of township and village enterprises is not different from the commune system. Most township and village enterprises in post–Mao China are collective and controlled by local rural governments as much as were land and production brigade and team enterprises in Mao's China,[11] to the extent that some China scholars call rural enterprises in post–Mao China "local state corporatism".[12]

Moreover, township and village enterprises did not simply spring up in China after Mao. The roots of their success can be traced back to past experience and the legacies of Mao's reign.[13] Most successful township enterprises have grown from the initiatives of production brigade and team enterprises developed during the Great Leap Forward and the Cultural Revolution. During the Great Leap Forward, a policy of "walking on two legs" (a policy to balance the relationship between industry and agriculture, between heavy and light industries and between centrally planned and local industries) was carried out. In 1958, 885 of the 1,165 enterprises run by the central government were devolved to the local authorities.[14] Under the policy of "industry run by communes", the communes took the initiative to run small foundries, coal mines, power stations, cement factories, and fertiliser, agricultural tool and food processing workshops. Six million commune factories

[11] Louis Putterman, "The Role of Ownership and Property Rights in China's Economic Transition", *China Quarterly*, no. 144, Dec. 1995, pp. 1047-64.

[12] Jean C. Oi, "Fiscal Reform and the Economic Foundations of Local State Corporatism", *World Politics*, vol. 45, no. 1, October 1992, pp. 99-126; Jonathan Unger and Anita Chan, "Corporatism and the East Asian Model", *Australian Journal of Chinese Affairs*, no. 33, Jan. 1995, pp. 29-54.

[13] For the connection between Maoist legacies and the post-Mao rural development see Carl Riskin, *China's Political Economy*, New York, 1987; Elizabeth J. Perry and Christine P.W. Wong (eds), *The Political Economy of Reform in Post-Mao China*, Cambridge, MA, 1985; Carl Riskin, "Small Industry and the Chinese Model of Development", *China Quarterly*, no. 46, April-June 1971, pp. 245-73; Dwight Pekins (ed.), *Rural Small-Scale Industry in the People's Republic of China*, Berkeley, 1977. Christine P.W. Wong, "Ownership and Control in Chinese Industry: the Maoist legacy and Prospects for the 1980s" in Joint Economic Committee, Congress of the United States, *China's Economy Looks Towards the Year 2000*, vol. 1; David Granick, *Chinese State Enterprises: A Regional Property Rights Analysis*, Chicago, 1990.

[14] Bo Yibo, *Luogan Zhongda Shijian Yu Juece de Huiguo* (Reflections on Several important Events and Decisions), vol. II, Beijing, 1993, p. 798.

were set up in 1958.[15] By the end of the first half of 1959, enterprises run by communes numbered 700,000, with a total production value of 7,100 million *yuan*, or 10 per cent of China's total industrial output.[16]

Because of readjustment policies carried out by Liu Shaoqi and Deng Xiaoping in the early 1960s, most of these enterprises were closed down. However, the local authorities had the experience and retained some of the technology, and this proved useful during the Cultural Revolution when decentralisation was again stressed and local initiatives again encouraged. By 1976, the industrial output of production brigade and team enterprises had already reached 12.39 billion *yuan*.[17] By 1978 when the reform which followed Mao's death was about to start there were already 1.52 million production brigade and team enterprises which were later called township enterprises. By 1990, the number of enterprises had in fact declined to 1.45 million. It is not the number of enterprises but their overall scale which really took off after 1978. In 1978, 1.52 million local enterprises employed 28.27 million workers whereas in 1990 the number of workers employed in 1.45 million enterprises reached 45.92 million.[18]

According to Wong, by 1979 production brigade and team enterprises already ran 90,000 small hydro-electric stations, produced all of the farm tools, nearly all the small and medium-sized farm machineries, more than 50 per cent of fertilisers, one-third of cement and 45 per cent of coal output in China.[19] A case study of Wenzhou by Kristen Parris also supports this general picture. According to Parris, household production and trade "were characteristic of Wenzhou during the Cultural Revolution when,

---

[15] Edward Friedman *et al.*, *Chinese Village Socialist State*, New Haven and London, 1991, p. 227.

[16] Huang Daoxia *et al.*, *Jidang Zhongguo Nongcun De Biange* (The reform that shook the Chinese countryside), Beijing, 1988, p. 115.

[17] Huang Daoxia, *et al.*, *ibid.*

[18] *Xiangzhen Qiye Nianjian 1978-1987* (Township Enterprises Year Book 1978-1987), Beijing 1989, and *Zhongguo Tongji Nianjian 1991* (China Statics Year Book 1991), Beijing, 1991, pp. 315-78.

[19] Christine P.W. Wong, 'The Maoist 'Model' Reconsidered: Local Self-Reliance and the Financing of Rural Industrialisation" in William Joseph *et al.*, *New Perspectives on the Cultural Revolution*, 1991, pp. 153-82.

as in some other areas, state control weakened considerably. By the mid-1970s most of eastern Wenzhou prefecture had developed an alternative economy that was the basis of what would become known as the Wenzhou model in the 1980s".[20]

These enterprises in areas such as Jiangsu, Zhejiang, Guangdong and Shandong have developed rapidly since the 1980s because of opportunities that had not existed in areas like Boyang County in Jiangxi Province. Unlike the areas surrounding Shanghai and Guangzhou, there had never been a tradition of commerce in the Qinglin area and the economy had always been enclosed and self-sufficient. Transportation was backward, and there was no market. Nor was there any information technology available for new development. It is not that there was no attempt to establish production brigade and team enterprises in Qinglin. For example, one oil mill owned and operated by the brigade was set up in 1974, employing seven people. In 1975, another associate enterprise, a rice mill, was set up. By 1978, there were seven production brigade and team enterprises in Qinglin, including a tile and brick kiln, altogether employing 116 people, with an annual gross income of 40,000 *yuan*. However, by the time the commune system was disbanded in 1981, these enterprises all had deficits and were thus dismantled.

The explanation for the dismal situation of these enterprises is not hard to find. First of all, most of the enterprises such as flour mills, oil mills and cotton gins were processing rather than manufacturing workshops. Therefore, no manufacturing value was added in Qinglin. The only manufacturing workshop, the tile and brick kiln, was doomed to run at a loss because there was a lack of fuel. All hills and mountains had been stripped bare as a result of firewood being needed for cooking in the area. By the late 1960s, most households in Qinglin had to purchase firewood from far away. The villagers used to pull a wheelbarrow to transport firewood for cooking from as far as 50 kilometres away. There was no coal available and the cost of firewood for a kiln was prohibitive. These enterprises could keep on running for a number of years largely because of the support of the collective system. Once that support was gone, there was no economic basis for

---

[20] Kristen Parris, "Local Initiative and National Reform: the Wenzhou Model of Development", *China Quarterly*, no. 134, June 1993, pp. 244-5.

their existence. With no access to markets, technology, information or external investment, it was very difficult, if not impossible, to develop local enterprises in the Qinglin area.

By the late 1980s, pressure and hardships had been mounting from all directions on Gao villagers. Because of the population expansion, which by now had lasted for four decades, ecological pressures had reached a potentially disastrous level. The forest and bushes around the village had been destroyed as a result of the increasing demand for firewood. As a consequence of the increasing application of chemical fertilisers and insecticides to produce more grain for a rapidly increasing population, aquatic life which in the past had been an important source of nutritious food had been wiped out. The villagers had to rely on crop production alone to survive.

By the end of the Cultural Revolution, the rural situation in Gao Village was indeed on the brink of disaster, but it was not for the reason proclaimed by the post-Mao Chinese authorities and their Establishment intelligentsia. It was not because of the political movement of the Cultural Revolution, which was said to have led to leadership chaos. Nor was it because of the commune system, which was said to have encouraged laziness and discouraged incentives. The two main reasons were the ecological pressure which had resulted from a doubling of the population, and the exploitative pricing system imposed by the government.

The post-Mao reform of the pricing system did provide a breathing space for several years for Gao villagers in the early 1980s. However, with the rapid rise in agricultural input costs since the late 1980s and the re-introduction of mandatory procurement by the state, the effect of the increase in prices for agricultural produce had been cancelled out. By the late 1980s, a large amount of surplus labour had been accumulated as a result of the population increase. Yet there was no local industry which could absorb the surplus labour and which could provide a source of revenue for the local authorities. Most serious of all, the decentralisation of responsibility for revenue and expenditure had enabled the local authorities to resort to plundering measures to squeeze as much as possible out of the already poverty-stricken villagers. It was under these circumstances that industrial development far away from Gao Village in the coastal south provided families with a solution which averted an explosive situation.

By 1995, eighty-five young men and thirteen young women had left Gao Village as migrant workers. They were all aged between fourteen and twenty-five. The only old villager was Gao Renfeng who was forty-eight. Gao Renfeng was able to find work as a migrant worker at this age because he had acquired some skills as a mechanic during the commune period. At that time he was assigned to look after an engine and water pump for paddy irrigation for Gao Village. Now he works as a mechanic in a workshop in Guangzhou. There are also nine Gao villagers who were apprenticed as carpenters, painters and bamboo crafts people before they left Gao Village, and most of them were able to use their skills as migrant workers. But for the majority the work they do usually demands very little skill. They are mostly engaged in making shoes, garments, toys, kitchenware or simple tools. The work is repetitive and monotonous, demanding physical attention rather than mental agility.

By 1995, thirty-four Gao villagers had gone to the city of Shantou in Guangdong Province, eighteen to Hainan, fourteen to the city of Xiamen in Fujian Province, seven to Nanchang, the capital of Jiangxi Province, four to Jiujiang, four to Jingdezhen,

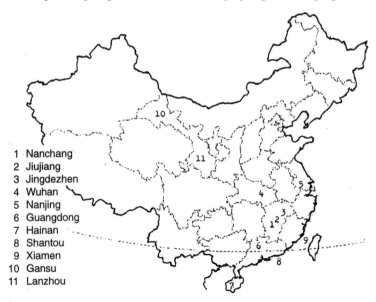

1 Nanchang
2 Jiujiang
3 Jingdezhen
4 Wuhan
5 Nanjing
6 Guangdong
7 Hainan
8 Shantou
9 Xiamen
10 Gansu
11 Lanzhou

Places where Gao villagers went as migrant workers

three to Nanjing, one to Wuhan and two to Lanzhou. The rest
still do not have a fixed place of work, but roam around to look
for temporary jobs. Those who went to the three nearest places
(Nanchang, Jiujiang and Jingdezhen) are mostly working as nannies
if they are female and carpenters and painters if they are male.
The accompanying map shows where Gao villagers have gone as
migrant workers. The way these Gao villagers got to work in
these places is typical of rural migration in present China. First
of all, they went where they had relatives and friends. Those
who went to Nanchang, Jingdezhen and Jiujiang all had some
relationship with former Gao villagers who lived in these places.
Five Gao villagers had been able to move to Jingdezhen and
Jiujiang in the 1950s and two went to Nanchang during the
Cultural Revolution. In the 1980s, these people themselves, or
their connections in these cities, were able to find work for Gao
villagers who had some relationship with them.

Second, enterprises in coastal south China do not usually need
to advertise for positions. There are always many young people
from rural areas looking for work. When these enterprises want
to recruit more workers, they tend to ask their employees to
nominate their fellow villagers. By doing this, the employers are
not only able to avoid any cost of advertising, but also avoid
government scrutiny in terms of working conditions and tax arrangements. By avoiding the official channel of advertisement the
employers can get away with not having to sign a contract with
migrant workers. Furthermore, the existing employees are required
to act as guarantors for their fellow villagers. The guarantees required
cover labour discipline, workshop theft, level of education and
age. If anything goes wrong, not only the new employee but also
his or her guarantor is punished. As a result of this system, there
is usually a group of migrant workers who are fellow villagers in
one workshop. For instance, all the eight migrant workers from
Gao Village in Xiamen work in one kitchenware factory, and
they were all nominated by Gao Changwen.

It is also typical that the villagers do not just support any fellow
villager but tend to support those from the same genealogical
branch. Thus, those who went to Xiamen are of one genealogical
branch, those in Shantou another branch and those in Hainan
still another branch. Gao Changwen is a case in point. Every
Spring Festival when he goes back to Gao Village for a visit,

parents come to him and beg him to take their children to Xiamen to work. However, Gao Changwen can only nominate one or two a year. Usually, his choice is made on the basis of genealogical proximity.

During the 1990s, earnings by migrant workers ranged from 300 to 400 *yuan* a month, or 8 to 10 *yuan* a day. Some may earn a little more than 400 if they are engaged in piece work. However, the rate of piece work is always set so that to earn more than 600 *yuan* a month is rare, even if the workers push themselves to their physical limit. The best accommodation for migrant workers are factory dormitories. A standard dormitory is a room of 10 to 16 square meters shared by ten to sixteen people of the same sex. There are usually bunk beds of two layers, and migrant workers have to bring their own bedding. There is usually nothing except a bare bulb hanging in the middle of the room. All their belongings are either placed on the bed or under it. Everyone has a mosquito net to ensure some privacy.

They all have to pay for the lodging, which ranges from 30 to 50 *yuan* a month. Some enterprises do not provide lodging, and their employees have to live in shelters they build themselves. These are usually built from a cardboard box, bamboo poles or whatever can be picked up from the rubbish dump. These shelters can be seen in Shenzhen, Shantou and Xiamen. Every migrant worker has a plastic basin and bucket to fetch water from a nearby tap or well to drink and to wash. Migrant workers all eat in a factory canteen which provides the same basic food every day: porridge and pickled vegetables for breakfast, some steamed rice with whatever seasonal vegetables are available mixed with a few pieces of meat, mostly pork fat, for lunch and supper. Most migrant workers have to buy food from a street corner shop to supplement their diet.

These migrant workers have to work six or seven days a week. A typical working day is ten to fourteen hours and some work as long as twenty hours. For most migrant workers, any time that can be spared is spent sleeping. Occasionally they play poker or mahjong. A local resident may set up a couple of snooker tables near the factory for the workers to play on. One in Xiamen charged each player half a *yuan* a go and another in Shenzhen charged 1 *yuan* for a game. Some youngsters get so bored that they spend all their savings on gambling. The most popular leisure activity is visiting and chatting with fellow workers from the same place of origin. Occasionally, they may have a glimpse of television programmes in a corner shop. In some factories, a television set is provided for the workers in the canteen.

It is not possible for a migrant worker to determine their hourly rate of pay. This is because there is no such thing as an eight-hour working day. With or without a contract, migrant workers are not told about the hours of work at the start of employment. Only a monthly wage is determined in advance. Therefore, the most common way for private enterprises to extract as much as possible from migrant workers is to make them work as long as possible. If any migrant workers refuse to work overtime, they can either be dismissed straight away or be punished by having their wages reduced. Piece work is just as exploitative because no piece rate is stipulated and migrant workers are only told that if they produce so many pieces they will receive so much.

A survey by the Guangdong Provincial Trade Union shows that 60 per cent of workers work seven days a week without any holiday, more than half of the workers work an average of ten to twelve hours a day and more than half of the workers do more than three hours' overtime a day. One factory in Longhuazhen was found to make workers work 244 hours overtime a month.[21] The kitchenware factory in Xiamen where eight Gao villagers are working had a profit of more than 20 million *yuan* in 1993. On paper, the basic wage of an average worker in this factory was 250 *yuan* a month in 1993. Another 100 *yuan* is added for overtime work to make a package of 350 *yuan* a month. However, the number of hours of overtime work was not specified either orally or on paper. The average overtime was four hours a day and thirty hours a week. Sometimes when told by the boss that there was an increase in customer orders, overtime could be as long as eight hours a day. If a worker refused to work overtime, a penalty of 5-10 *yuan* a day was deducted from the so-called basic wage. Refusal to work overtime several times would result in dismissal. A migrant worker does not have the option to refuse

---

[21] Xu Tingfei, *Yangcheng Wanbao* (Yangcheng Evening News), 21 May 1994, p. 2.

to work overtime for thirty-odd hours a week for an extra of 100 *yuan* a month.

Working conditions in these private factories are primitive at best and at worst very dangerous. Workshops are crowded, polluted, and extremely hot in summer. In some workshops that I visited in 1994, the level of noise was unbearable. A survey of seven Taiwan-funded factories in Zhuhai showed that the level of chemicals in the air, such as methylbenzene and ethylbenzene, were eight to ten times higher than the internationally accepted standards.[22] According to Li Niangui, a journalist from the Chinese official Xinhua News Agency who wrote a report for "internal reference", of the 260 workers who had a physical examination, forty-six were found to have either anaemia or abnormalities in their white blood cells. Of the 486 migrant workers who had a physical examination in Cheshi *xiang*, 83 per cent were found to be sick, 27 per cent had contracted occupational diseases and 17 per cent had work-related injuries or suffered from depression.[23]

There are frequent reports of the poor standards of work safety and mistreatment of migrant workers. The most frequently reported accidents involve injuries such as losing fingers or arms. In a hardware factory in Shenzhen, there were five accidents in the space of a single week in which workers' fingers were cut off. The boss refused to take any measures to prevent further accidents. An investigation in the city of Dongguan in Guangdong Province showed that within two months in 1993, sixty workers lost fingers, ten workers lost arms and there were two deaths.[24]

There are no national statistics available on the injuries and deaths caused by such accidents. However, figures from a specific area may indicate the seriousness of the situation. By 1994, when 4,000 villagers had left Yinbaohu as migrant workers, six migrant worker villagers from Yinbaohu *xiang* had died as a result of

[22] Yu Jiwen, "Waishang Qiye Qinhai Laogong Shili Zongshu" (A general sketch of the violation of workers' rights by foreign enterprises), *Jiushi Niandai* (The Nineties), April 1994, pp. 56-9.

[23] Li Niangui, *Yixie Waishang Touzi Qiye Yanzhong Qinfan Zhigong Hefa Quanyi* (Serious violation of the legal rights and interests of the workers by some foreign business enterprises). An extract of the report was published in the April issue of *Jiushi Niandai* 1994.

[24] *Dalu Xiaoxi, Gongdang Wenti Yanjiu* (Mainland News: Studies of the problems of the Communist Party of China), vol. 12, no. 4, 1994, p. 88.

work related accidents. According to this rate, of the 100 million migrant workers all over China, 15,000 deaths would have been caused by work related accidents by 1994.

Settlement for such accidents varies from place to place. On the basis of the death compensation paid to the six villagers in Yinbaohu *xiang*, an average death compensation in the 1990s was 10,000 *yuan* (according to the current exchange rate US $1 equals a bit more than 8 *yuan*). A boy from Jiang Village was crippled by an industrial accident in 1990 and is now unable to move. He was made a one-off compensation payment of 5,000 *yuan*. Gao Yuangui broke his left foot while working in Shantou in 1991. The boss only paid 80 per cent of his hospital costs and he was subsequently dismissed. In some places, the injured worker is hospitalised at the cost of the employer until they are well enough to work. If the worker is not able to resume work, he or she will be dismissed, some with a little compensation, and others with nothing. In the Xiamen kitchenware factory where Gao villagers work, a worker once lost all the fingers of one hand. Apart from the hospital cost, the worker was paid six months' basic wage, that is six times 250 *yuan*.

In another case in the same factory, the skin of a worker's whole arm was accidentally peeled off by a machine lathe. The factory owner paid the worker 20,000 *yuan* for hospital costs – more than two death compensation payments.[25] According to the same informants, the boss in their factory would rather see a worker die in an accident than live with a serious injury because the survivors cost more. Once when a forest area was being cleared for the expansion of a factory site, a migrant worker was struck by a falling tree. The boss laughed when he saw that the worker was dead and was pleased because death compensation was cheaper than hospital costs. The boss, a man from Hong Kong, said the worker's red blood prophesied a lucky beginning for the new factory site.

Migrant workers are victims of other forms of mistreatment and exploitation. One common practice is that of "dodging payment". A factory owner may make the workers work for unreasonably long hours, to the extent that they cannot cope physically. As a result the workers' so-called normal wages are

[25] Interviews with four Gao Village migrant workers in May 1994.

docked as punishment. According to one report, eighty-nine factories in Guangdong were found to have used this method to
deduct a total of 850,000 *yuan* from their workers' earnings in
1993. One factory in Henggangzhen deducted 130,000 *yuan* in
two months.[26] Another method is to delay payment or break the
promise of a pay rise. In the kitchenware factory in Xiamen, for
instance, whenever customers' orders come in and the boss wants
the workers to work hard, he will promise everyone a pay rise.
However, for two consecutive years this had never eventuated.
Some employers find excuses not to pay the workers. A leather
factory in Shenzhen only gave 100 *yuan* a month to its workers
as a living allowance for the whole of 1993. The reason given
to the workers was that the boss was not around.[27] The boss in
a Huatai electronics factory was reported to have deducted half
a month's wages from his workers because they went home for
their traditional Spring Festival in February. Workers in a garment
factory in Fuyongzhen went on strike many times because their
wages were always in arrears. Their wages for August 1993 were
not paid until the end of October, and those for November and
December had not been paid when the workers were preparing
to go home for the Spring Festival in February.[28]

In many cases, factory rules and discipline are arbitrary, without
any external accountability. In a factory in Baoan in Guangdong,
one of the thirteen factory rules is that anyone who violates the
rules will be caned like a dog.[29] Most factories use fines as a
major method of management. Workers may be fined for going
to the toilet, for being sick, or for leave of absence. One Taiwan-
funded factory in Fuzhou stipulates that sick leave of one hour
incurs a fine of 2 *yuan*, and any sick leave longer than one hour
is taken to be an absence of a whole day, the penalty for which
is to deduct three days' wage.

Other measures employed by the factory owners to intimidate
migrant workers and to make them submit to the boss's orders include
various kinds of deposits. Upon employment migrant workers are
required to pay, or have deducted from their first payments, a

[26] *Shenzhen Tequ bao* (Shenzhen Special Economic Zone Daily), 3 Jan. 1993.

[27] *Shenzhen Shangbao* (Shenzhen Commercial Daily), 14 Jan. 1994, p. 1.

[28] *Ibid.*, 1 Feb. 1994, p. 11.

[29] *Yangcheng Wanbao* (Yangcheng Evening News), 29 Mar. 1994, p. 8.

security deposit, a contract deposit if there is a contract, a tool deposit, a temporary residence nomination deposit and a resignation deposit. These deposits can total between 400-1,000 *yuan*. Some migrant workers are stuck with their employers because of these outrageous deposits.

Even without these deposits, private enterprises in China do not have difficulty in finding rural residents who are willing to work like slaves. The huge surplus of labour in China provides a "reserve army" of a limitless number of workers. Cash payments, however low and exploitative by Western standards, are very attractive to rural residents in China. Until they become migrant workers they have never seen so much cash in their lives. Out of the 300-400 *yuan* earned per month, most can save at least 100 *yuan* and some can save up to 200 *yuan* a month. Back home, an annual remittance of 1,200-2,400 *yuan* is of great value to the rural villagers. As for the working conditions in these private enterprises, they do not seem harsher than those in the paddy fields. At least they are away from the sun in summer and cold and wet in winter. In any case these rural youngsters are not aware of the health hazards caused by unhealthy working conditions – partly because of their ignorance and partly because it may take a number of years for the symptoms to appear. As for accidents, these youngsters, like drivers, tend to think that they are lucky, and that accidents will not happen to them. On top of the incentive of cash earnings and their lack of awareness of health problems, there is a sense of excitement for the rural young to be able to travel far and work in big cities.

However migrant workers think and feel about their work and conditions, it is a *laissez-faire* style of capitalism similar to that witnessed in eighteenth- and nineteenth-century Europe. However, there are "Chinese characteristics" that alleviate the pain and hardship of migrant workers. One of these is the sense of obligation towards one's fellow villagers. Because of the recruitment process, workers tend to form groups whose members are from the same place of origin. Traditional Chinese culture is such that even someone from the same province gives a migrant worker some sense of identity and obligation. Once outside their home town enclosure, villagers from the same county, and especially from the same village, treat each other as members of the same family. If someone is sick, the others can be relied on to stand in; they lend money to each other in cases of emergency; they may fight together to defend themselves from outside bullying and even fight together with the boss. Without a trade union to back them up, this group identity can sometimes act as a deterrent to the boss, who may find it more difficult to deal with a group of discontented young workers than with an individual.

The case of Gao Changwen is an example. Because Gao Changwen was the first to leave Gao village as a migrant worker, and because he is the most educated of the Gao Village migrant workers, almost every other day there is somebody coming to him for help. They come to him if they want to find a job, to borrow money, or when they want a place to sleep. During the five years that he worked as an assistant manager for a salary of more than 800 *yuan* a month he lent a couple of thousand *yuan* to those who came to seek help without expecting them ever to pay it back. Sometimes, a Gao villager, or a villager from Qinglin may just arrive at his door unannounced and expect him to fix everything. In such a case, Gao Changwen has either to find a job for the villager or buy a train ticket to send the villager back home. If he failed to do this, Gao Changwen would not have the face to go back to Gao Village. All seven migrant workers from Gao Village in the kitchenware factory were introduced by Gao Changwen, who acted as their guarantor. In return, these villagers are fiercely loyal to Gao Changwen to the extent that whatever Gao Changwen needs to be done his "followers" are ready to help. Gao Changwen said that if the boss sacked him all his people would leave at once. This prospect, Gao Changwen said, has made his boss treat him rather cautiously.

The "push and pull" factors are such that a young Gao villager is considered odd if he or she stays in the village. In fact, virtually all the young people in Gao village have gone. The very few who remain are considered to be incompetent. Every household has at least one youngster who has left. In some households as many as three in the family have left. By 1996, there were only four households in Gao Village which did not include migrant workers. Two of these do not yet have children big enough to be migrant workers while the parents are too old to go. Each of the other two households has a young man who could leave Gao Village as a migrant worker but have not left because one is the village head and the other is the village accountant. One of these two households is that of Gao Changquan, a member of the village committee and a heavy smoker and drinker. His son is at home because he is the head of Gao Village. Together, they virtually run Gao Village. The rest of the villagers are either middle aged or elderly men and women who work on the land to pay agriculture taxes and use remittance money from their sons and daughters to pay the local levies.

Most migrant workers from Gao Village can send some money home. In 1993 the average annual remittance was 2,000 *yuan*. There were three villagers who each managed to send 5,000 *yuan* back to Gao Village in 1993. One is a bricklayer whose skills are in demand in Shantou. The other two villagers succeeded in contracting some building work for which they acted as sub-agents. As sub-agents they employed groups of migrant workers. Their income came from the difference between what they paid the migrant workers and what they were paid under the contract. 5,000 *yuan* is a large amount of money by any standard in Gao Village. The villagers use the money sent by the migrant workers to build houses, to send little sisters and brothers to school, to pay the local levies, and most important of all, to save to get their sons married. The young men are supposed to work as migrant workers for several years after which they will have saved enough for them to come back and get married.

The fact that so many people have left Gao Village and that their earnings add an unprecedented amount of cash income to the village has brought about a number of changes, some immediate, others slower and possibly more far-reaching. The most immediate effect is that life is possible in Gao Village in spite of the harsh local levies. The villagers (except Gao Chaodian who does not have a child big enough to be a migrant worker) are now not only able to pay the levies but can also afford to send children to school at least from Grade 1 to Grade 3.

By 1994, all children of school age from grades one to three were at school. Some villagers have been able to build a house for their sons' marriage. More visibly, the villagers wear better clothing. They can afford rubber boots and bicycles and small items such as torchlights, gloves and even sunglasses. Wearing a watch is not rare any more and by 1996 there were more than twenty television sets in the village, mostly black and white.

Thanks to my own assistance as a migrant worker, for the first time since 1949 there is a village shop owned by a Gao villager, my brother Gao Changxian. The majority of the customers are Gao villagers and consumption of industrial goods has increased at a rapid rate. By 1994 the annual turnover of the village shop reached 30,000 *yuan*. What is most surprising is that Gao villagers no longer grow everything for their own consumption. Not only do they no longer make cloth, they do not even grow things such as garlic and sugar cane. Instead, they buy these things from the village shop! My brother travels regularly to Boyang County Town, not only to purchase goods such as paper, processed sugar, soy sauce, cigarettes, beer and shoes but also produce such as seasonal vegetables to sell to Gao villagers. One would have thought that peasants would grow things and then sell them to the town and urban people. The current situation is the reverse: seasonal vegetables are transported 100 kilometres from Boyang County Town to be sold in a rural village. If it were not for the cash income from migrant workers, Gao villagers would go without these seasonal vegetables.

The agricultural produce that Gao Changxian purchases at street markets in Boyang County Town are grown and sold by specialised household farmers who live near by, and who carry their produce to the town market on their shoulder poles or on a wheelbarrow every day. It was like this in Mao's China. As for industrial goods, many items such as shoes, garments, and plastic utensils are produced in the costal south and sold to the Boyang Town retailers by retailers in Guangzhou, Shenzhen or Xiamen.

Therefore, by the time my brother sells these commodities to Gao villagers, five transactions have taken place in the sales chain: from the factory to the wholesaler, from the wholesaler to the local retailer, from the local retailer to the Boyang retailer, from the Boyang retailer to my brother, and finally to the ultimate consumer.

The chain shows the extent to which the market mechanism in China stretches today across regions from the costal south to inland China. By Western standards, this mechanism is chaotic and very costly. The product will sell much better if it can reach the consumer directly. Second, this chain market mechanism has had a wave-like effect on China's economy, spreading from the coastal south to the remote corners of China. Thirdly it indicates regional differences in terms of industrial development and personal income. In Boyang there has been hardly any change in terms of industrial development since the end of Mao's reign. In 1985, not only did Boyang County not collect a cent in tax revenue from industrial enterprises, but lost 423,000 *yuan*.[30]

As a result of this lack of industrial development, the personal income of town residents has hardly increased since Mao's time. By 1985, an average town worker's annual wage in the state-owned sector was 695.1 *yuan* while that in the collective sector was 608 *yuan*. In 1993, the average town worker's wage in Jiangxi Province was 1,799 *yuan* a year.[31] This was a mere 157.8 *yuan* a month, compared with average earnings of 300-400 *yuan* a month by migrant workers, whose earnings are the very lowest in coastal China. For the first time in its history, Gao villagers, thanks to cash income from migrant workers, can earn more than town residents.

The fact that so many villagers have left as migrant workers has also had a range of social and political effects, some of which are immediately obvious. If the process continues, migrant work will cause changes ranging from social values and attitudes to demography and economic structures. One immediately visible impact is that there are no young males in the village. Except during the Spring Festival every year, Gao Village is quieter. However, this apparent peacefulness also gives them a sense of the village being abandoned. Materially the villagers are better off; but the village is lifeless and listless. The centre of activities is no longer located in the village and the aspirations and expectations of the whole village lie thousands of miles away. In fact, the villagers' view of the world and their value systems are undergoing a profound change. For the first time in Gao Village's history, the villagers have realised that they do not have to rely on the territory's land and water for a living. Ecological and resource pressures have been reduced dramatically. 30 per cent of Gao villagers no longer depend on the land for a livelihood. They therefore have more grain per capital and can afford to be less exploitative of local land and water.

There are other visible impacts. For instance, the young migrant workers are beginning to shake the very foundation of the lineage

---

[30] *Boyang Xianzhi* (Boyang County Annals), p. 516.

[31] *Jiangxi Tonji Nianjian 1994* (Jiangxi Statistics Year Book 1994), p. 70.

and kinship system. They have absorbed new ideas from the outside and consider local clan rituals as silly. During the Spring Festival in 1993 when I was in Gao Village, very few migrant workers bothered to pay their respects to the genealogy. Some went along simply because they thought it was harmless fun. When the village elders tried to talk the young villagers into organising some resources to fight Wang Village over the long-standing water territory dispute, the young migrant workers paid no attention to them, regarding their words as typical old people's irrelevant mumbling. It is now impossible to launch a clan fight in the area simply because there are virtually no young men anymore. Juvenile crimes such as that committed by Gao Zhanglin, which had increased sharply during the late 1980s, have decline dramatically in the early 1990s due to the simple fact that young people are not around.

Some of the consequences of migrant labour are not immediately transparent but are more far reaching. In spite of the political change in this century, including the violent 1949 Communist revolution, tradition dies hard in rural China. For instance, sons must be obedient to fathers and wives to husbands. However, since the late 1980s, the major source of family income is no longer the father but one of the migrant worker children. Since the family is less reliant on the father, the mother's ties with her sons and daughters, who are a major source of cash income, provide her with an emotional anchor, and hence assertiveness. The young people themselves are more independent in relation to their fathers in terms of thinking, values and behaviour. This almost invisible change will have serious political and social im-plications, because these young people will be more restless, less obedient and far more difficult to manipulate than the former generations of peasants. The young migrant workers have begun to let their hair grow long and wear thick sunglasses. They have begun to assert their own identity by not wanting to marry local girls any more.

Four Gao villagers married women from other parts of China whom they had met at their work place without consulting their parents. Gao Changwen married on educated woman from Boyang County Town who also went to Xiamen as a migrant worker. No woman of urban residence would previously have married a man of rural residence. Many of the migrant workers have boy-friends or girlfriends without necessarily intending to get married.

The only middle-aged Gao Village migrant worker who is married with three children in Gao Village had a mistress in Guangdong. A young woman from Gao Village who had worked as a nanny in Jingdezhen for a number of years said to me during an interview in 1993 that she did not want to get married because she wanted to be free. In 1992 during the Spring Festival, Gao Chaolin brought a wife home unannounced, to the great surprise and consternation of his parents. The elderly villagers, without knowing what to anticipate any more, feel confused and cannot make sense of what is happening.

The demographic changes are sweeping but unsettling for Gao Village. If the present process continues, more and more young people will leave Gao village. Where are these people eventually going to settle down? The current assumption by both the government and Gao villagers is that these young people will eventually get married and come back home. However, not a single young migrant worker from Gao Village has yet done this. It used to be the case that the villagers would get married young and have children when young. Since the 1990s, however, they tend to marry late and have children even later largely because they are too busy "making money". If China's economy goes bankrupt suddenly, or if all foreign businesspeople withdraw their investments, or civil wars break out in China, or if the Chinese government decides to force all rural migrant workers back to the villages, these young migrant workers may have to go back to where they come from. Otherwise, it is difficult to see why these young people will want to return permanently to Gao Village.

It is still too early to predict what will happen, because the process has been going on for only under a decade. Some will not come back to Gao Village in any case. Gao Changwen, for instance, has already bought a flat in Boyang County Town and he intends to set up his own business when and if he and his wife quit migrant work. Others who married women from other parts of China are unlikely to go back. If the present process continues, given that China remains stable and its economy keeps its present rate of growth, Gao Village as an entity will eventually disappear. The Chinese government, on the other hand, has to find a solution to enable these young people to become part of the urban population. So far, the government seems unsure of what to do with them. If, however, for whatever reason, these young people do go back to Gao Village, the situation is no less unsettling: they will be unwilling to tolerate the same pattern of life as previous generations and they will return with new ideas which will have profound political implications.

Ecological changes and an exploitative pricing system brought rural communities like Gao Village to the edge of disaster by the end of the Mao era. The price reform of the early 1980s provided some breathing space, but by the end of the 1980s, the situation had deteriorated rapidly. It was the opportunity offered by rapid industrial development far away from Gao Village in the coastal south that gave Gao villagers a chance of new development. Migrant work not only reduced the ecological burden on Gao Village but also provided valuable cash income for Gao villagers to pay local levies, to buy modern consumer goods and to pay for education and health care.

It is clear that the improvement in standards of living in Gao Village is built upon the blood and sweat of migrant workers. Though the life and working conditions of the migrant workers are horrendous by "Western" standards it is likely that they may not want to return to Gao Village if they are given a choice. There are many good reasons for this. First, migrant working is necessary for survival. The economic "pull" and "push" factors are such that the cash income from migrant labour is very attractive. Second, it is considered to be "prestigious" to travel and to work in urban areas. The young people feel proud that they are the main providers of their family income. Third, the young workers themselves do not find working in a factory necessarily harsher than labouring in the fields – at least it is under cover, in contrast to agricultural work. As for health hazards and poor working conditions, they are not immediately apparent to the young people from rural areas like Gao Village, who therefore choose to ignore them. It is matter of perception. There is a "psychological gap", so to speak, in that migrant workers do not take health hazards and working conditions as their life priority. Finally, there is the excitement of seeing a different world, of being able to afford things such as fashionable clothing which are otherwise unattainable.

12

CHANGE AND CONTINUITY: CULTURE AND CUSTOMS

Despite the social upheavals, the revolutionary change in land ownership and political structure – despite the vicissitudes of more than forty years – Gao Village appears to have changed little. If it were not for the industrial expansion along the south coast of China, which has attracted a substantial number of Gao villagers as migrant workers, the policy U-turns by the authorities after Mao would have only brought Gao Village back to where it started in 1950: household ownership of land and self-sufficiency at subsistence level.

In terms of culture and customs, so much has happened, and yet so little has changed. Although, thanks to the earnings of migrant workers, improvement has occurred which has taken the village beyond basic self-sufficiency, continuity is firmly demonstrated by the fact that forms of ownership and methods of production still remain essentially the same as before 1949. It is a continuity arrived at through a U-turn which ended four decades of radicalism. Continuity has persisted in other areas of life as well, in both local cultural activities and in social customs.

Clan culture and village affairs

One important aspect of continuity is clan culture in village affairs. Though in Gao Village this is not outwardly shown by symbols such as a clan temple or a formal patriarchal structure, its influence penetrates subtly into almost all aspects of village life. Gao Village has never had a clan temple, nor has there ever been a formal patriarchal social structure; but informally, clan structure was at work in village affairs before 1949 and has been since. However, the mechanisms of clan influence cannot be described by any straightforward configuration. There have always been different forces which interact to counterbalance one aspect of village life against another.

There are the interests and influences of different genealogical branches in the village which counterbalance each other; there are various inter-village relationships which take priority when and if conflicts arise; and there have been political changes and policies imposed from outside, the implementation of which not only counterbalance the first and second set of relationships but are also counterbalanced by them. All these forces interact with each other to govern village life. A few examples will show how intricate this can be.

Gao Changming, who later left Gao Village and became a porcelain maker in Jingdezhen, was considered a trouble maker. He was a rebel who set out to make trouble for other villagers and so when he was a child he was given the nickname *haijing* ("the wicked one who does harm to others"). He has been called *haijing* ever since. As discussed in Chapter 7, by refusing to give back a piece of land that Gao Tianqiang lent to him and by accusing Gao Tianqiang of being a "class enemy who was counterattacking to settle old scores" (meaning he wanted to take back the land that was confiscated during the land reform), Gao Changming was largely responsible for classifying Gao Tianqiang as a landlord, a class enemy label that had tremendous political implications.

Gao Changming's act was vicious and totally unjustified. Yet he himself was a victim of repressive clan culture. In the early 1930s, his father had died when he was a child. According to the Confucian code of behaviour at that time, his mother had to remain a widow in Gao Village to bring the child up for the clan. However, his mother had a passionate affair with one Wang Dieying from neighbouring Wang Village. It is not unusual to have affairs in the village. For example, Gao Changyin had an affair with Gao Renkai's wife, my mother had an affair with Gao Renyun, and at least two men had affairs with the widow of the rich peasant Gao Jingxiang. However Gao Changming's mother was so indiscreet that she lived with Wang openly in Gao Village. The clan powerholders of Gao Changming's genealogical branch could not tolerate this. The two oldest men of the branch, Gao Renhui and Gao Renkun, decided to sell Gao Changming's mother to end the scandal. When Gao Changming's mother heard of this she ran away to her parents in Duan Village. Duan Village happened to be twice as big as Gao Village and there was nothing that Gao Village could do to get her back. Eventually Gao Changming's mother married Wang Dieying and Gao Changming became parentless. Understandably, he became very bitter and grew up as a rebel in Gao Village.

The story of my father Gao Renfa is another example of how the complicated clan culture and inter-village relationships worked in this area. My father was the youngest of his generation in the clan. According to the behavioural code of clan culture, he had to do what he was told by the men in his genealogical branch who were older than him. In the 1940s the Nationalist government reinstated what was called the *baojia* system in the area to consolidate its control. Under this system, a village the size of Gao Village was to form a *jia*, and a head of the *jia* must be appointed, to be responsible to the government for collecting taxes and especially for enlisting soldiers to fight the Communists. A village that was three or four times bigger than Gao Village, or three or four villages of the same size, would form a *bao*, and the head of a *bao* would have power over the head of a *jia*. My father, illiterate and weak, was told by the village elders to be the head of the *jia* because nobody else wanted the job.

In 1944, the *bao* authorities gave an order that to fulfil the government's quota, the *jia* of Gao Village had to enlist one man in the Nationalist army. The responsibility fell on my father. As no Gao villagers wanted to be in the army, my father had to buy a man. Duan Benyi, a rich and powerful person who was classified as a landlord later during the land reform, promised that he would deliver Duan Village man to be enlisted at a price of 500 silver dollars.[1] The idea was that my father would pay the money first and when the man was enlisted the *bao* authority would pay my father back. However, when the time came for the man to be sent to the army he was nowhere to be seen. My father went to Duan Village to look for the man. Duan villagers not only refused to hand over the man for whom the price had been paid but also threatened to tie my father up and give him a good beating if he did not forget the whole thing. Gao Village of course was too small to fight against Duan Village. Not only

---

[1] Coinage still used at the time which was made of silver.

was my father unable to retrieve the 500 dollars from Duan Benyi, he was also forced to spend another 100 dollars on another man who also ran away without trace. My father spent hundreds of dollars buying another two men, who also disappeared before being enlisted in the Nationalist army.

Because of Gao Village's failure to fulfil the quota, the county authorities sent several policemen carrying rifles to Gao Village to hold my father responsible, and so my father had to offer himself to be enlisted. He was taken to Boyang County to have a physical check-up, but was disqualified because he was short-sighted. Penniless, he then had to walk back, begging in order to survive a 100 kilometre journey home. Eventually, Gao Renchang, who was married to my mother's sister, offered himself to be enlisted. He was enlisted and as a result my father was released of the responsibility. Gao Renchang did not participate in any fighting because he somehow found a chance to run away from the army and returned home.

As a result of doing what he was told by the clan elders, my father went bankrupt. He spent altogether several hundred silver dollars, sold all the furniture that was worth selling as well as all my mother's jewellery, and in addition incurred a debt of 1,500 kilograms of rice to fulfil the responsibility of being the head of the *jia*.

Again in 1950 my father was told to take on a responsibility which was beyond him. When the Communists organised the Poor Peasant Association, the clan elders Gao Renkun and Gao Renhui told my father to represent Gao Village. At the very beginning the villagers did not know what the Communists were like and they were as afraid of them as they were of the Nationalists. The clan elders asked my father to represent Gao Village not only because he was the youngest and therefore had to do what he was told, but also because he was the poorest. The only thing the villagers knew about Communists was that they would not harm the poor. The authorities accepted my father because he had also helped a Communist troop in 1949. So my father became the representative of Gao Village in the Guantian Peasant Association. Only half a year later, the ambitious Gao Changyin replaced my father. Gao Changyin, because of his active participation in land reform and other activities, became the Party secretary of Guantian brigade.

As discussed previously, during the Cultural Revolution there was again interaction between political influences imposed by the government and clan culture in village affairs. Teenage Red Guards of two conflicting villages went to persecute and beat up each other's landlords and rich peasants. Thus, teenage Red Guards from Gao Village beat up "the counter- revolutionary" Xu Tianyun of Xu Village and Red Guards of Xu village beat up landlord Gao Tianqiang from Gao Village. Political direction of the Cultural Revolution lent a legitimacy to and provided an excuse for new expressions of long-standing inter-village clan feuds. However, this legitimacy had its limits. Reciprocal persecution of "class enemies" did not take place between Gao Village and Wang Village, though the two villages had a much more serious account to settle. This was because Wang and Gao villages belonged to different production brigades. Neither did political climate give rise to reciprocal persecution of "class enemies" between Lai Village and Gao Village, because the two villages belonged to different counties.

Local religion or superstition?

One important indication of continuity in Gao Village is the U-turn since the 1980s in the area of religious practices, which were considered by the authorities in Maoist China as superstitions. About half a kilometre to the west of Gao Village there used to be a Buddhist temple, *tao hua an,* in which there were a dozen colourful wooden bodhisattvas. According to my childhood memories, the place was ghastly and the bodhisattvas were grotesque. During the Great Leap Forward, they were taken away and burned. The temple house remained and villagers in the Qinglin area still went there to pray from time to time discreetly, as if the bodhisattvas had still been there.

Surrounding the temple was a bamboo forest, which together with the house and land, belonged to the Qinglin brigade collectively. Bamboo is a valuable resource for the area. Bamboo shoots, which are a delicacy in the Chinese diet, can be harvested twice a year, once in spring and once in winter. More importantly, two crucial farming tools were and are still made of bamboo; the baskets used on shoulder poles to carry rice from the field, and a sort of mattress on which rice is dried. Rice has to be dried under the summer sun for at least two days before it can be stored for a long time. An ex-serviceman from the Korean War was assigned to live in the house and to look after the bamboo. The man, whose leg was slightly crippled by a war wound, was not a believer, yet even he gave consent to discreet prayers. Officially, however, *tao hua an* ceased to be a place for local religious practice for more than twenty years. Since the 1980s, the place has been restored as a temple, and half a dozen bodhisattvas have been placed there for villagers to pray to. The temple burned down in 1995, yet the site is still used for prayers in the open air. Some activists were collecting money to re-build it.

The villagers do not seem to practise Buddhism for spiritual sustenance, but for practical benefits, such as good fortune, luck, or to cure a sick person. Indeed, for the villagers, the word *pusa* which is translated as "bodhisattva" or "Buddha", means a statue of any kind. A statue of Mao is a *pusa*, as would be a statue of Jesus Christ. The villagers might pray to any statue for practical purposes. Some *pusa* are simply popular figures from Chinese history, such as Guan Yunchang (a general) and Zhu Geliang, a prime minister from the period of the Three Kingdoms (AD 220-65). This practice of syncretism is perhaps one reason why the Chinese government's suppression of religious practices is not so hurtful to rural people of Han ethnic communities. The fact that the dozen or so bodhisattvas in *tao hua an* were burned did not bother Gao villagers because they had their own *pusa* to turn to, which was *Wang Taigong*, literally the 'great grandfather Wang". Even during the height of the Cultural Revolution, nothing was done to harm Wang Taigong, a statue which was passed on from one household to another for prayers. Though Gao Renwei did not practice the embodiment of Wang Taigong any more after the fiasco of 1964, described in Chapter 6, he was never victimised for his role in what was officially considered to be "feudalist superstition".

Another prevalent religious practice in the area is ancestor worship, a practice which again has never been uprooted and which has returned with stronger force since the 1980s. Ancestor worship is practised in two main ways. One is to burn paper money, joss sticks on *Qingming* Festival at ancestors' graves and again on the New Year's Day of the Lunar Calendar. Those families which can afford it will also set fireworks in front of their ancestors' graves as a way of worshipping. The longer the fireworks last and the louder the sound, the more sincere and genuine the feeling shown is supposed to be. Another practice of ancestor worship is to offer food to the dead. During the Spring Festival, every household gets together to have three banquets, one on each day from the 28th to the 30th of the Twelfth Month of the Lunar Calendar. Immediately before each banquet, all the food is placed in front of the altar for the ancestors to consume first. While joss sticks are burned, all the family members will do obeisance by bowing three times with hands clasped. On New Year's Day, usually in the morning, all male members of Gao Village gather together to perform the ceremony of clan worship, which mainly consists of doing obeisance in the above manner. During the Great Leap Forward and the Cultural Revolution clan worship was stopped, but family worship of ancestors continued, and the villagers were only obliged to do it more discreetly during the most radical periods.

The general theme of change and continuity in village life is exemplified by the location and maintenance of graves. For the villagers, the bigger the grave and the better the maintenance the more sincere and genuine their filial piety.[2] The usual practice is to place the dead in a coffin which is placed in a hole dug in the ground. Then earth is piled on to it so that a dome is formed. The bigger and higher the dome the better the family feels about it. Digging up the grave of someone's ancestor is one of the worst moral crimes that can be committed. However, in the past forty years or so many graves have been levelled and removed and grave domes have become smaller and smaller. This has happened gradually, mainly for practical reasons based on the necessity of survival. As the population grew in Gao Village, every inch of land had to be made use of on the village's definitive territory. Some graves were levelled for growing crops while others were removed for irrigation construction. All this was done gradually, without external interference.

Without the political climate, there might have been resistance by the villagers, but the destruction of graves was not for the

---

[2] Filial piety is one of the major tenets of Confucianism, according to which a very well ordered society is based on a hierarchy in which every one should be piously obedient and deferential to an authority. Thus imperial officials should be deferential to the emperor; son to father, wife to husband and the young to the old. The practice of ancestor worship stems directly from this doctrine.

sake of politics. Like many things which have happened in rural China, this change can be interpreted as the destruction of religion by the Communist regime. However, it can equally be interpreted as a result of interacting forces, some of which are not political but rather developmental and economic.

The practice of burying the dead in a coffin made of timber continues to this day. Cremation has never been practised in this area. There has never been a crematorium and the villagers would be horrified even to contemplate the idea. They consider the preservation of the whole body as representing the continuation of life. Therefore, it is the duty of the offspring to preserve the dead body of the old in the family as long as possible. This practice is the result of centuries of indoctrination in Confucianist ideas of filial piety. For the same reason, a child has no authority of any kind in the hierarchy. Hence the practice is that the dead body of a child is never considered worth preserving, and the coffin for a child is usually made only of some wooden boards.

For the elderly, however, the better and thicker the timber and the heavier the coffin, the more filial the offspring and hence the more honoured and respected the family is in the eyes of the villagers. The best coffin is considered to be one made of Chinese fir trunks. The trunks must remain whole and be as wide as possible. Small pieces of timber panelled together are not considered to make a proper coffin. The villagers make comparisons and talk and gossip about how much has been spent on a coffin in such and such a family.

There is therefore enormous pressure on the family to find the best coffins it can afford for the elderly. Sometimes, a coffin made of huge Chinese fir trunks enclosing the corpse and some lime used to preserve the body requires twenty-four strong men to be carried to the grave. The cost of coffins is one of the three most burdensome expenditures in a family, the other two being marriage costs for a son and the building of a house. Indeed, for most couples their lifetime ambition is to fulfil the three obligations of building a house for the offspring, getting children married and having their parents properly buried. Enormous sacrifices will be made to achieve these three ambitions.

As wood is becoming more scarce and timber more precious, the cost of a coffin is rising. Even during the 1960s a good coffin would cost more than 300 *yuan*, an enormous amount by village standards, and this did not even include the cost of transportation. Because there was no such wood in the area, the villagers would push a wheelbarrow to transport the coffin from more than 60 kilometres away. The transportation of each coffin would require two strong men, each pushing a wheelbarrow on which there were two pieces of the coffin. The journey would usually take three to four days. As more and more forests have disappeared nearby, places where coffins can be purchased are further and further away. Since the 1980s, a good quality coffin can cost several thousand *yuan* and one has to travel as far as 200 kilometres to buy it. Nowadays, those families who can afford it hire a truck. But there are still those who cannot afford it, and therefore have to transport coffins by wheelbarrow! The burden of tradition is heavy and certainly not as pleasant as the romanticised scholarly view of China sometimes suggests.

There are other traditional practices such as fortune-telling, and again the practice has never been uprooted from the village. Even during the most radical period, fortune-tellers wandered from village to village. Usually blind males who travelled around to get some food from the villagers, they would pass a door and would be called to come into a household. They would be given some food to eat, after which the fortune-telling would start. All the client had to do was to state the hour and the date of birth. The fortune-teller would say something about what had happened in the past and what would happen in the future to the person in question. Usually, what the fortune-teller said was vague and ambiguous, and very often so general that it could apply to anyone. Every villager must have had his or her fortune told a couple of times. Whenever a fortune-teller passed Gao Village, he would be called in by my mother and my fortune would be told, because I had such an unusual career.

Marriage and women

The cost for a marriage has always been considerable, and the financial burden is especially great for a family with many sons. Usually, the burden falls on the groom's family: he has to prepare a marriage room, which is furnished with a bed, a mosquito net, a dressing table, a cupboard and a couple of wooden cases. In the 1960s and '70s, some families would also buy a sewing machine.

Nowadays, consumer goods such as a watch, a bicycle and a television set or an electric fan are also required. The groom is also responsible for the dowry, which includes a bridal suit, a dozen or more dresses, socks and shoes for the bride, wash basins, chairs, towels, toothpaste and brushes, scarves, gloves, boots, quilts, bedding made of silk, pillows and so on. Very often, a necklace and a pair of bracelets for the bride made of silver are also required. Two banquets, one at the engagement and one on the day before the wedding at the bride's parents' house, are also paid for by the groom. There is also a bigger banquet held at the groom's home on the wedding day. The scale of the two banquets depends on the number of relatives and guests invited. The bigger the banquet and the more lavish the food the more esteemed the wedding in the eyes of the villagers.

The average cost of getting married during the 1960s and 1970s was around 2,000 *yuan*. Since the 1980s, spending 10,000 *yuan* is considered ordinary. In some exceptional cases, the bride's family will contribute a part or even all of the cost. This will happen if the bride's family is wealthy while the bride herself is considered unworthy, either because of looks or character. Sometimes the bride's family is also ready to foot the bill for the dowry, and even to bear some of the costs of the marriage room if the groom is considered to be outstandingly promising. All dowry items have to be agreed upon and prepared well in advance, and kept in the bride's home. On the wedding day, the groom and a team of musicians and strong men who are to carry the dowry items arrive at the bride's home early in the morning. They then return to the groom's home for the ceremony and banquet. Sedan chairs are no longer used. Instead, the bride is carried on a wheelbarrow or a bicycle. Since the late 1980s, some wealthy families have used motorbikes. The procession starts as soon as the team leaves the bride's family door. Loud music played on gongs and trumpets declares the occasion when the team leaves. If the journey from the bride's home to the groom's home is long and passes many villages, the procession starts very early and the musicians start playing their instruments as soon as they enter a village. The team proceeds right though the middle of a village with pride. Villagers all come out to watch and to comment on the couple and on the substance of the dowry. If the marriage is exceptional in terms of dowry, the villagers in the area will pass on the legend for years or even generations, hence the esteem for the family and pride of its members. When the procession reaches the groom's home, the noise of fireworks fills the sky and the whole village comes out to watch the bride and to look at the dowry, which is placed in the house for everyone to see and make comments about it.

After a while, the master of ceremonies (usually an elderly clan power-holder or someone else with status or education) starts the ceremony by saying a few formal words. Then the couple stand together facing the altar in the house and are first told by the master to kowtow to the groom's ancestors three times.[3] After that, they are told to kowtow to the groom's parents three times. Next come the groom's relatives. The whole process can last a good half hour if the groom has many relatives. Finally, the groom and bride are asked to eat or drink something together; but they are never asked to kiss in public.

By the time all this is done, the banquet is ready. Eight people sit at one square table and on each table at least twelve dishes must be served. Some families serve as many as twenty-four dishes. Again, the more dishes and the better the food the more prestige and glory for the family. Since the 1980s, some wealthy families have started to serve as many as thirty-six dishes for a marriage banquet. The number of dishes should never be odd because marriage involves a couple, an even number. The number of tables served also indicates the status of the occasion: the higher the number the more prestigious the family. During the 1990s, a marriage banquet for which more than a hundred tables are served is not unheard of in the area, though there has never been such a marriage banquet in Gao Village. Guests at the banquet include at least one member from each household in the groom's village, local officials if they care to come, clan powerholders (always males), half a dozen of the oldest villagers (including females) and anyone of status, such as the village teacher. Those who come to the banquet must give the groom's family some cash, nothing else, as a gift. During the 1960s and '70s a gift of 2-5 *yuan* was the average amount. In the 1990s, 20-50 *yuan* is considered

---

[3] By kneeling on the floor, the couple are required to lower their heads to touch the ground three times.

normal. Some groom's families are known to make a profit out of the banquet.

On the evening of the wedding day, village musicians are called together to perform for the occasion. The orchestra usually consists of six to eight self-taught musicians: one playing the drum, another playing the gongs, two Chinese violinists and a number of trumpet players. They sing local operas while playing the instruments. Each has a role, and no rehearsal is ever needed. There has never been a written record of either the word, or the tunes for the local operas. They are passed on through listening and practice. The opera singing will go on and on until midnight when the bride and groom are supposed to go to bed.

However, the couple will not be allowed to have any time to themselves until a final act is played out. One bedroom item, such as a shoe or a dress, has to be taken out of the marriage bedroom without being detected by the married couple. The task is usually performed by a group of youngsters who stay up the whole night. When that is done the couple are awakened from their sleep and thus the wedding day ends. Usually the couple deliberately leave the bedroom door unlocked and pretend to sleep so that the final act can be played out quickly. However, they never know when the villagers will take action and therefore remain awake all night.

Instances of arranged marriages are still frequent in the area. In most cases, marriage takes place after a quite elaborate process of introduction. Usually one family requests someone as a go-between to go to the other family to sound out the possibility. The person who initiates the process can be either the young person or the parents. The other family may reject the proposal straight away, or may remain vague so as to find out more, or to keep a negotiating advantage. Only when the two families agree on the betrothal are the young man and woman allowed to see each other. Usually it is the man who visits the woman's family, often during a festival. The woman does not visit the man's family until an engagement has been concluded. Usually the go-between fixes both the engagement and financial arrangements for both families.

The man and woman are not allowed to talk in private until after their engagements, and it is considered imprudent for the woman to look at the man straight in the eyes. Privately, however, both the man and woman are asked about their opinions of each-other, and this is fed back through the go-between. Very often, the woman has a great deal of say in matters such as whether the engagement should take place and items of dowry. Once the woman is satisfied with the man's appearance, her next objective is to extract as much as possible from her future husband's family. Sometimes, negotiations can drag on for a couple of years and the woman usually wants to strike the best financial bargain for her parents. Some even demand that the groom's family should provide support for the cost of the education of the bride's younger siblings. Mutual understanding, feelings and love have to develop after the marriage.

There has not been a child bride in Gao Village since the 1950s, Gao Lingli being the last one. Daughter adoption, however, is quite common. Because of infertility, two families in Gao Village each adopted a daughter. The two women later married two men from outside Gao Village by way of *zhaozhui*. When a family has no son, a daughter's husband has to live with her parents' family, and their children are given the surname Gao.

The most visible change in the marriage pattern in Gao Village is that there have been nine marriages since the late 1960s in which both the bride and groom are Gao villagers. All of them knew each other well and liked each other before marriage. No villager can remember a single case of marriage of this kind before the early 1960s. As more and more villagers went to school, the idea of a marriage arranged by parents began to be resisted and disliked more and more by young villagers. Another important factor was that the collective system had provided opportunities for young villagers to work together and get to know each other better. Two marriages took place after the couples fell in love through rehearsing and performing Peking Operas during the Cultural Revolution.

Tradition, however, persists and many marriages are still arranged by parents. Since the 1950s there have been three marriages arranged by parents in Gao Village which involved the union of cousins. This was very unfortunate because four children from two such marriages have been born either crippled or mentally retarded. The third couple was lucky and their children are healthy and fine because the husband and wife are remote cousins. The three marriages were arranged by the parents primarily for financial reasons, and the women had no say over the dowry. Because they were relatives who had maintained a good relationship, neither side wanted to bargain, and the marriage ceremony was kept as simple as possible, thus saving a great deal of money. In fact, in two of these marriages, the husband and wife have been happy together. Only one woman, Gui Yuan, stated clearly that she had not wanted the marriage in the first place and that it was all her parent's fault.

Gui Yuan's husband Gao Renfang has gone to Guangdong as a migrant worker. He is the only migrant worker in Gao Village who is over forty years old, married and with children. Gao Renfang has been a migrant worker for more than five years now. He used to come home once a year during the Spring Festival. Since 1994, however, he has not come back home once, nor has he sent much money. It is rumoured that he has a mistress in Guangdong. There is nothing that Gui Yuan can do about the situation. She has to work on the land allocated to the family and look after her mentally retarded daughter. Gui Yuan, as a woman, is not in a position to initiate a divorce. Indeed, the only case of divorce in Gao Village was before 1949, when the landlord Gao Tianqiang divorced his wife and married again.

It is not just a matter of Confucian morality which only allows a husband to divorce his wife; it is also a matter of cost. The landlord Gao Tianqiang could afford a divorce, whereas other men could not. In this respect, the Communist revolution has left rural China unchanged. As long as they are trapped in a life of survival hardly anyone can afford a divorce, and therefore they have to make the best of what they think is their fate. In the 1990s, however, change is on the horizon. The case of Gao Renfang may well be the beginning of this change. Thanks to the earnings from migrant working, Gao Renfang can afford to and may indeed decide to divorce his wife and marry another woman. If this happens it is not necessarily better for Gui Yuan, who is trapped in Gao Village. It is conceivable however that female migrant workers from Gao Village can also assert themselves as a result of their cash earnings, although women have a long way to go before this happens. Currently, those who have left Gao Village as migrant workers are mostly teenage boys; parents tend to keep their teenage girls at home for various reasons such as safety and the greater readiness of girls to help their mothers with housework.

On the whole, the Communist regime has taken a giant step towards the emancipation of women in rural China. One important factor in this is that the idea of women being equal is not only officially recognised, but has actually spread among rural villagers. Women can and sometimes do challenge the village authorities and their husbands by saying "I am not afraid of you! Women are equal!" If a Gao Village woman wants to have a divorce there is nothing official, either morally or politically, that can stop her. It is only practical and economic factors which constrain her will and determination to initiate it.

Once a woman is married into another village, her name is cancelled from the register of her home village. She is not entitled to any resources in her home village, nor is she entitled to any inheritance from her parents. Household property has traditionally been passed on equally among the male children and this is still the practice. A divorced woman has nowhere to go unless she can remarry straight away. She is more or less trapped.

One last instance can be cited to illustrate the point. The daughter of the richest man in Gao Village, Gao Hanzheng, ran away with her lover from another village and obtained approval from the village committee for a marriage without Gao Hanzheng's permission. Two years after the marriage, the man was arrested and put into prison for committing a crime. Gao Hanzheng was furious and he held Xu Xianxiu, the village committee official who gave approval for the marriage, responsible for marrying his daughter to a criminal. Xu Xianxiu, of course, had the right to give the marriage approval, and there was nothing Gao Hanzheng could do about it. Gao Hanzheng went to Xu Village, slapped Xu Xianxiu's face and boxed his ears and then quickly ran back to Gao Village. Had he not run away quickly he might have been beaten up by the Xu villagers.

Officially, a woman shares the ownership of the family's property with her husband. Theoretically at least a divorced woman can have her share and live separately, with or without children. However, practically everything works against a woman who wants a divorce. To start with, in most cases, there are several families in one house and one woman's share is too little to be significant. Second, even if the family owns a house, no party can afford to pay the other party in order to keep it. Selling or dismantling the house for sub-division will, for all practical purposes, make husband, wife and children homeless. The third possibility is that the husband and wife remain friends, but live separately under the same roof, in which case the issue of divorce never arises. Equally, financial and practical restrictions apply to men, though to a lesser extent. Even if a man disregards the financial implications, he cannot divorce his wife on the basis that he does not love her any more. That would be considered to be too foolish and irrational to be taken seriously by the villagers or the local authorities. All other considerations will point to reconciliation and making do with each other. Adultery by either party is not a sufficient basis for a divorce.

Young rural women are very loyal to their parents, especially when they are not happy with their marriage. For the first couple of years of marriage, the woman treats herself as a guest in her husband's home. Parents-in-law are usually very polite and sometimes coaxing. The young woman herself feels detached and usually has no say in family affairs. If she wants to have any input in running the family it has to go through her husband. One consequence of this rather cautious and yet distant relationship between the in-laws is that the young woman may pack and leave for her parents any time she wishes. By staying with her parents, the young woman will work and contribute to the family income. Sometimes, a married woman may stay with her parents for months on end, either because of a fight with her husband or with her in-laws. When the man's family becomes anxious about this, local officials from both villages have to be mobilised to find a solution. In most cases, once a baby is born the young woman's emotional tie with her parents begins to fade; and because she is now the mother of an heir in the household, her status begins to increase.

Women in Gao Village have made progress in improving their status in two respects: education and participation in production activities. As discussed in the chapter on education, there was only one woman in Gao Village who was as much as semi-literate before the 1950s. Nowadays, most women under the age of thirty-five have had some education, ranging from two to five years. Before 1949 women of my mother's generation were mostly kept at home. Nowadays, all women work in the fields like men. During the collective period from the 1960s to the early 80s, women participated in village affairs and made their voices heard, although most decisions were still made by the men. Since the late 1980s, whenever there is an election for village head and members of the village committee, women have equal rights and an equal vote.[4] However, no woman has ever been elected or appointed as the village head, even though the female population overwhelms the male population in Gao Village, as most of those who have left as migrant workers are young males.

In fact no woman seems willing to come forward as a candidate. Even during the collective period when every production team (by stipulation of the government) had to appoint a woman as a deputy, it was always difficult to find a woman who was willing to take up the position. It is easy to see why this was the case. To start with, women were discouraged by their elders and their families from being active in public affairs. Second, in a male dominated environment women do not feel confident and determined. Third, during the collective period there were no material rewards for a woman to be a production team deputy. Instead, she had to work harder and set herself up as a model for others to follow. Since the 1980s, being a village head or member of

---

[4] Election of local village officials is one of the policies pursued by the central government and has taken place from time to time since the 1980s. I have opted not to spend much time discussing this aspect of village life for a number of reasons. The first is that elections are not held regularly as stipulated by the government. The local authorities will organise an election when they are earnestly urged by their superiors. Once the monitoring from above is not visible the local authorities tend to appoint their own officials. Secondly and more importantly, whether there is an election does not make a difference to village life. As production activities are primarily household based since the dismantling of the commune system, the responsibilities of the village officials are mainly on collecting taxes and levies and on imposing family planning policies. For those who become village officials, either elected or appointed, the behavioural pattern is the same: they tend to extract as much as possible from the villagers for themselves through taxes and levies. As for family planning, all village officials, past or present, try to obstruct the central government's efforts as much as possible. The degree of their success depends on the policies imposed from above which change from time to time. In any case, the current mentality as well as practice is that everyone grabs whatever is available for him or herself. Each villager is finding his or her own way to defend themselves. Thirdly, since the late 1980s, most young and able male Gao villagers have left as migrant workers. There is not much choice in terms of male candidates among those who have remained in Gao Village. No woman has so far been willing to stand as candidate, likewise the elderly and the middle aged.

the village committee has entailed material benefits; but women have not been on an equal footing to compete with men for a position. Men are free of responsibilities for housework and looking after children. They have no difficulty in leaving home for days to take part in a conference, nor in walking alone at night to attend a meeting in another village. When collecting taxes and levies and implementing family planning policies a village official often meets with resistance from local villagers, and this sometimes leads to physical fighting, or at least to shouting and quarrelling. All these aspects of the job are daunting for a woman. Since the 1980s, village officials have spent a lot of money and time on eating, drinking and smoking, which is inextricably associated with the job. Again, a rural woman is not supposed to be involved in such activities.

Participation in productive activities by women does raise women's status, if not publicly at least domestically. This can be seen by comparing those women who have worked in the field with those who have not. During the commune period, there were altogether fourteen women who either never worked or worked very little in the field. These were women of older genera- tions, all of whom had bound feet. Having bound feet alone was not sufficient reason to not work in the field. My mother had bound feet and she had to go out to work to pay the family debts. Some of these women were too old, or too weak to work like men. Others did not have to work because their families had enough labourers and their household account was always in credit with the production team. Only one woman refused to work and always claimed to be sick. This was Rongxiu, a domineer- ing woman and wife of the production team leader, Gao Changyao, who was one of the only two members of the Communist Party in Gao Village. Though the household was always in the red, Rongxiu's husband's status protected her from having to work in the fields.

Apart from Rongxiu and another woman whose husband was quiet and did not have a forceful personality, the remaining twelve women were docile and obedient to their husbands. Of these, two had husbands who had had affairs with Gao Village women, and this was public knowledge. These two women dared not even complain. In comparison, none of the women who had participated in working in the fields appeared to be obedient to their husbands. They would appear in public like men; their mannerisms and their ways of speaking showed a confidence and assertiveness that was lacking in the other group of women. They had a greater say in the family budget and in what to do or not to do in the family. None of the husbands in this group had committed adultery.

The rise in status, however, also had a cost. These women had to work much harder than the other group of women, on top of housework and care of children. Farm work can be very hard, and weather conditions are harsh. However, during the collective period, women were often assigned less physically demanding work or offered better work conditions. Very often, women also worked for shorter hours in the fields and had more breaks. They could, for instance, return home in the middle of work to feed a baby when required.

While women are expected to do all the housework such as cooking and washing, men in Gao Village also work extremely hard. Usually they work in the fields for a couple of hours before breakfast while women wash and cook at home. At noon, while women go back home to cook men continue their work in the fields. In the early evening when it is not yet dark, women will start cooking while their men are still working in the fields. During the collective period, farm work on the family private plots was mainly carried out by men either before or after their participation in collective farming. Men in Gao Village do not get drunk, and they do not spend time in a tea house because there has never been one. Until the late 1980s Gao Village men also did not gamble. Since then, however, a number of men have started to gamble by playing mahjoing and poker. Some Gao Village women do the same. There are always family quarrels in Gao Village, but domestic violence and physical abuse are rare.

Festivals

The Communist regime introduced four new holidays in China: March 8 (Women's Day) May 1 (Labour Day), June 1 (Children's Day) and October 1 (the National Day). However, these holidays are only for urban people and for those who earn a government salary. They do not have much significance for the villagers. Most villagers have no spiritual or emotional attachment to these holidays, which are not celebrated in any material way in village life. Only for a couple of years during the height of the Cultural Revolution, were women villagers asked to rest at home on Women's Day with a full day's work points. As for the other three holidays the only impact they have on the villagers is that school children do not have to go to school.

The villagers do, however, attach great importance to traditional festivals. Of all the traditional festival occasions, the Spring Festival is the most important. The festival starts on the 28th day of the Twelfth Month and ends on the 15th day of the First Month of the Lunar Calendar. Rural villagers can afford to have such a long holiday because the festival falls in the slack season around February of the Solar Calendar when there is no farming work to do. There are three family dinners on the 28th to the 30th day of the Twelve Month. These three dinners are the most lavish and most expensive in a year. The villagers will save every penny they can throughout the whole year to prepare for the occasion. Almost nothing is spent throughout the year, but nothing will be spared during the Spring Festival. Chickens are raised to be killed for the occasion, as are the pigs. New clothing will be made, if affordable, for the occasion. Marriages are arranged to take place during the period. Every member of a household is expected to come back home for the occasion.

Since the 1980s millions of migrant workers have travelled home and then back to work during this period, some from as far as 1,000 kilometres away, even for just a couple of days. Every year during this time, the Chinese government has to organise thousands of trains and millions of buses to cope with the un-stoppable flow of people. Candies, wine and cakes are made, and sugar and cigarettes are bought in huge quantities for the occasion. For the average rural villagers, this is the only time they do not mind consuming and spending for the sheer pleasure of it.

On New Year's Eve, that is the 30th day of the Twelfth Month, every child expects to receive some cash as a gift. There are fireworks every night for the three dinners, after which children may hold their lanterns, roving around the village. For three consecutive nights before each dinner starts, the food has to be offered first to the ancestors, to whom all family members are to kowtow three times. On the early morning of New Year's Day, every household sets off fireworks to declare the coming of a lucky new year. The louder the sound and the longer the fireworks last the better for the family. After a breakfast of rice cakes cooked in home-made wine flavoured porridge, the male villagers will do obeisance to the clan book. After that, villagers start to visit each other. They chat away while eating peanuts, home made crackers and cakes. From the second day of the new year onwards, villagers start paying visits to relatives and friends in other villages. The first visit is always to the parents-in-law and the next visit to other close relatives. Each visit will last for half or even a whole day if the journey is long. This will go on right up to the 15th day of the First Month of the new year, and until everyone has visited everyone else. Everyone wears their best and indeed this is the only time of the year when most villagers wear new clothes.

Another important festival for the villagers is *qingming* which falls on the Third Month of the Lunar Calendar (April of the Solar Calendar). Rice cakes with both sweet and savoury filling will be made for the occasion. The cakes will be taken to the graveside and offered to the ancestors and paper money and joss sticks will be burned. This is also the time when maintenance of ancestral graves such as adding more earth to the grave dome or patching a hole dug by rabbits or rats, is carried out. The next important festival is *duanwu* (Dragon Boat Festival), which falls on the 5th day of the Fifth Month (July of the Solar Calendar). The atmosphere of *duanwu* is more cheerful. While *qingming* is more of a family affair *duanwu* is more public. Every family will make bread and sticky rice cakes wrapped in bamboo leaves for the occasion. By then the weather is bright and warm. Along the river and lake banks thousands of villagers will watch the dragon boat races. Sometimes, local operas and Peking operas will be performed on an open ground.

In Qinglin area, dragon boat races were not held every year. In some years, floods were too serious, and when there was no good crop harvest in sight the villagers did not have the heart to be festive. Also during a couple of years when Maoist politics were at their most radical, dragon boat races were forbidden by local authorities. One of the primary reasons for the suppression of dragon boat races was that they tended to arouse inter-village disputes. Very often, villagers compete in dragon boat races to win honours for their own villages. Those villages that have a history of disputes will fight to win a race. In the Youdunjie area on a couple of occasions, the race led to serious fighting in which many villagers were wounded. Gao Village has never taken part in any race, and it could not even afford to own a dragon boat.

The last traditional festival is *zhongqiu*, or the Mid-Autumn Festival. This festival falls in the Eighth Month and is the least eventful, but it is very much discussed and celebrated in classical Chinese literature. This was the festival for the gentry and the educated, who were supposed to appreciate the beauty and spirit of a perfect autumn moon. The inspired poet would write a few lines to show his friends while walking or sitting in an elegant garden. For the rural villagers, this was a luxury that they could not afford, either before or since 1949. However, every household will buy some moon cakes to please the children. To the Chinese the round moon symbolises unity and hence the Mid-Autumn Festival is a festival for family members and relatives to get together.

On each of these traditional festivals, the man of an engaged couple has to pay a visit to his parents-in-law. The amount and quality of the gift he brings each time is closely scrutinised not only by his fiancé, and by her parents but also by her fellow villagers. Sometimes, in order to win face for her fiancé as well as herself and her family, the woman will misinform her fellow villagers by telling them that more has been brought to the family than is actually the case. But misinformation can work both ways. If the engaged woman or the family ever intends to break up the engagement, she or her family will spread the word that the man's family is too poor or too mean, and that the gifts are not worth mentioning. Once married, the husband does not visit his wife's parents on every festival. For the first couple of years he may visit them, usually with his wife, a couple of times a year. Finally, it becomes a routine, once every year during the Spring Festival.

On the whole, the so-called Communist onslaught on Chinese tradition has not been very vicious in rural areas like Gao Village. There have been changes with respect to culture and customs, some driven by Communist ideology and some by economic imperatives. For instance, the removal of graves and shrinkage of space for burying the dead took place largely because of economic necessity. Some of the changes, such as education for women and women's participation in agricultural production, have improved their lot. The retreat of religious practices in Mao's era and their revival since Mao's death show clearly how ideology and socio-economic conditions work hand in hand in rural society. When affordable health care was organised and made accessible to the villagers, traditional practices such as praying to the Buddha fell into decline. When affordable health care disappeared, traditional religious practices revived.

The same applies to marriage customs and the Chinese desire for male children. Economic imperatives have been inherently related to arranged marriages and the practice of dowry. Once a woman is married she cannot contribute to the well-being of her parent's household. Therefore, the family wants to get as much as possible out of the dowry arrangement, both for the sake of the woman's future material well-being and to compensate for the household's cost of having brought the woman up. Love-marriages which have no regard for economic considerations therefore tend not to be entertained by parents. Equally, arranged marriages through relatives save marriage costs for both sides. The preference for male children is partly a Chinese tradition; but the practice continues largely because of a lack of a social security system. In urban areas, where there was a comprehensive social security system, at least in Mao's era, the prejudice against female children was not a serious problem. The Communist onslaught on tradition has brought about changes only when there was a socio-economic back up. Otherwise traditions continue and revivals of traditional practices take place once the ideological grip is loosened.

13

GAO VILLAGE AND THE OUTSIDE WORLD

Until the early 1980s when many left the village to become migrant workers, Gao villagers knew very little of the outside world. Most of them had never got on a bus. They could not afford to travel and indeed there was not much need for them to do so. My mother travelled the most among all the villagers. She went to cities like Jingdezhen, Nanchang (the capital of Jiangxi Province), and even Shanghai because she could travel free on her son-in-law's cargo ship during business trips. She was also the only one of her generation to have ever travelled on a train when she came to Xiamen to visit me.

The villagers cared very little about the outside world beyond village borders. The changes in the village in the past forty odd years were more than enough to occupy them. By the early 1980s just as they were getting used to Mao's policies in the collective system, the system was dismantled. They can only base their world view on their life experience and their scope of vision cannot go beyond what they are allowed to see. For generations their life centred around how to survive. They therefore tended to judge other people in a pragmatic way. For instance, in the eyes of the villagers Mao was an emperor who could eat the best food and wear the best clothes. They thought Mao, like other emperors, had *jin kou yin ya* ("gold mouth and silver teeth") which meant whatever he said must be the final judgement and ultimate truth. They knew and cared little about ideology or élite political struggles. They took it for granted that whatever has happened should have happened. From time to time they were unhappy and would complain about policies imposed on them, such as not being allowed to sell an egg in the market. They wanted more private plots and they did not want too many meetings. But they did not see those impositions and restrictions as Mao's fault. Mostly they blamed the local party officials.

During Mao's era policies changed continually, and no single policy could be said specifically to have brought the villagers substantial material improvement. The most visible benefits were Mao's education and health care policies. Therefore they respected him. The villagers heard of Liu Shaoqi and his downfall. But they did not really know what Liu Shaoqi's policies meant for them. They thought Liu must be a *jian chen* ("disloyal court official") or else things would not have happened to him the way they did.

The villagers do not think much of Deng Xiaoping. The post-Mao reform policies of the early 1980s such as the increase in the price of agricultural produce brought some benefits to the villagers. However, these reform policies were not carried out in the name of Deng Xiaoping because officially Deng never occupied the number one position of the country. In any case, the benefits brought about by these reform policies were short-lived. The cost of agricultural input shot up quickly, blatant corruption by local party officials soon followed and polarisation manifested itself on a large scale. When Deng Xiaoping was known to wield power behind the scenes he was blamed for all the adverse developments. The villagers still think of and talk about Mao affectionately and respectfully. When I visited the villagers in the 1990s I noticed that some of them still hang Mao's portrait in their house. They refer to Deng as Deng *Aizi* (the "short" Deng) while Mao appeared overpowering and his behaviour showed style and dignity. The villagers think Deng does not even look like an emperor.

The negative attitude towards Deng by the local party officials is even more striking. Almost all of them became wealthier since the death of Mao. They have built large houses; they now ride on motorbikes whereas in Mao's time some of them could not even afford a push bike. There is undeniable material improvement in post-Mao China, and this can even be seen in the Qinglin area: more houses have been built and everyone is better dressed. Yet nobody likes Deng. When asked for an explanation of this apparent paradox, the local government officials invariably answer that there is too much corruption in present-day China, though they themselves may be the culprits! They also complain that there are too many crimes and nobody feels safe any more. It is true that migrant workers bring in income to the villagers. However, the villagers feel the changes profoundly unsettling and life

precarious. Both the migrant workers and the villagers do not
know what they will end up with. Some local officials who know
a little about politics talk of China as going back to the "old
society". Even the illiterate old villagers would complain that "*xian-
zai de shehui tai hei'an*" (the present society is too dark) and "*ren
xin tai huai*" (people's hearts are too evil). Some believe that
government officials in south China sell land to foreigners to
enrich themselves.

While everyone seems to blame someone else for the "darkness"
prevailing in the present-day Chinese society some villagers will
not hesitate to engage in "evil" activities to make fast money.
Two incidents may illustrate the situation. In 1996, a textile factory
from Guangdong, in order to reduce transaction costs, sent someone
to purchase cotton direct from Yu Village (from 1,000 households)
of Yinbaohu. Having inspected the cotton, negotiated the price,
signed the contract and paid the money, the person from the
factory went home happy. It was a huge deal, involving thousands
of tons of cotton. When the cargo finally arrived in Guangdong,
the factory discovered to their horror that enough bricks to build
a house had been carefully wrapped in the cotton! A similar
incident happened in a neighbouring village when the villagers
mixed sesame seeds with coal dust, which they then sold to an
oil mill enterprise.

The villagers know less about the world outside China. In
1994, however, I was surprised to be asked about the 2000 Olympics
and about Sydney. By 1994 there were electricity and television
sets in Gao Village, and the Chinese mass media had launched a
huge national campaign to promote China's bid for the 2000
Olympics. I did not realise the degree of humiliation and hurt
many Chinese must have suffered from China's failure in its bid
for the games until I discovered that even Gao villagers were
tuned in to the event. Another thing which astonished me was
the way the villagers asked about Hong Kong. They wanted to
know whether the British would fight a war to keep Hong Kong
and, if they did, whether China could win. Once I had trouble
in getting through when I tried to ring from Australia to Boyang
County. My sister wanted to know whether the telephone problem
had anything to do with China's quarrel with Britain over Hong
Kong.

Ever since China's defeat in the Opium Wars the Chinese

have had complex feelings and attitudes towards "foreigners". This is also true of Gao villagers. They know very little of what a foreign country is like and their overwhelming impression of a foreign country or a foreigner is of their wealth and material superiority. They believe that foreign goods have a magic quality. They have one word for everything foreign, which is *yang* (literally meaning "ocean", therefore from overseas). The Chinese used to and Gao villagers still call matches *yang huo* ("foreign fire"), petrol *yang you* ("foreign oil"), motor boats *yang chuan* ("foreign boats"), guns *yang qiang* ("foreign guns), soap *yang zao* ("foreign soap"), and synthetic fabric *yang bu* ("foreign cloth"). All these goods seem better than their traditional equivalents. The Chinese invented gunpowder, but their guns could not even kill a rabbit. A petrol lamp is much brighter than an oil lamp, and *yang bu* looks shiny and is much easier to wash. They therefore have this built-in notion that "foreign" means "wealth".

The villagers do not know anything about Africa or South America. Their overall impression of the world outside China is the "white" person. They have heard about *yang fang* ("foreign houses") built by foreigners in Shanghai and cities like Qingdao, which are colourful, with two or more storeys and gardens. It is like fairy tales to the villagers because their own houses are grey, functional and have mud floors. Occasionally they would hear that an overseas Chinese from Hong Kong or the United States has come back with a lot of money.

Even the government propaganda give the villagers this impression. In the film *The Red Detachment of Woman Soldiers*, very popular during the late 1960s, a Communist Red Army officer dressed himself up as a rich overseas Chinese from Hong Kong in order to get into a landlord's fortified house to organise a revolutionary uprising. This Communist officer looked very rich and glamorous as an overseas Chinese and even the landlord respected him.

When I returned to Gao Village after I had settled as an overseas Chinese in Australia, the villagers thought I must be very rich as well. The village and local government officials either explicitly or implicitly asked me to donate money for setting up a school and for some irrigation projects. Rumours went around that I had given so much money to my brothers and sister that they were going to build a large "foreign"−style house.

The villagers know so little about "foreigners" that they did not know what to ask me about when I first returned from abroad. A common question was what people eat in Britain. They commented that those foreigners must smell when I told them that they ate lamb and mutton. To them eating raw vegetables and drinking cold milk is uncivilised. They cannot understand why these foreigners do not eat fish heads, or a pig's head, feet or heart. When I gave them some chocolate to taste, none of them liked it. It was too bitter, they said.

The villagers, after they had acquired electricity and television sets, came to know what foreigners looked like. But the images seemed alien. They cannot understand how a black person can be so black. They think that the "whites" are generally too big, too hairy, their eyes too deep-set and their noses too long. In 1994 Cao Junrong, a local government official with whom I was friendly when I was a "barefoot teacher" in the 1970s, asked me what I thought of *waiguoren* ("the foreigners"). After I mumbled something I asked him the same question. This man, who had six years' education and had served in the army for three years and therefore had travelled quite a bit in China, said that these foreigners looked so ugly and yet they would often kiss openly on television. How, he exclaimed, could anyone kiss a woman like that?

During one trip to Gao Village I took along two Australian colleagues of mine. It was an unforgettable event in the village, one that they would keep on talking about for years to come. Everyone, man or woman, old or young, rushed out to look at the two foreigners. It was the first time in their lives that they saw two real "foreigners" in person. One of my colleagues has quite a prominent beer belly, like a happy Buddha. The village kids followed him wherever he went and kept on saying that he was pregnant. On another trip I took a student, a beautiful twenty-year-old woman with blue eyes and blonde hair. When I introduced her to a group of villagers, Gao Renyun, the man who long ago had an affair with my mother but is now eighty years old, said to me that he did not realise that was a young woman. He thought it was an elderly man with white hair!

The older generations of Gao villagers have very definite ideas of themselves and about the world around them though they do not not know much about it. Some of their ideas are derived from their own life experience whereas some are traditional, passed down for generations. For instance, in traditional China *xue er you ze shi* ("distinguished scholarship leads to a privileged career of a government official") had been a practice as well as ideology for more than a thousand years. The Gao villagers still believe that. When I returned from Britain in 1981, they all expected me to be appointed to an important official position in the government. When I got off a crowded dirty bus with no one to help with my suitcase, they were terribly disappointed. They thought that I should have been driven home in a car by a chauffeur with a couple of bodyguards. One of them assured the crowd surrounding me that I was already a member of the Central Committee of the Chinese Communist Party. One day in 1981 when I was at my mother's house, a villager walked in casually. When he saw I was reading a book he was puzzled and asked me why I still needed to read books. He commented with a tone of authority that I must have already read all the books there were to read in the world.

While the urban residents in China are fascinated by things foreign, from motorcars to cosmetics, Gao villagers do not seem affected by the trend. When I offered my brother a watch as a gift, he chose a Chinese watch instead of a foreign one. In 1994 when I offered to buy him a colour television my brother again asked me to buy a Chinese made one. He said a Chinese one was better because if something went wrong he could at least find someone to repair it. The villagers have to be practical because they are so poor. A single shopping spree by a young lady in Shanghai could be the equivalent of a poor villager's hard savings of many years.

The villagers have to be practical in order to survive. Some years ago, I offered to invite my mother to visit Australia. Though my mother was toying with the idea, all other members of the family were against it. They argued that so much money could be better spent on more essential things. If I wanted to spend that kind of money, a trip around China was better than a trip abroad, they said. Things outside their scope of life tend to be either irrelevant or do not make much sense. When I first went home from my studies in Britain the villagers wanted to hear me speak English. Then they would say to themselves that it was a "ghost language" that did not make any sense.

To the establishment Chinese intelligentsia, and to some extent urban residents, rural people like Gao villagers are just ignorant and stupid. They would say these villagers do not know anything about the outside world and stubbornly hold to their own way of life. In some sense this is true. However, if we are willing to be sympathetic we may see it in a different light. The villagers' values in life and attitudes towards the outside world reveal a sense of dignity, and even a degree of pride. They are very sure of themselves and proud of their way of life. Their life has indeed been an enclosed one and they were not given a chance to be otherwise until very recently.

It is not that the villagers want to be indifferent to the outside world. Rather, they do not see the point in being otherwise. They are always treated as beasts of burden. Who cares what they think? For most of Chinese history, the Chinese élite just wanted to exploit as much as possible the labour of the villagers. Rural conditions became a worry for the élite only when there was a famine which might lead to a peasant uprising. It is true that some of Mao's policies, such as the Great Leap Forward, brought disaster to the villagers, but Mao did take the initiative to change the patterns of their life. He wanted the villagers to get organised and he wanted them to run industry as well as agriculture in order to narrow the differences between the urban and the rural. As part of this effort Mao also urged the urban youths to go to live and work in rural areas to "learn from the peasants". Mao's policies were reversed by post-Mao reforms and were interpreted as disastrous for China's modernisation. However, the development of township enterprises is definitely a part of Mao's legacy. Yet the present Chinese élite do not see it that way.

That the villagers are treated with contempt and callousness can be illustrated by what I encountered in 1996. Gao Changsen, an old man of seventy, came to me, begging me to help rescue his grandson. This is the story he told. His grandson worked as a migrant worker in Beijing. He came home on a visit and a marriage with a rural girl was arranged. The family needed some money for the engagement. The young man did not arrange for the money to be sent from Beijing either because he did not know how, or the system could not do it, or he simply did not trust the system (it is quite common, and it has been reported in the official press, that many villagers are unable to cash their savings through the post office or bank). So he went to Beijing to get the money which he had saved. While waiting for his grandson to return with the money, Gao Changsen did not hear anything from the young man until he received an envelope from the Beijing police. In the envelope there was no letter, but a note stating that his grandson had been arrested. The note, which I examined, had an official police stamp but no more than a dozen words. No explanation was given of why the young man was arrested. Nor was there a hint of what the police were going to do with him. There was no contact telephone number, nor was an address attached. Gao Changsen did not know how to get to Beijing. He could not afford the trip anyway. In any case, even if a villager was going to Beijing it would be almost impossible to find the right people there. Other villagers helped him by making enquiries and visited the local government officials, but nobody knew anything about it. Gao Changsen was sobbing miserably in front of me and a group of villagers and hoped that I could help. On my way to Hong Kong I stopped at Nanchang, the capital of Jiangxi Province. I requested the people I knew in Nanchang to look into the matter, but no one knew even how to start.

Gao villagers' indifference towards the outside world has been conditioned by their economic circumstances and their way of life. Education has some effect on their world outlook, but the effect is very limited. The main reason is that, despite great progress made in Mao's era, most of them have had only a very basic level of education. For these villagers, most of what they learned at school becomes irrelevant as soon as they leave. For those whose economic circumstances have changed as a result of their education Gao village life has become irrelevant because they, like me and Gao Chaodong, have left the village. They are not Gao villagers any more.

Since the late 1980s, however, two developments have emerged which can potentially change the villagers' outlook. One is the villagers' access to television and the other is migrant work. However, change in the villagers' mentality as a result of these two developments has yet to manifest itself. A genuine change of mentality, for better or for worse, takes a long time to take effect. Gao villagers may amuse themselves with television, but they have yet to connect their own life with what appears on the screen. It is still too remote and too irrelevant. For instance, the urban Chinese may aspire for a Western style of life and Chinese students may be attracted by concepts such as democracy, but the thinking of rural residents like Gao villagers cannot be channelled towards this kind of aspiration by watching television. I have encountered numerous urban residents who asked me to help them migrate to or study in Australia. Gao villagers, however, think that this kind of idea is simply silly.

Migrant workers, on the other hand, are different. Gao Changwen, my migrant worker brother in Xiamen, wants to go to Australia to be a worker because he thinks he will earn much more there. Economic circumstances of migrant workers have changed and they have seen and experienced different styles of life. As long as they remain migrant workers they are not Gao villagers anymore. They are all young and their mentality is in the process of being formed. Will they have to go back to Gao Village when they reach the age of marriage? What do they think of themselves and the outside world after many years in urban areas? The answers to these questions may have profound implications for the future of China and therefore the outside world.

14

CONCLUSION

The history of Gao Village from 1949 onwards is not a history of the People's Republic of China. It is not the intention in this book to make generalisations about all of rural China. On the contrary, one main aim of this case study is to show that what has happened in one village can be different from the general picture of post-1949 China that has been conventionally presented.

Post-1949 China provides the non-academic community with some simple but enduring generalisations. When they think of it, some pictures always appear: backyard furnaces making useless iron and steel, and everyone beating a gong to kill sparrows during the Great Leap Forward; Red Guards burning books and beating up their teachers and Party officials during the Cultural Revolution; and everyone shouting with a *Little Red Book* and dancing to show their loyalty to the Great Leader Chairman Mao. Or, more recently, tanks running over students in Tiananmen Square and police beating up Tibetans. However, none of these pictures fits in with what has happened in Gao Village.

Of course, there is a methodological question of what value a case study like Gao Village has in interpreting China. While admitting that a case study of this kind cannot be used to prove any generalisation about China, it aims to provide insights. Any generalisation about China as a whole can be argued to be "scientifically" flawed. This is because China is so vast and there are always regional differences and variations. All we can hope for is to provide insights for understanding.

There are many factors contributing to regional differences in China. One primary factor to be taken into consideration is that there are two Chinas: a rural and an urban China. Rural China is not only different from urban China economically, but also politically. What has happened in urban China can never be taken as the same as in rural China, or vice versa.

Coastal China is different from central China which is in turn different from the north-west of China. Pre-1949 history may have left social and economic conditions that are different in coastal China. For instance, the fact that Guangdong is near Hong Kong and that many families in Guangdong have overseas Chinese relatives can have a range of social, political and economic implications that are absent in Gao Village. What has happened in Gao Village may in many ways mirror what has happened in rural Hunan, Anhui, Henan, and Sichuan where historical and economic conditions are similar. But they may be very different from what has happened in Guangdong or in Gansu and Xinjiang Provinces.

Even within the same region, differences may arise as a result of policy implementation. Because of the informal, personal, and autocratic style of Communist Party politics, the character and inclination of the number one leader in a province can have great differential policy consequences. For instance, the leadership in Anhui Province was more adventurous than in Jiangxi during the Great Leap Forward. As a result, the famine was far worse in Anhui than that in Jiangxi. In fact, a large number of peasants fled from Anhui to Jiangxi to beg for food during the most difficult years of the Great Leap Forward.

Because China is a so-called Communist country, there is a tendency by the mainstream media in the West to perceive China as an undifferentiated block in which everyone everywhere has to be the same. The fact that there is a world of difference between urban and rural China and that local governments can and do respond to and implement central policies differently tends to be ignored. Because of their eagerness to condemn Communist ideas and practice there is a tendency by the mainstream Western media not to take into consideration how local conditions and traditional influences have interacted in rural development since 1949.

The Gao villagers are mostly illiterate or semi-literate; but they are not, as some Marxists and élite Chinese intelligentsia would like us to believe, a backward-looking or feudalist reactionary mass which is supposed to be an obstacle to the advance of socialist history – "sacks of potatoes". Unlike the Chinese scholar-gentry class, the villagers were not die-hard traditionalists although the burden of tradition still weighs heavily on them. Unlike the urban educated who were once romantic about socialist China, they were not fanatical Maoists. The villagers were rational and pragmatic, although bullied and manipulated from time to time by the local officials.

The Chinese peasantry have made great contributions to China's industrialisation and to a welfare system that benefits the urban sector. Yet, instead of being sympathetic and grateful for the contributions made by the Chinese peasantry, the urban community in general and the Chinese élite in particular have a contemptuous attitude towards the Chinese peasantry whom they blame for China's backwardness. They claim that the "feudalist residue of the Chinese peasant consciousness" is to blame for the lack of democratic tradition in China and therefore for the personal and authoritarian style of CCP politics.

Several specific points can be made about developments in Gao Village since 1949. Gao villagers made great strides in production output as a result of the introduction of new crops and new technology as well as the more intensive exploitation of land. However, increases in output did not lead to visible improvements in material living standards for the Gao villagers. This was due to two main factors. One was the demand placed on the peasantry to contribute to China's industrialisation. The government had, until the early 1980s, always prescribed how much grain consumption *per capita* was allowed for the rural population. Any "surplus" grain had to be sold to the state at the state controlled price. The second main factor was that the population in Gao Village doubled in forty years. Like farmers anywhere in the world, the livelihood of the Gao villagers depended on their land. Twice as many people living on the same amount of land meant a 100 per cent reduction of income if the output remained the same. A one-fold increase in production output meant that only the same level of income could be maintained.

Therefore, an improvement in living standards for villagers in Gao Village depends on many interacting factors. If everything remains unchanged, the population has to be checked. In order to enable the villagers to check the birth rate voluntarily there needs to be a social security system and the population needs to be educated. In order to have sound social security and an educated population a breakthrough in the village's economy has to be brought about. In order to bring about an economic breakthrough, commercialisation and external capital are required. For all kinds of reasons, some of which are hinted at and some discussed, while others such as international factors are not discussed, commercialisation did not take place and external capital was not available. On the contrary, Gao villagers had no cash to spend because the pricing system was discriminatory and the government needed funds for other priorities. Thus, having to be dependent entirely on the limited amount of land with shrinking resources, Gao villagers were kept in a poverty trap from which they could not escape.

The rapid increase in population in Gao Village was the result of improvements in health care and a dramatic reduction of child mortality. One of the most visible benefits brought about by the Communist revolution in 1949 was the introduction of elementary health care technology such as immunisation and the control of plagues such as "snail fever". Another area of visible improvement in Gao Village since 1949 was education. There was a great increase in literacy in Gao Village in Mao's time. It has to be emphasised that it was during the period of the Cultural Revolution that these strides were made in improving health care and education in Gao Village. Both health care and education in Gao Village deteriorated since the 1980s, largely due to the detrimental rural policies since the late 1970s. Education only began to improve again since the early 1990s as a consequence of remittances from migrant workers and the demand for literate migrant workers.

Another important point to be made about Gao Village since 1949 were the environmental and ecological consequences. The increasing demand for grain to feed the ever increasing population has led to two developments. One was the decrease of production of cash crops so that more and more land had been turned into rice paddy. As a result, the necessity for filling the stomachs of the population had to be accomplished through the loss of cash income. The suppression of cash crops and the increasing focus on grain production in Gao Village had nothing to do with agricultural radicalism as conventionally interpreted. According to this interpretation, the ideologically motivated Maoist agricultural radicalism intended to suppress cash crops because cash crops were supposed to breed commercialism which in turn would breed capitalism. In the case of Gao Village, the villagers turned most of the cash crop land into rice paddy driven by the necessity of feeding the population, not as a result of an ideological push.

The disappearance of cash crops not only meant shortage of

cash for Gao villagers but also had a more far reaching consequence: the destruction of rural self-sufficiency. Until the early 1970s, the commodity items Gao villagers spent most of their cash on were salt, soap and matches. They made most of the daily necessities themselves. By the late 1980s, Gao villagers had to buy most of these necessity items from shops. And by the 1990s, helped by remittances from their migrant workers, Gao Village families purchased most things except grain and a few vegetables, either from shops or specialised households in nearby villages.

The other development was ecological destruction. Because of the increasing application of chemicals for the sake of increased grain production, aquatic life has been destroyed in the area. Rice growing is closely bound up with a water system that connects paddy with ponds, streams and creeks with lakes and rivers. Fish, shrimps, crabs, and so on used to be a very low cost source of protein in the villagers' diet. Water weeds used to be natural food sources for pigs and other domestic animals. Chemical applications have destroyed almost all of them. The villagers can no longer hear the soothing noise made by frogs during summer nights. Fish is now available only from fish farms.

Because of the increasing exploitation of land, erosion has become more and more serious. As a result, river beds like those of the Yellow and the Yangtze rivers have kept on rising. Because of reclamation of land from Poyang Lake and its surrounding rivers, the size of Poyang Lake and that of rivers have been shrinking. The combined result is the reduction in the capacity of the land to hold water, reduction in water catchment by the rivers and lakes, and a slowing in the speed of water flowing from Poyang Lake into the Yangtze river. As a consequence we have been witnessing more and more frequent floods occurring in the areas surrounding Poyang Lake. By the 1990s, there was a flood almost every year.

One enduring feature of rural China is that many villages are clan villages: every male has the same surname and every child born in the village has the same surname. Moreover, every male of the same generation born in the village has the same second name. Until very recently when migrant work started to take place, every villager identified him or herself with a clan village. The clan village was their society and anything else was either unreal or beyond their reach. Every clan village has its own territory which has more or less remained unchanged since 1949. The Communist revolution in 1949 had neither changed the village based economy, nor clan identity in Gao Village.

Politically and socially, a clan village like Gao Village was an independent entity by and in itself. Apart from a brief period during the Great Leap Forward, the People's Commune, which was established throughout rural China, did not create much community life beyond the clan village. A small clan village used to form a production team, a bigger clan village two or three production teams and an even bigger clan village used to be a production brigade. Whether a clan village could do well economically depended on its leadership. Land resources had not been re-allocated among villages by the commune system. Only human resources had been re-allocated during the most radical period such as the Great Leap Forward and the Cultural Revolution, but mainly for irrigation projects. Those clan villages which performed poorly either because of poor management or because of poor resources were not supported by the villages which were doing better.

In a word, both in terms of community identity and economic well being, the Communist revolution had not gone beyond the framework of a clan village. Not surprisingly, clan and genealogical characteristics overlapped, interfered and interacted with CCP policies and politics throughout Gao Village's and its neighbouring villages' history since 1949. Be it in the selection of local Party officials, re-allocation of human resources for infrastructure projects such as irrigation or territorial dispute resolution, clan and genealogical relations had played their role in influencing the final outcome. The most unambiguous example in the present account is how clan and genealogical relations affected and influenced political development during the Cultural Revolution.

While clan power has been strong in protecting a village's interest when in conflict with other clan villages, it is in many ways weak in its resistance against the state. For example, during the commune period no village clan had even tried to resist the state's imposition of taxes and state controlled price system. This was the case because until recently the tax system had been transparent and stable. It is only since the late 1980s that the imposition of local levies has become arbitrary and abusive. Because of this there has been resistance. However, there have been only isolated cases, and organised resistance by clan power has yet to appear in the Gao Village area.

Even so, some villagers in some of the powerful clan villages can get away with refusing to pay some of the local levies while Gao villagers cannot. As for the state controlled price system, there simply was no avenue for resistance since the villagers either had nothing to sell or had nowhere else to sell anything. Nor has a clan tried to resist the state's policy of family planning, though it is fair to say that state policy in this respect had not had any serious effect in rural areas until recent years. Even during the late 1980s and 1990s when the family policy had become more effective, implementation measures had been inconsistent. At times it was tight and forceful, at others loose and relaxed. Therefore, even if a clan wanted to resist, it was at loss as to how to respond to an uncertain policy.

Aspects of Chinese tradition were also at work in rural villages, interacting with the Communist political economy. For instance, in the commune system households with better labour resources were clearly subsidising households with poor resources. This is often interpreted as a result of Mao's policy of egalitarianism. In fact, it was an openly declared policy that in a commune system, distribution was "to each according to work performed" and that those who had contributed more should get more reward. However, for years on end, those who had contributed more did not get rewarded because the households in debt had not paid the households in credit. Therefore, the principle of "to each according to work performed" had remained on paper, but was not carried out in practice. This had been the case partly because those who were in debt very often had no means to repay their debts. Another important reason was the complicated clan relationship. Because in a clan village all households were somehow related to each other, they were obliged by their sense of genealogical duty not to be too forceful in settling the accounts.

It is often argued in the post-Mao Chinese literature that rural residents remained poor because "the big pot" economy in a commune system discouraged the villagers to work hard. Gao Village does not seem to bear this argument out. There was an elaborate monitoring and evaluation system in the commune system, and production output did increase steadily since 1949 in Gao Village. What had kept rural income low was not a lack of motivation to work but the exploitative nature of the pricing system. What boosted rural income in the early 1980s was more a result of price reform than the dismantling of the collective system. Had the pricing system and compulsory purchases remained unchanged during the 1980s rural income might have been kept low in spite of household farming in Gao Village.

On the other hand, there is clear evidence of a breakdown of collective health care in the village. At the same time agricultural input costs kept on rising and incomes stagnated. Rural residents became discontented and restless, and as a consequence the crime rate in the rural areas started to rise rapidly. Further deterioration was only checked since the early 1990s because of the job opportunities provided by the rapid industrial development in south China.

Migrant workers from Gao Village have done many things to improve their family situation back home. First, because discontented young villagers have left the village to become migrant workers rural crimes have been checked. Second, as fewer people need to be fed on the village's limited stretch of land, the ecological and economic burden on the land resources has been reduced. Third, remittances from migrant workers have helped Gao Village families with their payments for local levies, for health care and for education costs. By the mid 1990s around 30 per cent of Gao villagers had left the village as migrant workers. These migrant workers not only have to endure harsh working conditions but also suffer emotional trauma and are often abused by the factory owners. Still, the young Gao villagers are more than happy to be employed in the industrial sector and their earnings continue to subsidise rural life back home.

Apart from improvement in health care and education from which Gao villagers have clearly benefited through the 1949 Communist revolution, rural development in Gao Village had been, until the 1990s, involutionary; increases in output were partly taken away by the state's discriminatory pricing system and partly offset by the rapid increase in population. China's industrial development since the late 1980s has offered Gao villagers opportunities to leave as migrant workers and thus the possibility of breaking the involution for the first time in Gao Village's history.

However, by 1996 this still remained only a possibility, and we cannot claim that involutionary development has been broken.

First, it is not clear whether China's industrial development will continue at a rate that is able to absorb China's surplus rural labour. Second, it is not clear what these migrant workers' destiny will be. The phenomenon of migrant workers from rural China on such a scale has developed only in recent years and these migrant workers are still young. What will they do when they get married? Where will they settle down eventually, in urban areas or back in the villages? Government policies are crucial in determining the final outcome. There are no clear signs yet of what the government policies are.

There are these scenarios about which we may speculate. First, let us suppose that China's industrial development continues at a rate that is able to absorb the young villagers who move to the urban sector as migrant workers, and further suppose that the government takes measures to allow migrant workers to marry and settle down where they work. According to this scenario, China's process of urbanisation and modernisation will be fast. In this process more and more Gao villagers will leave and few will return. As a result, the tradition of clan culture and customs will gradually die out. In the process, problems of urban infrastructure will be serious.

The second scenario is that young villagers will go back home after some years working as migrant workers. Having made enough to build a house and to get married, they will eventually settle down in the village. This is reported to have been taking place in some areas where there are opportunities for migrant workers to develop commercial and business activities in their home areas. Or alternatively, either because of the halt in industrial development as a result of which no employment can be found in the urban sector or because of government impositions, migrant workers are forced to go back to their villages. Rural to urban migration will come to a halt if no employment can be found in the urban sector. Migrant workers will be forced to return home if the government refuses to provide education, health and housing facilities for them when they start having families. Currently no systematic provision of such facilities is on the government's agenda, although the absence of such policies cannot be continued for much longer.

A third scenario is also possible, according to which China's industrialisation will continue, although not at a rate which is able to absorb all the surplus labour from the rural areas. Some migrant workers will return to the rural areas and some will settle down where they work as urban residents. China's urban sector will expand gradually, but not so radically as to create urban ghettos. Those who return to their home villages will, with their newly-acquired capital and expertise, set up local industries or enterprises which will benefit the local economy. Places like Gao Village will not disappear but will maintain a more sustainable ecological environment as a result of a less serious population pressure.

If and when migrant workers do go back, whether Gao villagers will tolerate the traditional ways of life is a big question. They have absorbed new ideas and they have seen alternative ways of life. Migrant work has broadened their horizons, and their expectations may not be the same as their predecessors. Rural residents like Gao villagers may demand their share of China's modernisation. It seems that whichever scenario is to prevail, profound social changes are on the horizon for rural residents. If the international environment is conducive and if government policies are beneficial, the change may be for the better. However, the opposite is not out of the question.

1

BIBLIOGRAPHY OF WORKS ON RURAL STUDIES REFERRED TO IN CHAPTER 1

Baum, R., *Prelude to Revolution: Mao, the Party and the Peasant Question, 1962-6*, New York, 1975.

Bernhardt, K., *Rents, and Peasant Resistance: The Lower Yangzi Region, 1940-1950*, Stanford, 1992.

Brandt, L., *Commercialisation and Agricultural Development in East-Central China, 1870-1937*, Cambridge, 1989.

Buck, J.L., *Land Utilization in China*, Nanking, 1937.

Chalmers, J., *Peasant Nationalism and Communist Power: The Emergence of Revolutionary China*, Stanford, CA, 1962.

Chan, A., R. Madsen, and J. Unger, *Chen Village: the Recent History of a Peasant Community In Mao's China*, Berkeley, CA, 1984.

Crook, D. and I., *The First Years of Yangyi Commune, London, 1966; and Revolution in an Chinese Village, Miles Inn*, London, 1959.

Endicott, S., *Red Earth: Revolution in a Sichuan Village*, London 1988.

Esherick, J., *The Origin of the Boxer Uprising*, Berkeley, CA, 1987.

Faure, D., *Rural Economy of Pre-Liberation China, Trade Increase and Peasant Livelihood in Jiangsu and Guangdong, 1870 to 1937*, Hong Kong, 1989.

Fei Xiaotung, *China's Gentry: Essays on Rural-Urban Relations*, Chicago, 1953.

Freedman, M., *Lineage Organization in Southern China*, London 1970.

Friedman, E., P.G. Pickowice and M. Selden, *Chinese Village and Socialist State*, New Haven and London, 1991.

He Liyi, with Claire Anne Chik, *Mr China's Son: A Villager's Life*, Boulder, CO, 1994.

Hinton, W., *Fanshen: A Documentary of Revolution in Chinese Village*, New York, 1966.

———, *The Great Reversal: The Privatization of China 1978-1989*, New York, 1990.

Howard, P., *Breaking the Iron Bowl: Prospects for Socialism in China's Countryside*, Armonk, NY, 1988.

Huang, P., *The Peasant Economy and Social Change in North China*, Stanford, CA., 1985.

———, *The Peasant Family and Rural Development in the Yangzi Delta*, Stanford, CA 1990.

Huang Shu-min, *The Spiral Road Change in a Chinese Village Through the Eyes of a CCP Leader*, San Francisco, 1987.

Hu Hsien-chin, *The Common Descent Group in China and Its Functions*, New York, 1948.

Kelliher, D., *Peasant Power in China: the Era of Rural Reform, 1979-1989*, New Haven, CY, 1992.

King, F.H., *Farmers of Forty Centuries or Peasant Agriculture in China, Korea and Japan*, London, 1927.

Kulp, D.H., *Phoenix Village, Country Life in South China: The Sociology of Familism*, New York, 1925.

Lardy, N.R., *Agriculture in China's Modern Economic Development*, Cambridge, 1983.

Lippit, V., *Land Reform and Economic Development in China*, New York, 1974.

Lyons, T.P., *Poverty and Growth in a South China County: Anxi, Fujian, 1949-1992*, Ithaca, NY: Cornell University East Asia Series no. 72, 1994.

Madsen, R., *Morality and Power in a Chinese Village*, Berkeley and London, 1984.

Myers, R., *The Chinese Peasant Economy: Agricultural Development in Hepei and Shantung, 1890-1949*, Cambridge, MA., 1970.

Oi, J., *State and Peasant in Contemporary China, the Political Economy of Village Government*, Berkeley, 1989.

Parish, A., and M. Whyte, *Village and Family in Contemporary China*, Chicago, 1978.

———, *Chinese Rural Development: the Great Transformation*, Armonk, NY, 1985.

Perkins, D., *Agricultural Development in China, 1368-1968*, Chicago, 1969.

———, and S. Yusuf, *Rural Development in China*, Baltimore, MD, 1984.

Perry, E., and C. Wong (eds), *The Political Economy of Reform in Post-Mao China*, Cambridge, MA, 1985.

Potter, S.H., and J.M. Potter, *China's Peasants, the Anthropology of a Revolution*, Cambridge and New York, 1990.

Powell, S., *Agricultural Reform in China: From Communes to Commodity Economy*, Manchester and New York, 1992.

Putterman, L., *Continuity and Change in China's Rural Development, Collective and Reform Eras in Perspective*, New York, 1993.

Rawski, T., *Economic Growth in Pre-War China*, Berkeley, CA, 1989.

Riskin, C., *China's Political Economy, the Quest for Development since 1949*, New York, 1987.

Stavis, B., *The Politics of Agricultural Mechanisation in China*, Ithaca, NY, 1978.

Tam, O.K. *China's Modernisation: the Socialist Mechanisation Scheme*, London, 1985.

Thiseau, I., 'Recent Change in a Guangdong Village', *Australian Journal of Chinese Studies*, 19, 20 (1988).

Unger, J., 'State and Peasant in Post-Revolutionary China', *Journal of Peasant Studies*, 17, 1 (1989).

Wang Hong Sheng, '*From Revolutionary Vanguards to Pioneer Entrepreneurs: A Study of Rural Elite in a Chinese Village*, unpubl. Ph.D. thesis, University of Amsterdam, 1995.

Wittfogel, K.A., *New Light on Chinese Society, An Investigation of China's Socio-Economic Structure*, New York, 1938.

Wong, J., *Land Reform in the People's Republic of China*, New York, 1973.

Wong, J., Rong Ma and Mu Yang, (eds), *China's Rural Entrepreneurs: Ten Case Studies*, Singapore, 1995.

Wou, O.Y.K., *Mobilising the Masses: Building Revolution in Henan*, Stanford, CA, 1994.

Yang, C.K., *A Chinese Village in Communist Transition*, London and Cambridge, Ma, Mass., 1959.

Zhu Ling, *Rural Reform and Peasant Income in China, Input of China's Post-Mao Rural Reforms in Selected Regions*, London, 1991.

Zweig, D., *Agrarian Radicalism in China, 1968-1981*, Cambridge MA, and London, 1989.

2

STATISTICAL TABLES

Table 1. INCOME INDICATORS OF QINGLIN BRIGADE

	Per capita annual grain consumption (jin)	Unit labour value (yuan)	Per capita annual income (yuan)
1969	398	0.90	61
1970	312	0.80	65
1971	595	0.85	71
1972	545	1.087	98
1973	169	0.56	43
1974	377	0.76	60
1975	310	0.74	57
1976	403	0.70	63
1977	342	0.61	50
1978	339	0.51	51

Source: Basic Brigade Statistics Record, pp. 66–8.

Table 2. PREVENTION AND TREATMENT OF SCHISTOSOMIASIS
IN BOYANG COUNTY, 1953–85

	No. of people checked	No. discovered to have the disease	injection rate (%)	No. of people treated	Size (mu) of areas where infested snails wiped out
1953	873	99	11.34		
1956	12,764	3,864	30.27	1,984	
1958	395,658	19,539	4.94	13,591	
1962	19,217	2,505	13.0	3,571	44,700
1963	30,371	4,578	15.07	3,185	58,660
1966	61,770	8,363	13.54	8,433	17,894
1968	26,543	4,845	18.25	4,000	
1970	412,986	22,963	5.56	23,211	172,181
1979	120,103	6,770	5.6	10,728	380,578
1985	54,163	7,380	13.63	6,359	9,182

Source: The Annuals of Boyang County, pp. 754–5.

Table 3. POPULATION IN QINGLIN AREA

	No. of brigades	No. of production teams	No. of households	Total population	Of which male	Of which female
1949			465	1,673	920	753
1950			470	1,723	947	756
1951			475	1,757	967	810
1952			490	1,822	984	838
1953			498	1,885	991	894
1954			504	1,949	998	951
1955	1	13	523	2,013	1,049	941
1956	1	13	569	2,141	1,115	1,026
1957	1	13	566	2,192	1,120	1,072
1958	1	13	519	2,229	1,133	1,096
1959	1	13	547	2,253	1,147	1,106
1960	1	14	563	2,253	1,125	1,128
1961	3	31	544	2,456	1,269	1,187
1962		32	551	2,530	1,285	1,245
1963		32	558	2,604	1,310	1,294
1964		32	565	2,678	1,337	1,341
1965		32	570	2,752	1,430	1,322
1966		32	571	2,826	1,420	1,406
1967		32	573	2,900	1,480	1,420
1968		32	583	2,974	1,507	1,467
1969		19	599	3,048	1,540	1,508
1970	1	19	623	3,050	1,563	1,487
1971	1	18	617	3,042	1,573	1,469
1972	1	23	625	3,161	1,683	1,477
1973	1	23	627	3,217	1,675	1,542
1974	1	22	615	3,251	1,696	1,555
1975	1	24	632	3,416	1,786	1,630
1976	1	24	651	3,532	1,811	1,721
1977	1	31	626	3,518	1,807	1,711
1978	1	31	593	3,612	1,903	1,709

Note: Blank spaces indicate no statistics available.

Source: Brigade Basic Statistics Record, pp. 5-6.

Table 4. HOUSEHOLDS AND POPULATION IN BOYANG
COUNTY IN SELECTED YEARS

	1949	*1953*	*1956*	*1958*	*1964*	*1982*	*1985*
No. of households	129,437	140,430	146,015	149,295	153,846	186,410	193,444
Total population	508,240	553,961	592,434	627,858	694,974	1,062,338	1,071,184
Average people per household	3.93	3.95	4.06	4.21	4.52	5.70	5.54

Source: Boyang County Annuals, p. 136.

Table 5. PRIVATE-RUN CROPS AND PRODUCTION OUTPUT[*]

	Grain		Cotton		Peanut		Rape seed		Sesame		Vegetable	
	Land (mu)	Total output	Land (mu)	Total output	Land (mu)	Total output	Land (mu)	Total output	Land (mu)	Total output	Land (mu)	Total output
1949	311	416	20	6	12	24	20	12	33	20	70	219
1950	310	416	20	6	12	24	20	12	30	18	70	220
1951	310	416	20	6	12	24	20	12	32	19	70	220
1952	310	416	20	6	12	24	20	12	35	21	80	240
1953	310	416	20	6	12	24	20	12	30	18	85	250
1954	310	416	20	6	14	28	20	12	30	18	90	270
1955	320	436	20	6	14	28	30	18	38	23	90	270
1956	320	436	26	6	13	26	30	18	32	19	90	290
1957	320	436	26	8	11	22	30	18	39	24	90	270
1958	320	426	24	8	11	22	30	18	30	18	90	270
1959	320	426	24	8	11	22	40	28	32	19	100	300
1960	320	426	25	8	15	30	40	28	38	23	80	240
1961	320	426	25	8	13	26	40	28	40	24	85	260
1962	320	426	25	8	10	20	40	28	40	24	85	260
1963	320	426	27	9	10	20	40	28	40	24	80	240
1964	320	426	28	10	10	20	40	28	40	24	90	270
1965	300	390	25	7	10	20	40	20	40	20	81	243
1966	300	390	25	7	10	20	40	20	40	20	81	243
1967	290	375	25	7	10	20	40	20	40	20	81	243
1968	290	375	25	7	10	20	40	20	40	20	81	243
1969	280	365	5	3	10	20	40	20	40	22	81	243
1970	280	365	5	3	10	20	40	20	40	20	81	243
1971	234	313	3	1	8	16	30	15	20	10	99	164[†]
1972	244	336	7	4	12	24	40	20	30	18	108	324
1973	278	344	7	4	9	18	30	15	70	35	167	500
1974	412	807	74	39	21	54	34	14	21	11	165	500
1975	242	426	11	3	10	25	5	3	10	6	170	500
1976	256	426	11	3	10	25	5	3	10	6	170	500
1977	256	352	32	13	16	40	15	8	30	18	100	300
1978	240	286	26	3	10	4	36	20	40	28	100	300

[*] The output unit is Chinese *dan*, which is exactly 50 kilos.

[†] This figure is apparently incorrect. There is a cross in front of this figure in the *Brigade Basic Statistics Record*. No other figure is offered.

Note: From 1961 on there is a record for tobacco produced by the villagers on their private plots, as well as a record for sugar cane production 1965 to 1970. These records are not included in the table.

Source: Brigade Basic Statistics Record, pp. 27-30.

Table 6. GRAIN OUTPUT IN QINGLIN BRIGADE, 1949-78

	Output (dan)
1949	9,420
1950	17,920
1951	17,920
1952	18,920
1953	15,920
1954	6,420
1955	18,510
1956	17,010
1957	17,010
1958	15,510
1959	15,510
1960	15,507
1961	16,840
1962	16,840
1963	16,840
1964	16,840
1965	18,012
1966	18,757
1967	19,521
1968	20,306
1969	21,390
1970	20,979
1971	27,454
1972	30,812
1973	14,399
1974	17,746
1975	19,018
1976	24,375
1977	18,220
1978	20,635

Note: Grain output here includes rice, wheat, sweet potatoes, soybeans and so on, but it does not include economic crops such as cotton, rape seed and sesame.
Source: Brigade Basic Statistics Record, pp. 11-14.

Table 7. CROPS DESTROYED BY FLOODS AND DROUGHTS IN
QINGLIN BRIGADE, 1949-78

	Total land affected (mu)	of which no crop was harvested (mu)	of which affected by droughts (mu)	of which affected by floods (mu)
1949	2,427	2,100	14	2,413
1950	321	290	10	311
1951	379	261	12	311
1952	295	238	7	288
1953	437	390	33	404
1954	2,773	2,773	43	2,730
1955	728	718	16	712
1956	206	160	6	200
1957	347	308	47	300
1958	987	760	10	977
1959	289	243	23	276
1960	306	247	6	300
1961	257	186	71	186
1962	1,762	1,630	11	1,751
1963	1,252	1,081	129	1,123
1964	1,930	1,251	70	1,860
1965	875	527	70	805
1966	785	607	80	705
1967	685	505	80	605
1968	565	325	60	505
1969	415	425	60	355
1970	525	515	70	455
1971	648	415	140	504
1972	114	94	120	94
1973	3,525	3,021	220	3,305
1974	1,608	1,713	94	1,514
1975	1,561	1,445	116	1,445
1976	652	541	142	541
1977	1,995	1,995		1,995
1978	2,245	1,476	2,245	

Source: Brigade Basic Statistics Record, pp. 9-10.

Table 8. OUTPUT OF ECONOMIC CROPS IN
QINGLIN BRIGADE, 1949-78

	Cotton output (dan)	Rape seed output (dan)	Sesame output (dan)	Peanut output (dan)
1949	36	210	75	50
1950	36	210	75	50
1951	36	210	75	50
1952	36	210	75	50
1953	36	210	75	50
1954	36	210	75	50
1955	36	210	75	50
1956	36	210	75	50
1957	36	210	75	50
1958	36	210	75	50
1959	36	210	75	50
1960	210	240	90	50
1961	210	240	1080	50
1962	210	240	1080	100
1963	210	280	126	50
1964	165	210	75	50
1964	268	259	100	50
1965	268	259	100	50
1966	268	259	100	50
1967	268	259	100	50
1968	268	259	100	50
1969	268	259	100	50
1970	331	284	140	71
1971	113	276	145	64
1972	451	397	66	157
1973	126	105	76	157
1974	211	95	63	358
1975	107	222	133	334
1976	116	162	117	211
1977	169	225	149	385
1978	98	231	52	111

Source: Basic Brigade Statistics Record, pp. 19-22.

Table 9. PRODUCTION OUTPUTS OF MAIN CROPS IN QINGLIN
Average unit yield (jin per mu)

	Grain	Cotton	Rice
1962	196	15	420
1971	354	13	475
1972	420	52	552
1973	369	21	480
1974	320	36	428
1975	394	21	515
1976	333	20	413
1977	336	34	446
1978	349	16	433
1979	466	24	569
1982	482	36	691
1983	414	9.4	383
1985	549	95	658

Note: Grain includes rice, wheat, sweet potatoes, and other crops such as soya beans and buckwheat. Rice includes the first and the second crops. The years listed in the Table are the only ones for which access was possible. These figures are not consistent with those listed in the *Brigade Basic Statistics Record*, which included the years from 1949 to 1978. One of the reasons for the inconsistency is that before 1967 there were three Production Brigades in Qinglin. During the Cultural Revolution, the three Brigades were amalgamated into one Brigade called Qinglin Brigade. After 1978, Qinglin Brigade was divided again into three Brigades. The figures in *the Brigade Basic Statistics Record* were collected in 1978 from various sources and then put together for the whole Qinglin area, whereas the figures in Table 8 are taken from the annual reports of each year listed in the table. Therefore, it is safe to assume that the figures in Table 8 are more accurate.

Source: Dadui nongye tongji nianbao (Annual Brigade Report on Rural Conditions), *1962, 1971, 1972, 1973, 1974, 1975, 1976, 1977, 1978, 1979, 1982, 1983, 1985.*

Table 10. ANNUAL RATES OF TAX AND LEVIES IMPOSED ON
PRODUCTION TEAMS AND RATE OF GROSS INCOME FOR
DISTRIBUTION IN QINGLIN

	Public accumulation fund	Public welfare fund	Agriculture tax	Contribution to local officials' salary	% of gross income for distribution
1961	4	3	10.8	n.a.	66.6
1962	4.5	3	2.6	n.a.	n.a.
1963	4	3	9.8	2	60
1964	4	3	10.5	2	n.a.
1965	4	3	7.2	2	67.6
1971	5	3	6.41	n.a.	n.a.
1978	3	2	16	2	n.a.
1979	6	4	7.8	n.a.	n.a.

Source: Dadui niandu fenpei biao (Annual Brigade Distribution Table), *1961, 1962, 1963, 1964, 1965, 1971, 1978, 1979.*

3

SELECT GLOSSARY OF TERMS
USED IN TEXT

People and places

Anhui	a province east of Jiangxi	安徽
Beidaihe	a seaside resort	北戴河
Boyang xian	Boyang County	波阳县
Bo Yibo	a CCP leader	薄一波
Chen Yi	a CCP leader	陈毅
Chen Yun	a CCP leader	陈云
Deng Xiaoping	a CCP leader	邓小平
Deng Zihui	a CCP leader	邓子恢
Dongguan	a city in Guangdong Province	东莞
Duchang xian	*Duchang* County	都昌县
Gaojiacun	Gao Village	高家村
Guantian	an area within Qinglin, in which Gao Village is located	官田
Guangdong	a province in south China	广东
Guangzhou	capital city of Guangdong	广州
Hebei	a province in north China	河北
Henan	a province south of Hebei	河南
Hongtashan	name of a cigarette brand	红塔山
Jiang Zemin	a CCP leader	江泽民

Jiangxi sheng	Jiangxi Province	江西省
Jingdezhen	a city in Jiangxi Provice	景德镇
Jiujiang	a city in Jiangxi Province	九江
Li Fuchun	a CCP leader	李富春
Li Rui	a CCP leader	李锐
Li Xiannian	a CCP leader	李先念
Liu Shaoqi	a CCP leader	刘少奇
Lushan	a mountain resort	庐山
Mao Yuanxin	Mao's nephew	毛远新
Nanchang	capital city of Jiangxi Province	南昌
Poyang hu	Poyang Lake	鄱阳湖
Qinglin	the area within which Gao Village is located	青林
Shajiabang	name of a Peking opera	沙家浜
Shandong	a province in north-east China	山东
Tan Qilong	a CCP leader	谭启龙
Tao Zhu	a CCP leader	陶铸
Wan Li	a CCP leader	万里
Wang Taigong	name of a village Buddha	王太公
Xiamen	a city on the south coast	厦门
Changjiang	Yangtze	长江
yinbaohu xiang	Yinbaohu township	银宝湖乡
Youdunjie	a town in the area of Gao Village	油墩街

Zhao Ziyang	a CCP leader	赵紫阳
Zhou Enlai	a CCP leader	周恩来
Zhuhai	a city on the south coast	珠海

Words and phrases

Aizi	dwarf	矮子
Baipu	pay respect to the clan book	拜谱
Bao	administration unit in old China	保
chijiao yisheng	Barefoot doctor	赤脚医生
chijiao laoshi	Barefoot teacher	赤脚老师
da dui	Brigade	大队
Caizheng baogan zhi	financial responsibility system	财政包干制
Changmao	long-haired	长毛
Chi le zui ruan	less critical of the host after a banquet	吃了嘴软
gongshe	Commune	公社
shedui qiye	Commune and brigade enterprises	社队企业
gongchan feng	Communist wind	共产风
Cunweihui	village committee	村委会
Da gou	throw food at the dog to stop it from barking	打狗
Dan	a weight unit equal to 50kg	担
Duanzi juesun	without a son to continue the family line	断子绝孙

Duanwu	a festival	端午
Duo zi duo fu	the more sons the more fortunate	多子多福
Fanxiao liang	grain resold to the farmers	返销粮
Fenjia	division of family inheritance	分家
Hukou	household registration	户口
Hua bing chong ji	to paint a cake to quench one's hunger	画饼充饥
Jianchen	treacherous court official	奸臣
Jin kou yin ya	one's words are sacrosanct	金口银牙
Loushang louxia diandeng dianhua	storeyed house with electrification and telephone	楼上楼下 电灯电话
Min yi shi wei tian	food is as important as the sky to the ordinary people	民以食为天
Mu	unit of area	亩
Na le shou ruan	less critical of the gift giver	拿了手软
nongmin	Peasant	农民
shengchan xiaodui	Production team	生产小队
Pusa	Buddha	菩萨
Qingming	a festival	清明
Quantou	fists	拳头
Renqing zhai	burden of gift giving	人情债
xuexichong bing	Schistosomiasis	血吸虫病
Sishu	private school in old China	私塾
Sishu wujing	the Four Books and Five Classics	四书五经
Doufu	Tofu	豆腐

xiangzhen qiye	Township enterprises	乡镇企业
Wang mei zhi ke	to quench one's thirst by looking at plums	望梅止渴
Xiang	township	乡
Xue er you ze shi	academic excellence leads to official position	学而优则仕
Yang	from across ocean - foreign	洋
Yuan	unit of Chinese currency	元
Zhaozhui	son-in-law living with wife's parents	招赘
Zhongqiu	a festival	中秋

INDEX

accountant, 42-3, 83, 92
adultery, 238
agrarian radicalism, 57-8, 143, 258
agriculture input cost, 66
army [PLA], 27-8, 95, 96
Australia, 89, 249, 250, 254

backyard furnace, 138
Banister, Judith, 127
baojia, 225
barefoot doctor, 68, 79-84, 173
barefoot teachers, 103, 104-5, 173
Basic Brigade Statistics Record, 42, 134, 135, 167
Beijing, 148, 149, 252, 253-4
Becker, Jasper, 122, 140
birth rate, 126-7
Bo Yibo, 124, 204
bourgeois, 147, *see also* Cultural Revolution
Boyang County Annuals, 84, 130
Boyang County Town, 4, 92, 130, 218

caizheng baogan zhi (financial contract system), 186, 201
brigade (production), 16-19, 79-84, 173
Britain, 248, 251
capitalism, 3, 258
Chan, Anita, 2
chemical fertilisers, 32, 180; *see also* pollution
Chen Ta (Chen Da), 127
Chen Yi, 124
Chen Yun, 122, 138
child mortality, 33-4, 72, 75
China, 2, 122, 142
cinema, 162
Chinese classics, 157
Chinese Communist Party (CCP), 1, 16, 37, 96
Chinese intellectuals, 108, 257
Christianity, *see* religion

Christ, Jesus, 89
clan culture, 9, 11-17, 152-3, 173-5, 223-7
clan solidarity: 209-10, 216; clan feud, 116, 144-6, 151-8, 173-4
class (social), 15, 94-5, 224
clinic, 77, 88, 167
close planting, 140
commercialisation, 202, 258
commune system, 1, 16-20, 36-37, 42-3, 61-3, 64, 79-84, 172, 207
communism, 135
Communist Wind, 138
Confucianism, 93
consumer goods, *see* living standards
crime, 181, 247; *see also* reforms
crops, 7, 31
crop options, 198
Cultural Revolution: 18, 23-4, 29-30, 57, 62, 63, 77, 87, 97, 99-103, 107, 104-14, 115, 142-71, 204, 205, 207 "class enemies", 151-5; – innovations: 159-69; cultural activities, 162-4; education, 159-61; health, *see* barefoot doctor; irrigation projects, 167; local enterprises, 168-9; state machinery, 166-7; sports, 164-5; – personal grudge, 149-151, 155-8; power struggle, 144-6; production, 143-4; Red Guards at school, 147-9, 154
customs, 230, *see also*, religion, tradition, festival

deep ploughing, 137
Deng Xiaoping, 63, 97, 172, 184, 205, 247
Deng Zihui, 122
diseases, *see* health
divorce, 236-7
drunk, 241

ecology, *see* pollution

283

PRESENTED TO: _____

FROM: _____

DATE: _____

HEALTHY CHOICES

FOR WOMEN

100 Days of Devotions

For
Mind,
Body,
and Spirit

The quoted ideas expressed in this book (but not Scripture verses) are not, in all cases, exact quotations, as some have been edited for clarity and brevity. In all cases, the author has attempted to maintain the speaker's original intent. In some cases, quoted material for this book was obtained from secondary sources, primarily print media. While every effort was made to ensure the accuracy of these sources, the accuracy cannot be guaranteed. For additions, deletions, corrections, or clarifications in future editions of this text, please write Freeman-Smith, LLC.

The Holy Bible, King James Version

The Holy Bible, New King James Version (NKJV) Copyright © 1982 by Thomas Nelson, Inc. Used by permission.

New Century Version®. (NCV) Copyright © 1987, 1988, 1991 by Word Publishing, a division of Thomas Nelson, Inc. All rights reserved. Used by permission.

The Holman Christian Standard Bible™ (HCSB) Copyright © 1999, 2000, 2001 by Holman Bible Publishers. Used by permission.

The Holy Bible, New International Version®. (NIV) Copyright © 1973, 1978, 1984 International Bible Society. Used by permission of Zondervan. All rights reserved.

The Holy Bible. New Living Translation (NLT) copyright © 1996 Tyndale Charitable Trust. Used by permission of Tyndale House Publishers.

The New American Standard Bible®, (NASB) Copyright © 1960, 1962, 1963, 1968, 1971, 1972, 1973, 1975, 1977, 1995 by The Lockman Foundation. Used by permission.

Scripture taken from The Message. (MSG) Copyright © 1993, 1994, 1995, 1996, 2000, 2001, 2002. Used by permission of NavPress Publishing Group.

Cover Design by Kim Russell / Wahoo Designs
Page Layout by Bart Dawson

ISBN 978-1-60587-305-3

Printed in the United States of America

HEALTHY CHOICES

FOR WOMEN

100 Days of Devotions

For
Mind,
Body,
and Spirit

A MESSAGE TO READERS

A wise man will hear and increase learning, and a man of understanding will attain wise counsel.

Proverbs 1:5 NKJV

The advice in this book is general in nature, and your circumstances are specific to you. For that reason, we strongly suggest that you consult your physician before beginning any new regimen of physical exercise or diet. Don't depend upon this book—or any other book like it—to be your sole source of information on matters pertaining to your health. Instead, consider Proverbs 1:5 and seek wise counsel from a variety of sources, especially your personal physician, before making major health-related decisions.

INTRODUCTION

Countless books have been written on the topics of health and fitness. But if you're a Christian, you probably already own at least one copy—and more likely several copies—of the world's foremost guide to spiritual, physical, and emotional fitness. That book is the Holy Bible. The Bible is the irreplaceable guidebook for faithful believers—like you—who seek God's wisdom and His truth.

God has a plan for every aspect of your life, including your food, your fitness, and your faith. But God will not force His plans upon you; to the contrary, He has given you the ability to make choices. The consequences of those choices help determine the quality and the tone of your life. This book is intended to help you make wise choices—choices that will lead to spiritual, physical, and emotional health—by encouraging you to rely heavily upon the promises of God's Holy Word.

Health is a gift from God. What we do with that gift is determined, to a surprising extent, by the person we see every time we gaze into the mirror. If we squander our health—or if we take it for granted—we do a profound disservice to ourselves and to our loved ones. But God has other plans. He commands us to treat our bodies, our minds, and our souls with the utmost care. And that's exactly what we should do.

If you seek to protect and to enhance your spiritual, emotional, and physical health, these pages will help, but they offer no shortcuts. Healthy living is a journey, not a destination, and that journey requires discipline. If you're willing to make the step-by-step journey toward improved health, rest assured that God is taking careful note of your progress . . . and He's quietly urging you to take the next step.

100 DAYS TO A NEW AND IMPROVED YOU

A prudent person foresees the danger ahead and takes precautions. The simpleton goes blindly on and suffers the consequences.

Proverbs 27:12 NLT

It takes time to change a habit, but it doesn't take forever. In fact, if you can do anything for 100 straight days, then there's a very good chance you can keep doing it on the 101st, the 102nd, and beyond. If you thought that you could establish a number of healthy habits, would you be willing to carve out a few minutes each day for the next few months in order to find out? If you answered yes, congratulations. You're about to embark on a grand adventure.

When you form a deeper relationship with God, you can start establishing healthier habits, starting now.

This book contains 100 chapters, each of which contains a devotional message about your mind, your body, and your spirit. If you read each devotional carefully—and if you implement the ideas that you find there—you can have a profound impact on your own life and upon the lives of your loved ones.

FOOD FOR THOUGHT

You can build up a set of good habits so that you habitually take the Christian way without thought.

E. Stanley Jones

You will never change your life until you change something you do daily.

John Maxwell

If you want to form a new habit, get to work. If you want to break a bad habit, get on your knees.

Marie T. Freeman

Do you not know that your body is a sanctuary of the Holy Spirit who is in you, whom you have from God? You are not your own, for you were bought at a price; therefore glorify God in your body.

1 Corinthians 6:19-20 HCSB

A HEALTHY-CHOICE TIP

Before you begin a major new exercise program, see your doctor: As the old saying goes, it's better to be safe than sorry.

FORMING HEALTHY HABITS

Dear friend, I pray that you may prosper in every way and be in good health, just as your soul prospers.

3 John 1:2 HCSB

First, you make your habits, and then your habits make you. Some habits will inevitably bring you closer to God; other habits will lead you away from the path He has chosen for you. If you sincerely desire to improve your spiritual health, you must honestly examine the habits that make up the fabric of your day. And you must abandon those habits that are displeasing to God.

Today, ask God to help you form healthier habits. If you ask for His help—if you petition Him sincerely and often—your Heavenly Father will guide your steps and protect you from harmful behaviors.

If you trust God, and if you keep asking for His help, He can transform your life. If you sincerely ask Him to help you, the same God who created the universe will help you defeat the harmful habits that have heretofore defeated you. So, if at first you don't succeed, keep praying. God is listening, and He's ready to help you become a better person if you ask Him . . . so ask today.

FOOD FOR THOUGHT

We are never out of reach of Satan's devices, so we must never be without the whole armor of God.

Warren Wiersbe

Begin to be now what you will be hereafter.

St. Jerome

Acquire wisdom—how much better it is than gold! And acquire understanding—it is preferable to silver.

Proverbs 16:16 HCSB

A HEALTHY-CHOICE TIP

Do you dine out often? If so, be careful. Most restaurants stay in business by serving big portions of tasty food. Unfortunately, most restaurant food is high in calories, sugar, and fat. You will probably eat healthier meals if you prepare those meals at home instead of eating out.

RESPECTING YOUR BODY

Therefore, brothers, by the mercies of God, I urge you to present your bodies as a living sacrifice, holy and pleasing to God; this is your spiritual worship.

Romans 12:1 HCSB

In the 12th chapter of Romans, Paul encourages us to take special care of the bodies God has given us. But it's tempting to do otherwise.

We live in a fast-food world where unhealthy choices are convenient, inexpensive, and tempting. And, we live in a digital world filled with modern conveniences that often rob us of the physical exercise needed to maintain healthy lifestyles. As a result, too many of us find ourselves glued to the television, with a snack in one hand and a clicker in the other. The results are as unfortunate as they are predictable.

If you're not determined to be the master of your body . . . then you might just become a slave to your impulses.

God's Word teaches us that our bodies are "temples" which belong to God (1 Corinthians 6:19-20). We are commanded (not encouraged, not advised—we are commanded!) to treat our bodies with respect and honor. We do so by making wise choices and by making those choices consistently: day by day, month by month, and year by year.

FOOD FOR THOUGHT

Eat to live, and not live to eat.

Poor Richard's Almanac

Our body is like armor, our soul like the warrior. Take care of both, and you will be ready for what comes.

Amma St. Syncletice

For it was You who created my inward parts; You knit me together in my mother's womb. I will praise You, because I have been remarkably and wonderfully made.

Psalm 139:13-14 HCSB

A HEALTHY-CHOICE TIP

Take a few minutes to examine your eating habits. Do you gobble down snack foods while watching television? If so, stop. Do you drink high-calorie soft drinks or feast on unhealthy snacks like potato chips or candy? If so, you're doing yourself a disservice. Do you load up your plate and then feel obligated to eat every last bite? If so, it's time to form some new habits.

Poor eating habits are usually well established, so they won't be easy to change, but change them you must if you want to enjoy the benefits of a healthy lifestyle.

FAITH AND FITNESS

*Cast your burden on the Lord, and He shall sustain you; He
shall never permit the righteous to be moved.*

Psalm 55:22 NKJV

Faith and fitness. These two words may seem disconnect-
ed, but they are not. If you're about to begin a regimen of
vigorous physical exercise, then you will find it helpful to
begin a regimen of vigorous spiritual exercise, too. Why?
Because the physical, emotional, and spiritual aspects of
your life are interconnected. In other words, you cannot
"compartmentalize" physical fitness in one category of
your being and spiritual fitness in another—every facet of
your life has an impact on the person you are today and the
person you will become tomorrow. That's why your body

Today, spend time
thinking about
God's plans for
your spiritual and
physical health.

is so important to God—your body is,
quite literally, the "temple" that houses
"the Spirit of God" that dwells within
you (1 Corinthians 3:16).

God's Word contains powerful lessons about every aspect of your life, including your health. So, if you're con-

cerned about your spiritual, physical, or emotional health,
the first place to turn is that timeless source of comfort
and assurance, the Holy Bible. When you open your Bible
and begin reading, you'll quickly be reminded of this fact:

when you face concerns of any sort—including health-related challenges—God is with you. And His healing touch, like His love, endures forever.

FOOD FOR THOUGHT

The Christian faith is meant to be lived moment by moment. It isn't some broad, general outline—it's a long walk with a real Person. Details count: passing thoughts, small sacrifices, a few encouraging words, little acts of kindness, brief victories over nagging sins.

Joni Eareckson Tada

Only by walking with God can we hope to find the path that leads to life.

John Eldredge

STRENGTHENING YOUR FAITH

God has given us the Bible for the purpose of knowing His promises, His power, His commandments, His wisdom, His love, and His Son. As we study God's teachings and apply them to our lives, we live by the Word that shall never pass away. So if you're about to begin a new fitness program, be sure that you also pay careful attention to God's program by studying His Word every day of your life.

DON'T GO ON A DIET, CHANGE YOUR LIFESTYLE

Their end is destruction; their god is their stomach; their glory is in their shame. They are focused on earthly things.

Philippians 3:19 HCSB

If you want to lose weight, don't dare go on a diet! It's a sad fact, but true: in the vast majority of cases, diets simply don't work. In fact, one study that examined the results of popular diets conducted that nearly 100% of dieters suffered almost "complete relapse after 3 to 5 years." In other words, dieters almost always return to their pre-diet weights (or, in many cases, to even higher weight levels).

If diets don't work, what should you do if you weigh more than you should? The answer is straightforward: If you need to lose weight, don't start dieting; change your lifestyle.

It takes wisdom to be moderate; moderation is wisdom in action.

Your current weight is the result of the number of calories that you have taken into your body versus the number of calories that you have burned. If you seek to lower your weight, then you must burn more calories (by engaging in more vigorous physical activities), or take in fewer calories (by eating more sensibly), or both. It's as simple as that.

FOOD FOR THOUGHT

It's not that some people have willpower and some don't.
It's that some people are ready to change and others are
not.

James Gordon, M.D.

We are all created differently. We share a common need to
balance the different parts of our lives.

Dr. Walt Larimore

You can look at your calorie count in the same way you
might look at a bank account. Every mouthful of food
is a deposit and every activity that requires energy is a
withdrawal. If we deposit more then we withdraw, our
surplus grows larger and larger.

John Maxwell

To many, total abstinence is easier than perfect moderation.

St. Augustine

A HEALTHY-CHOICE TIP

Are you skipping meals? Don't do it. Skipping meals isn't
healthy, and it isn't a sensible way to lose weight, either.

DAY 6

SAY NO TO UNHEALTHY FOODS

Don't you know that you are God's sanctuary and that the Spirit of God lives in you?

1 Corinthians 3:16 HCSB

Eating unhealthy foods is habit-forming. And if you have acquired the unfortunate habit of eating unhealthy foods, then God wants you start to making changes today.

Take a few more minutes than you did on day 3 to think about your eating habits. Are you really ready to improve your diet, your health, and your life?

Poor eating habits are easy to make and hard to break, but break them you must. Otherwise, you'll be disobeying God's commandments while causing yourself great harm.

Think about ways that your spiritual health impacts your physical health, and vice-versa.

Maintaining a healthy lifestyle is a journey, not a destination, and that journey requires discipline. But rest assured that if you and your loved ones are willing to make the step-by-step journey toward a healthier diet, God is taking careful note of your progress . . . and He's quietly urging you to take the next step.

FOOD FOR THOUGHT

Food ought to be a refreshment to the body, and not a burden.

St. Bonaventure

The key to healthy eating is moderation and managing what you eat every day.

John Maxwell

In general, mankind, since the improvement of cookery, eats twice as much as nature requires.

Ben Franklin

A HEALTHY-CHOICE TIP

Adopt healthy habits you can stick with. In other words, don't starve yourself. And if you're beginning an exercise regimen, start slowly. Be moderate, even in your moderation.

PUT GOD IN HIS RIGHTFUL PLACE

Do not have other gods besides Me.

Exodus 20:3 HCSB

As you think about the nature of your relationship with God, remember this: you will always have some type of relationship with Him—it is inevitable that your life must be lived in relationship to God. The question is not if you will have a relationship with Him; the burning question is whether that relationship will be one that seeks to honor Him . . . or not.

Are you willing to place God first in your life? And, are you willing to welcome Him into your heart? Unless you can honestly answer these questions with a resounding yes, then your relationship with God isn't what it could be or should be. Thankfully, God is always available, He's always ready to forgive, and He's waiting to hear from you now. The rest, of course, is up to you.

> You must guard your heart by putting God in His rightful place—first place.

FOOD FOR THOUGHT

It is when we come to the Lord in our nothingness, our powerlessness and our helplessness that He then enables us to love in a way which, without Him, would be absolutely impossible.

Elisabeth Elliot

When all else is gone, God is still left. Nothing changes Him.

Hannah Whitall Smith

If God has the power to create and sustain the universe, He is more than able to sustain your marriage and your ministry, your faith and your finances, your hope and your health.

Anne Graham Lotz

Love has its source in God, for love is the very essence of His being.

Kay Arthur

STRENGTHENING YOUR FAITH

As you establish priorities for your day and your life, God deserves first place. And you deserve the experience of putting Him there.

SO MANY TEMPTATIONS

The LORD is my strength and song, and He has become my salvation; He is my God, and I will praise Him…

Exodus 15:2 NKJV

Our world is teeming with temptations and distractions that can rob you of the physical, emotional, and spiritual fitness that might otherwise be yours. And if you're not careful, the struggles and stresses of everyday living can rob you of the peace that should rightfully be yours because of your personal relationship with Christ. So take time each day to have a personal training session with your Savior.

Today, think about the ways that your spiritual, emotional, and physical health are interconnected.

Don't be a woman who's satisfied with occasional visits to church on Sunday morning; build a relationship with Jesus that deepens day by day. When you do, you will most certainly encounter the subtle hand of the Father. Then, if you are wise, you will take His hand and follow God as He leads you on the path to a healthier, happier life.

FOOD FOR THOUGHT

Measure the size of the obstacles against the size of God.

Beth Moore

God wants to reveal Himself as your Heavenly Father. When you wonder which way to turn, you can grasp His strong hand, and He'll guide you along life's path.

Lisa Whelchel

Do not fight the temptation in detail. Turn from it. Look ONLY at your Lord. Sing. Read. Work.

Amy Carmichael

Temptation is not a sin. Even Jesus was tempted. The Lord Jesus gives you the strength needed to resist temptation.

Corrie ten Boom

A HEALTHY-CHOICE TIP

If life's inevitable temptations seem to be getting the best of you, try praying more often, even if many of those prayers are simply brief, "open-eyed" requests to your Father in heaven.

HAVE A REGULAR APPOINTMENT WITH GOD

But have nothing to do with irreverent and silly myths. Rather, train yourself in godliness.

1 Timothy 4:7 HCSB

Each new day is a gift from God, and if we are wise, we spend a few quiet moments each morning thanking the Giver. Daily life is woven together with the threads of habit, and no habit is more important to our spiritual health than the discipline of daily prayer and devotion to the Creator.

When we begin each day with heads bowed and hearts lifted, we remind ourselves of God's love, His protection, and His commandments. And if we are wise, we align our priorities for the coming day with the teachings and commandments that God has given us through His Holy Word.

You need a regular appointment with your Creator. God is ready to talk to you, and you should prepare yourself each morning to talk to Him.

Are you seeking to change some aspect of your life? Do you seek to improve the condition of your spiritual or physical health? If so, ask for God's help and ask for it many times each day . . . starting with your morning devotional.

FOOD FOR THOUGHT

I suggest you discipline yourself to spend time daily in a systematic reading of God's Word. Make this "quiet time" a priority that nobody can change.

Warren Wiersbe

We are meddling with God's business when we let all manner of imaginings loose, predicting disaster, contemplating possibilities instead of following, one day at a time, God's plain and simple pathway.

Elisabeth Elliot

Jesus challenges you and me to keep our focus daily on the cross of His will if we want to be His disciples.

Anne Graham Lotz

STRENGTHENING YOUR FAITH

Make a promise to yourself and keep it that you will begin each day with a morning devotional. A regular time of quiet reflection and prayer will allow you to praise your Creator and to focus your thoughts. A daily devotional is especially important during those times of your life when you're feeling discouraged or fearful.

DAY 10

IF NOT NOW, WHEN?

Therefore, get your minds ready for action, being self-disciplined, and set your hope completely on the grace to be brought to you at the revelation of Jesus Christ.

1 Peter 1:13 HCSB

If you're determined to improve the state of your physical, spiritual, or emotional health, the best time to begin is now. But if you're like most people, you'll be tempted to put things off until tomorrow, or the next day, or the next.

The habit of putting things off until the last minute, along with its first cousin, the habit of making excuses for work that was never done, can be detrimental to your life, to your character, and to your health. Are you in the habit of doing what needs to be done when it needs to be done, or are you a dues-paying member of the Procrastinator's Club? If you're a woman who has already acquired the habit of doing things sooner rather than later, congratulations! But, if you find yourself putting off all those unpleasant tasks until later (or never), it's time to think about the consequences of your behavior.

> When it comes to food, fitness, or faith, the best moment to begin major improvements is the present moment.

One way that you can learn to defeat procrastination is by paying less attention to the sacrifices you're making today and more attention to the rewards you'll receive to-morrow. So, if you're trying to improve your fitness, or any other aspect of your life, don't spend endless hours fretting over your fate. Simply seek God's counsel and get busy. When you do, you will be richly rewarded because of your willingness to act.

FOOD FOR THOUGHT

We spend our lives dreaming of the future, not realizing that a little of it slips away every day.

Barbara Johnson

Do noble things, do not dream them all day long.

Charles Kingsley

A HEALTHY-CHOICE TIP

Healthy choices are easy to put off until some future date. But procrastination, especially concerning matters of personal health, is, at best, foolish and, at worst, dangerous. If you feel the need to improve your physical health, don't wait for New Year's Day; don't even wait until tomorrow. The time to begin living a healthier life is the moment you finish reading this sentence.

TRUSTING GOD AND FINDING BALANCE

Don't burn out; keep yourselves fueled and aflame. Be alert servants of the Master, cheerfully expectant. Don't quit in hard times; pray all the harder.

Romans 12:11-12 MSG

Face facts: life is a delicate balancing act, a tightrope walk with over-commitment on one side and under-commitment on the other. And it's up to each of us to walk carefully on that rope, not falling prey to pride (which causes us to attempt too much) or to fear (which causes us to attempt too little).

God's Word promises us the possibility of abundance (John 10:10). And we are far more likely to experience that abundance when we lead balanced lives.

A regularly scheduled time of prayer, Bible reading, and meditation can help you prioritize your day and your life.

When you allow yourself to take on too many jobs, you simply can't do all of them well. That means that if you allow yourself to become overcommitted, whether at home, at work, at church, or anywhere in between, you're asking for trouble. So you must learn how to say no to the things you don't have the time or the energy to do.

Of course, sometimes, saying no can be tough. Why? Because well-meaning women (like you) genuinely want to help other people out. But if you allow yourself to become overworked, you may begin over-promising and under-serving—and you'll disappoint just about everybody, including yourself.

Are you and your loved ones doing too much—or too little? If so, it's time to have a little chat with God. And if you listen carefully to His instructions, you will strive to achieve a more balanced life, a life that's right for you and your loved ones. When you do, everybody wins.

FOOD FOR THOUGHT

Let's face it. None of us can do a thousand things to the glory of God. And, in our own vain attempt to do so, we stand the risk of forfeiting a precious thing.

Beth Moore

STRENGTHENING YOUR FAITH

Ruth Bell Graham, wife of evangelist Billy Graham, observed: "The Reference Point for the Christian is the Bible. All values, judgments, and attitudes must be gauged in relationship to this Reference Point." Make certain that you're an avid reader of God's bestseller, and make sure that you keep reading it as long as you live!

DO FIRST THINGS FIRST

Therefore, get your minds ready for action, being self-disciplined . . . .

1 Peter 1:13 HCSB

"First things first." These words are easy to speak but hard to put into practice. For a busy woman living in a demanding world, placing first things first can be difficult indeed. Why? Because so many people are expecting so many things from you!

If you're having trouble prioritizing your day, perhaps you've been trying to organize your life according to your own plans, not God's. A better strategy, of course, is to take your daily obligations and place them in the hands of the One who created you. To do so, you must prioritize your day according to God's commandments, and you must seek His will and His wisdom in all matters. Then, you can face the day with the assurance that the same God who created our universe out of nothingness will help you place first things first in your own life.

> Your Heavenly Father wants you to prioritize your day and your life. And the best place to start is by putting God first.

Do you feel overwhelmed or confused? Turn the concerns of this day over to God—prayerfully, earnestly, and often. Then listen for His answer . . . and trust the answer He gives.

FOOD FOR THOUGHT

Sin is largely a matter of mistaken priorities. Any sin in us that is cherished, hidden, and not confessed will cut the nerve center of our faith.

Catherine Marshall

Have you prayed about your resources lately? Find out how God wants you to use your time and your money. No matter what it costs, forsake all that is not of God.

Kay Arthur

There were endless demands on Jesus' time. Still he was able to make that amazing claim of "completing the work you gave me to do." (John 17:4 NIV)

Elisabeth Elliot

A HEALTHY-CHOICE TIP

If you're trying to reshape your physique or your life, don't try to do it alone. Ask for the support and encouragement of your family members and friends. You'll improve your odds of success if you enlist your own cheering section.

DAY 13

IT ALL STARTS WITH GOD

Now the God of all grace, who called you to His eternal glory in Christ Jesus, will personally restore, establish, strengthen, and support you.

1 Peter 5:10 HCSB

Physical fitness, like every other aspect of your life, begins and ends with God. If you'd like to adopt a healthier life-style, God is willing to help. In fact, if you sincerely wish to create a healthier you—either physically, emotionally or spiritually—God is anxious to be your silent partner in that endeavor, but it's up to you to ask for His help.

When you are tired, fearful, or discouraged, God can restore your physical strength and your emotional health.

The journey toward improved health is not only a common-sense exercise in personal discipline, it is also a spiritual journey ordained by our Creator. God does not intend that we abuse our bodies by giving in to excessive appetites or to slothful behavior. To the contrary, God has instructed us to pro-tect our physical bodies to the greatest extent we can. To do otherwise is to disobey Him.

God has a plan for every facet of your life, and His plan includes provisions for your spiritual, physical, and emotional health. But, He expects you to do your fair share of the work! In a world that is chock-full of tasty temptations, you may find it all too easy to make unhealthy choices. Your challenge, of course, is to resist those unhealthy choices by every means you can, including prayer. And you can be sure that whenever you ask for God's help, He will give it.

FOOD FOR THOUGHT

God uses our most stumbling, faltering faith-steps as the open door to His doing for us "more than we ask or think."

Catherine Marshall

Faith is not merely you holding on to God—it is God holding on to you.

E. Stanley Jones

The love of God is so vast, the power of His touch so invigorating, we could just stay in His presence for hours, soaking up His glory, basking in His blessings.

Debra Evans

STRENGTHENING YOUR FAITH

Whatever your weaknesses, God is stronger. And His strength will help you measure up to His tasks.

THE RIGHT KIND OF EXERCISE FOR YOU

He gives strength to the weary and strengthens the powerless.

Isaiah 40:29 HCSB

If you want to attain and maintain a healthy lifestyle, it's important to engage in a consistent exercise program. Implementing a plan of regular, sensible exercise is one way of ensuring that you've done your part to care for the body that God has given you.

Dr. Kenneth Cooper observed, "Physical activity achieved at any level is an essential ingredient in slowing down the process of aging and turning life into a far more useful, enjoyable—and independent—affair." So what's the right kind of exercise for you? That's a question for you and your doctor. But whether you're running marathons or walking around the block, it's important to stay as active as you can, as long as you can.

> Your exercise regimen should be sensible, enjoyable, safe, and consistent.

No one can force you to exercise . . . you'll need to make that decision on your own. And if you genuinely desire to please God, it's a decision that you will make today.

FOOD FOR THOUGHT

People who exercise at least 3 hours a week tend to eat a more balanced and a healthier diet.

Dr. Walt Larimore

Give at least two hours every day to exercise, for health must not be sacrificed to learning. A strong body makes the mind strong.

Thomas Jefferson

It is remarkable how one's wits are sharpened by physical exercise.

Pliny the Younger

An early morning walk is a blessing for the whole day.

Henry David Thoreau

A HEALTHY-CHOICE TIP

The benefits of exercise are both both physical and emotional. But no one can exercise for you; it's up to you to exercise, or not.

FOOD MATTERS

Do not carouse with drunkards and gluttons, for they are on their way to poverty.

Proverbs 23:20-21 NLT

Many of us are remarkably ill-informed and amazingly apathetic about the foods we eat. We feast on high-fat fast foods. We swoon over sweets. We order up—and promptly pack away—prodigious portions. The result is a society in which too many of us become the human equivalents of the portions we purchase: oversized.

A healthier strategy, of course, is to pay more attention to the nutritional properties of our foods and less attention their taste. But for those of us who have become accustomed to large quantities of full-flavored, high-calorie foods, old memories indeed die hard.

Today, think carefully about the quality and the quantity of the foods you eat.

Should we count every calorie that we ingest from now until the day the Good Lord calls us home? Probably not. When we focus too intently upon weight reduction, we may make weight loss even harder to achieve. Instead, we should eliminate from our diets the foods that are obviously bad for us and we should eat more of the foods that are obviously good for us. And of course, we should eat sensible amounts, not prodigious portions.

FOOD FOR THOUGHT

Moderation is better than muscle, self-control better than political power.

Proverbs 16:32 MSG

Now the God of all grace, who called you to His eternal glory in Christ Jesus, will personally restore, establish, strengthen, and support you.

1 Peter 5:10 HCSB

Every achievement worth remembering is stained with the blood of diligence and scarred by the wounds of disappointment.

Charles Swindoll

Failure is the path of least persistence.

Anonymous

A HEALTHY-CHOICE TIP

Since God loves you, and since He wants the very best for you, don't you believe that He also wants you to enjoy a healthy lifestyle? Of course He does. And since a healthy lifestyle is what God wants for you, isn't it what you should want, too?

YOUR PARTNERSHIP WITH GOD

So now we can rejoice in our wonderful new relationship with God—all because of what our Lord Jesus Christ has done for us in making us friends of God.

Romans 5:11 NLT

If you're like most women, you've already tried, perhaps on many occasions, to form healthier habits. You've employed your own willpower in a noble effort to create a new, improved, healthier you. You've probably tried to improve various aspects of your spiritual, physical, or emotional health. Perhaps you've gone on diets, or made New Year's resolutions, or tried the latest self-help fad in an attempt to finally make important changes in your life. And if you're like most women, you've been successful . . . for a while. But eventually, those old familiar habits came creeping back into your life, and the improvements that you had made proved to be temporary. This book is intended to help you build a series of healthy habits for your Christian walk . . . and make those habits stick.

> Your journey toward improved health can be, and should be, a journey that you make with God.

As you read through the pages of this book, you will be asked to depend less upon your own willpower and more upon God's power. For 100 days, you'll be asked to focus on three major areas of your life: mind, body, and spirit. And, of this you can be sure: When you form a working relationship with the Creator, there's no limit to the things that the two of you, working together, can do in just 100 days.

FOOD FOR THOUGHT

Measure the size of the obstacles against the size of God.

Beth Moore

God uses our most stumbling, faltering faith-steps as the open door to His doing for us "more than we ask or think."

Catherine Marshall

A HEALTHY-CHOICE TIP

Perhaps you have tended to divide the concerns of your life into two categories: "spiritual" and "other." If so, it's time to reconsider. God intends you to integrate His commandments into every aspect of your life, and that includes your physical and emotional health, too.

DAY 17

ASKING FOR GOD'S HELP

So I say to you, ask, and it will be given to you; seek, and you will find; knock, and it will be opened to you. For everyone who asks receives, and he who seeks finds, and to him who knocks it will be opened.

Luke 11:9-10 NKJV

Do you genuinely want to strengthen your fitness and your faith? If the answer to that question is yes, then you should set aside ample time each morning to ask for God's help.

Is prayer an integral part of your daily life, or is it a hit-or-miss habit? Do you "pray without ceasing," or is your prayer life an afterthought? Do you regularly pray in the quiet moments of the early morning, or do you bow your head only when others are watching?

> Today, make certain that you ask God specifically for the things you need.

As Christians, we are instructed to pray often. But it is important to note that genuine prayer requires much more than bending our knees and closing our eyes. Heartfelt prayer is an attitude of the heart.

If your prayers have become more a matter of habit than a matter of passion, you're robbing yourself of a deeper relationship with God. And how can you rectify that situation? By praying more frequently and more fervently.

When you do, God will shower you with His blessings, His grace, and His love.

FOOD FOR THOUGHT

What God gives in answer to our prayers will always be the thing we most urgently need, and it will always be sufficient.

Elisabeth Elliot

God says we don't need to be anxious about anything; we just need to pray about everything.

Stormie Omartian

Are you weak? Weary? Confused? Troubled? Pressured? How is your relationship with God? Is it held in its place of priority? I believe the greater the pressure, the greater your need for time alone with Him.

Kay Arthur

STRENGTHENING YOUR FAITH

There's no corner of your life that's too unimportant to pray about, so pray about everything.

GUARD YOUR HEART AND MIND

Finally, brethren, whatever things are true, whatever things are noble, whatever things are just, whatever things are pure, whatever things are lovely, whatever things are of good report, if there is any virtue and if there is anything praiseworthy— meditate on these things.

Philippians 4:8 NKJV

You are near and dear to God. He loves you more than you can imagine, and He wants the very best for you. And one more thing: God wants you to guard your heart.

Every day, you are faced with choices . . . more choices than you can count. You can do the right thing, or not. You can be prudent, or not. You can be kind, and generous, and obedient to God. Or not.

Today, think about ways that you can guard your heart from temptation and stress.

Today, the world will offer you countless opportunities to let down your guard and, by doing so, make needless mistakes that may injure you or your loved ones. So be watchful and obedient. Guard your heart by giving it to your Heavenly Father; it is safe with Him.

FOOD FOR THOUGHT

He doesn't need an abundance of words. He doesn't need a dissertation about your life. He just wants your attention. He wants your heart.

Kathy Troccoli

Be sober! Be on the alert! Your adversary the Devil is prowling around like a roaring lion, looking for anyone he can devour.

1 Peter 5:8 HCSB

Becoming pure is a process of spiritual growth, and taking seriously the confession of sin during prayer time moves that process along, causing us to purge our life of practices that displease God.

Elizabeth George

Holiness has never been the driving force of the majority. It is, however, mandatory for anyone who wants to enter the kingdom.

Elisabeth Elliot

STRENGTHENING YOUR FAITH

You should do whatever it takes to guard your heart—and with God's help, you can do it.

MODERATION LEADS TO ABUNDANCE

Don't associate with those who drink too much wine, or with those who gorge themselves on meat. For the drunkard and the glutton will become poor, and grogginess will clothe [them] in rags.

Proverbs 23:20-21 HCSB

If you sincerely seek the abundant life that Christ has promised, you must learn to control your appetites before they control you. Good habits, like bad ones, are habit-forming. The sooner you acquire the habit of moderation, the better your chances for a long, happy, abundant life.

Today, think of at least one step you can take to become a more moderate person.

Are you running short on willpower? If so, perhaps you haven't yet asked God to give you strength. The Bible promises that God offers His power to those righteous men and women who earnestly seek it. If your willpower has failed you on numerous occasions, then it's time to turn your weaknesses over to God. If you've been having trouble standing on your own two feet, perhaps it's time to drop to your knees, in prayer.

FOOD FOR THOUGHT

God wants to revolutionize our lives—by showing us how knowing Him can be the most powerful force to help us become all we want to be.

Bill Hybels

Believe and do what God says. The life-changing consequences will be limitless, and the results will be confidence and peace of mind.

Franklin Graham

Peace, peace to you, and peace to your helpers! For your God helps you.

1 Chronicles 12:18 NKJV

A HEALTHY-CHOICE TIP

Life is a gift—health must be earned. We earn good health by cultivating healthy habits. This is the right time for you to commit yourself to a more sensible lifestyle. So take a close look at your habits: how you eat, how you exercise, and how you think about your health. The only way that you'll revolutionize your physical health is to revolutionize the habits that make up the fabric of your day.

LISTENING TO GOD

The one who is from God listens to God's words. This is why you don't listen, because you are not from God.

John 8:47 HCSB

Sometimes God speaks loudly and clearly. More often, He speaks in a quiet voice—and if you are wise, you will be listening carefully when He does. To do so, you must carve out quiet moments each day to study His Word and sense His direction.

Can you quiet yourself long enough to listen to your conscience? Are you attuned to the subtle guidance of your intuition? Are you willing to pray sincerely and then to wait quietly for God's response? Hopefully so. Usually God refrains from sending His messages on stone tablets or city billboards. More often, He communicates in subtler ways. If you sincerely desire to hear His voice, you must listen carefully, and you must do so in the silent corners of your quiet, willing heart.

Today, find time to be quiet and still. Then, in the silence, listen carefully to your Creator.

FOOD FOR THOUGHT

God is always listening.

Stormie Omartian

The center of power is not to be found in summit meetings or in peace conferences. It is not in Peking or Washington or the United Nations, but rather where a child of God prays in the power of the Spirit for God's will to be done in her life, in her home, and in the world around her.

Ruth Bell Graham

When we come to Jesus stripped of pretensions, with a needy spirit, ready to listen, He meets us at the point of need.

Catherine Marshall

We must leave it to God to answer our prayers in His own wisest way. Sometimes, we are so impatient and think that God does not answer. God always answers! He never fails! Be still. Abide in Him.

Mrs. Charles E. Cowman

STRENGTHENING YOUR FAITH

God is trying to get your attention. Are you listening?

BITTERNESS PUTS DISTANCE BETWEEN YOU AND GOD

Hatred stirs up conflicts, but love covers all offenses.

Proverbs 10:12 HCSB

Are you mired in the quicksand of bitterness or regret? If so, it's time to free yourself from the mire. The world holds few if any rewards for those who remain angrily focused upon the past. Still, the act of forgiveness is difficult for all but the most saintly men and women.

Being frail, fallible, imperfect human beings, most of us are quick to anger, quick to blame, slow to forgive, and even slower to forget. Yet we know that it's best to forgive others, just as we, too, have been forgiven.

You can never fully enjoy the present if you're bitter about the past. Instead of living in the past, make peace with it . . . and move on.

If there exists even one person—including yourself—against whom you still harbor bitter feelings, it's time to forgive and move on. Bitterness, and regret are not part of God's plan for you, but God won't force you to forgive others. It's a job that only you can finish, and the sooner you finish it, the better.

FOOD FOR THOUGHT

Forgiveness is the key that unlocks the door of resentment and the handcuffs of hate. It is a power that breaks the chains of bitterness and the shackles of selfishness.

Corrie ten Boom

Bitterness is a spiritual cancer, a rapidly growing malignancy that can consume your life. Bitterness cannot be ignored but must be healed at the very core, and only Christ can heal bitterness.

Beth Moore

When you harbor bitterness, happiness will dock elsewhere.

Anonymous

Bitterness is the price we charge ourselves for being unwilling to forgive.

Marie T. Freeman

A HEALTHY-CHOICE TIP

Holding a grudge? Drop it! Remember, holding a grudge is like letting somebody live rent-free in your brain . . . so don't do it!

DAY 22

BE AWARE OF YOUR BLESSINGS

Therefore, get your minds ready for action, being self-disciplined, and set your hope completely on the grace to be brought to you at the revelation of Jesus Christ.

1 Peter 1:13 HCSB

Psalm 145 makes this promise: "The LORD is gracious and compassionate, slow to anger and rich in love. The LORD is good to all; he has compassion on all he has made" (vv. 8-9 NIV). As God's children, we are blessed beyond measure, but sometimes, as busy women in a demanding world,

> God blesses us in spite of our lives and not because of our lives.
>
> *Max Lucado*

we are slow to count our gifts and even slower to give thanks to the Giver. Our blessings include life and health, family and friends, freedom and possessions—for starters. And, the gifts we receive from God are multiplied when we share them with others. May we always give thanks to God for our blessings, and may we always demonstrate our gratitude by sharing them.

FOOD FOR THOUGHT

When you and I are related to Jesus Christ, our strength and wisdom and peace and joy and love and hope may run out, but His life rushes in to keep us filled to the brim. We are showered with blessings, not because of anything we have or have not done, but simply because of Him.

Anne Graham Lotz

There is no secret that can separate you from God's love; there is no secret that can separate you from His blessings; there is no secret that is worth keeping from His grace.

Serita Ann Jakes

Jesus intended for us to be overwhelmed by the blessings of regular days. He said it was the reason he had come: "I am come that they might have life, and that they might have it more abundantly."

Gloria Gaither

STRENGTHENING YOUR FAITH

God gives each of us countless blessings. We, in turn, should give Him our thanks and our praise. So remember: the best moment to give thanks is always the present moment.

PRAY CONSTANTLY ABOUT EVERYTHING, INCLUDING YOUR HEALTH

Rejoice always! Pray constantly. Give thanks in everything, for this is God's will for you in Christ Jesus.

1 Thessalonians 5:16-18 HCSB

Too many of us, even well-intentioned believers, tend to "compartmentalize" our waking hours into a few familiar categories: work, rest, play, family time, and worship. To do so is a mistake. Worship and praise should be woven into the fabric of our lives; prayer should never be relegated to a weekly three-hour visit to church on Sunday morning.

Today, spend time thinking about the power of prayer and the role that prayer plays in your life.

Theologian Wayne Oates once admitted, "Many of my prayers are made with my eyes open. You see, it seems I'm always praying about something, and it's not always convenient—or safe—to close my eyes." Dr. Oates understood that God always hears our prayers and that the relative position of our eyelids is of no concern to Him.

Today, find a little more time to lift your concerns to God in prayer. Pray about everything you can think of, including your spiritual, emotional, and physical health.

FOOD FOR THOUGHT

I am able to do all things through Him who strengthens me.

Philippians 4:13 HCSB

What God gives in answer to our prayers will always be the thing we most urgently need, and it will always be sufficient.

Elisabeth Elliot

Pour out your heart to God and tell Him how you feel. Be real, be honest, and when you get it all out, you'll start to feel the gradual covering of God's comforting presence.

Bill Hybels

And He said to me, "My grace is sufficient for you, for My strength is made perfect in weakness."

2 Corinthians 12:9 NKJV

STRENGTHENING YOUR FAITH

When you've got a choice to make, pray about it—one way to make sure that your heart is in tune with God is to pray often. The more you talk to God, the more He will talk to you.

IT TAKES DISCIPLINE

Apply your heart to discipline and your ears to words of knowledge.

Proverbs 23:12 NASB

Physical fitness requires discipline: the discipline to exercise regularly and the discipline to eat sensibly—it's as simple as that. But here's the catch: understanding the need for discipline is easy, but leading a disciplined life can be hard for most of us. Why? Because it's usually more fun to eat a second piece of cake than it is to jog a second lap around the track. But, as we survey the second helpings that all too often find their way on to our plates, we should consider this: as Christians, we are instructed to lead disciplined lives, and when we behave in undisciplined ways, we are living outside God's will.

Today, think about the costs and the benefits of discipline.

God's Word reminds us again and again that our Creator expects us to be disciplined in our thoughts and disciplined in our actions. God doesn't reward laziness, misbehavior, apathy, or shortsightedness. To the contrary, He expects believers to behave with dignity and self-control.

We live in a world in which leisure is glorified and consumption is commercialized. But God has other plans.

He did not create us for lives of gluttony or sloth; He created us for far greater things.

Life's greatest rewards seldom fall into our laps; to the contrary, our greatest accomplishments usually require lots of work, which is perfectly fine with God. After all, He knows that we're up to the task, and He has big plans for us; may we, as disciplined believers, always be worthy of those plans.

FOOD FOR THOUGHT

Work is doing it. Discipline is doing it every day. Diligence is doing it well every day.

Dave Ramsey

No discipline seems enjoyable at the time, but painful. Later on, however, it yields the fruit of peace and righteousness to those who have been trained by it.

Hebrews 12:11 HCSB

A HEALTHY-CHOICE TIP

Discipline matters. It takes discipline to strengthen your faith; it takes discipline to improve your fitness.

TOO BUSY?

Be careful not to forget the Lord.

Deuteronomy 6:12 HCSB

Has the busy pace of life robbed you of the peace that might otherwise be yours through Jesus Christ? If so, you are simply too busy for your own good. Through His Son Jesus, God offers you a peace that passes human understanding, but He won't force His peace upon you; in order to experience it, you must slow down long enough to sense His presence and His love.

> Frustration is not the will of God. There is time to do anything and everything that God wants us to do.
>
> *Elisabeth Elliot*

Today, as a gift to yourself, to your family, and to the world, slow down and claim the inner peace that is your spiritual birthright: the peace of Jesus Christ. It is offered freely; it has been paid for in full; it is yours for the asking. So ask. And then share.

FOOD FOR THOUGHT

If you can't seem to find time for God, then you're simply too busy for your own good. God is never too busy for you, and you should never be too busy for Him.

Marie T. Freeman

The demand of every day kept me so busy that I subconsciously equated my busyness with commitment to Christ.

Vonette Bright

In our tense, uptight society where folks are rushing to make appointments they have already missed, a good laugh can be as refreshing as a cup of cold water in the desert.

Barbara Johnson

We often become mentally and spiritually barren because we're so busy.

Franklin Graham

STRENGTHENING YOUR FAITH

The world wants to grab every spare minute of your time, but God wants some of your time, too. When in doubt, trust God.

DAY 26

TACKLING TOUGH TIMES

God is our refuge and strength, a very present help in trouble.

Psalm 46:1 NKJV

Women of every generation have experienced adversity, and this generation is no different. But, today's women face challenges that previous generations could have scarcely imagined. Thankfully, although the world continues to change, God's love remains constant. And, He remains ready to comfort us and strengthen us whenever we turn to Him.

Psalm 147 promises, "He heals the brokenhearted, and binds their wounds" (v. 3). When we are troubled, we must call upon God, and, in His own time and according to His own plan, He will heal us.

> If you're having tough times, don't hit the panic button and don't keep everything bottled up inside. Talk things over with people you can really trust.

If you are like most women, it is simply a fact of life: from time to time, you worry. You worry about health, about finances, about safety, about relationships, about family, and about countless other challenges of life, some great and some small. Where is the best place to take your worries? Take them to God. Take your troubles to Him, and your fears, and your sorrows. Seek protection from the One who cannot be moved.

FOOD FOR THOUGHT

If God sends us on stony paths, he provides strong shoes.

Corrie ten Boom

We all go through pain and sorrow, but the presence of God, like a warm, comforting blanket, can shield us and protect us, and allow the deep inner joy to surface, even in the most devastating circumstances.

Barbara Johnson

Add to your faith virtue; and to virtue, knowledge; and to knowledge, temperance; and to temperance, patience; and to patience, godliness; and to godliness, brotherly kindness; and to brotherly kindness, charity.

2 Peter 1:5-7 KJV

A HEALTHY-CHOICE TIP

If you're trying to remodel yourself, you'll need to remodel your environment, too. In order to decrease temptations and increase the probability of success, you should take a long, hard look at your home, your office, and the places you frequently visit. Then, you must do whatever you can to move yourself as far as possible from the temptations that you intend to defeat.

BIG DREAMS

With God's power working in us, God can do much, much more than anything we can ask or imagine.

Ephesians 3:20 NCV

Are you willing to entertain the possibility that God has big plans in store for you? Hopefully so. Yet sometimes, especially if you've recently experienced a life-altering disappointment, you may find it difficult to envision a brighter future for yourself and your family. If so, it's time to reconsider your own capabilities . . . and God's.

Your Heavenly Father created you with unique gifts and untapped talents; your job is to tap them. When you do, you'll begin to feel an increasing sense of confidence in yourself and in your future.

> You can dream big dreams, but you can never out-dream God. His plans for you are even bigger than you can imagine.

It takes courage to dream big dreams. You will discover that courage when you do three things: accept the past, trust God to handle the future, and make the most of the time He has given you today.

Nothing is too difficult for God, and no dreams are too big for Him—not even yours. So start living—and dreaming—accordingly.

FOOD FOR THOUGHT

Sometimes our dreams were so big that it took two people to dream them.

Marie T. Freeman

Always stay connected to people and seek out things that bring you joy. Dream with abandon. Pray confidently.

Barbara Johnson

The future lies all before us. Shall it only be a slight advance upon what we usually do? Ought it not to be a bound, a leap forward to altitudes of endeavor and success undreamed of before?

Annie Armstrong

Allow your dreams a place in your prayers and plans. God-given dreams can help you move into the future He is preparing for you.

Barbara Johnson

A HEALTHY-CHOICE TIP

Educate yourself on which foods are healthy and which foods aren't. Read labels and learn the basics of proper nutrition. Then, use common sense and discipline in planning your diet.

GOD'S PROTECTION

The Lord is my strength and my song; He has become my salvation.

Exodus 15:2 HCSB

In a world filled with dangers and temptations, God is the ultimate armor. In a world filled with misleading messages, God's Word is the ultimate truth. In a world filled with more frustrations than we can count, God's Son offers the ultimate peace. Will you accept God's peace and wear God's armor against the dangers of our world?

Sometimes, in the crush of everyday life, God may seem far away, but He is not. God is everywhere you have ever been and everywhere you will ever go. He is with you night and day; He knows your thoughts and your prayers. He is your ultimate Protector. And, when you earnestly seek His protection, you will find it because He is here—always—waiting patiently for you to reach out to Him.

Today, pray for God's protection and God's guidance. You need both.

FOOD FOR THOUGHT

God will never let you sink under your circumstances. He always provide a safety net and His love always encircles.

Barbara Johnson

Only believe, don't fear. Our Master, Jesus, always watches over us, and no matter what the persecution, Jesus will surely overcome it.

Lottie Moon

Our future may look fearfully intimidating, yet we can look up to the Engineer of the Universe, confident that nothing escapes His attention or slips out of the control of those strong hands.

Elisabeth Elliot

Worries carry responsibilities that belong to God, not to you. Worry does not enable us to escape evil; it makes us unfit to cope with it when it comes.

Corrie ten Boom

STRENGTHENING YOUR FAITH

You are protected by God . . . now and always. The only security that lasts is the security that flows from the loving heart of God.

YOUR BODY, YOUR CHOICES

So then each of us shall give account of himself to God.

Romans 14:12 NKJV

As adults, each of us bears a personal responsibility for the general state of our own physical health. Certainly, various aspects of health are beyond our control: illness sometimes strikes even the healthiest men and women. But for most of us, physical health is a choice: it is the result of hundreds of small decisions that we make every day of our lives. If we make decisions that promote good health, our bodies respond. But if we fall into bad habits and undisciplined lifestyles, we suffer tragic consequences.

God has entrusted you with the responsibility of caring for your body. So it's always the right time to become proactive about your health.

When our unhealthy habits lead to poor health, we find it all too easy to look beyond ourselves and assign blame. In fact, we live in a society where blame has become a national obsession: we blame cigarette manufacturers, restaurants, and food producers, to name only a few. But to blame others is to miss the point: we, and we alone, are responsible for the way that we treat our bodies. And the sooner that we accept that responsibility, the sooner we can assert control over our bodies and our lives.

Do you sincerely desire to improve your physical fitness? If so, start by taking personal responsibility for the body that God has given you. Then, make the solemn pledge to yourself that you will begin to make the changes that are required to enjoy a longer, healthier, happier life.

FOOD FOR THOUGHT

Even a child is known by his actions, by whether his conduct is pure and right.

Proverbs 20:11 NIV

Although God causes all things to work together for good for His children, He still holds us accountable for our behavior.

Kay Arthur

A HEALTHY-CHOICE TIP

It's easy to blame other people for the current state of your health. You live in a world where it's fashionable to blame food manufacturers, doctors, and fast food restaurants, to mention but a few. Yet none of these folks force food into your mouth, and they don't force you to sit on the sofa when you should be exercising! So remember: it's your body . . . and it's your responsibility.

HEALTHY PRIORITIES

Beloved, I pray that in all respects you may prosper and be in good health, just as your soul prospers.

3 John 1:2 NASB

When it comes to matters of physical, spiritual, and emotional health, Christians possess an infallible guidebook: the Holy Bible. And, when it comes to matters concerning fitness—whether physical, emotional, or spiritual fitness—God's Word can help us establish clear priorities that can guide our steps and our lives.

It's easy to talk about establishing clear priorities for maintaining physical and spiritual health, but it's much more difficult to live according to those priorities. For busy believers living in a demanding world, placing first things first can be difficult indeed. Why? Because so many people are expecting so many things from us!

Time is a non-renewable resource. Today, think about the ways to spend your time more wisely.

If you're having trouble prioritizing your day—or if you're having trouble sticking to a plan that enhances your spiritual and physical health—perhaps you've been trying to organize your life according to your own plans, not God's. A better strategy, of course, is to take your daily obligations and place them in the hands of the

One who created you. To do so, you must prioritize your day according to God's commandments, and you must seek His will and His wisdom in all matters.

FOOD FOR THOUGHT

Ultimate healing and the glorification of the body are certainly among the blessings of Calvary for the believing Christian. Immediate healing is not guaranteed.

Warren Wiersbe

A HEALTHY-CHOICE TIP

High blood pressure can cause heart attacks, strokes, and plenty of other serious health problems. The good news is that high blood pressure is usually treatable with medication, or lifestyle changes, or both. But you won't know you need treatment unless you know your blood pressure. Thankfully, blood pressure cuffs can be found just about everywhere, in many drug stores and even in some supermarkets. So remember this: you don't have to wait for a doctor's appointment to check your blood pressure. You can monitor your own blood pressure in between visits to the doctor's office, and that's precisely what you should do.

THE WORLD CHANGES,
BUT GOD DOES NOT

There is a time for everything, and a season for every activity under heaven.

Ecclesiastes 3:1 NIV

Our world is in a state of constant change. God is not. At times, the world seems to be trembling beneath our feet. But we can be comforted in the knowledge that our Heavenly Father is the rock that cannot be shaken. His Word promises, "I am the Lord, I do not change" (Malachi 3:6 NKJV).

> Change is inevitable; growth is not. God will come to your doorstep on countless occasions with opportunities to learn and to grow.

Every day that we live, we mortals encounter a multitude of changes—some good, some not so good. And on occasion, all of us must endure life-changing personal losses that leave us breathless. When we do, our loving Heavenly Father stands ready to protect us, to comfort us, to guide us, and, in time, to heal us.

Are you facing difficult circumstances or unwelcome changes? If so, please remember that God is far bigger than any problem you may face. So, instead of worrying about life's inevitable challenges, put your faith in the Father and His only begotten Son: "Jesus Christ is the same yesterday, today, and forever" (Hebrews 13:8 HCSB). And rest assured: It is precisely because your Savior does not change that you can face your challenges with courage for this day and hope for the future.

FOOD FOR THOUGHT

Mere change is not growth. Growth is the synthesis of change and continuity, and where there is no continuity there is no growth.

C. S. Lewis

With God, it isn't who you were that matters; it's who you are becoming.

Liz Curtis Higgs

More often than not, when something looks like it's the absolute end, it is really the beginning.

Charles Swindoll

STRENGTHENING YOUR FAITH

Your journey with God unfolds day by day, and that's precisely how your journey to an improved state of physical fitness must also unfold: moment by moment, day by day, year by year.

DAY 32

CHOOSING TO LET GOD TRANSFORM YOUR LIFE

Your old life is dead. Your new life, which is your real life—even though invisible to spectators—is with Christ in God. He is your life.

Colossians 3:3 MSG

Think, for a moment, about the "old" you, the person you were before you invited Christ to reign over your heart. Now, think about the "new" you, the person you have become since then. Is there a difference between the "old" you and the "new and improved" version? There should be! And that difference should be noticeable not only to you but also to others.

Unless you're a radically different person because of your relationship with Jesus, your faith isn't what it could be . . . or should be.

The Bible clearly teaches that when we welcome Christ into our hearts, we become new creations through Him. Our challenge, of course, is to behave ourselves like new creations. When we do, God fills our hearts, He blesses our endeavors, and transforms our lives . . . forever.

FOOD FOR THOUGHT

Repentance involves a radical change of heart and mind in which we agree with God's evaluation of our sin and then take specific action to align ourselves with His will.

Henry Blackaby

If we accept His invitation to salvation, we live with Him forever. However, if we do not accept because we refuse His only Son as our Savior, then we exclude ourselves from My Father's House. It's our choice.

Anne Graham Lotz

If you are God's child, you are no longer bound to your past or to what you were. You are a brand new creature in Christ Jesus.

Kay Arthur

There is so much Heaven around us now if we have eyes for it, because eternity starts when we give ourselves to God.

Gloria Gaither

A HEALTHY-CHOICE TIP

If you're serious about improving your fitness or your faith, pray about it.

DAY 33

GETTING ENOUGH REST?

Come to Me, all you who are weary and burdened, and I will give you rest.

Matthew 11:28-30 NKJV

Even the most inspired Christians can, from time to time, find themselves running on empty. The demands of daily life can drain us of our strength and rob us of the joy that is rightfully ours in Christ. When we find ourselves tired, discouraged, or worse, there is a source from which we can draw the power needed to recharge our spiritual batteries. That source is God.

God wants you to get enough rest. The world wants you to burn the candle at both ends. Trust God.

God intends that His children lead joyous lives filled with abundance and peace. But sometimes, abundance and peace seem very far away. It is then that we must turn to God for renewal, and when we do, He will restore us.

God expects us to work hard, but He also intends for us to rest. When we fail to take the rest that we need, we do a disservice to ourselves and to our families.

Is your spiritual battery running low? Is your energy on the wane? Are your emotions frayed? If so, it's time to turn your thoughts and your prayers to God. And when you're finished, it's time to rest.

FOOD FOR THOUGHT

And be not conformed to this world: but be ye transformed by the renewing of your mind.

Romans 12:2 KJV

And the apostles gathered themselves together unto Jesus, and told him all things, both what they had done, and what they had taught. And he said unto them, Come ye yourselves apart into a desert place, and rest a while.

Mark 6:30-31 HCSB

I will lift up mine eyes unto the hills, from whence cometh my help. My help cometh from the Lord, which made heaven and earth.

Psalm 121:1-2 KJV

A HEALTHY-CHOICE TIP

Most adults need about eight hours of sleep each night. If you're depriving yourself of much needed sleep in order to stay up and watch late night television, you've developed a bad habit. Instead, do yourself a favor: turn off the TV and go to bed.

THE TRAGEDY OF ADDICTION

Let us walk with decency, as in the daylight: not in carousing and drunkenness.

Romans 13:13 HCSB

The dictionary defines addiction as " the compulsive need for a habit-forming substance; the condition of being habitually and compulsively occupied with something." That definition is accurate, but incomplete. For Christians, addiction has an additional meaning: it means compulsively worshipping something other than God.

Ours is a highly addictive society. Why? The answer is straightforward: supply and demand. The supply of addictive substances continues to grow; the affordablity and availability of these substances makes them highly attractive to consumers; and the overall demand for addictive substances has increased as more users have become addicted to an ever-expanding array of substances and compulsions.

> You must guard your heart against addiction . . . or else.

You know people who are full-blown addicts—probably lots of people. If you, or someone you love, is suffering from the blight of addiction, the following ideas are worth remembering:

1. For the addict, addiction comes first. In the life of an addict, addiction rules. God, of course, commands otherwise. God says, "You shall have no other gods before Me," and He means precisely what He says (Exodus 20:3 NKJV). Our task, as believers, is to put God in His proper place: first place. 2. You cannot cure another person's addiction, but you can encourage that person to seek help. Addicts are cured when they decide, not when you decide. What you can do is this: you can be supportive, and you can encourage the addict to find the help that he or she needs (Luke 10:25-37). 3. If you are living with an addicted person, think about safety: yours and your family's. Addiction is life-threatening and life-shortening. Don't let someone else's addiction threaten your safety or the safety of your loved ones (Proverbs 22:3). 4. Don't assist in prolonging the addiction: When you interfere with the negative consequences that might otherwise accompany an addict's negative behaviors, you are inadvertently "enabling" the addict to continue the destructive cycle of addiction. So don't be an enabler (Proverbs 15:31). 5. Help is available: Lots of people have experienced addiction and lived to tell about it. They want to help. Let them (Proverbs 27:17). 6. A cure is possible. With God's help, no addiction is incurable. And with God, no situation is hopeless (Matthew 19:26).

YOUR CHOICES MATTER

I am offering you life or death, blessings or curses. Now, choose life! . . . To choose life is to love the Lord your God, obey him, and stay close to him.

Deuteronomy 30:19-20 NCV

Each day, we make thousands of small choices concerning the things that we do and the things we think. Most of these choices are made without too much forethought. In fact, most of us go about our daily lives spending a significant portion of our lives simply reacting to events. Often, our actions are simply the result of impulse or habit. God asks that we slow down long enough to think about the choices that we make, and He asks that we make those choices in accordance with His commandments.

First you make choices . . . and soon those choices begin to shape your life. That's why you must make smart choices . . . or face the consequences.

The Bible teaches us that our bodies are "temples" which belong to God (1 Corinthians 6:19-20). We are commanded (not encouraged, not advised, commanded!) to treat our bodies with respect and honor. We do so by making wise choices and by making those choices consistently over an extended period of time.

Do you sincerely seek to improve the overall quality of your health? Then vow to yourself and to God that you will begin making the kind of wise choices that will lead to a longer, healthier, happier life. The responsibility for those choices is yours. And so are the rewards.

FOOD FOR THOUGHT

Every day of our lives we make choices about how we're going to live that day.

Luci Swindoll

There may be no trumpet sound or loud applause when we make a right decision, just a calm sense of resolution and peace.

Gloria Gaither

A HEALTHY-CHOICE TIP

Do you think God wants you to develop healthy habits? Of course He does! Physical, emotional, and spiritual fitness are all part of God's plan for you. But it's up to you to make certain that a healthy lifestyle is a fundamental part of your plan, too.

THE POWER OF DAILY WORSHIP AND MEDITATION

Man shall not live by bread alone, but by every word that proceeds from the mouth of God.

Matthew 4:4 NKJV

Are you concerned about your spiritual, physical, or emotional fitness? If so, there is a timeless source of advice and comfort upon which you can—and should—depend. That source is the Holy Bible.

God's Word has much to say about every aspect of your life, including your health. If you face personal health challenges that seem almost insoluble, have faith and seek God's wisdom. If you can't seem to get yourself on a sensible diet or on a program of regular physical exercise, consult God's teachings. If your approach to your physical or emotional health has, up to this point, been undisciplined, pray for the strength to do what you know is right.

> God's Word has the power to change every aspect of your life, including your health.

God has given you the Holy Bible for the purpose of knowing His promises, His power, His commandments, His wisdom, His love, and His Son. As you seek to improve the state of your own health, study God's teachings and apply them to your life. When you do, you will be blessed, now and forever.

FOOD FOR THOUGHT

He awakens Me morning by morning, He awakens My ear to hear as the learned. The Lord God has opened My ear.

Isaiah 50:4-5 NKJV

Lord, You are my lamp; the Lord illuminates my darkness.

2 Samuel 22:29 HCSB

Teach me Your way, Lord, and I will live by Your truth. Give me an undivided mind to fear Your name.

Psalm 86:11 HCSB

I will instruct you and show you the way to go; with My eye on you, I will give counsel.

Psalm 32:8 HCSB

STRENGTHENING YOUR FAITH

Find the best time of the day to spend with God. Hudson Taylor, an English missionary, wrote, "Whatever is your best time in the day, give that to communion with God." That's powerful advice that leads to a powerful faith.

FINDING CONTENTMENT

I am the door. If anyone enters by Me, he will be saved, and will come in and go out and find pasture.

John 10:9 HCSB

Where can you find contentment? Is it a result of wealth, or power, or beauty, or fame? Hardly. Genuine contentment springs from a peaceful spirit, a clear conscience, and a loving heart (like yours!).

Our modern world seems preoccupied with the search for happiness. We are bombarded with messages telling us that happiness depends upon the acquisition of material possessions. These messages are false. Enduring peace is not the result of our acquisitions; it is the inevitable result of our dispositions. If we don't find contentment within ourselves, we will never find it outside ourselves.

God offers you His peace, His protection, and His promises. If you accept these gifts, you will be content.

Thus the search for contentment is an internal quest, an exploration of the heart, mind, and soul. You can find contentment—indeed you will find it—if you simply look in the right places. And the best time to start looking in those places is now.

FOOD FOR THOUGHT

I believe that in every time and place it is within our power to acquiesce in the will of God—and what peace it brings to do so!

Elisabeth Elliot

The key to contentment is to consider. Consider who you are and be satisfied with that. Consider what you have and be satisfied with that. Consider what God's doing and be satisfied with that.

Luci Swindoll

Father and Mother lived on the edge of poverty, and yet their contentment was not dependent upon their surroundings. Their relationship to each other and to the Lord gave them strength and happiness.

Corrie ten Boom

STRENGTHENING YOUR FAITH

Be contented where you are, even if it's not exactly where you want to end up. God has something wonderful in store for you—and remember that God's timing is perfect—so be patient, trust God, do your best, and expect the best.

DAY 38

MAKING THE RIGHT CHOICES

A wise man will hear and increase learning, and a man of understanding will attain wise counsel.

Proverbs 1:5 NKJV

Life is a series of choices. Each day, we make countless decisions that can bring us closer to God . . . or not. When we live according to God's commandments, we earn for ourselves the abundance and peace that He intends for us to experience. But, when we turn our backs upon God by disobeying Him, we bring needless suffering upon ourselves and our families.

Today, think about unwise choices you've made in the past and wise choices you intend to make in the future.

Do you seek God's peace and His blessings? Then obey Him. When you're faced with a difficult choice or a powerful temptation, seek God's counsel and trust the counsel He gives. Invite God into your heart and live according to His commandments. When you do, you will be blessed today, tomorrow, and forever.

God has given you a guidebook for righteous living called the Holy Bible. It contains thorough instructions which, if followed, lead to fulfillment and salvation. But, if you choose to ignore God's commandments, the results are as predictable as they are tragic.

So here's a surefire formula for a happy, abundant life: live righteously.

And for further instructions, read the manual.

FOOD FOR THOUGHT

Wisdom is the God-given ability to see life with rare objectivity and to handle life with rare stability.

Charles Swindoll

Wisdom is knowledge applied. Head knowledge is useless on the battlefield. Knowledge stamped on the heart makes one wise.

Beth Moore

A HEALTHY-CHOICE TIP

John Maxwell observed, "The key to healthy eating is moderation and managing what you eat every day." And he was right. Crash diets don't usually work, but sensible eating habits do work, so plan your meals accordingly.

DAY 39

KNOW WHAT YOU EAT

Acquire wisdom—how much better it is than gold! And acquire understanding—it is preferable to silver.

Proverbs 16:16 HCSB

How hard is it for us to know the nutritional properties of the foods we eat? Not very hard. In the grocery store, almost every food item is clearly marked. In fast-food restaurants, the fat and calorie contents are posted on the wall (although the print is incredibly small, and with good reason: the health properties of these tasty tidbits are, in most cases, so poor that we should rename them "fat foods").

Today, make it a point to measure every calorie you consume. Then, at the end of the day, ask yourself if your food choices have been wise, unwise, or disastrous.

As informed adults, we have access to all the information that we need to make healthy dietary choices. Now it's up to each of us to make wise dietary choices, or not. Those choices are ours, and so are their consequences.

FOOD FOR THOUGHT

But also for this very reason, giving all diligence, add to your faith virtue, to virtue knowledge.

2 Peter 1:5 NKJV

Let the word of Christ dwell in you richly in all wisdom, teaching and admonishing one another in psalms and hymns and spiritual songs, singing with grace in your hearts to the Lord.

Colossians 3:16 NKJV

Those who are wise shall shine like the brightness of the firmament, and those who turn many to righteousness like the stars forever and ever.

Daniel 12:3 NKJV

STRENGTHENING YOUR FAITH

Wisdom 101: If you're looking for wisdom (health or otherwise), the Book of Proverbs is a wonderful place to start. It has 31 chapters, one for each day of the month. If you read Proverbs regularly, and if you take its teachings to heart, you'll gain timeless wisdom from God's unchanging Word.

THE FUTILITY OF BLAME

People's own foolishness ruins their lives, but in their minds they blame the Lord.

Proverbs 19:3 NCV

When our unhealthy habits lead to poor health, we find it all too easy to look beyond ourselves and assign blame. In fact, we live in a society where blame has become a national obsession: we blame cigarette manufacturers, restaurants, and food producers, to name only a few. But to blame others is to miss the point: we, and we alone, are responsible for the way that we treat our bodies. And the sooner that we accept that responsibility, the sooner we can assert control over our bodies and our lives.

Today, ask God to help you take responsibility for the current state of your health. And while you're at it, ask Him to help you make wise choices in the future.

So, when it comes to your own body, assume control and accept responsibility. It's a great way to live and a great way to stay healthy.

FOOD FOR THOUGHT

The main thing is this: we should never blame anyone or anything for our defeats. No matter how evil their intentions may be, they are altogether unable to harm us until we begin to blame them and use them as excuses for our own unbelief.

A. W. Tozer

The single most important element in any human relationship is honesty—with oneself, with God, and with others.

Catherine Marshall

Never use your problem as an excuse for bad attitudes or behavior.

Joyce Meyer

A HEALTHY-CHOICE TIP

The road to poor health is paved with good intentions. Until you make exercise a high priority in your life, your good intentions will soon give way to old habits. So give your exercise regimen a position of high standing on your daily to-do list.

DAY 41

SENSIBLE EXERCISE

No discipline seems pleasant at the time, but painful. Later on, however, it produces a harvest of righteousness and peace for those who have been trained by it.

Hebrews 12:11 NIV

A healthy lifestyle includes regular, sensible physical exercise. How much exercise is right for you? That's a decision that you should make in consultation with your physician.

God rewards wise behaviors and He punishes misbehavior. A commitment to a sensible exercise program is one way of being wise, and it's also one way of pleasing God.

But make no mistake: if you sincerely desire to be a thoughtful caretaker of the body that God has given you, exercise is important.

Once you begin a regular exercise program, you'll discover that the benefits to you are not only physical but also psychological. Regular exercise allows you to build your muscles while you're clearing your head and lifting your spirits.

So, if you've been taking your body for granted, today is a wonderful day to change. You can start slowly, perhaps with a brisk walk around the block. As your stamina begins to build, so will your sense of satisfaction. And, you'll be comforted by the knowledge that you've done your part to protect and preserve the precious body that God has entrusted to your care.

FOOD FOR THOUGHT

The effective Christians of history have been men and women of great personal discipline—mental discipline, discipline of the body, discipline of the tongue, and discipline of the emotion.

Billy Graham

Sow righteousness for yourselves and reap faithful love; break up your untilled ground. It is time to seek the Lord until He comes and sends righteousness on you like the rain.

Hosea 10:12 HCSB

Don't you know that you are God's temple and that God's Spirit lives in you?

1 Corinthians 3:16 NCV

A HEALTHY-CHOICE TIP

Make exercise enjoyable. Your workouts should be a source of pleasure and satisfaction, not a form of self-imposed punishment. Find a way to exercise your body that is satisfying, effective, and fun.

SPIRITUAL HEALTH, SPIRITUAL GROWTH

But the fruit of the Spirit is love, joy, peace, long-suffering, gentleness, goodness, faith, meekness, temperance . . . .

Galatians 5:22-23 KJV

Are you as "spiritually fit" as you're ever going to be? Hopefully not! When it comes to your faith (and, by the way, when it comes to your fitness), God isn't done with you yet.

The journey toward spiritual maturity lasts a lifetime: As Christians, we can and should continue to grow in the love and the knowledge of our Savior as long as we live. But, if we cease to grow, either emotionally or spiritually, we do ourselves and our families a profound disservice.

> Wherever you are in your spiritual journey, it's always the right time to take another step toward God.

If we study God's Word, if we obey His commandments, and if we live in the center of His will, we will not be "stagnant" believers; we will, instead, be growing Christians . . . and that's exactly what God wants for our lives.

In those quiet moments when we open our hearts to God, the Creator who made us keeps remaking us. He gives us direction, perspective, wisdom, and courage. He encourages us to become more fit in a variety of ways: more spiritually fit, more physically fit, and more emotionally fit.

God is willing to do His part to ensure that you remain fit. Are you willing to do yours?

FOOD FOR THOUGHT

If all struggles and sufferings were eliminated, the spirit would no more reach maturity than would the child.

Elisabeth Elliot

We set our eyes on the finish line, forgetting the past, and straining toward the mark of spiritual maturity and fruitfulness.

Vonette Bright

STRENGTHENING YOUR FAITH

Spiritual growth is not instantaneous . . . and neither, for that matter, is the attainment of a physically fit body. So be patient. You should expect a few ups and downs along the way, but you should also expect to see progress over time.

DAY 43

HAVE THE COURAGE TO TRUST GOD

Trust in the Lord with all your heart, and do not rely on your own understanding; think about Him in all your ways, and He will guide you on the right paths.

Proverbs 3:5-6 HCSB

When our dreams come true and our plans prove successful, we find it easy to thank our Creator and easy to trust His divine providence. But in times of sorrow or hardship, we may find ourselves questioning God's plans for our lives.

On occasion, you will confront circumstances that trouble you to the very core of your soul. It is during these difficult days that you must find the wisdom and the courage to trust your Heavenly Father despite your circumstances.

Are you a woman who seeks God's blessings for yourself and your family? Then trust Him. Trust Him with your relationships. Trust Him with your priorities. Follow His commandments and pray for His guidance. Trust Your Heavenly Father day by day, moment by moment—in good times and in trying times.

> What is courage? It is the ability to be strong in trust, in conviction, in obedience. To be courageous is to step out in faith—to trust and obey, no matter what.
>
> Kay Arthur

Then, wait patiently for God's revelations . . . and prepare yourself for the abundance and peace that will most certainly be yours when you do.

FOOD FOR THOUGHT

Sometimes the very essence of faith is trusting God in the midst of things He knows good and well we cannot comprehend.

Beth Moore

Are you serious about wanting God's guidance to become the person he wants you to be? The first step is to tell God that you know you can't manage your own life; that you need his help.

Catherine Marshall

Brother, is your faith looking upward today? / Trust in the promise of the Savior. / Sister, is the light shining bright on your way? / Trust in the promise of thy Lord.

Fanny Crosby

STRENGTHENING YOUR FAITH

Because God is trustworthy—and because He has made promises to you that He intends to keep—you are protected.

IN SEARCH OF WISDOM AND BALANCE

Now if any of you lacks wisdom, he should ask God, who gives to all generously and without criticizing, and it will be given to him. But let him ask in faith without doubting. For the doubter is like the surging sea, driven and tossed by the wind.

James 1:5-6 HCSB

To find balance, you must find wisdom. Where will you find wisdom today? Will you seek it from God or from the world? As a thoughtful woman living in a society that is filled with temptations and distractions, you know that the world's brand of "wisdom" is everywhere . . . and it is dangerous. You live in a world where it's all too easy to stray far from the ultimate source of wisdom: God's Holy Word.

God makes His wisdom available to you. Your job is to acknowledge, to understand, and (above all) to use that wisdom.

When you commit yourself to the daily study of God's Word—and when you live according to His commandments—you will become wise . . . in time. But don't expect to open your Bible today and be wise tomorrow. Wisdom is not like a mushroom; it does not spring up overnight. It is, instead, like a majestic oak tree that starts as a tiny acorn, grows into a sapling, and eventually reaches up to the sky, tall and strong.

Today and every day, as a way of understanding God's plan for your life, you should study His Word and live by it. When you do, you will accumulate a storehouse of wisdom that will enrich your own life and the lives of your family members, your friends, and the world.

FOOD FOR THOUGHT

This is my song through endless ages: Jesus led me all the way.

Fanny Crosby

If we neglect the Bible, we cannot expect to benefit from the wisdom and direction that result from knowing God's Word.

Vonette Bright

Knowledge can be found in books or in school. Wisdom, on the other hand, starts with God . . . and ends there.

Marie T. Freeman

A HEALTHY-CHOICE TIP

An exercise program that starts slowly and builds over time is far better than an exercise program that starts—and ends—quickly.

PRAY CONSTANTLY

Rejoice in hope; be patient in affliction; be persistent in prayer.

Romans 12:12 HCSB

God's Word promises that prayer is a powerful tool for changing your life and your world. So here's a question: Are you using prayer as a powerful tool to improve your world, or are you praying sporadically at best? If you're wise, you've learned that prayer is indeed powerful and that it is most powerful when it is used often.

Prayer changes things—and you—so pray.

Today, if you haven't already done so, establish the habit of praying constantly. Don't pray day-to-day; pray hour-to-hour. Start each day with prayer, end it with prayer, and fill it with prayer. That's the best way to know God; it's the best way to change your world; and it is, quite simply, the best way to live.

FOOD FOR THOUGHT

What God gives in answer to our prayers will always be the thing we most urgently need, and it will always be sufficient.

Elisabeth Elliot

Your family and friends need your prayers and you need theirs. And God wants to hear those prayers. So what are you waiting for?

Marie T. Freeman

We must leave it to God to answer our prayers in His own wisest way. Sometimes, we are so impatient and think that God does not answer. God always answers! He never fails! Be still. Abide in Him.

Mrs. Charles E. Cowman

Is anyone among you suffering? He should pray. Is anyone cheerful? He should sing praises.

James 5:13 HCSB

STRENGTHENING YOUR FAITH

Don't ever be embarrassed to pray: Are you embarrassed to bow your head in a restaurant? Don't be; it's the people who aren't praying who should be embarrassed!

DAY 46

PROTECTING YOUR EMOTIONAL HEALTH

And the peace of God, which surpasses every thought, will guard your hearts and your minds in Christ Jesus. Finally brothers, whatever is true, whatever is honorable, whatever is just, whatever is pure, whatever is lovely, whatever is commendable—if there is any moral excellence and if there is any praise—dwell on these things.

Philippians 4:7-8 HCSB

Emotional health isn't simply the absence of sadness; it's also the ability to enjoy life and the wisdom to celebrate God's gifts. Christians have every reason to be optimistic about life. As John Calvin observed, "There is not one blade of grass, there is no color in this world that is not intended to make us rejoice." But sometimes, when we are tired or frustrated, rejoicing seems only a distant promise. Thankfully, God stands ready to restore us: "I will give you a new heart and put a new spirit in you...." (Ezekiel 36:26 NIV). Our task, of course, is to let Him.

> When negative emotions threaten to hijack your day, lift your thoughts—and your prayers—to God.

If you're feeling deeply discouraged or profoundly depressed, then it is time to seriously address the state of your emotional health. First, open your heart to God in prayer. Then, talk with trusted family members, friends, and your pastor. And, if you or someone close to you considers it wise, seek advice from your physician or make an appointment with a licensed mental health professional.

When your emotional health is at stake, you should avail yourself of every reasonable resource. Then, armed with the promises of your Creator and the support of family and friends, you can go about the business of solving the challenges that confront you. When you do, the clouds will eventually part, and the sun will shine once more upon your soul.

FOOD FOR THOUGHT

Worry does not empty tomorrow of its sorrow; it empties today of its strength.

Corrie ten Boom

A HEALTHY-CHOICE TIP

John Maxwell observed, "The key to healthy eating is moderation and managing what you eat every day." And he was right. Crash diets don't usually work, but sensible eating habits do work, so plan your meals accordingly.

TRUSTING GOD'S WILL

God is my shield, saving those whose hearts are true and right.
Psalm 7:10 NLT

God has will, and so do we. He gave us the power to make choices for ourselves, and He created a world in which those choices have consequences. The ultimate choice that we face, of course, is what to do about God. We can cast our lot with Him by choosing Jesus Christ as our personal Savior, or not. The choice is ours alone.

We also face thousands of small choices that make up the fabric of daily life. When we align those choices with God's commandments, and when we align our lives with God's will, we receive His abundance, His peace, and His joy. But when we struggle against God's will for our lives, we reap a bitter harvest indeed.

When God's will becomes your will, good things happen.

Today, you'll face thousands of small choices; as you do, use God's Word as your guide. And, as you face the ultimate choice, place God's Son and God's will and God's love at the center of your life. You'll discover that God's plan is far grander than any you could have imagined.

FOOD FOR THOUGHT

To yield to God means to belong to God, and to belong to God means to have all His infinite power. To belong to God means to have all.

Hannah Whitall Smith

The will of God is never exactly what you expect it to be. It may seem to be much worse, but in the end it's going to be a lot better and a lot bigger.

Elisabeth Elliot

The center of power is not to be found in summit meetings or in peace conferences. It is not in Peking or Washington or the United Nations, but rather where a child of God prays in the power of the Spirit for God's will to be done in her life, in her home, and in the world around her.

Ruth Bell Graham

A HEALTHY-CHOICE TIP

Exercising discipline should never be viewed as an imposition or as a form of punishment; far from it. Discipline is the means by which you can take control of your life (which, by the way, is far better than letting your life control you).

FOLLOW HIM

If anyone serves Me, let him follow Me; and where I am, there My servant will be also. If anyone serves Me, him My Father will honor.

John 12:26 NKJV

Jesus walks with you. Are you walking with Him? Hopefully, you will choose to walk with Him today and every day of your life.

Jesus loved you so much that He endured unspeakable humiliation and suffering for you. How will you respond to Christ's sacrifice? Will you take up His cross and follow Him (Luke 9:23), or will you choose another path? When you place your hopes squarely at the foot of the cross, when you place Jesus squarely at the center of your life, you will be blessed. If you seek to be a worthy disciple of Jesus, you must acknowledge that He never comes "next." He is always first.

It takes a genuine commitment— and significant sacrifices—to really follow Jesus. And it's worth it.

Do you hope to fulfill God's purpose for your life? Do you seek a life of abundance and peace? Do you intend to be Christian, not just in name, but in deed? Then follow Christ. Follow Him by picking up His cross today and every day that you live. When you do, you will quickly discover that Christ's love has the power to change everything, including you.

FOOD FOR THOUGHT

Will you, with a glad and eager surrender, hand yourself and all that concerns you over into his hands? If you will do this, your soul will begin to know something of the joy of union with Christ.

Hannah Whitall Smith

Peter said, "No, Lord!" But he had to learn that one cannot say "No" while saying "Lord" and that one cannot say "Lord" while saying "No."

Corrie ten Boom

The love life of the Christian is a crucial battleground. There, if nowhere else, it will be determined who is Lord: the world, the self, and the devil—or the Lord Christ.

Elisabeth Elliot

STRENGTHENING YOUR FAITH

Following Christ is a matter of obedience. If you want to be a little more like Jesus . . . learn about His teachings, follow in His footsteps, and obey His commandments.

START MAKING CHANGES NOW

But be doers of the word and not hearers only.

James 1:22 HCSB

Warren Wiersbe correctly observed, "A Christian should no more defile his body than a Jew would defile the temple." Unfortunately, too many of us have allowed our temples to fall into disrepair. When it comes to fitness and food, it's easy to fall into bad habits. And it's easy to convince ourselves that we'll start improving our health "some day."

Today, pick out one important obligation that you've been putting off. Then, take at least one specific step toward the completion of the task you've been avoiding.

If we are to care for our bodies in the way that God intends, we must establish healthy habits, and we must establish them sooner rather than later.

Saint Jerome advised, "Begin to be now what you will be hereafter." You should take his advice seriously, and you should take it NOW. When it comes to your health, it's always the right time to start establishing the right habits.

FOOD FOR THOUGHT

Let us not be content to wait and see what will happen, but give us the determination to make the right things happen.

Peter Marshall

Therefore, get your minds ready for action, being self-disciplined, and set your hope completely on the grace to be brought to you at the revelation of Jesus Christ.

1 Peter 1:13 HCSB

When you make a vow to God, don't delay fulfilling it, because He does not delight in fools. Fulfill what you vow.

Ecclesiastes 5:4 HCSB

For the hearers of the law are not righteous before God, but the doers of the law will be declared righteous.

Romans 2:13 HCSB

A HEALTHY-CHOICE TIP

When important work needs to be done, it's tempting to procrastinate. But God's Word teaches us to be "doers of the Word," which means taking action even when we might prefer to do nothing.

DAY 50

BE ENTHUSIASTIC

Whatever you do, do it enthusiastically, as something done for the Lord and not for men.

Colossians 3:23 HCSB

Are you passionate about your faith, your fitness, and your future? Hopefully so. But if your zest for life has waned, it is now time to redirect your efforts and recharge your spiritual batteries. And that means refocusing your priorities by putting God first.

Look at your life and your challenges as exciting adventures. Don't wait for life to spice itself; spice things up yourself.

Each day is a glorious opportunity to serve God and to do His will. Are you enthused about life, or do you struggle through each day giving scarcely a thought to God's blessings? Are you constantly praising God for His gifts, and are you sharing His Good News with the world? And are you excited about the possibilities for service that God has placed before you, whether at home, at work, or at church? You should be.

Nothing is more important than your wholehearted commitment to your Creator and to His only begotten Son. Your faith must never be an afterthought; it must be your ultimate priority, your ultimate possession, and your ultimate passion. When you become passionate about your faith, you'll become passionate about your life, too.

FOOD FOR THOUGHT

God is the giver, and we are the receivers. And His richest gifts are bestowed not upon those who do the greatest things, but upon those who accept His abundance and His grace.

Hannah Whitall Smith

Living life with a consistent spiritual walk deeply influences those we love most.

Vonette Bright

A HEALTHY-CHOICE TIP

You don't have to attend medical school to understand the basic principles of maintaining a healthy lifestyle. In fact, many of the things you need to know are contained in this text. But don't stop here. Vow to make yourself an expert on the care and feeding of the body that God has given you. In today's information-packed world, becoming an expert isn't a very hard thing to do.

DON'T OVERESTIMATE THE IMPORTANCE OF APPEARANCES

Man does not see what the Lord sees, for man sees what is visible, but the Lord sees the heart.

1 Samuel 16:7 HCSB

Are you worried about keeping up appearances? And as a result, do you spend too much time, energy, or money on things that are intended to make you look good? If so, you are certainly not alone. Ours is a society that focuses intently upon appearances. We are told time and again that we can't be "too thin or too rich." But in truth, the important things in life have little to do with food, fashion, fame, or fortune.

How you appear to other people doesn't make much difference, but how you appear to God makes all the difference.

Today, spend less time trying to please the world and more time trying to please your earthly family and your Father in heaven. Focus today on pleasing your God and your loved ones, and don't worry too much about trying to impress the folks you happen to pass on the street. It takes too much energy—and too much life—to keep up appearances. So don't waste your energy or your life.

FOOD FOR THOUGHT

Comparison is the root of all feelings of inferiority.

James Dobson

Fashion is an enduring testimony to the fact that we live quite consciously before the eyes of others.

John Eldredge

Outside appearances, things like the clothes you wear or the car you drive, are important to other people but totally unimportant to God. Trust God.

Marie T. Freeman

If the narrative of the Scriptures teaches us anything, from the serpent in the Garden to the carpenter in Nazareth, it teaches us that things are rarely what they seem, that we shouldn't be fooled by appearances.

John Eldredge

STRENGTHENING YOUR FAITH

If you find yourself focussing too much on your appearance, it's time to find a different focus.

THE DECISION TO CELEBRATE LIFE

This is the day the Lord has made; let us rejoice and be glad in it.

Psalm 118:24 HCSB

God gives us this day; He fills it to the brim with possibilities, and He challenges us to use it for His purposes. The 118th Psalm reminds us that today, like every other day, is a cause for celebration. The day is presented to us fresh and clean at midnight, free of charge, but we must beware: Today is a non-renewable resource—once it's gone, it's gone forever. Our responsibility, of course, is to use this day in the service of God's will and according to His commandments.

By celebrating the gift of life, you protect your heart from the dangers of pessimism, regret, hopelessness, and bitterness.

Today, treasure the time that God has given you. Give Him the glory and the praise and the thanksgiving that He deserves. And search for the hidden possibilities that God has placed along your path. This day is a priceless gift from God, so use it joyfully and encourage others to do likewise. After all, this is the day the Lord has made.

FOOD FOR THOUGHT

Christ is the secret, the source, the substance, the center, and the circumference of all true and lasting gladness.

Mrs. Charles E. Cowman

When the dream of our heart is one that God has planted there, a strange happiness flows into us. At that moment, all of the spiritual resources of the universe are released to help us. Our praying is then at one with the will of God and becomes a channel for the Creator's purposes for us and our world.

Catherine Marshall

If you can forgive the person you were, accept the person you are, and believe in the person you will become, you are headed for joy. So celebrate your life.

Barbara Johnson

STRENGTHENING YOUR FAITH

God has given you the gift of life (here on earth) and the promise of eternal life (in heaven). Now, He wants you to celebrate those gifts.

BE A CHEERFUL CHRISTIAN

A cheerful heart has a continual feast.

Proverbs 15:15 HCSB

On some days, as every woman knows, it's hard to be cheerful. Sometimes, as the demands of the world increase and our energy sags, we feel less like "cheering up" and more like "tearing up." But even in our darkest hours, we can turn to God, and He will give us comfort.

Few things in life are more sad, or, for that matter, more absurd, than a grumpy Christian. Christ promises us lives of abundance and joy, but He does not force His joy upon us. We must claim His joy for ourselves, and when we do, Jesus, in turn, fills our spirits with His power and His love.

Cheerfulness is its own reward—but not its only reward.

How can we receive from Christ the joy that is rightfully ours? By giving Him what is rightfully His: our hearts and our souls.

When we earnestly commit ourselves to the Savior of mankind, and when we place Jesus at the center of our lives and trust Him as our personal Savior, He will transform us, not just for today, but for all eternity. Then we, as God's children, can share Christ's joy and His message with a world that needs both.

FOOD FOR THOUGHT

Joy is the serious business of heaven.

C. S. Lewis

God is good, and heaven is forever. And if those two facts don't cheer you up, nothing will.

Marie T. Freeman

We may run, walk, stumble, drive, or fly, but let us never lose sight of the reason for the journey, or miss a chance to see a rainbow on the way.

Gloria Gaither

When we bring sunshine into the lives of others, we're warmed by it ourselves. When we spill a little happiness, it splashes on us.

Barbara Johnson

A HEALTHY-CHOICE TIP

God has given you many blessings, and you have many reasons to be cheerful. So what are you waiting for?

ASK HIM FOR THE THINGS YOU NEED

You do not have because you do not ask.

James 4:2 HCSB

God gives the gifts; we, as believers, should accept them—but oftentimes, we don't. Why? Because we fail to trust our Heavenly Father completely, and because we are, at times, surprisingly stubborn. Luke 11 teaches us that God does not withhold spiritual gifts from those who ask. Our obligation, quite simply, is to ask for them.

If you sincerely want to find balance, ask for God's help.

Are you a woman who asks God to move mountains in your life, or are you expecting Him to stumble over molehills? Whatever the size of your challenges, God is big enough to handle them. Ask for His help today, with faith and with fervor, and then watch in amazement as your mountains begin to move.

FOOD FOR THOUGHT

Often I have made a request of God with earnest pleadings even backed up with Scripture, only to have Him say "No" because He had something better in store.

Ruth Bell Graham

By asking in Jesus' name, we're making a request not only in His authority, but also for His interests and His benefit.

Shirley Dobson

When will we realize that we're not troubling God with our questions and concerns? His heart is open to hear us— his touch nearer than our next thought—as if no one in the world existed but us. Our very personal God wants to hear from us personally.

Gigi Graham Tchividjian

A HEALTHY-CHOICE TIP

If you want more from life, ask more from God. If you're searching for peace and abundance, ask for God's help— and keep asking—until He answers your prayers. If you sincerely want to rise above the stresses and complications of everyday life, ask for God's help many times each day.

GOD'S PLAN
FOR YOUR HEALTH

Who are those who fear the Lord? He will show them the path they should choose. They will live in prosperity, and their children will inherit the Promised Land.

Psalm 25:12-13 NLT

The journey toward improved health is not only a common-sense exercise in personal discipline, it is also a spiritual journey ordained by our Creator. God does not intend that we abuse our bodies by giving in to excessive appetites or to slothful behavior. To the contrary, God has instructed us to protect our physical bodies to the greatest extent we can. To do otherwise is to disobey Him.

God has a plan for your spiritual, physical, and emotional health.

When you make the decision to seek God's will for your life—and you should—then you will contemplate His Word, and you will be watchful for His signs. God intends to use you in wonderful, unexpected ways if you let Him. But be forewarned: the decision to seek God's plan and fulfill His purpose is ultimately a decision that you must make by yourself and for yourself. The consequences of that decision have implications that are both profound and eternal, so choose carefully. And then, as you go about your daily activities, keep your eyes and ears open, as well as your heart, because God is patiently trying to get His message through . . . and there's no better moment than this one for you to help Him.

FOOD FOR THOUGHT

God has a plan for the life of every Christian. Every circumstance, every turn of destiny, all things work together for your good and for His glory.

Billy Graham

God's all-sufficiency is a major. Your inability is a minor. Major in majors, not in minors.

Corrie ten Boom

A HEALTHY-CHOICE TIP

We live in a junk-food society, but you shouldn't let your house become junk-food heaven. Make your home a haven of healthy foods. And remember, it's never too soon to teach your kid good habits . . . and that includes the very good habit of sensible eating.

YOU'RE ACCOUNTABLE

But each person should examine his own work, and then he will have a reason for boasting in himself alone, and not in respect to someone else. For each person will have to carry his own load.

Galatians 6:4-5 HCSB

We humans are masters at passing the buck. Why? Because passing the buck is easier than fixing, and criticizing others is so much easier than improving ourselves. So instead of solving our problems legitimately (by doing the work required to solve them) we are inclined to fret, to blame, and to criticize, while doing precious little else. When we do, our problems, quite predictably, remain unsolved.

> It's easy to hold other people accountable, but real accountability begins with the person in the mirror.

Whether you like it or not, you (and only you) are accountable for your actions. But because you are human, you'll be sorely tempted to pass the blame. Avoid that temptation at all costs.

Problem-solving builds character. Every time you straighten your back and look squarely into the face of Old Man Trouble, you'll strengthen not only your backbone but also your spirit. So, instead of looking for someone to blame, look for something to fix, and then get busy fixing it. And as you consider your own situation, remember this: God has a way of helping those who help themselves, but He doesn't spend much time helping those who don't.

FOOD FOR THOUGHT

Generally speaking, accountability is a willingness to share our activities, conduct, and fulfillment of assigned responsibilities with others.

Charles Stanley

We urgently need people who encourage and inspire us to move toward God and away from the world's enticing pleasures.

Jim Cymbala

STRENGTHENING YOUR FAITH

If you want to build character, you need to assume responsibility for your actions. Once you begin to hold yourself accountable, you'll begin to grow emotionally and spiritually.

PUT FAITH ABOVE FEELINGS

Now the just shall live by faith.

Hebrews 10:38 NKJV

Who is in charge of your emotions? Is it you, or have you formed the unfortunate habit of letting other people— or troubling situations—determine the quality of your thoughts and the direction of your day? If you're wise— and if you'd like to build a better life for yourself and your loved ones—you'll learn to control your emotions before your emotions control you.

Here are the facts: God's love is real; His peace is real; His support is real. Don't ever let your emotions obscure these facts.

Human emotions are highly vari-able, decidedly unpredictable, and of-ten unreliable. Our emotions are like the weather, only far more fickle. So we must learn to live by faith, not by the ups and downs of our own emotional roller coasters.

Sometime during this day, you will probably be gripped by a strong negative feeling. Distrust it. Reign it in. Test it. And turn it over to God. Your emotions will inevitably change; God will not. So trust Him completely as you watch those negative feelings slowly evaporate into thin air—which, of course, they will.

FOOD FOR THOUGHT

The only serious mistake we can make is the mistake that Psalm 121 prevents: the mistake of supposing that God's interest in us waxes and wanes in response to our spiritual temperature.

Eugene Peterson

Before you can dry another's tears, you too must weep.

Barbara Johnson

I may no longer depend on pleasant impulses to bring me before the Lord. I must rather respond to principles I know to be right, whether I feel them to be enjoyable or not.

Jim Elliot

Emotions we have not poured out in the safe hands of God can turn into feelings of hopelessness and depression. God is safe.

Beth Moore

A HEALTHY-CHOICE TIP

Fitness is a journey, not a destination. Achieving physical fitness—and maintaining it—is a seven-day-a-week assignment. If you don't make physical fitness a priority, your health will suffer.

MAKE THE MOST OF WHATEVER COMES

A man's heart plans his way, but the Lord determines his steps.
Proverbs 16:9 HCSB

Sometimes, we must accept life on its terms, not our own. Life has a way of unfolding, not as we will, but as it will. And sometimes, there is precious little we can do to change things.

When events transpire that are beyond our control, we have a choice: we can either learn the art of acceptance, or we can make ourselves miserable as we struggle to change the unchangeable.

When you encounter situations that you cannot change, you must learn the wisdom of acceptance . . . and you must learn to trust God.

We must entrust the things we cannot change to God. Once we have done so, we can prayerfully and faithfully tackle the important work that He has placed before us: doing something about the things we can change . . . and doing it sooner rather than later.

Can you summon the courage and the wisdom to accept life on its own terms? If so, you'll most certainly be rewarded for your good judgment.

FOOD FOR THOUGHT

We must meet our disappointments, our persecutions, our malicious enemies, our provoking friends, our trials and temptations of every sort, with an attitude of surrender and trust. We must spread our wings and "mount up" to the "heavenly places in Christ" above them all, where they will lose their power to harm or distress us.

Hannah Whitall Smith

The one true way of dying to self is the way of patience, meekness, humility, and resignation to God.

Andrew Murray

It is always possible to do the will of God. In every place and time it is within our power to acquiesce in the will of God.

Elisabeth Elliot

A HEALTHY-CHOICE TIP

If you're genuinely planning on becoming a disciplined person "some day" in the distant future, you're deluding yourself. The best day to begin exercising self-discipline is this one.

RECHARGING YOUR SPIRITUAL BATTERIES

Those who hope in the LORD will renew their strength. They will soar on wings like eagles; they will run and not grow weary, they will walk and not be faint

Isaiah 40:31 NIV

As you make the journey toward improved fitness, you'll undoubtedly run out of energy from time to time. When it happens, you can turn to God for strength and for guidance.

For the journey through life, you need energy. If you're wise, you'll ask the Creator to energize you and guide you.

Andrew Murray observed, "Where there is much prayer, there will be much of the Spirit; where there is much of the Spirit, there will be ever-increasing power." These words remind us that the ultimate source of our strength is God. When we turn to Him—for guidance, for enlightenment, and for strength—we will not be disappointed.

Are you feeling exhausted? Are your emotions on edge? If so, it's time to turn things over to God in prayer. Are you weak or worried? Take the time—or, more accurately, make the time—to delve deeply into God's Holy Word. Are you spiritually depleted? Call upon fellow believers to support you, and call upon Christ to renew your spirit and your life. When you do, you'll discover that the Creator of the universe has the power to make all things new . . . including you.

FOOD FOR THOUGHT

Jesus taught us by example to get out of the rat race and recharge our batteries.

Barbara Johnson

Troubles we bear trustfully can bring us a fresh vision of God and a new outlook on life, an outlook of peace and hope.

Billy Graham

A HEALTHY-CHOICE TIP

God wants you to experience abundant life, but He will not force you to adopt a healthy lifestyle. Managing your food and your fitness is up to you.

If you want more from life, ask more from God. D. L. Moody observed, "Some people think God does not like to be troubled with our constant asking. But, the way to trouble God is not to come at all." So, if you seek an improved level of fitness—or if you seek any other worthy goal—ask God (and keep asking Him) until He answers your prayers.

DAY 60

PERSPECTIVE AND BALANCE

Come to Me, all you who labor and are heavy laden, and I will give you rest. Take My yoke upon you and learn from Me, for I am gentle and lowly in heart, and you will find rest for your souls. For My yoke is easy and My burden is light.

Matthew 11:28-30 NKJV

Sometimes, amid the demands of daily life, we lose perspective. Life seems out of balance, and the pressures of everyday living seem overwhelming. What's needed is a fresh perspective, a restored sense of balance...and God.

Life is a balancing act. To improve your balance, consult your Heavenly Father many times each day.

If a temporary loss of perspective has robbed you of the spiritual fitness that should be yours in Christ, it's time to re-adjust your thought patterns. Negative thoughts are habit-forming; thankfully, so are positive ones. With practice, you can form the habit of focusing on God's priorities and your possibilities. When you do, you'll soon discover that you will spend less time fretting about your challenges and more time praising God for His gifts.

When you call upon the Lord and prayerfully seek His will, He will give you wisdom and perspective. When you make God's priorities your priorities, He will direct your steps and calm your fears. So today and every day hereafter, pray for a sense of balance and perspective. And remember: your thoughts are intensely powerful things, so handle them with care.

FOOD FOR THOUGHT

Prescription for a happier and healthier life: resolve to slow down your pace; learn to say no gracefully; resist the temptation to chase after more pleasure, more hobbies, and more social entanglements.

James Dobson

Notice what Jesus had to say concerning those who have wearied themselves by trying to do things in their own strength: "Come to me, all you who labor and are heavy laden, and I will give you rest."

Henry Blackaby and Claude King

A HEALTHY-CHOICE TIP

Need balance? Have a daily planning session with God. A regularly scheduled time of prayer, Bible reading, and meditation can help you prioritize your day and your life. And what if you're simply too busy to spend five or ten minutes with God? If so, it's time to reorder your priorities.

BEYOND THE SETBACKS

Peace, peace to you, and peace to him who helps you, for your God helps you.

1 Chronicles 12:18 HCSB

It's simply a fact of life: Not all of your health-related plans will succeed, and not all of your goals will be met. Life's occasional setbacks are simply the price that we must pay for our willingness to take risks as we follow our dreams. But even when we encounter bitter disappointments, we must never lose faith.

> Remember that failure isn't permanent . . . unless you fail to get up. So pick yourself up, dust yourself off, and trust God.

Hebrews 10:36 advises, "Patient endurance is what you need now, so you will continue to do God's will. Then you will receive all that he has promised" (NLT). These words remind us that when we persevere, we will eventually receive the rewards which God has promised us. What's required is perseverance, not perfection.

When we face hardships, God stands ready to protect us. Our responsibility, of course, is to ask Him for protection. When we call upon Him in heartfelt prayer, He will answer—in His own time and according to His own plan—and He will do His part to heal us. We, of course, must do our part, too.

And, while we are waiting for God's plans to unfold and for His healing touch to restore us, we can be comforted in the knowledge that our Creator can overcome any obstacle, even if we cannot.

FOOD FOR THOUGHT

What may seem defeat to us may be victory to him.

C. H. Spurgeon

Success or failure can be pretty well predicted by the degree to which the heart is fully in it.

John Eldredge

A HEALTHY-CHOICE TIP

If you're on a new health regimen, you may relapse back into your old, unhealthy habits. If so, don't waste time or energy beating yourself up. If you've "fallen off the wagon," simply pick yourself up, dust yourself off, and get back on it. God was with you when you were riding that wagon the first time, He was with you when you fell, and He'll welcome you back on the wagon when you're wise enough to climb back on.

LASTING PEACE

Be of good comfort, be of one mind, live in peace; and the God of love and peace will be with you.

2 Corinthians 13:11 NKJV

Have you found the lasting peace that can—and should—be yours through Jesus Christ? Or are you still chasing the illusion of "peace and happiness" that the world promises but cannot deliver?

The beautiful words of John 14:27 promise that Jesus offers peace, not as the world gives, but as He alone gives: "Peace I leave with you. My peace I give to you. I do not give to you as the world gives. Your heart must not be troubled or fearful" (HCSB). Your challenge is to accept Christ's peace into your heart and then, as best you can, to share His peace with your neighbors. But sometimes, that's easier said than done.

God offers peace that passes human understanding . . . and He wants you to make His peace your peace.

If you are a person with lots of obligations and plenty of responsibilities, it is simply a fact of life: You worry. From time to time, you worry about finances, safety, health, home, family, or about countless other concerns, some great and some small. Where is the best place to take your worries? Take them to God . . . and leave them there.

Today, as a gift to yourself, to your family, and to your friends, claim the inner peace that is your spiritual birthright: the peace of Jesus Christ. Christ is standing at the door, waiting patiently for you to invite Him to reign over your heart. His eternal peace is offered freely. Claim it today.

FOOD FOR THOUGHT

The fruit of our placing all things in God's hands is the presence of His abiding peace in our hearts.

Hannah Whitall Smith

I believe that in every time and place it is within our power to acquiesce in the will of God—and what peace it brings to do so!

Elisabeth Elliot

STRENGTHENING YOUR FAITH

Does peace seem to be a distant promise? It is not. God's peace is available to you this very moment if you place absolute trust in Him. Today, let go of your concerns by turning them over to God. Trust Him in the present moment, and accept His peace . . . in the present moment.

MODERATION IS WISDOM IN ACTION

Now if any of you lacks wisdom, he should ask God, who gives to all generously and without criticizing, and it will be given to him.

James 1:5 HCSB

Moderation and wisdom are traveling companions. If we are wise, we must learn to temper our appetites, our desires, and our impulses. When we do, we are blessed, in part, because God has created a world in which temperance is rewarded and intemperance is inevitably punished.

Moderation pays. Excess doesn't. Behave accordingly.

When we allow our appetites to run wild, they usually do. When we abandon moderation, we forfeit the inner peace that God offers—but does not guarantee—to His children. When we live intemperate lives, we rob ourselves of countless blessings that would have otherwise been ours.

God's instructions are clear: if we seek to live wisely, we must be moderate in our appetites and disciplined in our behavior. To do otherwise is an affront to Him . . . and to ourselves.

FOOD FOR THOUGHT

Teach me, O Lord, the way of Your statutes, and I shall keep it to the end.

Psalm 119:33 NKJV

So teach us to number our days, that we may gain a heart of wisdom.

Psalm 90:12 NKJV

Acquire wisdom—how much better it is than gold! And acquire understanding—it is preferable to silver.

Proverbs 16:16 HCSB

A HEALTHY-CHOICE TIP

Of a thousand American adults who were surveyed in a recent poll, eighty-eight percent were unable to accurately estimate how many calories they should consume each day to maintain their weight. Consequently, these adults didn't know how many calories they should consume if they wanted to lose weight. Thankfully, in these days of easy Internet information, it isn't very difficult to discover how many calories you need. So do the research and find your calorie target. Then, aim for the bull's-eye that leads to better health and a longer life.

BEYOND COMPLAINING

Be hospitable to one another without complaining.

1 Peter 4:9 HCSB

Most of us have more blessings than we can count, yet we can still find reasons to complain about the minor frustrations of everyday life. To do so, of course, is not only shortsighted, but it is also a serious roadblock on the path to spiritual abundance.

Would you like to feel more comfortable about your circumstances and your life? Then promise yourself that you'll do whatever it takes to ensure that you focus your thoughts and energy on the major blessings you've received (not the minor inconveniences you must occasionally endure).

If you're wise, you'll fill your heart with gratitude. When you do, there's simply no room left for complaints.

So the next time you're tempted to complain about the inevitable frustrations of everyday living, don't do it! Today and every day, make it a practice to count your blessings, not your hardships. It's the truly decent way to live.

FOOD FOR THOUGHT

It's your choice: you can either count your blessings or recount your disappointments.

Jim Gallery

He wants us to have a faith that does not complain while waiting, but rejoices because we know our times are in His hands—nail-scarred hands that labor for our highest good.

Kay Arthur

I am sure it is never sadness—a proper, straight, natural response to loss—that does people harm, but all the other things, all the resentment, dismay, doubt and self-pity with which it is usually complicated.

C. S. Lewis

When you're on the verge of throwing a pity party thanks to your despairing thoughts, go back to the Word of God.

Charles Swindoll

A HEALTHY-CHOICE TIP

If you're wise, you'll spend more time counting your blessings and less time counting your problems.

FOLLOW YOUR CONSCIENCE

Let us draw near with a true heart in full assurance of faith, our hearts sprinkled clean from an evil conscience and our bodies washed in pure water.

Hebrews 10:22 HCSB

God gave you a conscience for a very good reason: to make your path conform to His will. Billy Graham correctly observed, "Most of us follow our conscience as we follow a wheelbarrow. We push it in front of us in the direction we want to go." To do so, of course, is a profound mistake.

Listen carefully to your conscience. That little voice inside your head will seldom lead you astray.

Yet all of us, on occasion, have failed to listen to the voice that God planted in our hearts, and all of us have suffered the consequences.

Wise believers make it a practice to listen carefully to that quiet internal voice. Count yourself among that number. When your conscience speaks, listen and learn. In all likelihood, God is trying to get His message through. And in all likelihood, it is a message that you desperately need to hear.

FOOD FOR THOUGHT

My conscience is captive to the word of God.

Martin Luther

God desires that we become spiritually healthy enough through faith to have a conscience that rightly interprets the work of the Holy Spirit.

Beth Moore

If I am walking along the street with a very disfiguring hole in the back of my dress, of which I am in ignorance, it is certainly a very great comfort to me to have a kind friend who will tell me of it. And similarly, it is indeed a comfort to know that there is always abiding with me a divine, all-seeing Comforter, who will reprove me for all my faults and will not let me go on in a fatal unconsciousness of them.

Hannah Whitall Smith

A HEALTHY-CHOICE TIP

Here's a time-tested formula for success: have faith in God and do the work. It has been said that there are no shortcuts to any place worth going, and those words apply to your physical fitness, too. There are simply no shortcuts to a healthy lifestyle.

TRUST GOD'S PROMISES

For you need endurance, so that after you have done God's will, you may receive what was promised.

Hebrews 10:36 HCSB

What do you expect from the day ahead? Are you expecting God to do wonderful things, or are you living beneath a cloud of apprehension and doubt? The familiar words of Psalm 118:24 remind us of a profound yet simple truth: "This is the day which the LORD hath made; we will rejoice and be glad in it" (KJV).

God has made many promises to you, and He will keep every single one of them. Your job is to trust God's promises and live accordingly.

For Christian believers, every day begins and ends with God's Son and God's promises. When we accept Christ into our hearts, God promises us the opportunity for earthly peace and spiritual abundance. But more importantly, God promises us the priceless gift of eternal life.

As we face the inevitable challenges of life here on earth, we must arm ourselves with the promises of God's Holy Word. When we do, we can expect the best, not only for the day ahead, but also for all eternity.

FOOD FOR THOUGHT

Our future may look fearfully intimidating, yet we can look up to the Engineer of the Universe, confident that nothing escapes His attention or slips out of the control of those strong hands.

Elisabeth Elliot

Worries carry responsibilities that belong to God, not to you. Worry does not enable us to escape evil; it makes us unfit to cope with it when it comes.

Corrie ten Boom

God will never let you sink under your circumstances. He always provide a safety net and His love always encircles.

Barbara Johnson

Only believe, don't fear. Our Master, Jesus, always watches over us, and no matter what the persecution, Jesus will surely overcome it.

Lottie Moon

STRENGTHENING YOUR FAITH

Of this you can be sure: God's faithfulness is steadfast, unwavering, and eternal.

HE IS SUFFICIENT

And He said to me, "My grace is sufficient for you, for My strength is made perfect in weakness."

2 Corinthians 12:9 NKJV

Of this you can be certain: God is sufficient to meet your needs. Period.

Do the demands of life seem overwhelming at times? If so, you must learn to rely not only upon your own resources, but also upon the promises of your Father in heaven. God will hold your hand and walk with you and your family if you let Him. So even if your circumstances are difficult, trust the Father.

The Psalmist writes, "Weeping may endure for a night, but joy comes in the morning" (Psalm 30:5 NKJV). But when we are suffering, the morning may seem very far away. It is not. God promises that He is "near to those who have a broken heart" (Psalm 34:18 NKJV). When we are troubled, we must turn to Him, and we must encourage our friends and family members to do likewise.

> If you'd like infinite protection, there's only one place you can receive it: from an infinite God.

If you are discouraged by the inevitable demands of life here on earth, be mindful of this fact: the loving heart of God is sufficient to meet any challenge . . . including yours.

FOOD FOR THOUGHT

Jesus has been consistently affectionate and true to us. He has shared his great wealth with us. How can we doubt the all-powerful, all-sufficient Lord?

C. H. Spurgeon

God's saints in all ages have realized that God was enough for them. God is enough for time; God is enough for eternity. God is enough!

Hannah Whitall Smith

God will call you to obey Him and do whatever he asks of you. However, you do not need to be doing something to feel fulfilled. You are fulfilled completely in a relationship with God. When you are filled with Him, what else do you need?

Henry Blackaby and Claude King

Yes, God's grace is always sufficient, and His arms are always open to give it. But, will our arms be open to receive it?

Beth Moore

STRENGTHENING YOUR FAITH

Whatever you need, God can provide. He is always sufficient to meet your needs.

STUDY GOD'S WORD

You will be a good servant of Christ Jesus, nourished by the words of the faith and of the good teaching that you have followed.

1 Timothy 4:6 HCSB

God's Word is unlike any other book. The Bible is a roadmap for life here on earth and for life eternal. As Christians, we are called upon to study God's Holy Word, to trust its promises, to follow its commandments, and to share its Good News with the world.

Life is a balancing act, and the Bible can help you stay balanced. So let God's Word guide your path today and every day.

As women who seek to follow in the footsteps of the One from Galilee, we must study the Bible and meditate upon its meaning for our lives. Otherwise, we deprive ourselves of a priceless gift from our Creator. God's Holy Word is, indeed, a transforming, life-changing, one-of-a-kind treasure. And, a passing acquaintance with the Good Book is insufficient for Christians who seek to obey God's Word and to understand His will.

FOOD FOR THOUGHT

I need the spiritual revival that comes from spending quiet time alone with Jesus in prayer and in thoughtful meditation on His Word.

Anne Graham Lotz

God can see clearly no matter how dark or foggy the night is. Trust His Word to guide you safely home.

Lisa Whelchel

The Bible is God's Word to man.

Kay Arthur

Weave the unveiling fabric of God's word through your heart and mind. It will hold strong, even if the rest of life unravels.

Gigi Graham Tchividjian

STRENGTHENING YOUR FAITH

Even if you've been studying the Bible for many years, you've still got lots to learn. Bible study should be a lifelong endeavor; make it your lifelong endeavor.

DAY 69

REBELLION INVITES DISASTER

You must follow the Lord your God and fear Him. You must keep His commands and listen to His voice; you must worship Him and remain faithful to Him.

Deuteronomy 13:4 HCSB

For most of us, it is a daunting thought: one day, perhaps soon, we'll come face to face with our Heavenly Father, and we'll be called to account for our actions here on earth. Our personal histories will certainly not be surprising to God; He already knows everything about us. But the full scope of our activities may be surprising to us: some of us will be pleasantly surprised; others will not be.

Be honest with yourself as you consider ways that you have, in the last few days, disobeyed God. Then, think about specific ways that you can be more obedient in the future.

God's commandments are not offered as helpful hints or timely tips. God's commandments are not suggestions; they are ironclad rules for living, rules that we disobey at our own risk.

The English clergyman Thomas Fuller observed, "He does not believe who does not live according to his beliefs." These words are most certainly true. We may proclaim our beliefs to our hearts' content, but our proclamations will mean nothing—to others or to ourselves—unless we accompany our words with deeds that match. The sermons that we live are far more compelling than the ones we preach.

So today, do whatever you can to ensure that your thoughts and your deeds are pleasing to your Creator. Because you will, at some point in the future, be called to account for your actions. And the future may be sooner than you think.

FOOD FOR THOUGHT

Only he who believes is obedient, and only he who is obedient believes.

Dietrich Bonhoeffer

Obedience is the outward expression of your love of God.

Henry Blackaby

STRENGTHENING YOUR FAITH

Every day of your life, you will be tempted to rebel against God's teachings. Your job, simply put, is to guard your heart against the darkness as you focus on the light.

SMALL STEPS

So we must not get tired of doing good, for we will reap at the proper time if we don't give up.

Galatians 6:9 HCSB

If you want to become more physically fit, you don't have to make one giant leap. You can start with many small steps, and you should. When it comes to any new exercise regimen, starting slowly and improving gradually is the smart way to do it.

> Think of one or two small steps you can take to improve your physical and spiritual health.

Crash diets usually crash. And fitness fads fade. But sensible exercise, when combined with a moderate diet, produces results that last.

So if you're determined to improve the state of your health, remember that consistency is the key. Start slowly, avoid injury, be consistent, and expect gradual improvement, not instant success.

FOOD FOR THOUGHT

Do you not know that the runners in a stadium all race, but only one receives the prize? Run in such a way that you may win. Now everyone who competes exercises self-control in everything. However, they do it to receive a perishable crown, but we an imperishable one.

1 Corinthians 9:24-25 HCSB

It is better to finish something than to start it. It is better to be patient than to be proud.

Ecclesiastes 7:8 NCV

Battles are won in the trenches, in the grit and grime of courageous determination; they are won day by day in the arena of life.

Charles Swindoll

By perseverance the snail reached the ark.

C. H. Spurgeon

A HEALTHY-CHOICE TIP

Becoming fit and staying fit is an exercise in perseverance. If you give up at the first sign of trouble, you won't accomplish much. But if you don't give up, you'll eventually improve your health and your life.

ENTRUSTING
YOUR HOPES TO GOD

You, Lord, give true peace to those who depend on you, because they trust you.

Isaiah 26:3 NCV

Have you ever felt hope for the future slipping away? If so, you have temporarily lost sight of the hope that we, as believers, must place in the promises of our Heavenly Father. If you are feeling discouraged, worried, or worse, remember the words of Psalm 31: "Be of good courage, and He shall strengthen your heart."

Since God has promised to guide and protect you— now and forever— you should never lose hope.

Because we are saved by a risen Christ, we can have hope for the future, no matter how desperate our circumstances may seem. After all, God has promised that we are His throughout eternity. And, He has told us that we must place our hopes in Him.

Of course, we will face disappointments and failures, but these are only temporary defeats. Of course, this world can be a place of trials and tribulations, but we are secure. God has promised us peace, joy, and eternal life. And God keeps His promises today, tomorrow, and forever.

FOOD FOR THOUGHT

I discovered that sorrow was not to be feared but rather endured with hope and expectancy that God would use it to visit and bless my life.

Jill Briscoe

Never yield to gloomy anticipation. Place your hope and confidence in God. He has no record of failure.

Mrs. Charles E. Cowman

The best we can hope for in this life is a knothole peek at the shining realities ahead. Yet a glimpse is enough. It's enough to convince our hearts that whatever sufferings and sorrows currently assail us aren't worthy of comparison to that which waits over the horizon.

Joni Eareckson Tada

A HEALTHY-CHOICE TIP

If you genuinely want to exercise more, find exercise that you enjoy. And if you can't seem to find exercise that you enjoy, search for ways to make your current exercise program a little less painful and a little more fun.

ACCEPTING GOD'S CALLING

But as God has distributed to each one, as the Lord has called each one, so let him walk.

1 Corinthians 7:17 NKJV

God is calling you to follow a specific path that He has chosen for your life. And it is vitally important that you heed that call. Otherwise, your talents and opportunities may go unused.

Have you already heard God's call? And are you pursuing it with vigor? If so, you're both fortunate and wise. But if you have not yet discovered what God intends for you to do with your life, keep searching and keep praying until you discover why the Creator put you here.

God has a plan for your life, a divine calling that you can either answer or ignore. Your choice to respond to it will determine the direction you take and the contributions you make.

Remember: God has important work for you to do—work that no one else on earth can accomplish but you. The Creator has placed you in a particular location, amid particular people, with unique opportunities to serve. And He has given you all the tools you need to succeed. So listen for His voice, watch for His signs, and prepare yourself for the call that is sure to come.

FOOD FOR THOUGHT

God never calls without enabling us. In other words, if he calls you to do something, he makes it possible for you to do it.

Luci Swindoll

When you become consumed by God's call on your life, everything will take on new meaning and significance. You will begin to see every facet of your life, including your pain, as a means through which God can work to bring others to Himself.

Charles Stanley

If God has called you, do not spend time looking over your shoulder to see who is following you.

Corrie ten Boom

A HEALTHY-CHOICE TIP

If someone else is cooking your meals, ask that person to help you plan a healthier diet. Without the cooperation of the person who cooks your food, you'll have an incredibly difficult time sticking to a healthier diet.

THE GOOD NEWS

Grace to you and peace from God our Father and the Lord Jesus Christ.

Philippians 1:2 HCSB

God's grace is not earned . . . thank goodness! To earn God's love and His gift of eternal life would be far beyond the abilities of even the most righteous man or woman. Thankfully, grace is not an earthly reward for righteous behavior; it is a blessed spiritual gift which can be accepted by believers who dedicate themselves to God through Christ. When we accept Christ into our hearts, we are saved by His grace.

God's grace isn't earned, but freely given—what an amazing, humbling gift.

The familiar words of Ephesians 2:8 make God's promise perfectly clear: It is by grace we have been saved, through faith. We are saved not because of our good deeds but because of our faith in Christ.

God's grace is the ultimate gift, and we owe to Him the ultimate in thanksgiving. Let us praise the Creator for His priceless gift, and let us share the Good News with all who cross our paths. We return our Father's love by accepting His grace and by sharing His message and His love. When we do, we are eternally blessed . . . and the Father smiles.

FOOD FOR THOUGHT

God forgets the past. Imitate him.

Max Lucado

I believe that forgiveness can become a continuing cycle: because God forgives us, we're to forgive others; because we forgive others, God forgives us. Scripture presents both parts of the cycle.

Shirley Dobson

God does what few men can do—forgets the sins of others.

Anonymous

Forgiveness is God's command.

Martin Luther

A HEALTHY-CHOICE TIP

Physical fitness is not the result of a single decision that is made "once and for all." Physical fitness results from thousands of decisions that are made day after day, week after week, and year after year.

LEARNING WHEN TO SAY NO

So let us run the race that is before us and never give up. We should remove from our lives anything that would get in the way and the sin that so easily holds us back.

Hebrews 12:1 NCV

You live in a busy world, a world where many folks may be making demands upon your time. If you're like most women, you've got plenty of people pulling you in lots of directions, starting, of course, with your family—but not ending there.

> You have a right to say no. Don't feel guilty about asserting that right. When your conscience says no, then you must say it, too.

Perhaps you also have additional responsibilities at work or at church. Maybe you're active in community affairs, or maybe you're involved in any of a hundred other activities that gobble up big portions of your day. If so, you'll need to be sure that you know when to say enough is enough.

When it comes to squeezing more and more obligations onto your daily to-do list, you have the right to say no when you simply don't have the time, the energy, or the desire to do the job. And if you're wise, you'll learn so say no as often as necessary . . . or else!

FOOD FOR THOUGHT

Prescription for a happier and healthier life: resolve to slow down your pace; learn to say no gracefully; resist the temptation to chase after more pleasure, more hobbies, and more social entanglements.

James Dobson

Judge everything in the light of Jesus Christ.

Oswald Chambers

Life is built on character, but character is built on decisions.

Warren Wiersbe

Great relief and satisfaction can come from seeking God's priorities for us in each season, discerning what is "best" in the midst of many noble opportunities, and pouring our most excellent energies into those things.

Beth Moore

A HEALTHY-CHOICE TIP

Remember that you have a right to say "No" to requests that you consider unreasonable or inconvenient. Don't feel guilty for asserting your right to say "No," and don't feel compelled to fabricate excuses for your decisions.

THE GIFT OF LIFE

What a gift life is to those who stay the course! You've heard, of course, of Job's staying power, and you know how God brought it all together for him at the end. That's because God cares, cares right down to the last detail.

James 5:11 MSG

Life is a glorious gift from God. Treat it that way.

This day, like every other, is filled to the brim with opportunities, challenges, and choices. But, no choice that you make is more important than the choice you make concerning God. Today, you will either place Him at the center of your life—or not—and the consequences of that choice have implications that are both temporal and eternal.

> Your life is a priceless opportunity, a gift of incalculable worth. You should thank God for the gift of life . . . and you should use that gift wisely.

Sometimes, we don't intentionally neglect God; we simply allow ourselves to become overwhelmed with the demands of everyday life. And then, without our even realizing it, we gradually drift away from the One we need most. Thankfully, God never drifts away from us. He remains always present, always steadfast, always loving.

As you begin this day, place God and His Son where they belong: in your head, in your prayers, on your lips, and in your heart. And then, with God as your guide and companion, let the journey begin.

FOOD FOR THOUGHT

Jesus wants Life for us, Life with a capital L.

John Eldredge

You have a glorious future in Christ! Live every moment in His power and love.

Vonette Bright

Our Lord is the Bread of Life. His proportions are perfect. There never was too much or too little of anything about Him. Feed on Him for a well-balanced ration. All the vitamins and calories are there.

Vance Havner

STRENGTHENING YOUR FAITH

Life is a priceless gift from God. Spend time each day thanking God for His gift.

THE SOURCE OF STRENGTH

And He said to me, "My grace is sufficient for you, for My strength is made perfect in weakness."

2 Corinthians 12:9 NKJV

Where do you go to find strength? The gym? The health food store? The espresso bar? There's a better source of strength, of course, and that source is God. He is a never-ending source of strength and courage if you call upon Him.

Today, think about ways that you can tap into God's strength: try prayer, worship, and praise, for starters.

Are you an energized Christian? You should be. But if you're not, you must seek strength and renewal from the source that will never fail: that source, of course, is your Heavenly Father. And rest assured—when you sincerely petition Him, He will give you all the strength you need to live victoriously for Him.

Have you "tapped in" to the power of God? Have you turned your life and your heart over to Him, or are you muddling along under your own power? The answer to this question will determine the quality of your life here on earth and the destiny of your life throughout all eternity. So start tapping in—and remember that when it comes to strength, God is the Ultimate Source.

FOOD FOR THOUGHT

The God we seek is a God who is intrinsically righteous and who will be so forever. With His example and His strength, we can share in that righteousness.

Bill Hybels

By ourselves we are not capable of suffering bravely, but the Lord possesses all the strength we lack and will demonstrate His power when we undergo persecution.

Corrie ten Boom

Cast yourself into the arms of God and be very sure that if He wants anything of you, He will fit you for the work and give you strength.

Philip Neri

A HEALTHY-CHOICE TIP

As you petition God each morning, ask Him for the strength and the wisdom to treat your body as His creation and His "temple." During the day ahead, you will face countless temptations to do otherwise, but with God's help, you can treat your body as the priceless, one-of-a-kind gift that it most certainly is.

BE PATIENT AND TRUST GOD

Be still before the Lord and wait patiently for Him.

Psalm 37:7 NIV

Psalm 37:7 commands us to wait patiently for God. But as busy women in a fast-paced world, many of us find that waiting quietly for God is difficult. Why? Because we are fallible human beings seeking to live according to our own timetables, not God's. In our better moments, we realize that patience is not only a virtue, but it is also a commandment from God.

When you learn to be more patient with others, you'll make your world—and your heart—a better place.

We human beings are impatient by nature. We know what we want, and we know exactly when we want it: NOW! But, God knows better. He has created a world that unfolds according to His plans, not our own. As believers, we must trust His wisdom and His goodness.

God instructs us to be patient in all things. We must be patient with our families, our friends, and our associates. We must also be patient with our Creator as He unfolds His plan for our lives. And that's as it should be. After all, think about how patient God has been with us.

FOOD FOR THOUGHT

Wisdom always waits for the right time to act, while emotion always pushes for action right now.

Joyce Meyer

How do you wait upon the Lord? First you must learn to sit at His feet and take time to listen to His words.

Kay Arthur

Let me encourage you to continue to wait with faith. God may not perform a miracle, but He is trustworthy to touch you and make you whole where there used to be a hole.

Lisa Whelchel

Waiting is the hardest kind of work, but God knows best, and we may joyfully leave all in His hands.

Lottie Moon

A HEALTHY-CHOICE TIP

Every step of your life's journey is a choice . . . and the quality of those choices determines the quality of the journey.

CONTAGIOUS CHRISTIANITY

We are therefore Christ's ambassadors, as though God were making his appeal through us. We implore you on Christ's behalf: Be reconciled to God.

2 Corinthians 5:20 NIV

Genuine, heartfelt Christianity can be highly contagious. When you've experienced the transforming power of God's love, you feel the need to share the Good News of His only begotten Son. So, whether you realize it or not, you can be sure that you are being led to share the story of your faith with family, with friends, and with the world.

> If you want to be more like Jesus . . . follow in His footsteps every day, obey His commandments every day, and share His never-ending love every day.

Every believer, including you, bears responsibility for sharing God's Good News. And it is important to remember that you share your testimony through words and actions, but not necessarily in that order.

Today, don't be bashful or timid: Talk about Jesus and, while you're at it, show the world what it really means to follow Him. After all, the fields are ripe for the harvest, time is short, and the workers are surprisingly few. So please share your story today because tomorrow may indeed be too late.

FOOD FOR THOUGHT

It has been the faith of the Son of God who loves me and gave Himself for me that has held me in the darkest valley and the hottest fires and the deepest waters.

Elisabeth Elliot

Live your lives in love, the same sort of love which Christ gives us, and which He perfectly expressed when He gave Himself as a sacrifice to God.

Corrie ten Boom

This hard place in which you perhaps find yourself is the very place in which God is giving you opportunity to look only to Him, to spend time in prayer, and to learn long-suffering, gentleness, meekness—in short, to learn the depths of the love that Christ Himself has poured out on all of us.

Elisabeth Elliot

A HEALTHY-CHOICE TIP

Take a careful look inside your refrigerator. Are the contents reflective of a healthy lifestyle? And if your fridge is overflowing with junk foods, it's time to rethink your shopping habits.

DAY 79

GET INVOLVED
IN A CHURCH

*And I also say to you that you are Peter, and on this rock I will
build My church, and the forces of Hades will not overpower it.
I will give you the keys of the kingdom of heaven, and whatever
you bind on earth will have been bound in heaven, and whatever
you loose on earth will have been loosed in heaven.*

Matthew 16:18-19 HCSB

If you want to find balance, the church is a wonderful
place to discover it.

Are you an active, contributing, member of your local
fellowship? The answer to this simple question will have a
profound impact on the direction of your
spiritual journey and the content of your
character.

God intends for
you to be actively
involved in His
church. Your
intentions should
be the same.

If you are not currently engaged in a
local church, you're missing out on an array of blessings that include, but are certainly not limited to, the life-lifting relationships that you can—and should—be
experiencing with fellow believers.

So do yourself a favor: Find a congregation you're
comfortable with, and join it. And once you've joined,
don't just attend church out of habit. Go to church out of

a sincere desire to know and worship God. When you do, you'll be blessed by the men and women who attend your fellowship, and you'll be blessed by your Creator. You deserve to attend church, and God deserves for you to attend church, so don't delay.

FOOD FOR THOUGHT

Every time a new person comes to God, every time someone's gifts find expression in the fellowship of believers, every time a family in need is surrounded by the caring church, the truth is affirmed anew: the Church triumphant is alive and well!

Gloria Gaither

In God's economy you will be hard-pressed to find many examples of successful "Lone Rangers."

Luci Swindoll

STRENGTHENING YOUR FAITH

Make church a celebration, not an obligation: What you put into church determines what you get out of it. Your attitude towards worship is vitally important . . . so celebrate accordingly!

DURING DIFFICULT DAYS

We also have joy with our troubles, because we know that these troubles produce patience. And patience produces character, and character produces hope.

Romans 5:3-4 NCV

All of us face those occasional days when the traffic jams and the dog gobbles the homework. But, when we find ourselves overtaken by the minor frustrations of life, we must catch ourselves, take a deep breath, and lift our thoughts upward. Although we are here on earth struggling to rise above the distractions of the day, we need never struggle alone. God is here—eternally and faithfully, with infinite patience and love—and, if we reach out to Him, He will restore perspective and peace to our souls.

> Difficult days come and go. Stay the course. The sun is shining somewhere, and will soon shine on you.

Sometimes even the most devout Christians can become discouraged, and you are no exception. After all, you live in a world where expectations can be high and demands can be even higher.

If you find yourself enduring difficult circumstances, remember that God remains in His heaven. If you become discouraged with the direction of your day or your life, lift your thoughts and prayers to Him. He is a God of possibility, not negativity. He will guide you through your difficulties and beyond them. Then, you can thank the Giver of all things good for blessings that are simply too numerous to count.

FOOD FOR THOUGHT

Are you weak? Weary? Confused? Troubled? Pressured? How is your relationship with God? Is it held in its place of priority? I believe the greater the pressure, the greater your need for time alone with Him.

Kay Arthur

The strengthening of faith comes from staying with it in the hour of trial. We should not shrink from tests of faith.

Catherine Marshall

A HEALTHY-CHOICE TIP

Many of the messages that you receive from the media are specifically designed to sell you products that interfere with your spiritual, physical, or emotional health. God takes great interest in your health; the moguls from Madison Avenue take great interest in your pocketbook. Trust God.

THE POWER OF OPTIMISM

I am able to do all things through Him who strengthens me.

Philippians 4:13 HCSB

As each day unfolds, you are quite literally surrounded by more opportunities than you can count—opportunities to improve your own life and the lives of those you love. God's Word promises that you, like all of His children, possess the ability to experience earthly peace and spiritual abundance. Yet sometimes—especially if you dwell upon the inevitable disappointments that may, at times, befall even the luckiest among us—you may allow pessimism to invade your thoughts and your heart.

> Be a realistic optimist. Think realistically about yourself and your situation while making a conscious effort to focus on hopes, not fears.

The self-fulfilling prophecy is alive, well, and living at your house. If you constantly anticipate the worst, that's what you're likely to attract. But, if you make the effort to think positive thoughts, you'll increase the probability that those positive thoughts will come true.

So here's a simple, character-building tip for improving your life: put the self-fulfilling prophecy to work for you. Expect the best, and then get busy working to achieve it.

When you do, you'll not only increase the odds of achieving your dreams, but you'll also have more fun along the way.

FOOD FOR THOUGHT

The popular idea of faith is of a certain obstinate optimism: the hope, tenaciously held in the face of trouble, that the universe is fundamentally friendly and things may get better.

J. I. Packer

It is a remarkable thing that some of the most optimistic and enthusiastic people you will meet are those who have been through intense suffering.

Warren Wiersbe

Christ can put a spring in your step and a thrill in your heart. Optimism and cheerfulness are products of knowing Christ.

Billy Graham

A HEALTHY-CHOICE TIP

Learn to look for opportunities, not obstructions; and while you're at it, look for possibilities, not problems.

ACCEPTING LIFE

Do not remember the past events, pay no attention to things of old. Look, I am about to do something new; even now it is coming. Do you not see it? Indeed, I will make a way in the wilderness, rivers in the desert.

Isaiah 43:18-19 HCSB

If you're like most people, you like being in control. Period. When you're trying to improve your health—or any other aspect of your life, for that matter—you want things to happen in accordance with your own specific timetable. But sometimes, God has other plans . . . and He always has the final word.

Think of at least one aspect of your life that you've been reluctant to accept, and then prayerfully ask God to help you trust Him more by accepting the past.

All of us experience adversity and pain. As human beings with limited comprehension, we can never fully understand the will of our Father in Heaven. But as believers in a benevolent God, we must always trust His providence.

When Jesus went to the Mount of Olives, as described in Luke 22, He poured out His heart to God. Jesus knew of the agony that He was destined to endure, but He also knew that God's will must be done. We, like our Savior, face trials that bring fear and trembling to the very depths of our souls, but like Christ, we too must ultimately seek God's will, not our own.

Are you embittered by a personal tragedy that you did not deserve and cannot understand? If so, it's time to make peace with life. It's time to forgive others, and, if necessary, to forgive yourself. It's time to accept the unchangeable past, to embrace the priceless present, and to have faith in the promise of tomorrow. It's time to trust God completely. And it's time to reclaim the peace—His peace—that can and should be yours.

FOOD FOR THOUGHT

What cannot be altered must be borne, not blamed.

Thomas Fuller

Prayer may not get us what we want, but it will teach us to want what we need.

Vance Havner

A HEALTHY-CHOICE TIP

Are you chained to a desk or trapped in a sedentary lifestyle? And are you waiting for something big to happen before you revolutionize your exercise habits? If so, wait no more. In fact, you can start today by substituting a light snack and a healthy walk for that calorie-laden lunch.

CONSIDER
THE POSSIBILITIES

But Jesus looked at them and said, "With men this is impossible, but with God all things are possible."

Matthew 19:26 HCSB

All of us face difficult days. Sometimes even the most optimistic women can become discouraged, and you are no exception. If you find yourself enduring difficult circumstances, perhaps it's time for an extreme intellectual make-over—perhaps it's time to focus more on your strengths and opportunities, and less on the challenges that confront you. And one more thing: perhaps it's time to put a little more faith in God.

Don't invest large quantities of your life focusing on past misfortunes. On the road of life, regret is a dead end.

Every day, including this one, is brimming with possibilities. Every day is filled opportunities to grow, to serve, and to share. But if you are entangled in a web of negativity, you may overlook the blessings that God has scattered along your path. So don't give in to pessimism, to doubt, or to cynicism. Instead, keep your eyes upon the possibilities, fix your heart upon the Creator, do your best, and let Him handle the rest.

FOOD FOR THOUGHT

Here lies the tremendous mystery—that God should be all-powerful, yet refuse to coerce. He summons us to cooperation. We are honored in being given the opportunity to participate in His good deeds. Remember how He asked for help in performing His miracles: Fill the water pots, stretch out your hand, distribute the loaves.

Elisabeth Elliot

God specializes in things fresh and firsthand. His plans for you this year may outshine those of the past. He's prepared to fill your days with reasons to give Him praise.

Joni Eareckson Tada

I could go through this day oblivious to the miracles all around me or I could tune in and "enjoy."

Gloria Gaither

A HEALTHY-CHOICE TIP

The cure for obesity is simple, but implementing that cure isn't. Weight loss requires lots of planning and lots of self-discipline. But with God's help, you're up to the task.

NEW BEGINNINGS

Then the One seated on the throne said, "Look! I am making everything new."

Revelation 21:5 HCSB

Each new day offers countless opportunities to serve God, to seek His will, and to obey His teachings. But each day also offers countless opportunities to stray from God's commandments and to wander far from His path.

Sometimes, we wander aimlessly in a wilderness of our own making, but God has better plans for us. And, whenever we ask Him to renew our strength and guide our steps, He does so.

If you're graduating into a new phase of life, be sure to make God your partner. If you do, He'll guide your steps, He'll help carry your burdens, and He'll help you focus on the things that really matter.

Consider this day a new beginning. Consider it a fresh start, a renewed opportunity to serve your Creator with willing hands and a loving heart. Ask God to renew your sense of purpose as He guides your steps. Today is a glorious opportunity to serve God. Seize that opportunity while you can; tomorrow may indeed be too late.

FOOD FOR THOUGHT

Whoever you are, whatever your condition or circumstance, whatever your past or problem, Jesus can restore you to wholeness.

Anne Graham Lotz

Walking with God leads to receiving his intimate counsel, and counseling leads to deep restoration.

John Eldredge

God is not running an antique shop! He is making all things new!

Vance Havner

The amazing thing about Jesus is that He doesn't just patch up our lives, He gives us a brand new sheet, a clean slate to start over, all new.

Gloria Gaither

STRENGTHENING YOUR FAITH

How do you know if you can still keep growing as a Christian? Check your pulse. If it's still beating, then you can still keep growing.

MOVING MOUNTAINS

If you have faith as a mustard seed, you will say to this mountain, "Move from here to there," and it will move; and nothing will be impossible for you.

Matthew 17:20 NKJV

Every life—including yours—is a series of successes and failures, celebrations and disappointments, joys and sorrows. Every step of the way, through every triumph and tragedy, God will stand by your side and strengthen you . . . if you have faith in Him. Jesus taught His disciples that if they had faith, they could move mountains. You can too.

> The quality of your faith will help determine the quality of your day and the quality of your life.

When a suffering woman sought healing by merely touching the hem of His cloak, Jesus replied, "Daughter, be of good comfort; thy faith hath made thee whole" (Matthew 9:22 KJV). The message to believers of every generation is clear: we must live by faith today and every day.

When you place your faith, your trust, indeed your life in the hands of Christ Jesus, you'll be amazed at the marvelous things He can do with you and through you. So strengthen your faith through praise, through worship, through Bible study, and through prayer. And trust God's plans. With Him, all things are possible, and He stands ready to open a world of possibilities to you . . . if you have faith.

FOOD FOR THOUGHT

Faith is seeing light with the eyes of your heart, when the eyes of your body see only darkness.

Barbara Johnson

Grace calls you to get up, throw off your blanket of helplessness, and to move on through life in faith.

Kay Arthur

Just as our faith strengthens our prayer life, so do our prayers deepen our faith. Let us pray often, starting today, for a deeper, more powerful faith.

Shirley Dobson

STRENGTHENING YOUR FAITH

If you don't have faith, you'll never move mountains. But if you do have faith, there's no limit to the things that you and God, working together, can accomplish.

LIVE ON PURPOSE

I, therefore, the prisoner in the Lord, urge you to walk worthy of the calling you have received.

Ephesians 4:1 HCSB

"What on earth does God intend for me to do with my life?" It's an easy question to ask but, for many of us, a difficult question to answer. Why? Because God's purposes aren't always clear to us. Sometimes we wander aimlessly in a wilderness of our own making. And sometimes, we struggle mightily against God in an unsuccessful attempt to find success and happiness through our own means, not His.

> God has a plan for your life, a definite purpose that you can fulfill. Your challenge is to pray for God's guidance and to follow wherever He leads.

If you're a woman who sincerely seeks God's guidance, He will give it. But, He will make His revelations known to you in a way and in a time of His choosing, not yours, so be patient. If you prayerfully petition God and work diligently to discern His intentions, He will, in time, lead you to a place of joyful abundance and eternal peace.

Sometimes, God's intentions will be clear to you; other times, God's plan will seem uncertain at best. But even on those difficult days when your life seems dangerously out of balance, you must never lose sight of these overriding facts: God created you for a reason; He has important work for you to do; and He's waiting patiently for you to do it. The next step is up to you.

FOOD FOR THOUGHT

Only God's chosen task for you will ultimately satisfy. Do not wait until it is too late to realize the privilege of serving Him in His chosen position for you.

Beth Moore

His life is our light—our purpose and meaning and reason for living.

Anne Graham Lotz

Yesterday is just experience but tomorrow is glistening with purpose—and today is the channel leading from one to the other.

Barbara Johnson

A HEALTHY-CHOICE TIP

God's Word is full of advice about health, moderation, and sensible living. When you come across these passages, take them to heart and put them to use.

SAFETY FIRST

The sensible see danger and take cover; the foolish keep going and are punished.

Proverbs 27:12 HCSB

We live in a world that can be a dangerous place, especially for those who are inclined toward risky behaviors. Some risk takers are easy to spot: they jump out of little airplanes, scurry up tall mountains, or race very fast automobiles.

Most risk takers, however, are not so bold; instead, they take more subtle risks that endanger themselves, their friends, and their families. They drink and drive, or they smoke cigarettes, or they neglect to fasten their seatbelts, or they engage in countless other behaviors that, while not as glamorous as mountain climbing, are equally as dangerous.

Put the brakes on risky behaviors . . . before risky behaviors put the brakes on you.

This world holds enough hazards of its own without our adding to those risks by foolishly neglecting our own personal safety and the safety of those around us. So, the next time you're tempted to do something foolish, remember that the body you're putting at risk belongs not only to you, but also to God. And He hopes that you'll behave wisely.

FOOD FOR THOUGHT

Sometimes, being wise is nothing more than slowing down long enough to think about things before you do them.

Jim Gallery

If we neglect the Bible, we cannot expect to benefit from the wisdom and direction that result from knowing God's Word.

Vonette Bright

Wisdom is knowledge applied. Head knowledge is useless on the battlefield. Knowledge stamped on the heart makes one wise.

Beth Moore

The more wisdom enters our hearts, the more we will be able to trust our hearts in difficult situations.

John Eldredge

A HEALTHY-CHOICE TIP

Remember: life is God's gift to you—taking good care of yourself is your gift to God.

YOU DON'T HAVE TO BE PERFECT

To acquire wisdom is to love oneself; people who cherish understanding will prosper.

Proverbs 19:8 NLT

You don't have to be perfect to be wonderful. The difference between perfectionism and realistic expectations is the difference between a life of frustration and a life of contentment. Only one earthly being ever lived life to perfection, and He was the Son of God. The rest of us have fallen short of God's standard and need to be accepting of our own limitations as well as the limitations of others.

If you find yourself frustrated by the unrealistic demands of others (or by unrealistic pressures of the self-imposed variety) it's time to ask yourself who you're trying to impress, and why. Your first responsibility is to the Heavenly Father who created you and to the Son who saved you. Then, you bear a powerful responsibility to be true to yourself. And of course you owe debts of gratitude to friends and family members. But, when it comes to meeting society's unrealistic expectations, forget it! Those expectations aren't just unrealistic; they're detrimental to your spiritual health.

So, if you've become discouraged with your inability to be perfectly fit, remember that when you accepted

Christ as your Savior, God accepted you for all eternity. Now, it's your turn to accept yourself. When you do, you'll feel a tremendous weight being lifted from your shoulders. After all, pleasing God is simply a matter of obeying His commandments and accepting His Son. But as for pleasing everybody else? That's impossible . . . so why even try?

FOOD FOR THOUGHT

A perfectionist resists the truth that growing up in Christ is a process.

Susan Lenzkes

STRENGTHENING YOUR FAITH

As you begin to work toward improved physical and emotional health, don't expect perfection. Of course you should work hard; of course you should be disciplined; of course you should do your best. But then, when you've given it your best effort, you should be accepting of yourself, imperfect though you may be. In heaven, we will know perfection. Here on earth, we have a few short years to wrestle with the challenges of imperfection. Let us accept these lives that God has given us—and these bodies which are ours for a brief time here on earth—with open, loving arms.

TOO FRIENDLY WITH THE WORLD?

Let no one deceive himself. If anyone among you seems to be wise in this age, let him become a fool that he may become wise. For the wisdom of this world is foolishness with God. For it is written, "He catches the wise in their own craftiness."

1 Corinthians 3:18–19 NKJV

We live in the world, but we should not worship it—yet at every turn, or so it seems, we are tempted to do otherwise.

As Warren Wiersbe correctly observed, "Because the world is deceptive, it is dangerous."

> The world makes plenty of promises that it can't keep. God, on the other hand, keeps every single one of His promises.

The 21st-century world in which we live is a noisy, distracting place, a place that offers countless temptations and dangers. The world seems to cry, "Worship me with your time, your money, your energy, your thoughts, and your life!" But if we are wise, we won't fall prey to that temptation.

If you wish to build your character day-by-day, you must distance yourself, at least in part, from the temptations and distractions of modern-day society. But distancing yourself isn't easy, especially when so many societal forces are struggling to capture your attention, your participation, and your money.

C. S. Lewis said, "Aim at heaven and you will get earth thrown in; aim at earth and you will get neither." That's good advice. You're likely to hit what you aim at, so aim high . . . aim at heaven. When you do, you'll be strengthening your character as you improve every aspect of your life. And God will demonstrate His approval as He showers you with more spiritual blessings than you can count.

FOOD FOR THOUGHT

The more we stuff ourselves with material pleasures, the less we seem to appreciate life.

Barbara Johnson

A HEALTHY-CHOICE TIP

In the good old days, dining out used to be an occasional treat for most families. Now, it's more of an everyday occurrence. But there's a catch: most restaurants aim for taste first, price second, and health a distant third. But you should think health first. So the next time you head out for a burger, a bagel, or any other fast food, take a minute to read the fine print that's usually posted on the wall. You may find out that the healthy-sounding treat is actually a calorie-bomb in disguise.

GETTING ENOUGH REST?

Come to Me, all you who labor and are heavy laden, and I will give you rest. Take My yoke upon you and learn from Me, for I am gentle and lowly in heart, and you will find rest for your souls. For My yoke is easy and My burden is light.

Matthew 11:28-30 NKJV

Even the most inspired Christians can, from time to time, find themselves running on empty. The demands of daily life can drain us of our strength and rob us of the joy that is rightfully ours in Christ. When we find ourselves tired, discouraged, or worse, there is a source from which we can draw the power needed to recharge our spiritual batteries. That source is God.

God wants you to get enough rest. The world wants you to burn the candle at both ends. Trust God.

God intends that His children lead joyous lives filled with abundance and peace. But sometimes, abundance and peace seem very far away. It is then that we must turn to God for renewal, and when we do, He will restore us.

God expects us to work hard, but He also intends for us to rest. When we fail to take the rest that we need, we do a disservice to ourselves and to our families.

Is your spiritual battery running low? Is your energy on the wane? Are your emotions frayed? If so, it's time to turn your thoughts and your prayers to God. And when you're finished, it's time to rest.

FOOD FOR THOUGHT

Satan does some of his worst work on exhausted Christians when nerves are frayed and their minds are faint.

Vance Havner

Jesus taught us by example to get out of the rat race and recharge our batteries.

Barbara Johnson

Life is strenuous. See that your clock does not run down.

Mrs. Charles E. Cowman

A HEALTHY-CHOICE TIP

You live in a world that tempts you to stay up late—very late. But too much late-night TV, combined with too little sleep, is a prescription for exhaustion, ill health, ill temper, or all three. So do yourself, your boss, and your loved ones a big favor. Arrange your TV schedule and your life so you get eight hours of sleep every night.

MAKING GOD'S PRIORITIES YOUR PRIORITIES

Draw near to God, and He will draw near to you.

James 4:8 HCSB

Have you fervently asked God to help prioritize your life? Have you asked Him for guidance and for the courage to do the things that you know need to be done? If so, then you're continually inviting your Creator to reveal Himself in a variety of ways. As a follower of Christ, you must do no less.

The priorities you choose will dictate the life you live. So choose carefully. And don't be afraid to say no when you begin to feel overcommitted.

When you make God's priorities your priorities, you will receive God's abundance and His peace. When you make God a full partner in every aspect of your life, He will help you keep things in balance. When you allow God to reign over your heart, He will honor you with spiritual blessings that are simply too numerous to count. So, as you plan for the day ahead, make God's will your ultimate priority. When you do, every other priority will have a tendency to fall neatly into place.

FOOD FOR THOUGHT

Blessed are those who know what on earth they are here on earth to do and set themselves about the business of doing it.

Max Lucado

The essence of the Christian life is Jesus: that in all things He might have the preeminence, not that in some things He might have a place.

Franklin Graham

How important it is for us—young and old—to live as if Jesus would return any day—to set our goals, make our choices, raise our children, and conduct business with the perspective of the imminent return of our Lord.

Gloria Gaither

A HEALTHY-CHOICE TIP

Simply put, it's up to you to assume the ultimate responsibility for your health. So if you're fighting the battle of the bulge (the bulging waistline, that is), don't waste your time blaming the fast food industry—or anybody else, for that matter. It's your body, and it's your responsibility to take care of it.

PAYING ATTENTION TO GOD

For where your treasure is, there your heart will be also.

Luke 12:34 HCSB

Who is in charge of your heart? Is it God, or is it something else? Have you given Christ your heart, your soul, your talents, your time, and your testimony? Or are you giving Him little more than a few hours each Sunday morning?

In the book of Exodus, God warns that we should place no gods before Him. Yet all too often, we place our Lord in second, third, or fourth place as we worship other things. When we unwittingly place possessions or relationships above our love for the Creator, we create big problems for ourselves.

Because God is infinite and eternal, you cannot comprehend Him. But you can understand your need to praise Him, to love Him, and to obey His Word.

Does God rule your heart? Make certain that the honest answer to this question is a resounding yes. In the life of every Christian, God should come first. And that's precisely the place that He deserves in your heart.

FOOD FOR THOUGHT

In heaven, we will see that nothing, absolutely nothing, was wasted, and that every tear counted and every cry was heard.

Joni Eareckson Tada

God loves each of us as if there were only one of us.

St. Augustine

He treats us as sons, and all he asks in return is that we shall treat Him as a Father whom we can trust without anxiety. We must take the son's place of dependence and trust, and we must let Him keep the father's place of care and responsibility.

Hannah Whitall Smith

He is always thinking about us. We are before his eyes. The Lord's eye never sleeps, but is always watching out for our welfare. We are continually on his heart.

C. H. Spurgeon

A HEALTHY-CHOICE TIP

Don't worship food. Honor the body that God gave you by eating sensible portions of sensible foods.

DAY 93

SEEK FELLOWSHIP

Then all the people began to eat and drink, send portions, and have a great celebration, because they had understood the words that were explained to them.

Nehemiah 8:12 HCSB

Fellowship with other believers should be an integral part of your everyday life. Your association with fellow Christians should be uplifting, enlightening, encouraging, and consistent.

Are you an active member of your own fellowship? Are you a builder of bridges inside the four walls of your church and outside it? Do you contribute to God's glory by contributing your time and your talents to a close-knit band of believers? Hopefully so. The fellowship of believers is intended to be a powerful tool for spreading God's Good News and uplifting His children. And God intends for you to be a fully contributing member of that fellowship. Your intentions should be the same.

If you're experiencing a strained relationship with someone, take steps to mend that relationship . . . and do it now.

FOOD FOR THOUGHT

In God's economy you will be hard-pressed to find many examples of successful "Lone Rangers."

Luci Swindoll

Christians are like coals of a fire. Together they glow—apart they grow cold.

Anonymous

Be united with other Christians. A wall with loose bricks is not good. The bricks must be cemented together.

Corrie ten Boom

One of the ways God refills us after failure is through the blessing of Christian fellowship. Just experiencing the joy of simple activities shared with other children of God can have a healing effect on us.

Anne Graham Lotz

STRENGTHENING YOUR FAITH

You need fellowship with men and women of faith. And your Christian friends need fellowship with you. So what are you waiting for?

REMEMBER THE SABBATH

Remember the Sabbath day, to keep it holy.

Exodus 20:8 NKJV

When God gave Moses the Ten Commandments, it became perfectly clear that our Heavenly Father intends for us to make the Sabbath a holy day, a day for worship, for contemplation, for fellowship, and for rest. Yet we live in a seven-day-a-week world, a world that all too often treats Sunday as a regular workday.

One way to strengthen your faith is by giving God at least one day each week. If you carve out the time for a day of worship and praise, you'll be amazed at the impact it will have on the rest of your week. But if you fail to honor God's day, if you treat the Sabbath as a day to work or a day to party, you'll miss out on a harvest of blessings that is only available one day each week.

> The Sabbath is unlike the other six days of the week, and it's up to you to treat it that way.

How does your family observe the Lord's day? When church is over, do you treat Sunday like any other day of the week? If so, it's time to think long and hard about your family's schedule and your family's priorities. And if you've been treating Sunday as just another day, it's time to break that habit. When Sunday rolls around, don't try to fill every spare moment. Take time to rest . . . Father's orders!

FOOD FOR THOUGHT

Jesus taught us by example to get out of the rat race and recharge our batteries.

Barbara Johnson

Jesus gives us the ultimate rest, the confidence we need, to escape the frustration and chaos of the world around us.

Billy Graham

It is what Jesus is, not what we are, that gives rest to the soul. If we really want to overcome Satan and have peace with God, we must "fix our eyes on Jesus." Let his death, his suffering, his glories, and his intercession be fresh on your mind.

C. H. Spurgeon

STRENGTHENING YOUR FAITH

Working seven days a week may impress your boss . . . but it isn't the way God intends for you to live your life. You live in a world that doesn't often honor the Sabbath, but God wants you to treat the Sabbath as a day of rest, no exceptions. So next Sunday, do yourself and your family a favor: take God at His Word by making the Sabbath a special day for you and your family.

EXPERIENCING SILENCE

Be still, and know that I am God.

Psalm 46:10 NKJV

The world seems to grow louder day by day, and our senses seem to be invaded at every turn. If we allow the distractions of a clamorous society to separate us from God's peace, we do ourselves a profound disservice. Our task, as dutiful believers, is to carve out moments of silence in a world filled with noise.

If we are to maintain righteous minds and compassionate hearts, we must take time each day for prayer and for meditation. We must make ourselves still in the presence of our Creator. We must quiet our minds and our hearts so that we might sense God's will and His love.

Spend a few moments each day in silence. You owe it to your Creator . . . and to yourself.

Has the busy pace of life robbed you of the peace that God has promised? If so, it's time to reorder your priorities and your life. As you try to balance the priorities on your daily to-do list, remember that nothing is more important than the time you spend with your Heavenly Father. So be still and claim the inner peace that is found in the silent moments you spend with God.

FOOD FOR THOUGHT

It is in that stillness that the Voice will be heard, the only voice in all the universe that speaks peace to the deepest part of us.

Elisabeth Elliot

Let your loneliness be transformed into a holy aloneness. Sit still before the Lord. Remember Naomi's word to Ruth: "Sit still, my daughter, until you see how the matter will fall."

Elisabeth Elliot

Because Jesus Christ is our Great High Priest, not only can we approach God without a human "go-between," we can also hear and learn from God in some sacred moments without one.

Beth Moore

A HEALTHY-CHOICE TIP

If you place a high value on the body God has given you, then place high importance on the foods you use to fuel it.

KEEPING IN BALANCE BY KEEPING IT SIMPLE

But godliness with contentment is a great gain. For we brought nothing into the world, and we can take nothing out. But if we have food and clothing, we will be content with these. But those who want to be rich fall into temptation, a trap, and many foolish and harmful desires, which plunge people into ruin and destruction.

1 Timothy 6:6-9 HCSB

You live in a world where simplicity is in short supply. Think for a moment about the complexity of your everyday life and compare it to the lives of your ancestors. Certainly, you are the beneficiary of many technological innovations, but those innovations have a price: in all likelihood, your world is highly complex. Consider the following:

Simplicity and peace are two concepts that are closely related. Complexity and peace are not.

1. From the moment you wake up in the morning until the time you lay your head on the pillow at night, you are the target of an endless stream of advertising information. Each message is intended to grab your attention in order to convince you to purchase things you didn't know you needed (and probably don't!).

2. Essential aspects of your life, including personal matters such as health care, are subject to an ever-increasing flood of rules and regulations.

3. Unless you take firm control of your time and your life, you may be overwhelmed by the tidal wave of complexity that threatens your happiness.

Your Heavenly Father understands the joy of living simply, and so should you. So do yourself a favor: keep your life as simple as possible. Simplicity is, indeed, genius. By simplifying your life, you are destined to improve it.

FOOD FOR THOUGHT

There is absolutely no evidence that complexity and materialism lead to happiness. On the contrary, there is plenty of evidence that simplicity and spirituality lead to joy, a blessedness that is better than happiness.

Dennis Swanberg

A HEALTHY-CHOICE TIP

If you're in reasonably good shape, a nice healthy walk can be a great substitute for a big sit-down meal. So don't underestimate the benefits of a good walk. It's a great way to burn a few calories, to get some fresh air, and to improve your life.

DAY 97

LIFETIME LEARNING

The wise person makes learning a joy; fools spout only foolishness.

Proverbs 15:2 NLT

When it comes to learning life's lessons, we can either do things the easy way or the hard way. The easy way can be summed up as follows: when God teaches us a lesson, we learn it . . . the first time! Unfortunately, too many of us—both parents and children alike—learn much more slowly than that.

God still has important lessons to teach you. Your task is to be open to His instruction.

When we resist God's instruction, He continues to teach, whether we like it or not. And if we keep making the same old mistakes, God responds by rewarding us with the same old results.

Our challenge, then, is to discern God's lessons from the experiences of everyday life. Hopefully, we learn those lessons sooner rather than later because the sooner we do, the sooner He can move on to the next lesson and the next, and the next . . .

FOOD FOR THOUGHT

True learning can take place at every age of life, and it doesn't have to be in the curriculum plan.

Suzanne Dale Ezell

While chastening is always difficult, if we look to God for the lesson we should learn, we will see spiritual fruit.

Vonette Bright

The wonderful thing about God's schoolroom is that we get to grade our own papers. You see, He doesn't test us so He can learn how well we're doing. He tests us so we can discover how well we're doing.

Charles Swindoll

STRENGTHENING YOUR FAITH

Today is your classroom: what will you learn? Will you use today's experiences as tools for personal, spiritual, and physical improvement, or will you ignore the lessons that life and God are trying to teach you? Will you carefully study God's Word, and will you apply His teachings to the experiences of everyday life? The events of today have much to teach. You have much to learn. May you live—and learn—accordingly.

FITNESS IS A FORM OF WORSHIP

Worship the Lord your God and . . . serve Him only.

Matthew 4:10 HCSB

What does worship have to do with fitness? That depends on how you define worship. If you consider worship to be a "Sunday-only" activity, an activity that occurs only inside the four walls of your local church, then fitness and worship may seem totally unrelated. But, if you view worship as an activity that impacts every facet of your life—if you consider worship to be something far more than a "one-day-a week" obligation—then you understand that every aspect of your life is a form of worship. And that includes keeping your body physically fit.

> When you worship God with a sincere heart, He will guide your steps and bless your life.

Every day provides opportunities to put God where He belongs: at the center of our lives. When we do so, we worship not just with our words, but also with our deeds. And one way that we can honor our Heavenly Father is by treating our bodies with care and respect.

The Bible makes it clear: "Your body is the temple of the Holy Spirit" (1 Corinthians 6:19 NLT). Treat it that way. And consider your fitness regimen to be one way—a very important way—of worshipping God.

FOOD FOR THOUGHT

It's the definition of worship: A hungry heart finding the Father's feast. A searching soul finding the Father's face. A wandering pilgrim spotting the Father's house. Finding God. Finding God seeking us. This is worship. This is a worshiper.

Max Lucado

There is no division into sacred and secular; it is all one great, glorious life.

Oswald Chambers

God asks that we worship Him with our concentrated minds as well as with our wills and emotions. A divided and scattered mind is not effective.

Catherine Marshall

A HEALTHY-CHOICE TIP

Consider your healthy lifestyle a form of worship: When God described your body as a temple, He wasn't kidding. Show your respect for God's Word by keeping your temple in tip-top shape.

YOUR PHYSICAL AND SPIRITUAL FITNESS: WHO'S IN CHARGE?

But seek ye first the kingdom of God, and his righteousness; and all these things shall be added unto you.

Matthew 6:33 KJV

One of the surest ways to improve your health and your life—and the best way—is to do it with God as your partner. When you put God first in every aspect of your life, you'll be comforted by the knowledge that His wisdom is the ultimate wisdom and that His plans are the right plans for you. When you put God first, your outlook will change, your priorities will change, your behaviors will change, and your health will change. When you put Him first, you'll experience the genuine peace and lasting comfort that only He can give.

> God deserves first place in your life . . . and you deserve the experience of putting Him there.

In the book of Exodus, God instructs us to place no gods before Him (20:3). Does God rule your heart? Make certain that the honest answer to this question is a resounding yes. And then prepare yourself for the cascade of spiritual and emotional blessings that are sure to follow.

FOOD FOR THOUGHT

The LORD is my strength and my song; he has become my victory. He is my God, and I will praise him.

Exodus 15:2 NLT

Love the Lord your God with all your heart, with all your soul, and with all your strength.

Deuteronomy 6:5 HCSB

Make God's will the focus of your life day by day. If you seek to please Him and Him alone, you'll find yourself satisfied with life.

Kay Arthur

Jesus Christ is the first and last, author and finisher, beginning and end, alpha and omega, and by Him all other things hold together. He must be first or nothing. God never comes next!

Vance Havner

STRENGTHENING YOUR FAITH

God has a plan for the world and for you. When you discover His plan for your life—and when you follow in the footsteps of His Son—you will be rewarded. The place where God is leading you is the place where you must go.

DAY 100

GIVE HIM YOUR HEART

For God so loved the world that He gave His only begotten Son, that whoever believes in Him should not perish but have everlasting life.

John 3:16 NKJV

Your decision to allow Christ to reign over your heart is the pivotal decision of your life. It is a decision that you cannot ignore. It is a decision that is yours and yours alone.

God's love for you is deeper and more profound than you can imagine. God's love for you is so great that He sent His only Son to this earth to die for your sins and to offer you the priceless gift of eternal life. Now, you must decide whether or not to accept God's gift. Will you ignore it or embrace it? Will you return it or neglect it? Will you accept Christ's love and build a lifelong relationship with Him, or will you turn away from Him and take a different path?

> The ultimate choice for you is the choice to invite God's Son into your heart. Choose wisely . . . and immediately.

Accept God's gift now: allow His Son to preside over your heart, your thoughts, and your life, starting this very instant.

FOOD FOR THOUGHT

Choose Jesus Christ! Deny yourself, take up the Cross, and follow Him—for the world must be shown. The world must see, in us, a discernible, visible, startling difference.

Elisabeth Elliot

The most profound essence of my nature is that I am capable of receiving God.

St. Augustine

It's your heart that Jesus longs for: your will to be made His own with self on the cross forever, and Jesus alone on the throne.

Ruth Bell Graham

The amount of power you experience to live a victorious, triumphant Christian life is directly proportional to the freedom you give the Spirit to be Lord of your life!

Anne Graham Lotz

STRENGTHENING YOUR FAITH

If you've already accepted Christ into your heart, congratulations! If you haven't, the appropriate moment to do so is this one.

MORE FROM GOD'S WORD

Verses by Topic

FAITH

If you do not stand firm in your faith, then you will not stand at all.

Isaiah 7:9 HCSB

Be alert, stand firm in the faith, be brave and strong.

1 Corinthians 16:13 HCSB

For we walk by faith, not by sight.

2 Corinthians 5:7 HCSB

Now faith is the reality of what is hoped for, the proof of what is not seen.

Hebrews 11:1 HCSB

Now without faith it is impossible to please God, for the one who draws near to Him must believe that He exists and rewards those who seek Him.

Hebrews 11:6 HCSB

GOD'S LOVE

For God loved the world in this way: He gave His only Son, so that everyone who believes in Him will not perish but have eternal life.

John 3:16 HCSB

For the Lord is good, and His love is eternal; His faithfulness endures through all generations.

Psalm 100:5 HCSB

The one who has My commandments and keeps them is the one who loves Me. And the one who loves Me will be loved by My Father. I also will love him and will reveal Myself to him.

John 14:21 HCSB

We love Him because He first loved us.

1 John 4:19 NKJV

Draw near to God, and He will draw near to you.

James 4:8 HCSB

WISDOM

Therefore, everyone who hears these words of Mine and acts on them will be like a sensible man who built his house on the rock. The rain fell, the rivers rose, and the winds blew and pounded that house. Yet it didn't collapse, because its foundation was on the rock.

Matthew 7:24–25 HCSB

But from Him you are in Christ Jesus, who for us became wisdom from God, as well as righteousness, sanctification, and redemption.

1 Corinthians 1:30 HCSB

For God has not given us a spirit of fearfulness, but one of power, love, and sound judgment.

2 Timothy 1:7 HCSB

Now if any of you lacks wisdom, he should ask God, who gives to all generously and without criticizing, and it will be given to him.

James 1:5 HCSB

THE SIMPLE LIFE

A simple life in the Fear-of-God is better than a rich life with a ton of headaches.

Proverbs 15:16 MSG

Do not love the world or the things in the world. If anyone loves the world, the love of the Father is not in him.

1 John 2:15 NKJV

We brought nothing into the world, so we can take nothing out. But, if we have food and clothes, we will be satisfied with that.

1 Timothy 6:7-8 NCV

So think clearly and exercise self-control. Look forward to the special blessings that will come to you at the return of Jesus Christ.

1 Peter 1:13 NLT

For the grace of God has been revealed, bringing salvation to all people. And we are instructed to turn from godless living and sinful pleasures. We should live in this evil world with self-control, right conduct, and devotion to God.

Titus 2:11-12 NLT

RIGHTEOUSNESS

The righteous one will live by his faith.

Habakkuk 2:4 HCSB

And the world is passing away, and the lust of it; but he who does the will of God abides forever.

1 John 2:17 NKJV

Because the eyes of the Lord are on the righteous and His ears are open to their request. But the face of the Lord is against those who do evil.

1 Peter 3:12 HCSB

Flee from youthful passions, and pursue righteousness, faith, love, and peace, along with those who call on the Lord from a pure heart.

2 Timothy 2:22 HCSB

And now, Israel, what does the Lord your God ask of you except to fear the Lord your God by walking in all His ways, to love Him, and to worship the Lord your God with all your heart and all your soul?

Deuteronomy 10:12 HCSB

YOUR PRIORITIES

Don't abandon wisdom, and she will watch over you; love her, and she will guard you.

Proverbs 4:6 HCSB

And I pray this: that your love will keep on growing in knowledge and every kind of discernment, so that you can determine what really matters and can be pure and blameless in the day of Christ.

Philippians 1:9 HCSB

So teach us to number our days, that we may gain a heart of wisdom.

Psalm 90:12 NKJV

For where your treasure is, there your heart will be also.

Luke 12:34 HCSB

He said to them all, "If anyone desires to come after Me, let him deny himself, and take up his cross daily, and follow Me. For whoever desires to save his life will lose it, but whoever loses his life for My sake will save it."

Luke 9:23-24 NKJV

ASKING FOR GOD'S HELP

If you remain in Me and My words remain in you, ask whatever you want and it will be done for you.

John 15:7 HCSB

What father among you, if his son asks for a fish, will, instead of a fish, give him a snake? Or if he asks for an egg, will give him a scorpion? If you then, who are evil, know how to give good gifts to your children, how much more will the heavenly Father give the Holy Spirit to those who ask Him?

Luke 11:11-13 HCSB

Don't worry about anything, but in everything, through prayer and petition with thanksgiving, let your requests be made known to God.

Philippians 4:6 HCSB

You do not have because you do not ask.

James 4:2 HCSB

For the Lord gives wisdom; from His mouth come knowledge and understanding.

Proverbs 2:6 NKJV

GOD'S STRENGTH

Be of good courage, and let us be strong for our people and for the cities of our God. And may the Lord do what is good in His sight.

1 Chronicles 19:13 NKJV

Do you not know? Have you not heard? The Everlasting God, the LORD, the Creator of the ends of the earth does not become weary or tired. His understanding is inscrutable. He gives strength to the weary, and to him who lacks might He increases power. Though youths grow weary and tired, and vigorous young men stumble badly, yet those who wait for the LORD will gain new strength; they will mount up with wings like eagles, they will run and not get tired, they will walk and not become weary.

Isaiah 40:28–31 NASB

He said unto me, My grace is sufficient for thee: for my strength is made perfect in weakness.

2 Corinthians 12:9 KJV

The LORD is my strength and my song....

Exodus 15:2 NIV

LIFE

I urge you now to live the life to which God called you.

Ephesians 4:1 NKJV

Shout triumphantly to the Lord, all the earth. Serve the Lord with gladness; come before Him with joyful songs.

Psalm 100:1-2 HCSB

Rejoice in the Lord always. Again I will say, rejoice!

Philippians 4:4 NKJV

Jesus told him, "I am the way, the truth, and the life. No one comes to the Father except through Me."

John 14:6 HCSB

He who follows righteousness and mercy finds life, righteousness and honor.

Proverbs 21:21 NKJV

LIFETIME LEARNING

A wise person pays attention to correction that will improve his life.

Proverbs 15:31 ICB

Remember what you are taught, and listen carefully to words of knowledge.

Proverbs 23:12 NCV

The fear of the Lord is the beginning of knowledge, but fools despise wisdom and discipline.

Proverbs 1:7 NIV

The knowledge of the secrets of the kingdom of heaven has been given to you....

Matthew 13:11 NIV

It is not good to have zeal without knowledge, nor to be hasty and miss the way.

Proverbs 19:2 NIV

SILENCE

Be still, and know that I am God.

Psalm 46:10 NKJV

Be silent before the Lord and wait expectantly for Him.

Psalm 37:7 HCSB

In quietness and confidence shall be your strength.

Isaiah 30:15 NKJV

I am not alone, because the Father is with Me.

John 16:32 HCSB

Draw near to God, and He will draw near to you.

James 4:8 HCSB

VALUES

God's Way is not a matter of mere talk; it's an empowered life.

1 Corinthians 4:20 MSG

Walk in a manner worthy of the God who calls you into His own kingdom and glory.

1 Thessalonians 2:12 NASB

Therefore, since we have this ministry, as we have received mercy, we do not give up. Instead, we have renounced shameful secret things, not walking in deceit or distorting God's message, but in God's sight we commend ourselves to every person's conscience by an open display of the truth.

2 Corinthians 4:1-2 HCSB

We must not become tired of doing good. We will receive our harvest of eternal life at the right time if we do not give up.

Galatians 6:9 NCV

Blessed are those who hunger and thirst for righteousness, because they will be filled.

Matthew 5:6 HCSB

DOING THE RIGHT THING

The righteous one will live by his faith.

Habakkuk 2:4 HCSB

And the world is passing away, and the lust of it; but he who does the will of God abides forever.

1 John 2:17 NKJV

Because the eyes of the Lord are on the righteous and His ears are open to their request. But the face of the Lord is against those who do evil.

1 Peter 3:12 HCSB

Flee from youthful passions, and pursue righteousness, faith, love, and peace, along with those who call on the Lord from a pure heart.

2 Timothy 2:22 HCSB

Sow righteousness for yourselves and reap faithful love; break up your untilled ground. It is time to seek the Lord until He comes and sends righteousness on you like the rain.

Hosea 10:12 HCSB

PEACE

And the peace of God, which surpasses every thought, will guard your hearts and your minds in Christ Jesus. Finally brothers, whatever is true, whatever is honorable, whatever is just, whatever is pure, whatever is lovely, whatever is commendable—if there is any moral excellence and if there is any praise—dwell on these things.

Philippians 4:7-8 HCSB

Abundant peace belongs to those who love Your instruction; nothing makes them stumble.

Psalm 119:165 HCSB

You will keep in perfect peace him whose mind is steadfast, because he trusts in you.

Isaiah 26:3 NIV

I have told you these things so that in Me you may have peace. In the world you have suffering. But take courage! I have conquered the world.

John 16:33 HCSB

GOD'S GRACE

But God, who is abundant in mercy, because of His great love that He had for us, made us alive with the Messiah even though we were dead in trespasses. By grace you are saved!

Ephesians 2:4-5 HCSB

My grace is sufficient for you, for My strength is made perfect in weakness.

2 Corinthians 12:9 NKJV

And we have seen and testify that the Father has sent the Son as Savior of the world.

1 John 4:14 NKJV

For by grace you are saved through faith, and this is not from yourselves; it is God's gift—not from works, so that no one can boast.

Ephesians 2:8-9 HCSB

In Him we have redemption through His blood, the forgiveness of our trespasses, according to the riches of His grace that He lavished on us with all wisdom and understanding.

Ephesians 1:7-8 HCSB

THE DIRECTION OF YOUR THOUGHTS

Set your minds on what is above, not on what is on the earth.

Colossians 3:2 HCSB

Brothers, don't be childish in your thinking, but be infants in evil and adult in your thinking.

1 Corinthians 14:20 HCSB

Guard your heart above all else, for it is the source of life.

Proverbs 4:23 HCSB

May the words of my mouth and the meditation of my heart be acceptable to You, Lord, my rock and my Redeemer.

Psalm 19:14 HCSB

Commit your works to the Lord, and your thoughts will be established.

Proverbs 16:3 NKJV

TRUSTING GOD

Lord, I turn my hope to You. My God, I trust in You. Do not let me be disgraced; do not let my enemies gloat over me.

Psalm 25:1-2 HCSB

He granted their request because they trusted in Him.

1 Chronicles 5:20 HCSB

The one who understands a matter finds success, and the one who trusts in the Lord will be happy.

Proverbs 16:20 HCSB

The fear of man is a snare, but the one who trusts in the Lord is protected.

Proverbs 29:25 HCSB

Those who trust in the Lord are like Mount Zion. It cannot be shaken; it remains forever.

Psalm 125:1 HCSB

GOD'S FAITHFULNESS

I will sing of the tender mercies of the Lord forever! Young and old will hear of your faithfulness. Your unfailing love will last forever. Your faithfulness is as enduring as the heavens.

Psalm 89:1-2 NLT

God is faithful, by whom you were called into the fellowship of His Son, Jesus Christ our Lord.

1 Corinthians 1:9 NKJV

Because of the LORD'S great love we are not consumed, for his compassions never fail. They are new every morning; great is your faithfulness.

Lamentations 3:22-23 NIV

Blessed is he whose help is the God of Jacob, whose hope is in the LORD his God, the Maker of heaven and earth, the sea, and everything in them—the LORD, who remains faithful forever.

Psalm 146:5-6 NIV

BIBLE STUDY

All Scripture is inspired by God and is profitable for teaching, for rebuking, for correcting, for training in righteousness, so that the man of God may be complete, equipped for every good work.

2 Timothy 3:16-17 HCSB

Man shall not live by bread alone, but by every word that proceeds from the mouth of God.

Matthew 4:4 NKJV

Heaven and earth will pass away, but My words will never pass away.

Matthew 24:35 HCSB

For the word of God is living and effective and sharper than any two-edged sword, penetrating as far as to divide soul, spirit, joints, and marrow; it is a judge of the ideas and thoughts of the heart.

Hebrews 4:12 HCSB

PRAISE AND THANKSGIVING

It is good to give thanks to the Lord, and to sing praises to Your name, O Most High.

Psalm 92:1 NKJV

And let the peace of the Messiah, to which you were also called in one body, control your hearts. Be thankful.

Colossians 3:15 HCSB

Therefore as you have received Christ Jesus the Lord, walk in Him, rooted and built up in Him and established in the faith, just as you were taught, and overflowing with thankfulness.

Colossians 2:6-7 HCSB

In everything give thanks; for this is the will of God in Christ Jesus for you.

1 Thessalonians 5:18 NKJV

So that at the name of Jesus every knee should bow—of those who are in heaven and on earth and under the earth—and every tongue should confess that Jesus Christ is Lord, to the glory of God the Father.

Philippians 2:10-11 HCSB

JOY

Rejoice in the Lord always. I will say it again: Rejoice!

Philippians 4:4 HCSB

You will show me the way of life, granting me the joy of your presence and the pleasures of living with you forever.

Psalm 16:11 NLT

David and the whole house of Israel were celebrating before the Lord.

2 Samuel 6:5 HCSB

Their sorrow was turned into rejoicing and their mourning into a holiday. They were to be days of feasting, rejoicing, and of sending gifts to one another and the poor.

Esther 9:22 HCSB

At the dedication of the wall of Jerusalem, they sent for the Levites wherever they lived and brought them to Jerusalem to celebrate the joyous dedication with thanksgiving and singing accompanied by cymbals, harps, and lyres.

Nehemiah 12:27 HCSB

ABUNDANCE

I have come that they may have life, and that they may have it more abundantly.

John 10:10 NKJV

And God is able to make every grace overflow to you, so that in every way, always having everything you need, you may excel in every good work.

2 Corinthians 9:8 HCSB

Until now you have asked for nothing in My name. Ask and you will receive, that your joy may be complete.

John 16:24 HCSB

Come to terms with God and be at peace; in this way good will come to you.

Job 22:21 HCSB

My cup runs over. Surely goodness and mercy shall follow me all the days of my life; and I will dwell in the house of the Lord forever.

Psalm 23:5-6 NKJV

ANXIETY

Therefore don't worry about tomorrow, because tomorrow will worry about itself. Each day has enough trouble of its own.

Matthew 6:34 HCSB

Anxiety in a man's heart weighs it down, but a good word cheers it up.

Proverbs 12:25 HCSB

Why am I so depressed? Why this turmoil within me? Put your hope in God, for I will still praise Him, my Savior and my God.

Psalm 42:11 HCSB

In the multitude of my anxieties within me, Your comforts delight my soul.

Psalm 94:19 NKJV

Be anxious for nothing, but in everything by prayer and supplication, with thanksgiving, let your requests be made known to God.

Philippians 4:6 NKJV

CONFIDENCE

God also bound himself with an oath, so that those who received the promise could be perfectly sure that he would never change his mind. So God has given us both his promise and his oath. These two things are unchangeable because it is impossible for God to lie. Therefore, we who have fled to him for refuge can take new courage, for we can hold on to his promise with confidence.

Hebrews 6:17-18 NLT

The result of righteousness will be peace; the effect of righteousness will be quiet confidence forever.

Isaiah 32:17 HCSB

I've told you all this so that trusting me, you will be unshakable and assured, deeply at peace. In this godless world you will continue to experience difficulties. But take heart! I've conquered the world.

John 16:33 MSG

You are my hope; O Lord GOD, You are my confidence.

Psalm 71:5 NASB

ENCOURAGING OTHERS

I want their hearts to be encouraged and joined together in love, so that they may have all the riches of assured understanding, and have the knowledge of God's mystery—Christ.

Colossians 2:2 HCSB

And let us be concerned about one another in order to promote love and good works.

Hebrews 10:24 HCSB

Carry one another's burdens; in this way you will fulfill the law of Christ.

Galatians 6:2 HCSB

But encourage each other daily, while it is still called today, so that none of you is hardened by sin's deception.

Hebrews 3:13 HCSB

Iron sharpens iron, and one man sharpens another.

Proverbs 27:17 HCSB

GOD'S COMMANDMENTS

If only you had paid attention to My commands. Then your peace would have been like a river, and your righteousness like the waves of the sea.

Isaiah 48:18 HCSB

This is how we are sure that we have come to know Him: by keeping His commands.

1 John 2:3 HCSB

For this is the love of God, that we keep His commandments. And His commandments are not burdensome.

1 John 5:3 NKJV

Follow the whole instruction the Lord your God has commanded you, so that you may live, prosper, and have a long life in the land you will possess.

Deuteronomy 5:33 HCSB

He who has My commandments and keeps them, it is he who loves Me. And he who loves Me will be loved by My Father, and I will love him and manifest Myself to him.

John 14:21 NKJV

GOD'S PRESENCE

Draw near to God, and He will draw near to you.

James 4:8 HCSB

You will seek Me and find Me when you search for Me with all your heart.

Jeremiah 29:13 HCSB

The Lord is near all who call out to Him, all who call out to Him with integrity. He fulfills the desires of those who fear Him; He hears their cry for help and saves them.

Psalm 145:18-19 HCSB

Surely goodness and mercy shall follow me all the days of my life: and I will dwell in the house of the Lord for ever.

Psalm 23:6 KJV

I am not alone, because the Father is with Me.

John 16:32 HCSB

GOD'S TIMING

He said to them, "It is not for you to know times or periods that the Father has set by His own authority."

Acts 1:7 HCSB

Therefore the Lord is waiting to show you mercy, and is rising up to show you compassion, for the Lord is a just God. Happy are all who wait patiently for Him.

Isaiah 30:18 HCSB

But those who wait on the LORD shall renew their strength; they shall mount up with wings like eagles, they shall run and not be weary, they shall walk and not faint.

Isaiah 40:31 NKJV

To everything there is a season, a time for every purpose under heaven.

Ecclesiastes 3:1 NKJV

I waited patiently for the LORD; and He inclined to me, and heard my cry.

Psalm 40:1 NKJV

JESUS

The next day John saw Jesus coming toward him and said, "Here is the Lamb of God, who takes away the sin of the world!"

John 1:29 HCSB

I am the door. If anyone enters by Me, he will be saved.

John 10:9 NKJV

I have come as a light into the world, so that everyone who believes in Me would not remain in darkness.

John 12:46 HCSB

I am the true vine, and My Father is the vineyard keeper. Every branch in Me that does not produce fruit He removes, and He prunes every branch that produces fruit so that it will produce more fruit.

John 15:1-2 HCSB

But we do see Jesus—made lower than the angels for a short time so that by God's grace He might taste death for everyone— crowned with glory and honor because of the suffering of death.

Hebrews 2:9 HCSB